MW01008661

Sons of the Father

Jeffersonian America

Jan Ellen Lewis, Peter S. Onuf, and
Andrew O'Shaughnessy, Editors

SONS OF THE FATHER

George Washington and His Protégés

EDITED BY

ROBERT M. S. McDONALD

University of Virginia Press   Charlottesville and London

University of Virginia Press

Printed in the United States of America on acid-free paper

First published 2013

3 5 7 9 8 6 4 2

LIBRARY OF CONGRESS CATALOGING-IN-PUBLICATION DATA

Sons of the father : George Washington and his protégés / edited by Robert M. S. McDonald.

pages cm. — (Jeffersonian America)

Includes bibliographical references and index.

ISBN 978-0-8139-3438-9 (cloth : alk. paper) — ISBN 978-0-8139-3439-6 (e-book)

1. Washington, George, 1732–1799—Friends and associates. 2. Washington, George, 1732–1799—Influence. 3. Founding Fathers of the United States—Biography. I. McDonald, Robert M. S., 1970– editor of compilation.

E312.17.S66 2013

973.3092'2—dc23

2012048814

In memory of Don Higginbotham

Be courteous to all, but intimate with few, and let those few be well tried before you give them your confidence.

—George Washington to Bushrod Washington, January 15, 1783

Contents

Preface

George Washington fathered no children, but he never lacked for sons. This volume considers his influence on the lives, careers, and characters of the members of a diverse fraternity of younger men that included military commanders such as Nathanael Greene as well as political figures such as Gouverneur Morris. With some, such as Henry Knox and the Marquis de Lafayette, he enjoyed especially close relationships. Others, such as Daniel Morgan and Anthony Wayne, received from him little affection. He could be a stern parent, scorning the disloyalty of James Monroe, but also an indulgent one, forgiving the insubordination of Alexander Hamilton, who, like Thomas Jefferson, possessed a capacity not only to serve Washington but also to appropriate his name for political advantage. One of the men under consideration in these pages, Captain Robert Kirkwood of Delaware, Washington may have never met. Yet Kirkwood knew Washington and, like others of various ranks who scrutinized the behavior of the Continental Army's commander in chief, followed his example of how to lead.

What was it like to serve under Washington? Whether acting as a military officer or civilian officeholder, he did not possess a reputation for gladhanding, easy confidences, or even much warmth. His greatest attributes as a commander might well have been his firm command over his own emotions and the way in which he held himself above if not apart from the men who looked to him for leadership. The artist Charles Willson Peale, who visited Mount Vernon in 1772, later remembered: "One afternoon, several young gentlemen . . . and myself were engaged in pitching the bar, one of the athletic sports common in those times, when suddenly the Colonel appeared among us. He requested to be shown the pegs that marked the bounds of our efforts; then, smiling, and without putting off his coat, held out his hand for the missile." As Peale recalled: "No sooner did the heavy iron bar feel the grasp of his mighty hand than it lost the power of gravitation, and whizzed through the air, striking the ground far, very far, beyond our utmost limits. We were indeed amazed, as we stood around, all stripped to the buff, with shirt sleeves rolled up, and having thought ourselves very clever fellows, while the Colonel, on retiring, pleasantly observed, 'When you beat my pitch, young gentlemen, I'll try again.'"[1]

At Mount Vernon to capture the likeness of the forty-year-old planter in the militia uniform that he had worn during the French and Indian War, Peale painted Washington's portrait in words at least as well as he did in oil. As his anecdote suggests, working for this man of exacting standards and prodigious talents could prove a humbling task. How to impress an individual who seemingly had no difficulty making the greatest challenges appear easy? Effective leadership, Washington believed, included an ability and a willingness to stand as a model of excellence for the emulation of others. As he reminded his subordinates in 1756, it was "the actions, and not the commission, that make the Officer." He noted later that only a "phenomenon in nature" could make possible "a well disciplin'd Soldiery, where Officers are relax'd and tardy in their duty." On the other hand, "when Officers set good Examples, it may be expected that the men will with zeal and alacrity follow them."[2]

These words of wisdom must have been difficult for Washington to swallow when, in September 1776, the imminent landing of 4,000 British and Hessian soldiers at Kip's Bay on Manhattan sparked panic among Connecticut militia manning the breastworks and the two Continental brigades that rushed to reinforce them. Washington, alerted to the attack by the roar of British warships' cannon, rode four miles from his command post to find a scene of utter disarray. Heedless of his calls to "Take the walls!" and "Take the cornfield!," soldiers retreated past him in full sprint. "I used every means in my power to rally and get them into some order," he reported to John Hancock, president of the Continental Congress. More specific accounts of his actions claim that he cast his hat on the ground, threatened his own troops with his sword, brandished his cocked pistol, and swatted some of his officers with his riding crop. Seething with rage and hurling obscenities, he ventured dangerously close to the enemy before his aides grabbed his horse by its bridle and pulled him toward safety. Washington described his soldiers' performance as "disgracefull and dastardly," but so, it appears, was his own. It was a bad day for his army, but a worse one for Washington, who on this rare occasion lost the composure for which he became famous.[3]

These really were times that tried men's souls. They also forged character. Washington learned from setbacks. He gained not only the wisdom and perspective to avoid future disasters, but also an even greater degree of self-possession. When crises confronted him—the capture of Philadelphia, starving troops at Valley Forge, and a possible coup at Newburgh, or, later, during his presidency, when he faced whiskey rebels, Democratic-Republican societies, and opponents of the Jay Treaty with Great Britain—Washington displayed far greater finesse. He had come to understand that "a people unused to restraint must be led, they will not be drove." It was not that he lost his appreciation for the efficacy of brute strength. At Valley Forge in 1778, for instance, he beseeched Congress to allow up to 500 rather than 100 lashes as punishment for soldiers' bad behavior. Yet here he not only ordered the immediate construction of huts to shelter his troops, but also promised a cash prize to "reward the party in each regiment, which finishes their hut in the quickest, most workmanlike manner."[4] In 1794, he dispatched a massive 13,000-man force into western Pennsylvania to crush the Whiskey Rebellion. The largest army assembled in North America since the siege of Yorktown never saw combat. Washington commanded it to act with a light touch and, at least initially, rode in the lead. Even earlier, his performance at Newburgh had perhaps provided the best example. When he addressed his officers in 1783, his perseverance in the war and near-constant rectitude had gained for him so much moral authority that all he needed to do was put on his spectacles.[5]

As the essays in this volume make clear, Washington often impressed his junior partners, but he seldom intimidated them. These men not only served as eyewitnesses to his leadership, but also contributed to his decision making. Washington, for his part, often invited such advice. He convened councils of war with his generals and meetings of his presidential cabinet. He reached out when faced with personal dilemmas, such as what to do about shares of the James River Company and Potomac River Company granted to him by the Virginia Assembly in 1784. He believed it wrong "to accept this gratuitous gift" or to appear to have a financial interest in the cause of river improvements, which he championed. He shared his predicament with James Madison, Thomas Jefferson, Patrick Henry, William Grayson, Benjamin Harrison, George William Fairfax, Nathanael Greene, and the Marquis de Lafayette, to whom he explained his desire to decline the gift, "without appearing to slight the favors of my Country—committing an act of disrespect to the Legislature—or having motives of pride, or an ostentatious display of disinterestedness ascribed to me." Following the advice of Madison (who ghostwrote his response to the state legislature), he ultimately donated the shares to further the cause of education. Some went to an academy that later became Washington and Lee University.[6]

Yet candid consultation could also cause friction, especially if it moved from confidential advice to open disagreement. Even before the 1790s, when Washington endured disputes with Jefferson, Madison, and James Monroe, he sought to minimize instances of conflict. In 1784, when he contemplated reforms for the Society of the Cincinnati, he advised eliminating its general meetings, which he described not only as "unnecessary" and "expensive," but also divisive, since "nothing loosens the bands of private friendship more, than for friends to pit themselves ag[ain]st each other in public debate."[7] His aversion to open dissent was almost congenital. Promoted to the rank of full colonel at the age of twenty-two, Washington had long been accustomed to other men taking his orders. This would have been the case even if he had never embarked on a military career, for Washington was one of Virginia's largest slaveholders. In 1785, Elkanah Watson, a Massachusetts-born merchant just a couple of days past his twenty-seventh birthday, observed during a visit to Mount Vernon that Washington's slaves "seemed to watch his eye, and to anticipate his every wish; hence a look was equivalent to a command. His servant Billy [Lee], the faithful companion of his military career, was always at his side. Smiling content animated and beamed on every countenance in his presence." On one level, Washington accepted the value of democratic dissonance, but on another, he relished the role of unquestioned patriarch. More than a century before Theodore Roosevelt employed the expression, Washington had enjoyed the benefits of speaking softly while carrying a big, metaphorical, stick.[8]

For the modern observer it is difficult to envision Washington, still the father of his country, in positions of command that gave him legal authority to whip the backs of either soldiers or slaves. At the same time, it seems almost impossible to imagine the scene recounted by Watson, the young visitor to Mount Vernon, who after taking ill with a cold found the former general, in the middle of the night, quietly opening Watson's door to bring hot tea to his bedside.[9] Washington helped to define a different time with a broader range of parameters. It was an increasingly fluid and democratic America, with more room for mobility and sincerity, but at the same time, some of the old rules, at least in his mind, still seemed inviolable.

Understanding the full range of Washington's leadership, which embraced all shades of persuasion and coercion as well as multiple modes of command and solicitude, requires the examination of his relationships with a particularly broad cast of characters. The men on whom this volume focuses were not all, at all times, his closest associates. Yet all are important figures in that their interactions with him provide glimpses into different aspects of Washington's capacities for management, motivation, control, and the cultivation of talent.

Fred Anderson's insightful first chapter on "George Washington's Mentors" highlights the ambitious young provincial's formative relationships, such as his sometimes strained interactions with Robert Dinwiddie, Virginia's lieutenant governor. The focus then turns toward Washington as the senior partner. As L. Scott Philyaw's essay suggests, the narrow discrepancy in age between Washington and Daniel Morgan made Washington more of a peer than a father, but the palpable distance in social status could not be overcome. The resulting separation between the two men seemed more or less mutually expected and agreeable, a dynamic that did not characterize Washington's relationship with Anthony Wayne, who, according to Mary Stockwell, appears to have yearned for Washington to reciprocate his diligent loyalty with recognition that never really came.

Thomas Jefferson, meanwhile, not only occupied an honored position within Washington's cabinet, but also played a pivotal role as a presidential advisor until partisanship undermined their relationship. Brian Steele's insightful analysis adds an important postmortem to this familiar story, highlighting Jefferson's efforts to render Washington, after he died in 1799, as a republican president above party. That Jefferson's efforts enjoyed a good degree of success testifies to Washington's sincere, if ultimately impossible, efforts to unite Americans of all persuasions. That Jefferson sought to close his distance with the real Washington by refashioning for posterity a less Federalist version speaks to the first president's enduring importance, a fact underscored by similar attempts by others, including Monroe, to elide political differences.

William Ferraro's perceptive chapter shows how Monroe, after his humiliating recall as minister to France, first lashed out at Washington, but then, later in life, regained an appreciation for his presidential predecessor. Henry Knox, the intellectual bookseller and workhorse artilleryman whom Washington called his best friend, endured similar disappointment, but did not display the same disloyalty. As Mark Thompson portrays this efficient New Englander, the time he wasted fretting over injured honor late in life paled in comparison to the warmth he had earlier felt as the beneficiary of the patrician's time and attention. Certainly, Nathanael Greene made the most of similar opportunities provided him. As John W. Hall demonstrates, he catapulted through the ranks to become Washington's most trusted general.

While the commander in chief may have considered Greene a younger version of himself, Washington seems to have admired Gouverneur Morris, on the other hand, in part because of their differences. Easygoing and affable, Morris charmed Washington from the start. Never a military man, he nonetheless endeared himself to Washington as a tireless advocate, first for the Continental Army and later for a firmer union. Although Washington enjoyed the gift of reticence, Morris suffered from a degree of verbal indiscretion that might have impaired a less stable relationship. Some of Morris's most significant slips, Mary-Jo Kline points out, occurred while he served as Washington's representative in France. Only a man so self-assured could handle with such modesty the president's resulting remonstrance and subsequent decision to replace him.

Alexander Hamilton, who possessed a much more prickly sense of honor, rebelled against such treatment when, during the Revolution, Washington retained him as an aide and denied him a field command. While their later partnership would prove pivotal in the development of the national government under a new Constitution, Hamilton sometimes professed less affection for his mentor than an appreciation for the leverage his connection with Washington gave him. As described by Peter Henriques, at times the relationship appears almost cold and calculating, especially when contrasted with Washington's friendship with Lafayette. While Washington's desire to secure a French alliance provided the impetus for the inclusion of the young nobleman within his circle of young assistants, Stuart Leibiger points out that, as time passed, the two men earned each other's respect and affection, although Washington characteristically never reciprocated in writing Lafayette's celebration of a father-son relationship between them. The association between Washington and Captain Robert Kirkwood, although the least direct and most implicit, may well have also been the most important. As Thomas Rider suggests, Kirkwood, while exemplary, is also the most representative of the tens of thousands of men whom Washington led.

Perhaps the most significant omission from this volume is Madison, whose relationship with Washington is already ably analyzed in Stuart Leibiger's *Founding Friendship: George Washington, James Madison, and the Creation of the American Republic.* Leibiger's book makes the case that the partnership of Washington and Madison, especially during "the all-important 1785–90 period"—when they helped lead the movement to envision, propose, approve, and implement a new framework for national government—stands as "the most important" of all the possible pairings of American founders. Leibiger, who traces the "parallel careers" of "these two crucially important Virginians," presents a compelling case that "Madison was Washington's ideal collaborator" in the project to find "a republican solution to the problems of republican government."[10]

While Leibiger's work is the most recent book to examine Washington's collaboration with another member of the Revolutionary generation, *George Washington's Generals,* edited by George Billias, at first glance seems perhaps most analogous to this volume, in that its authors focus on eleven of Washington's subordinates, including five (Greene, Knox, Lafayette, Morgan, and Wayne) also considered here. Yet its chapters, written in the early 1960s, focus more on these generals' contributions in the War for Independence than on their relationships with Washington. Moreover, while the essays it contains stand as excellent profiles of these men as military leaders, they provide little coverage of their interactions with the commander in chief and of their lives after the conclusion of the war.[11]

Leibiger's *Founding Friendship,* in contrast, applies to Washington's partnership with Madison some of the same questions raised in this volume about some of his other key associations. How did these personal alliances take root and develop? Were they based on common background, shared commitments, or complementary qualities that made them stronger together than apart? Did the nature of these relationships reflect or undermine the strictures of social, military, and political hierarchy? What do they tell us about Washington's leadership—as well as his willingness to defer to others who at least believed they possessed better information or a different perspective? Was his trust conditional? Did lines exist that could never be crossed? That Washington, senior in age to all of the individuals considered here, possessed superior status relative to his military comrades is incontrovertible. Even among the civilians with whom he collaborated—even when they were not serving in his presidential administration—the disparity of rank stood clear.

In these relationships, did Washington place himself, as Leibiger believes was the case with Madison, in the role of a friend? Or did he imagine himself as an older brother, as a patron interacting with clients, as a general commanding subordinates, or as a master steering his apprentices?

The answers to all these questions are multiple, conditional, and situational. The essays in this volume demonstrate Washington's consistency in treating all these men differently, for different reasons, at different times. It was perhaps part of his genius to recognize the individuality of the men with whom he interacted, as well as the shifting requirements of changing circumstances. After Monroe, the former minister to France, in 1797 published a pamphlet taking to task the Washington administration, the former president went to his grave speaking ill of the man who had once stood within his inner circle. As Don Higginbotham observes, "Washington had a tendency not to forgive and forget." "Keenly sensitive to criticism and possessed of a fiery temper that only rarely erupted," he "expected more from men he knew well, especially if they were Virginians."[12] Yet even after the New Yorker Hamilton, as a young lieutenant colonel, stormed out on his commander in chief and quit the army, Washington welcomed him back as if nothing had happened.

Theodore Crackel is certainly correct to note in the introduction that Washington's relationship with each and every man considered here is not entirely comparable to the interactions between a father and a son. But while Washington was only four years older than Morgan, he was between ten and twenty-three years older than the other men considered within this volume, many of whom at times looked up to him in much the same way he did to his half brother, Lawrence Washington. After their father's death, it was Lawrence, fourteen years his elder, who, according to Joseph Ellis, served as "a surrogate father" and took responsibility "for managing the career options of his young protégé" and introducing him to the wider world.[13]

George Washington played a similar role for several of the men analyzed in these pages. For others, his influence came later in their lives. For all of them, and for nearly all Americans, he assumed the role of national patriarch. Washington had been called the "Father of his Country" at least as early as 1783, when Lucretia Wilhelmina van Winter, a Dutch poet, penned for him a tribute of twenty stanzas ending with the words "Lo! Washington! the Father of his Country, the Protector of Liberty!"[14] The appellation took hold throughout the latter part of the 1780s—and especially after his inauguration—when he was saluted as the "Father of his Country" (or "our Country," "the Country," and "this Country") by correspondents and in newspapers.[15]

Washington provided paternalistic metaphors as well. During the American Revolution, he repeatedly referred to his group of military aides as "my family."[16] He accorded the same level of intimacy to the small coterie of clerks and other assistants employed during his presidential administration and living under his roof.[17] It is true that if Washington stood as a father figure to these men, he did so in a discernibly eighteenth-century pose. The men of his time, place, and class, according to Daniel Blake Smith, exemplified a "rather permissive" mode of parenthood that placed a high value on "the development of self-confidence, autonomy, and the reciprocal obligations of fathers and sons."[18] As a military leader, he displayed little reluctance to issue commands he considered prudent and consistent with the cause. Yet he had little appetite for micromanagement, and he spurned manipulation. Garry Wills observes that Washington earned the confidence of an independent-minded people by resigning his commission at the end of the War for Independence rather than clinging to authority, like Caesar or Cromwell. Wills's assertion that he gained power "by his readiness to give it up" also applies to his relationships with the men upon whom he relied.[19] He could even disown them when disappointed with their behavior, but the national father never treated these men like children.

Nearly all of these "protégés" at one point or another professed a level of respect for Washington that bordered on reverence, or even love. Morgan, for example, at a time during the war when Washington's leadership was under attack, reportedly avowed that "under no other man . . . would I ever serve." Not to be outdone, Wayne in 1789 described his old commander as America's "greatest soldier—ablest statesman—& truest friend." Jefferson, even when criticizing Washington, noted that he "errs as other men do, but errs with integrity." Monroe, also capable of finding fault with the first president, nonetheless lauded his many "virtues & services . . . especially in the course of our revolution." Knox, who, according to Timothy Pickering, was known for his "adulatory professions of respect, honor, and devotion to the great man," described Washington's "mature and wise" judgment as the product of "great deliberation and reflection." Greene confessed his opinion that "General Washington's influence will do more than all the Assemblies upon the Continent," while Morris eulogized him as a man possessing "the courage of a soldier, the intrepidity of a chief, the fortitude of a hero," and a "quick sense of what was just, and decent, and fit." Hamilton extolled Washington as "a kind and venerated Patron and father," who "consulted much, pondered much, resolved slowly, [and] resolved surely." Lafayette reported that "his genius, his greatness, and the nobility of his manners attach to him the hearts and veneration" of men from both sides of the Atlantic. Captain Kirkwood of Delaware, of course, did not know Washington personally. Although he left few written records, his meritorious career, distinguished by many of the most important values that Washington exemplified, nonetheless pays tribute to the leadership of the man who, during the War for Independence, represented the apogee of Kirkwood's military chain of command.[20]

The true greatness of George Washington, of course, is more than an amalgam of these men's praise, or even the sum total of tributes, public as well as private, tendered during his life and after his death.[21] Yet Washington's capacity for judgment stands out. As Morris remarked, "Of a thousand propositions he knew to distinguish the best." He also knew how to "select among a thousand the man most fitted for his purpose."[22] During the course of his career, he assumed multiple roles, performed multiple tasks, and chose multiple subordinates. In terms of potential protégés, he truly suffered an embarrassment of riches. Jack P. Greene's apt afterword makes this point quite clearly. Washington had many men of merit from whom to choose. Even accounting for the quantity and quality of free and responsible eighteenth-century Americans, Washington's selection of junior partners is perhaps his most remarkable achievement. Like him, they possessed not only raw talent, but also the desire to improve themselves and their world. He envisioned the Continental Army as a school for military professionalism, and his presidential administration as a laboratory of republican government. In these educational institutions, Washington served not only as dean, but also as a lifelong student. He even hoped to institutionalize this statesman-building process through the creation of a national university. In the end, through attitude and example, and through his open-minded application of principle, he served not only as the father of his country, but also as an indispensable mentor for a generation of leaders.

Given its focus on George Washington's mentorship, how fitting that this volume traces its origins to a June 18–20, 2010, conference held in memory of Don Higginbotham, who spent much of his life not only studying Washington but also mentoring students and scholars of the American Revolutionary era. Higginbotham twice interrupted his long career at the University of North Carolina at Chapel Hill by answering calls to serve as a visiting professor at the United States Military Academy, so it seems fitting, too, that the conference took place at West Point, the famed promontory in New York's Hudson Highlands, where, during the American Revolution, Washington ordered the construction of fortifications and later foiled the treasonous plot of Benedict Arnold.

"Sons of the Father," the first Sons of the American Revolution Annual Conference on the American Revolution, emerged as a manifestation of the continuing efforts of the National Society of the Sons of the American Revolution to encourage historical research—one of the purposes specified in the charter it received from Congress. Formed in 1889, this nonprofit patriotic and educational organization had long supported the study of history; it deepened its commitment in 2008 when its executive committee, led by David M. Appleby, its president general, accepted the proposal of Joseph W. Dooley to initiate the annual conference, and then named him its director. Were it not for Joe's vision, enthusiasm, and dedication, this project would never have materialized. For this volume, and for all subsequent projects presented under the banner of the SAR Annual Conference on the American Revolution, Joe is worthy of the appellation often bestowed on Washington: he is the indispensible man.

Others, if less indispensible, offered assistance that nonetheless proved crucial. First among them is James C. Rees, now the retired president of George Washington's Mount Vernon, the organization that cosponsored the conference and bestowed not only its imprimatur but also crucial financial support. Generous contributions helping to make the conference possible also came from the National Vietnam Veterans Foundation; Arlington Blue Top Cabs; the California Society SAR Ladies Auxiliary; J. Phillip London, PhD; David N. Appleby; Robert L. Bowen; Lindsey C. Brock; J. Thomas Burch Jr.; Judge Edward F. Butler Sr.; John H. Franklin; Judge Tom Lawrence; Stephen A. Leishman; Larry J. Magerkurth; S. John Massoud; Kim Honor Matkovsky; Larry D. McClanahan; Richard W. Sage; J. David Sympson; and Timothy E. Ward.

A number of people volunteered their time and hospitality. Elyse Goldberg and her team at Washington's Headquarters State Historic Site in Newburgh opened their doors to conference attendees for tours, and their scenic grounds for a cocktail reception. Not to be outdone, at the New Windsor

Cantonment State Historic Site, where the Continental Army spent the last winter of the War for Independence, the late Michael Clark and his colleagues Michael McGurty and Chad Johnson extended their welcome to the conference's final dinner at the reconstructed "Temple of Virtue," where Washington implored his officers to think less of their own interests and more of how they could best serve others. The commander in chief's call for selflessness still resonates. Christine Coalwell McDonald, who first met Don while serving as a research associate at Monticello's International Center for Jefferson Studies, and Alan Aimone, the long-standing United States Military Academy librarian who was also Don's long-standing friend, not only lent sage advice on matters of fact and interpretation, but also volunteered to drive presenters to and from conference events, the train station, and the airport. Among the many who traveled great distances were Kathy Higginbotham and Jean Vickery. Through their presence, Kathy, Don's widow, and Jean, the Higginbothams' dear friend, helped to ameliorate for many in attendance the palpable sense of Don's absence.

After the conference, the wonderful professionals at the University of Virginia Press—particularly Richard Holway, Raennah Mitchell, and Mark Mones—helped to transform a collection of papers into a coherent and cohesive book. So did Joseph Ellis and Rosemarie Zagarri, who served as (initially) anonymous readers and shared generously their enthusiasm for the manuscript, as well as ideas for its improvement. In addition, Major Adrienne Harrison, a faculty member in the West Point History Department, as well as Caleb Cage, Lieutenant Dylan Potter, and Lieutenant Michael Monty (each of whom, like Adrienne, graduated from West Point as American History majors), read portions of the manuscript or offered encouragement in other important ways.

Adrienne and Caleb met Don Higginbotham as undergraduates, but like Dylan and Michael, they knew him best as people will continue to know him—as a meticulous scholar whose work on the era of the American Revolution endures. Befitting his subject, he wrote less for the moment and more for the ages. Buffeting historiographical fashions, he sought neither to celebrate nor to scorn, and never wavered from his goals to understand and then explain. He had a fine-tuned appreciation for the role of individual agency and the reality of historical contingency, in part, perhaps, because of the trajectory of his own life, which took root in small-town Missouri, where for a while his main ambition was to drive a family friend's oil truck. His change of heart, as well as the contours of his long career and the importance of his legacy, have been documented elsewhere.[23] Here, it seems most appropriate to note that he possessed some of the best qualities of the man on whose life and times he focused much of his research and writing. Consider the high-ranking delegation of French military officers that met with Washington in 1780. Its members found themselves "enchanted" by Washington's "easy and noble bearing, extensive and correct views, [and] the art of making himself beloved."[24] Many of us, upon meeting Don Higginbotham, have had the same reaction. Those who have been privileged to know him well also discovered real warmth, an avuncular side, youthful mischievousness, an uncommon capacity for fairness, and a true friend. This book is dedicated to his memory.

Quoted material is reproduced exactly as it appears in the cited sources, including variant spelling and misspellings. We have, however, used "*sic*" to note the misspelling of proper names, and we have supplied missing letters within square brackets when necessary for clarity. Abbreviations for sources used throughout the volume are identified in the list of abbreviations on pages xxvii–xxviii.

Notes

1. Charles Coleman Sellers, *Charles Willson Peale* (New York, 1969), 100. See also Freeman, 3:292–93.

2. GW, Address, [8 January 1756], *PGW: Col. Ser.*, 2:257; GW, General Orders, 22 August 1775, *PGW: Rev. Ser.*, 1:347. See also Don Higginbotham, "George Washington and George Marshall," in *War and Society in Revolutionary America: The Wider Dimensions of Conflict*, by Don Higginbotham (Columbia, S.C., 1988), 223–25.

3. Don Higginbotham, *The War of American Independence: Military Attitudes, Policies, and Practice, 1763–1789* (New York, 1971), 160; Robert Middlekauff, *The Glorious Cause: The American Revolution, 1763–1789* (New York, 1982), 348–49; David McCullough, *1776* (New York, 2005), 210–16; Freeman, 4:191–97; GW to John Hancock, 16 September 1776, *PGW: Rev. Ser.*, 6:313–14.

4. GW to Major General Stirling, 19 January 1777, *PGW: Rev. Ser.*, 8:110; GW to a Continental Congress Camp Committee, [29 January 1778], ibid., 13:403; GW, General Orders, 18 December 1777, ibid., 12:627. On punishments, see also Charles Royster, *A Revolutionary People at War: The Continental Army and American Character* (Chapel Hill, N.C., 1979), 77–78.

5. Richard H. Kohn, *Eagle and Sword: The Federalists and the Creation of the Military Establishment in America, 1783–1802* (New York, 1975), 170, 17–39; Joseph J. Ellis, *His Excel-*

lency: George Washington (New York, 2004), 224–26, 141–44; Don Higginbotham, *George Washington and the American Military Tradition* (Athens, Ga., 1985), 96–100, 156n40.

6. Gordon S. Wood, *Revolutionary Characters: What Made the Founders Different* (New York, 2006), 44–45; Stuart Leibiger, *Founding Friendship: George Washington, James Madison, and the Creation of the American Republic* (Charlottesville, Va., 1999), 56–57; GW to Lafayette, 15 February 1785, *PGW: Conf. Ser.*, 2:364.

7. GW, Observations on the Institution of the Society, [ca. 4 May 1784], *PGW: Conf. Ser.*, 1:331.

8. Elkanah Watson, *Men and Times of the Revolution, or, Memoirs of Elkanah Watson . . .* , ed. Winslow C. Watson (New York, 1856), 244. Theodore Roosevelt first used the "big stick" analogy in 1900, attributing it to West African folklore (see T. Roosevelt to Henry L. Sprague, 26 January 1900, Carbon Copy Letterbook, Manuscript Division, Library of Congress).

9. Watson, *Men and Times of the Revolution*, 244. Watson's visit is summarized in Freeman, 6:36–37.

10. Leibiger, *Founding Friendship*, 1, 224.

11. George Athan Billias, ed., *George Washington's Generals* (New York, 1964).

12. Don Higginbotham, "Introduction: Washington and the Historians," in *George Washington Reconsidered*, ed. Don Higginbotham (Charlottesville, Va., 2001), 7.

13. Ellis, *His Excellency*, 9.

14. The poem, dated 20 October 1783, was enclosed in Gerard Vogels to GW, 10 March 1784, *PGW: Conf. Ser.*, 1:196n1. Washington wrote to van Winter, "The honor which your Pen has done me, so far exceeds my merits, that I am at a loss for words to express my sense of the compliment it conveys" (see GW to Lucretia Wilhelmina van Winter, 30 March 1785, ibid., 2:472).

15. For some of the earliest examples, see Francisco Rendon to GW, [ca. 31 December 1785], ibid., 3:485; Holland Masonic Lodge to GW, 7 March 1789, *PGW: Pres. Ser.*, 1:370; James Duane to GW, 9 May 1789, *Gazette of the United States* (Philadelphia), 13 May 1789; *Georgia Gazette* (Savannah), 14 May 1789; Nathaniel Sackett to GW, 23 May 1789, *PGW: Pres. Ser.*, 2:376; Josiah Crane to GW, [(?) June 1789], ibid., 3:88; and Charles Shnabell to GW, 16 July 1789, ibid., 3:218.

16. See, e.g., GW to Anthony White, 28 October 1775, *PGW: Rev. Ser.*, 2:249; GW to Lieutenant Colonel Joseph Reed, 23 January 1776, ibid., 3:172–73; GW to Major General Charles Lee, 10 February 1776, ibid., 3:283; GW to John Laurens, 5 August 1777, ibid., 10:509; GW to Major General Arthur St. Clair, 10 April 1778, ibid., 14:470; GW to Major General Lafayette, 25 September 1778, ibid., 17:131; and GW to Major General Benjamin Lincoln, 9 October 1778, ibid., 17:317.

17. See, e.g., GW to Thomas Nelson Jr., 27 July 1789, *PGW: Pres. Ser.*, 3:332; GW to William Jackson, 26 December 1791, ibid., 9:313; GW to Charles Carter of Ludlow, 19 May 1792, ibid., 10:397–98; GW, Certificate for William Jackson [his secretary], [12 June 1793], ibid., 13:65; GW to Nicholas Van Staphorst, 1 September 1793, ibid., 14:2; and GW to Edmund Randolph, 30 September 1793, ibid., 14:152.

18. Daniel Blake Smith, *Inside the Great House: Planter Family Life in Eighteenth-Century Chesapeake Society* (Ithaca, N.Y., 1980), 82.

19. Garry Wills, *Cincinnatus: George Washington and the Enlightenment* (Garden City, N.Y., 1984), 23.

20. James Graham, *The Life of General Daniel Morgan, of the Virginia Line of the Army of the United States, with Portions of His Correspondence; Compiled from Authentic Sources* (New York, 1856), 173; Anthony Wayne to GW, 6 April 1789, *PGW: Pres. Ser.*, 2:37; Thomas Jefferson to William Branch Giles, 31 December 1795, *PTJ*, 28:565; James Monroe to James Madison, 10 August 1804, in *The Papers of James Madison: Secretary of State Series*, ed. Robert J. Brugger et al., 9 vols. to date (Charlottesville, Va., 1986–), 7:583; Timothy Pickering to George Cabot, 20 September 1798, in *The Founders on the Founders: Word Portraits from the American Revolutionary Era*, ed. John P. Kaminski (Charlottesville, Va., 2008), 331; Henry Knox to Marquis de Lafayette, 25 July 1787, in Francis S. Drake, *Life and Correspondence of Henry Knox, Major-General in the American Revolutionary Army* (Boston, 1873), 144; Nathanael Greene to Alexander Hamilton, 10 January 1781, *PAH*, 2:530; Gouverneur Morris, *An Oration, Upon the Death of General Washington* (New York, 1800), 7; Hamilton, General Orders, 21 December 1799, *PAH*, 24:112; Hamilton, *Letter from Alexander Hamilton Concerning the Public Conduct and Character of John Adams, Esq., President of the United States* (New York, 1800), 29; Lafayette to the Prince de Poix, 20 October 1781, in *Lafayette in the Age of the American Revolution: Selected Letters and Papers, 1776–1790*, ed. Stanley I. Idzerda et al., 5 vols. (Ithaca, N.Y., 1977–83), 4:425.

21. For an ably selected sampling, see John P. Kaminski and Jill Adair McCaughan, eds., *A Great and Good Man: George Washington in the Eyes of His Contemporaries* (Madison, Wis., 1989).

22. Morris, *An Oration, Upon the Death of General Washington*, 6.

23. See Don Higginbotham, *Revolution in America: Considerations and Comparisons* (Charlottesville, Va., 2005), esp. 1–9; Harry L. Watson, "In Memoriam: R. Don Higginbotham," *JER* 28 (Winter 2008): 653; Richard H. Kohn, "Don Higginbotham," *Perspectives on History* 47 (February 2009): 42; and Jack P. Greene, "In Memorium: Robert Don Higginbotham," *Uncommon Sense*, no. 126 (Winter 2009), http://oieahc.wm.edu/uncommon/126/higginbotham.cfm.

24. *The Journal of Claude Blanchard: Commissary of the French Auxiliary Army Sent to the United States during the American Revolution, 1780–1783*, ed. Thomas Balch, trans. William Duane (Albany, N.Y., 1876), 67.

Abbreviations

FE	Paul Leicester Ford, ed., *The Works of Thomas Jefferson,* Federal Edition, 12 vols. (New York, 1904–5).
Fitzpatrick	John C. Fitzpatrick, ed., *The Writings of George Washington . . .*, 39 vols. (Washington, D.C., 1931–44).
Freeman	Douglas Southall Freeman, *George Washington: A Biography,* 7 vols. (New York, 1948–57).
GW	George Washington
JER	*Journal of the Early Republic*
NYPL	New York Public Library
PAH	*The Papers of Alexander Hamilton,* ed. Harold C. Syrett, 26 vols. (New York, 1961–79).
PGW	*The Papers of George Washington,* ed. W. W. Abbot et al., in progress (Charlottesville, Va., 1983–), cited by series:
PGW: Col. Ser.	*Colonial Series* (10 vols., completed)
PGW: Rev. Ser.	*Revolutionary War Series* (20 vols. to date)
PGW: Conf. Ser.	*Confederation Series* (6 vols., completed)
PGW: Pres. Ser.	*Presidential Series* (16 vols. to date)
PGW: Ret. Ser.	*Retirement Series* (4 vols., completed)
PGW: Diaries	*The Diaries of George Washington,* ed. Donald Jackson and Dorothy Twohig, 6 vols. (Charlottesville, Va., 1976–79).

PTJ	*The Papers of Thomas Jefferson*, ed. Julian P. Boyd et al., 36 vols. to date (Princeton, N.J., 1950–).
TJW	*Thomas Jefferson: Writings*, ed. Merrill D. Peterson (New York, 1984).
WMQ	*William and Mary Quarterly*
WPLC	George Washington Papers, Library of Congress

Sons of the Father

Introduction

THEODORE J. CRACKEL

When you read the essays in this volume, I believe you will agree with me that a circle encompassing all of Washington's "sons" would have to be rather widely drawn. In fact, let me suggest a relational construct that will define several of these characters outside the circle of "sons," and in two cases even outside the familial circle. These latter two are Daniel Morgan and Robert Kirkwood, men whose relationship with Washington was more that of neighbor than family.

The remaining figures discussed in this volume can be counted as members of Washington's extended family, but not nearly all were sons. There are several that I would rather categorize as cousins, sometimes distant cousins—family members whom one sees occasionally and who may or may not be close. Although sometimes irritants, they are kinfolk with whom one must at least share an occasional holiday or meal. Three of the men profiled here fall into this class: Anthony Wayne, Thomas Jefferson, and James Monroe.

The remaining five were truly "sons"—all loved and valued by the father, although they occasionally disappointed him and sometimes failed to return his affection and regard. Of course, he sometimes disappointed them, and may even have failed them—or so they may have thought. Such are the imperfect relations of sons and fathers.

Washington chose these "sons," in part at least, for the talents he saw in them. He tolerated them when they rebelled, protected and provided for them as best he could even when they didn't keep in touch as closely as he might have hoped, and welcomed them back whenever they returned home. Among these five, there were two elder "sons"—Henry Knox and Nathanael

Greene; two middle sons—Gouverneur Morris and Alexander Hamilton; and, finally, the "youngest" son—the Marquis de Lafayette.

In addition to the individual essays addressing these ten men, there are two contextual essays that help us better understand the papers that appear here. The first of these contextual essays, Fred Anderson's "George Washington's Mentors," serves as the lead chapter in this volume. His insightful interpretation of Washington's haphazard growth as both an officer and gentleman sets the stage for what follows. The second contextual essay, which concludes this work, is Jack P. Greene's afterword, "Unanticipated Challenges and Unexpected Talents—Leadership and the Colonial Matrix," which he offers as "a highly speculative effort to untangle and comment on some of the problems" associated with leadership in the American Revolution.

In the lead essay, Anderson writes that "patron-client relationships and the 'sponsored social mobility' that went with them, were central to life" in cultures like that of Virginia. Such relationships provided both "a means of demonstrating and reinforcing" the "status of the patron," and a way of "managing upward social mobility" among cohorts of young men. It also harnessed their ambitious impulses "to socially useful purposes" and controlled the "potentially destructive, negative effects." In Virginia, with its "weak, decentralized governing institutions" and its "rudimentary educational system," restraints on such ambition were essential. An aspiring "Virginia gentleman" had first to learn how to defer to those of his elders "who would vouch for him" and then "introduce him to the wider world of honor and offices."

For the young George Washington, who had at eleven years of age lost his father, access to such patron-client relationships came most directly through his older half brother, Lawrence, whose Fairfax connections (by marriage) and military connections (through Virginia Lieutenant Governor William Gooch) were particularly useful. They opened doors "into the circle of officers whom the Crown sent to govern Virginia and to defend the empire." "In effect," Anderson points out, the men at the top of Virginia's governing structure knew Washington "in all the ways that mattered" before they had ever laid eyes on him.

That the young Washington "understood his position as a client" to the Fairfax family was clear from his correspondence with the Fairfax men, "in which he took pains to offer help in any form they might require, and repeatedly expressed gratitude for their friendship." And at age twenty-three, in a letter to one of his younger brothers, he mapped out the path he intended to follow in this "tricky life passage."

As time went on, the "contradictions and complexities" of his "patronage relations" proved a challenge. They tied him to "Court" interests at a time when the backcountry, in which he surveyed and then commanded the Virginia Regiment, was dominated by "Country" politicians. Eventually, they complicated his life to such a degree that his original patron-client relationships no longer answered his needs. He had become a colonel in command of the Virginia Regiment, and had curried favor with two of Britain's more important generals, John Burgoyne and John Forbes, but still found the advancement he had hoped for in the British military establishment stymied. In part, as Anderson suggests, his problem lay in the fact that he had become "a commander, in effect, without first having mastered the art of being a subordinate." He had bypassed "the most fundamental principle of life in a regular army."

His old connections had given him status, but that could only carry him so far. As Anderson suggests, "his best hope for advancement lay in resigning" his command, "marrying well, and becoming a successful tobacco planter." And that is exactly what he did. Still, for all the "pressured, chaotic quality" of his "education in arms," Washington's experience in the Seven Years' War did teach him a number of "hard lessons about war and human nature" that cultivated skills and habits "crucial to his later career."

Finally, Anderson poses a question: "Did the leadership skills he developed at the head of the Virginia Regiment, and a sense of the reciprocal obligations of power and loyalty that emerged from his uneven experiences as both client and patron, combine" to make him a better mentor? The answer, he suggests, lies in the essays in this volume.

Let me begin my examination of these essays with two whose subjects I prefer to delineate as simply neighbors—and one of those a rather distant neighbor. The more senior, and closer neighbor, is Daniel Morgan. L. Scott Philyaw suggests that Morgan was likely known (if not known well) to Washington longer than any of the others considered here, and that is almost certainly correct. In 1753, Morgan settled in Winchester, Virginia—then a small town on the Great Wagon Road from Philadelphia down the Shenandoah Valley to the Carolina Piedmont. There he worked as a laborer and teamster. As Philyaw shows, it was in the latter capacity that he may have come to Washington's attention, during General Edward Braddock's march toward the Forks of the Ohio in the summer of 1755. When the French and Indians attacked and routed the British column, it was Washington's bravery, leadership, and composure, along with the steadfastness of the Virginia troops and teamsters like Morgan, that prevented a complete debacle.

Two decades later, in the summer of 1775, the two men's paths seem to have merged once more near Boston. When on July 3 Washington took command of the American forces around that city, Morgan was already raising a company of riflemen in Winchester. The newly minted captain arrived outside of Boston with his troops on August 6. Washington had been alerted to Morgan's arrival in a letter from Horatio Gates that probably arrived not long after the riflemen. Shortly thereafter, Morgan's company and two other rifle companies were selected to accompany Colonel Benedict Arnold on his expedition to Canada. Arnold put Morgan in command of all three. As it happened, Morgan's riflemen distinguished themselves in what was otherwise an unfortunate affair. "Morgan's meritorious conduct," writes Philyaw, "attracted the attention of General Washington, who recommended that the captain be promoted to colonel in command of a regiment of riflemen." After that, Morgan repeatedly caught Washington's attention, and when the war shifted to the south, he was sent to assist General Nathanael Greene. There, Morgan was given command of the light infantry corps and promoted to brigadier general. His brilliant tactical success at the Battle of Cowpens rewarded the faith placed in him.

Years later, in 1794, Washington again chose Morgan for a critical military assignment. This time the command was the left wing of the militia army sent into western Pennsylvania to suppress the Whiskey Rebellion. As Philyaw puts it, "Washington certainly understood" that the circumstances in those parts "called for Morgan's talents." In sum, the two men enjoyed mutual respect but were never close. As Philyaw understands, the two men simply moved in very different circles.

The more distant of the neighbors is Thomas Rider's Captain Robert Kirkwood. Kirkwood mustered into the service as a first lieutenant in January 1776 (barely six months after Morgan had raised his rifle company) and was promoted to captain at the end of that year. Yet, unlike Morgan, he hardly ever came to Washington's notice. Although Kirkwood's name appeared occasionally in correspondence that crossed the general's desk, there was nothing in that to call special attention to him.

That said, Kirkwood did prove a very competent junior officer—active, brave, and loyal—and capable of independent action and good judgment. In the spring of 1780, as action shifted to the South, Kirkwood's company, with Colonel Alexander Smallwood's Delaware Regiment and Baron Johan De Kalb's division, was sent to attack and harass the British forces that had defeated General Benjamin Lincoln at Charleston and were ravishing it. Once again, Kirkwood and his men performed admirably, but largely escaped notice.

In the aftermath, as Rider puts it, "Kirkwood's soldierly qualities, his sense of enterprise, his vigilance, and his courage, continued to serve him well in partisan operations in the Carolinas." There, Captain Kirkwood's company became a part of Brigadier General Morgan's "Flying Army." At Cowpens, Kirkwood, on the right wing, saw particularly intense fighting. "Despite witnessing as many as one-sixth of the members of the company killed or wounded," Rider writes, "Kirkwood's men maintained order . . . [and] contributed to a demoralizing Continental musket volley that broke the British advance." Lieutenant Colonel Henry Lee of Virginia, whose men were on the left, took particular note of that action and later wrote in his memoirs of his great regard for Kirkwood's skill and courage. Kirkwood (like many, we might suspect) was a fine company-grade officer, but was given no opportunity to be more.

Even a decade later, Washington seems to have known nothing of him that suggested he should be given greater responsibilities. In 1791, he nominated him to be a captain (once again) in the new United States Army. In mid-December of that year, when word of Arthur St. Clair's horrific defeat in westernmost Ohio reached Governor Henry Lee, he wrote to Washington mentioning just four of the officers killed that day—one of them "the entrepid Kirkwood."

As Lee summed up his career: "It was the thirty-third time he had risked his life for his country; and he died as he had lived, the brave, meritorious, unrewarded, Kirkwood." Washington could hardly have lamented his death, except in some general sense, for Kirkwood, the very distant neighbor, had simply resided too far from Washington to attract more particular notice.

Morgan and Kirkwood—and, I believe, most of the officer corps of Washington's army were *of* that neighborhood—men to be respected for their talents and service, but not members of even a broadly extended Washington circle. These officers may have admired—even loved—Washington (man or monument), but drew his notice only occasionally and, at that, all too often as correspondents lamenting the lack of promotion, carping about relative rank, or seeking arrears in pay. Still, most remained constant—as Kirkwood and Morgan did—and deserved and received Washington's gratitude and even solicitude, but only at arm's length, as is so often the case with mere neighbors.

Those within the family circle—even in the outer circles—did, as we should expect, receive more particular notice from Washington. The first of these—Mary Stockwell's Anthony Wayne—must be something like the cousin who really, really likes you, but can't stop talking, and keeps reminding you (without realizing that he's doing it) that he attended an Ivy League school and you didn't. He's maddening. How else can we explain Washington's treatment of him? Peter Henriques, in his Alexander Hamilton essay (about which more below), mentions Washington's habit of categorizing his correspondents by what might be called a friendship meter salutation: "Sir," for most; "Dear Sir," for those who were due respect (but who did not rank among his personal friends), and "My Dear Sir," for family and those others most close. In addition, as Henriques suggests, there was a further delineation in the closing—exhibiting varying degrees of respect and affection. Certainly after the Battle of Stony Point, and perhaps just a bit before, Wayne began to be addressed, in correspondence, as "Dear Sir," but he was never taken a step further to "My Dear Sir" (as were the majority of the "sons"). Nor did Washington ever add an expression of affection to the closing of his letters to Wayne.

Wayne's classical allusions may have tried Washington, but his drive and attention to detail elicited the general's respect, if not affection. As Stockwell suggests, Wayne did his duty passionately, but was neither promoted nor favored. In fact, Washington appears to have been so certain of the devotion of Wayne that he could ignore and at times even disparage him with no fear of ever losing his loyalty—or ever facing the slightest bit of criticism from him.

Of the "sons," the second whom I judge a "cousin" (a "second cousin" perhaps) is Brian Steele's most clever Jefferson—the one who could exploit, even turn Washington's postmortem to his own cause. "From the earliest decade of the nineteenth century," writes Steele, "Americans have always wanted to have their George Washington and their Thomas Jefferson too." Steele argues convincingly that "Jefferson recognized this as a problem and spent a not inconsiderable amount of energy and thought reconciling Washington to the republicanism that was sweeping the land in his own name after Washington's death."

Washington had clearly developed a certain esteem for Jefferson, most particularly in the years immediately after the Revolution, but it was not until he was brought into the cabinet that Jefferson was saluted in letters with "My

Dear Sir" and acknowledged with a closing note of affection.[1] Even then, however, this usage was often ignored, and both "Sir" and "Dear Sir" (particularly the latter) appeared more often than not—possibly an expedient brought on by the press of business. "My Dear Sir" disappeared entirely after 1792, but the assurance of mere esteem did not replace Washington's "affectionate" closing until just before Jefferson departed the government.

The two men's correspondence was later effectively terminated, on July 6, 1796, when Washington wrote Jefferson: "It would not be frank, candid, or friendly to conceal, that your conduct has been represented as derogating from that opinion *I* had conceived you entertained of me. That to your particular friends and connexions, you have described, and they have announced me, as a person under a dangerous influence." "I was no party man," continued Washington, "and the first wish of my heart was, if parties did exist, to reconcile them." Shortly thereafter, he dismissed the subject: "But enough of this; I have already gone farther in the expression of my feelings, than I intended." He then shifted the subject to agriculture and ended the letter thus: "If you can bring a moveable threshing Machine, constructed upon simple principles to perfection, it will be among the most valuable institutions in this Country; for nothing is more wanting, and to be wished for on our farms. Mrs. Washington begs you to accept her best wishes—and with very great esteem and regard I am—Dear Sir Your obedient Hble Servt."[2] There is no "affectionate" here, and one suspects that, in regard to Martha's wishes, Washington *could* tell a lie.

But, as Steele detected, the letter does suggest something that Jefferson could use. "As early as 1802," writes Steele, "Jefferson began looking for ways to challenge the Federalist memory of Washington." Washington, Jefferson calculated, could be shaped "into a symbol *transcending* party in a way that made the single greatest symbol of American nationhood safe for . . . Jeffersonian Republicanism." In an effort to recast the "collective memory of Washington," he turned him into a republican statesman. One source of Washington's appeal was that he was careful not to misuse his power. Jefferson used that perception to his advantage, Steele argues. If Federalists were, as depicted, "monarchists and partisans of England," how could they "ever claim the imprimatur of Washington?" Steele's Jefferson transformed Washington, in death, into what the general had striven for and usually succeeded in being in life: a "national symbol" of unity and republicanism.

The third of Washington's "cousins" is William Ferraro's James Monroe—a "second cousin once removed" in my schema. He wasn't going to get many invitations to dinner at Mount Vernon. He never made it to the "My Dear Sir" list. In fact, he exchanged very few letters with Washington. Although Monroe was elected to the Senate from Virginia in 1790, he was very much a backbencher. When, in May 1794, Washington asked him to replace Gouverneur Morris as minister to France, he felt shocked but elated. As a diplomat, however, he found the learning curve rather steep. As Ferraro writes, "Indiscreet communications with partisan friends and newspapers, and perceived embellishments in letters to the state department, already had compromised Monroe in the eyes of Washington. . . . Other than Monroe, few were stunned by his recall." Despite this, as Ferraro reports, Monroe still avowed "some tenderness" toward the president.

The operative word, however, must have been "some," for he was soon at work on a 473-page attack on Washington's foreign policy meant to justify his own actions in France. Washington made copious notes in the volume: for example, when Monroe noted that he had discussed with the ministry "the conduct of France in . . . harassing our commerce . . . and urged earnestly the immediate repeal of the decrees which authorized" violations of American trading rights, Washington observed that Monroe, at the same time, "told [the French] (contrary to express Instructions) that if it was not convenient to comply . . . the U States w[oul]d give . . . up [their demands]."[3] Washington seldom made notes as he read, but his annotation in this volume was by far the most extensive in any volume he owned.

Monroe's overgrown pamphlet enraged Washington, but as Ferraro points out, the old general preferred to let others make the public condemnation. Still, Monroe must have learned of Washington's attitude and of his efforts to encourage others to speak out. As Ferraro opines, at the time of Washington's death, in December 1799, Monroe hated no man more than the former president, and the feeling was mutual. The evening before his death, the desperately ill Washington was so irate when hearing news of Monroe that his bitter outbursts were, Ferraro writes, "almost certain[ly] . . . Washington's final statement on public affairs."

But that is not quite the end of the story. Years afterward, in the late years of his own life, Monroe seems to have reassessed Washington's contribution. Ferraro offers up Monroe's own words to make the point: "No person was ever called to a trust of greater delicacy and difficulty than . . . [Washington]. His greater dread was that of disunion, but it proceeded solely from a disinterested regard for the public welfare." "At bottom," writes Ferraro, "both Washington and Monroe believed in the potential unity and strength of a national government based on the sovereign people acting through duly elected leaders."

Finally, let me turn to those I judge to be the true "sons." Of these, there are two elder brothers—Henry Knox and Nathanael Greene. Mark Thompson's Henry Knox, although not the eldest of the two, was Washington's "first born." He was possibly the army's best-read officer in military matters—Washington excluded. He was a Boston bookseller—and, of the sons we will meet, the most constant and possibly the most perceptive of the "father's" wartime advisors.

Knox was an unapologetic intellectual. As Thompson writes, "Knox shared the Enlightenment's penchant for order, regularity, and rational inquiry. The same principles that promoted Knox's quest for an ordered world also shaped his approach to battle and his view of war along the lines countenanced by Enlightenment thinkers." When John Adams asked Knox for a list of military books that American officers should read, he ranked Maurice de Saxe's *Reveries on the Art of War* at the top. It was an informed selection, for it was among the five books most read and owned by British officers and, according to the eminent military historian Ira D. Gruber, one of those books "that not only embodied the prudential way of war that would encumber British operations in the War for American Independence—but also [mark] British officers' growing appreciation for a reflective approach to their service—an appreciation for a history and theory of war that would sustain a profession of arms."[4]

Washington valued Knox's contribution as chief of artillery, for Knox "was to draw . . . [on] recent European developments in artillery" that would bring "maneuverability and mobility to the artillery" that would allow it to "support Washington's strategy of attrition and keep pace with the infantry's quick strikes against the enemy." But there was more. Washington also valued him as a thinker—an intellectual counterpoint in the commander's war councils.

Indeed, Washington and Knox shared an almost unique friendship in the midst of the war and beyond. From the early days of their acquaintance, they both used the salutation "My Dear Sir" in their correspondence, and both came to add the assurance of great affection as they closed their letters. Among the "sons," only Lafayette (and he in a unique and abbreviated way) shared that distinction.

The friendship between Washington and Knox continued unabated until 1798, when Washington allowed Knox's name to be placed last on the list of three major generals to be appointed in the army to be raised in case of a French invasion—the Quasi-War. Knox was offended both by being placed below (and presumably subordinate to) Alexander Hamilton and by not having been given the opportunity of withdrawing his name before the list was made public, to avoid the embarrassment this placement caused him. Washington essentially brushed aside Knox's objections and simply explained how this had occurred. Knox, unsatisfied, concluded the exchange in a brief letter that ended: "I will not detain you one moment longer than to say in the presence of almighty God, that there is not a creature upon the surface of this globe, who was, is, and will remain, more your sincere friend than H. Knox."[5] Washington did not reply, but he did make his feelings about his friend very clear in a letter to President John Adams: "With respect to General Knox, I can say with truth, there is no man in the United States with whom I have been in habits of greater intimacy; no one whom I have loved more sincerely; nor any for whom I have had a greater friendship."[6] It is sad that he did not share those thoughts with this best of friends.

The second of the two older "sons" is John W. Hall's Nathanael Greene—the tireless quartermaster general and talented field commander. He was, if I may be excused the vernacular phrase, Washington's "go-to guy" when the problems were of *strategic* importance. Early in the war, as Hall writes, "despite his relative inexperience, [Greene] had become one of Washington's closest advisors." It is likely that, as Hall surmises, "Washington might have seen much of himself in the ambitious New Englander. Both men had lost a parent at the age of eleven, and although they came from the esteemed classes of their respective colonies, neither had the benefit of a formal education. They were both painfully conscious of this disadvantage, which contributed to similarly sensitive conceptions of pride and honor."

Hall finds that Greene and Washington, "on issues of administration and politics," were of the same mind, and on strategic matters, that the general "relied increasingly on the younger man's advice as the war progressed." In early 1778, as the quartermaster department sank into a morass of confusion and disorder, Washington ordered Greene to take on "this thankless yet crucial burden." It "played to Greene's strengths" and moved him into Washington's inner circle. Still, Greene craved "not only his master's approval, but also his affection," and, as Hall writes, "it was quite possibly beyond Washington to provide what Greene wanted." By his "nature and habit," Washington "exuded the aloofness and stoicism of a Roman senator."

In October 1780, Washington sent Greene to the southern theater with the "autonomy" to conduct "operations as he saw fit." Although Greene "scarcely ever won a tactical engagement," writes Hall, "he drove Cornwallis out of the Carolinas and then reduced the British army's hold on the South one post at a time until, in December 1782, the British at last evacuated Charles Town."

Greene's "meteoric rise" in just six years "from a militia private" was possible because of both his "natural talent and ambition" and Washington's "patronage." As Hamilton put it, "His abilities entitled him to a preeminent share in the councils of his chief." Perhaps, as Hall writes, he proved to be more than a "son." He had become "his own master."

There are also two middle "sons" who, in very different ways, maintained an independence from Washington—with very different results. The first of these is Mary-Jo Kline's Gouverneur Morris—an ever faithful "son," but one outside the military sphere. "What unlikely candidates for friendship," Kline suggests: a rake and "irrepressible jokester," on the one hand, and a gentleman famous for his "faultless rectitude and reserved behavior," on the other. At their first encounters, it is likely that the only lasting impression either made on the other was that they shared certain remarkable physical traits. Like Washington, Morris was over six feet and well built. As time went on, however, those impressions changed.

In April 1776, Morris had an occasion to write to Washington. This letter, however, established a level of cordiality that distinguished their relationship ever after. Its light, informal, and jovial manner must have startled Washington, but it must—ultimately, if not immediately—have come to please him. "I take the Liberty of addressing your Excellency upon a Subject so much out of my own Line, that I must be entirely in your Equity, as to the Charge of Impertinence. I hope to be acquitted." In the letter, he asks a favor of Washington that need not concern us (and that Washington ignored), and then concludes saying, "I receive Pleasure in furnishing the Occasion for that Happiness which you receive in doing Good."[7] Washington's reply has not been found, but whatever he wrote did nothing to discourage the New Yorker.

Morris was even more entertaining in person than in his letters, and the two men met more frequently beginning in May, when Morris was named to a committee "that would act as liaison with Washington as he prepared Manhattan's defenses." In those weeks, "Morris revealed another bond that linked him with Washington—a passionate, romantic nationalist fervor."

When the British forced the American army out of New York, the provincial congress left as well. Their next meeting was not until 1777, when Morris was elected to the Continental Congress and made a part of "the committee named to confer with Washington at his winter camp" at Valley Forge. Never was the army faced with so many problems. But "Washington never found," writes Kline, "a more receptive student, nor the army a more sympathetic witness than Gouverneur Morris," despite the fact that "the younger man always seemed on the verge of some dangerous blunder through his outspokenness or irreverence." Still, the relationship blossomed. "Indeed, by the fall of 1779, Washington had gone so far as to respond to one witticism with another."

In 1781, Gouverneur joined his friend Robert Morris in the Finance Office. After the British surrender at Yorktown, the two men, with allies like Hamilton, "embarked on a campaign to put Continental finances in order and to create a sense of nationalism." By mid-1782, Gouverneur had come to believe that a continuance of the war was the best "means to his ends of national unity and sound finance." As that seemed increasingly unlikely, in the fall of that year the men attempted to harness the unrest of army officers—opening a chain of events that led to Washington's Newburgh Address on March 15, 1783. Morris, Hamilton, and the others involved, Kline suggests, had "ignored the curt responses of men like Washington and Knox when hints [of what the schemers were up to] were dropped."

"For two years," Kline observes, "Morris and Washington seem to have suspended their friendship." But by July 1785, "whatever explanations or apologies were needed to restore friendship were made" and Morris joined Washington at Mount Vernon. When Morris departed, "Washington rode with him as far as Alexandria to extend their time together."

"The most lastingly productive part of their collaborations," Kline argues, was at "the Philadelphia Convention of 1787," with Washington as president of the convention and Morris in the unofficial role as advocate of the "programs they both longed to see in the new system of government." In the fall of 1788, the work of the convention behind them, Morris prepared to sail to Europe. "He bade farewell to Washington in a letter that combined a tribute to their friendship, ribald barnyard humor, and patriotic sentiment. Nothing could have been more characteristic," observes Kline.

In 1792, Morris became the American minister to France, but his unveiled opposition to the ongoing French Revolution made it necessary for Washington to send him a frankly worded letter of instruction. Morris replied that he appreciated Washington's friendship and counsel, but ultimately, in 1794, events in Paris forced Washington to replace him.

Morris did not return to the United States until the spring of 1799, but he was soon talking of a trip to Mount Vernon. "I assure you my dear Sir the Pleasure of passing a few Hours with you is among the greatest which I promised myself in returning to my native Country."[8] Washington replied that "if either business or inclination should induce you to look towds the South, that I shall be very happy to see you at this Seat of my retirement; where I rather hope, than expect, to spend the remnant of my life in tranquility."[9] Morris never made the trip, and his last letter, written on December 9, 1799, arrived at Mount Vernon just two days after Washington's death. "Washington and Morris," Kline submits, "were joined in a friendship based on shared opinions on public affairs and a mutual regard for each other's merits." She might have added "humor." It was a rare commodity in Washington's official circle, but one that Kline demonstrates he treasured in Morris.

The last of the middle sons is Peter Henriques's Hamilton. He was, writes Henriques, a man with an "unusually intense ambition" paired with "a touchy ego that made him querulous and . . . combative." The young artillery captain first came to Washington's attention in September 1776 at Harlem Heights, and again as the army retreated across New Jersey shortly thereafter. However, it was action with the two guns that he had ferried across the Delaware River on Christmas night 1776 and used effectively in support of Washington's attack on Trenton, that seems most likely to have recommended him for a position in Washington's official "family." On March 1, 1777, his new assignment, at the rank of lieutenant colonel, was announced in orders.

Although Washington later described Hamilton's duties as that of his "principal & most confidential aid," he would likely have described the work of Joseph Reed, Robert Hanson Hamilton, and others in much the same way.[10] Still, as Henriques maintains, Washington saw something special and detected unique abilities in Hamilton and, as a result, "placed him in situations where his talents could be developed and used." But there was another side to Hamilton, Henriques observes; his "personality was not that of an aide. . . . His inclination ran strongly to command." As such, "Hamilton was clearly ambivalent and conflicted in his feelings for Washington, torn between his desire to defer to him and please His Excellency . . . and his apparent need to resist being dependent on him."

To all appearances, the relationship between these two men during the

Revolution was based at best on a mutual esteem, but not deep affection. As Hamilton had neared three years as an aide, he approached Washington about a field assignment and the general appeared willing. But when none was forthcoming, he reminded Washington of his apparent promise and laid out a planned operation—after which, he would presumably return to his post.[11]

In mid-February 1781, when Washington proved unwilling to approve the action, Hamilton took umbrage to a critical remark and left the general's staff. In explaining the affair to his father-in-law, Philip Schuyler (an admirer and friend of Washington), he wrote that "for three years past I have felt no friendship for him and have professed none. The truth is our own dispositions are the opposites of each other. . . . I wished to stand rather upon a footing of military confidence than of private attachment."[12] In much the same way, writes Henriques, "Washington was never personally close to Hamilton in the way he was to Lafayette."

Later that year, Washington finally made good on his promise of a combat assignment and allowed Hamilton "to lead the assault on Redoubt No. 10 at Yorktown, one of the climactic moments of the campaign leading to the surrender of Cornwallis and the virtual end of the war." Yet, as Henriques writes, "there is no indication of any type of special and close relationship between the two men in the time between Yorktown and Washington's inauguration as the nation's first president."

The Constitutional Convention in 1787 might have brought the two men together again, for both were committed to remedying the fatal weakness of the government under the Articles of Confederation. Still, as Henriques puts it: "The bond between them was not so much one of personal intimacy as one of shared views and common goals for the country they both loved." When the new Constitution was ratified, "Hamilton was among those who wrote and forcefully argued that Washington, whatever his personal desires, *must* be president." When Washington appointed Hamilton his secretary of the treasury, the latter put forward a "far-reaching program" that "engendered great controversy and intense opposition." But in this, Hamilton had Washington's steadfast support. At Hamilton's departure in early 1795, he and Washington exchanged brief letters that contained words of perfunctory affection, and in their subsequent correspondence Washington began letters of substance with "My Dear Sir" and Hamilton closed his with words of affection. It would seem that as the years had passed, their relationship had moved beyond esteem and toward "attachment," to use Hamilton's word choice.

In the late summer of 1798 the Congress passed a bill authorizing an enlarged military establishment (much of it on paper only) that would be available should the war at sea with France spill over onto the land. Washington, with Hamilton as his second in command, would lead the force, but Washington would not play an active role until the French actually threatened. Hamilton worked tirelessly to organize the new forces and appoint officers. In that last point, Washington and Hamilton found something to unify them. Partisan spirit had grown so strong, with Jeffersonian Republicans seemingly in league with the French, that Hamilton was careful to exclude them from leadership roles in the new force. Washington agreed, and advised James McHenry, the secretary of war, that "the brawlers against Governmental measures . . . all of a sudden . . . are very desirous of obtaining Commissions in the Army, about to be raised." He advised "circumspection."[13] Jefferson's party seemingly finally drove Washington and Hamilton into each other's arms.

The final, youngest, "son" is Stuart Leibiger's Lafayette. His case is unique in a number of respects. He was a foreign officer—more particularly, French, at a time when French support was not simply desirable, but essential, to independence. He was also the youngest of the "sons." But, more particularly, his "father-son claim," Leibiger writes, "is based on the writings of both Lafayette and a few of his contemporaries. He described the commander in chief as his father, and himself as a son, in letters to Washington and others. Many firsthand observers also described the association in these terms."

Still, it was not love at first sight. "The relationship," says Leibiger, "seems to have developed by degrees, especially on Washington's end." For the general, such connections usually "started as marriages of convenience, and then only gradually became intimate." That seems to have been the case here, for, in letters, both men ultimately acknowledge that time had made the heart grow fonder.

There was also, Leibiger shows, reasonable self-interest at stake. For Lafayette, there was fame to be had; for Washington, possible access to French support in the war—"perhaps even" the good fortune "to obtain a French alliance." At the Battle of Brandywine, Lafayette displayed both valor and skill—beginning "as an observer," but ending up "as a participant, rallying retreating troops" before being wounded. Washington valued personal valor. By the end of 1777, Washington had arranged for him to command a division of Virginians—which the Frenchman then outfitted at his own expense.

Spring of 1778 brought word of the French alliance. By then, Lafayette was getting regular, if small, independent commands, which he handled with skill. When the British finally abandoned Philadelphia and pulled their troops back to New York, Washington followed, in the hope of finding some promising opportunity to exploit. Lafayette, in turn, hoped that this might be his chance. At Monmouth Court House, it looked as if both men might be rewarded. Washington ordered a force of 1,500 to make the attack. When Charles Lee, second in command, declined to command the force, the role fell to Lafayette. However, when the force was increased to 4,000, Lee suddenly had a change of mind. "Lafayette helped Washington out of an embarrassing dilemma by voluntarily stepping aside." A few weeks later, Lafayette was ordered "to march two Continental brigades to Providence, Rhode Island, and to place himself under the command of General John Sullivan." Lafayette's ready "willingness to accept a lesser command," wrote Washington, "'obviated every difficulty, and gave me singular pleasure.'"

In late 1778 Lafayette grew ill, and early the next year returned to France to regain his health. "Back in France," Leibiger notes, "Lafayette found himself a celebrity, not only because of his own exploits, but also because of his friendship with Washington. He relentlessly lobbied the French government for the loans, ships, and troops the Continental Army desperately needed." The result? "France not only promised to send an army to America, but agreed that Washington would be the supreme commander of allied forces."

In the fall of 1779, a son was born to Lafayette, and he, like so many American officers and families of all stations in life, named the lad after the great man. In March 1780, Lafayette was ordered "to return to America to confidentially notify Washington that France would, that spring, send six warships and 6,000 troops."

As Washington and the commander of the new French force, Jean-Baptiste Donatien de Vimeur, le comte de Rochambeau, debated how best to employ the American and French forces around New York and in Rhode Island, an unexpected target was shaping up in the South. In response, in February 1781, Washington sent Lafayette southward with 1,500 troops. When Cornwallis and his British force moved northward into Virginia, Lafayette was sent into that state to harasses the enemy. "Outnumbered six to one," writes Leibiger, "the young Frenchman . . . resorted to a Fabian strategy." Shortly thereafter, when Washington and Rochambeau received word that the French fleet was headed to the Chesapeake Bay, Washington ordered Lafayette to keep Cornwallis pinned at Yorktown, where, by this time, the English had encamped, and began to move the American and French forces south. Expecting to be rescued by the British fleet, Cornwallis was happy to preserve his force and await the transports.

Lafayette left for France shortly after the French fleet bottled Cornwallis up and forced his surrender, but he made his way back to America in 1784, after Washington returned to civilian life. He traveled widely in the new United States and made an extended visit to Mount Vernon. Leibiger digests effectively the conclusion of that visit. "Washington rode with Lafayette as far as Maryland before bidding his friend a tearful farewell. 'In the moment of our separation,' the Virginian sadly wrote, '& every hour since—I felt all that love, respect & attachment for you, with which length of years, close connexion & your merits, have inspired me.' Washington wondered whether he would never see Lafayette again. 'And tho' I wished to say no,' he mused, 'my fears answered yes.'"

In the next few years, the two men exchanged letters and presents, but the French Revolution was unkind to Lafayette and his family. Washington's instincts in 1784 were correct. He never saw Lafayette again. "During the Revolutionary War," writes Leibiger, "Lafayette got as close to Washington as any young man ever did, but he was never Washington's best friend." Of the ten "sons" considered at the conference and in this volume, it seems likely that Washington's "best friend" was Knox. We have his word on it. But it is equally clear that of these ten men, Lafayette was the only one he might have fully admitted into his private family.

The second contextual essay, Jack P. Greene's "Unanticipated Challenges and Unexpected Talents: Leadership and the Colonial Matrix," is what the author defines as "a highly speculative effort to untangle and comment on some of the problems" associated with leadership in the American Revolution. Most generally, it focuses on "how relatively new, dependent, and supposedly underdeveloped societies find leaders" who developed "resistance movements," steered these movements through a successful war to independence, and finally, "in the war's wake," created a new "extended" federal government that drew heavily on their colonial experience. Where, for example, he asks, did British Americans find not only Washington and his protégés, but also the much larger number of civil stewards who guided the mainland colonial polities "from resistance to Independence and on to republican statehood and national union?"

Greene suggests approaching the problem by focusing on a narrower question: Why did so many metropolitan (rather than colonial) Britons underestimate the colonial capability for resistance? Many political and military leaders underestimated the caliber of leadership that would be found—but why? It might have been that the leaders and citizens were simply ill-informed about the situation, location, and vulnerability of colonies, but Greene suggests that "a far better explanation" is an "ancient and categorical prejudice against colonials." The colonies were seen "as receptacles for those who had failed at home: the poor, the unemployed, the unwanted, and the outcasts—the very dregs of English society." It was a view ubiquitous in British publications and rooted in the conviction that no one would leave England unless compelled to do so.

"That societies composed of such false Britons could ever find the leadership or resolve to mount an effective resistance to a powerful state composed of *true* Britons seemed thoroughly problematic to many people in Britain," writes Greene. They ignored growing wealth and focused instead on the dissimilarities, extreme parochialism, internal division, and the apparent inability to put the common welfare above local interests. "Prejudice," argues Greene, "was the primary source of this fatal and massive miscalculation."

But, as Greene points out, most of the colonies had several generations of experience at governing their households, towns, counties, and provinces. They made and enforced laws, negotiated disputes, "catered to the needs and demands of a free citizenry," organized to keep the peace and protect themselves from local enemies, and drew on that experience to solve new problems. At the same time, an increasingly sophisticated press kept them informed.

Writes Greene, in conclusion: "My message here is that late-colonial societies were emphatically not underdeveloped politically and not lacking in leadership resources." "Politically competent civil societies were not the product of the American Revolution, but its precondition." And, "continuities, not disjunctures, characterize the transition from the colonial to the early national era in all areas of life."

As the reader will find, the essays in this volume seem to bear this out.

Notes

1. There was one earlier use of "affectionate" (abbreviated) in the closing, and that was in a letter of 2 June 1784—the exception, I suppose, that proves the rule.

2. GW to Thomas Jefferson, 6 July 1796, *Papers of George Washington Digital Edition,* ed. Theodore J. Crackel (Charlottesville, Va., 2008).

3. GW, "Comments on Monroe's A View of the Conduct of the Executive of the United States," March 1798, ibid.

4. Ira D. Gruber, *Books and the British Army in the Age of the American Revolution* (Chapel Hill, N.C., 2010), 32.

5. Henry Knox to GW, 4 November 1798, *Papers of George Washington Digital Edition.*

6. GW to John Adams, 25 September 1798, ibid.

7. Gouverneur Morris to GW, 20 April 1776, ibid.

8. Morris to GW, 9 May 1799, ibid.

9. GW to Morris, 26 May 1799, ibid.

10. GW to Adams, 25 September 1798, ibid. In this context, see also GW to Joseph Reed, 23 January 1776, ibid.

11. Alexander Hamilton to GW, 22 November 1780, *PAH,* 2:509–10.

12. Hamilton to Philip Schuyler, 18 February 1781, ibid., 2:566.

13. GW to James McHenry, 30 September 1798, *Papers of George Washington Digital Edition.* In this context, see also Theodore J. Crackel, *Mr. Jefferson's Army: Political and Social Reform of the Military Establishment, 1801–1809* (New York, 1987), 18–21.

avuncular - like an uncle, esp. in benevolence

George Washington's Mentors

FRED ANDERSON

Young people have always needed older ones to guide them, but if some kindly soul had taken George Washington aside at age sixteen and told him how much he would benefit from having a good "mentor," he wouldn't have had a clue what that person was talking about. At least according to the *Oxford English Dictionary,* the earliest recorded use of the word, in the sense of "a person who acts as guide and adviser to another person, esp. one who is younger and less experienced [or] . . . more generally, a person who offers support and guidance to another; an experienced and trusted counsellor or friend; a patron, a sponsor," came only in 1750, in Lord Chesterfield's *Letters to His Son.* If the word itself would have baffled the young Washington, however, we can be sure that he would have grasped the concept immediately, because he, like all his contemporaries, so thoroughly understood patronage. Patronage was woven into the very fabric of Virginia life, albeit in a form that might or might not carry the avuncular connotations of mentorship. An eighteenth-century patron, the *OED* tells us, was "a person standing in a role of oversight, protection, or sponsorship to another; a man of status or distinction who gives protection and aid to another person in return for deference and certain services."

In the stylized language of the day, patrons and their dependents often referred to each another as friends, but the affection we see as fundamental to friendship did not necessarily figure in a fundamentally unequal relationship. What *was* essential, that the patron give "protection and aid to another person in return for deference and certain services," defined the role of the client; and the client was simply a "hanger-on." A client enjoyed a protected position, but it would also be a galling one for an ambitious youth like the teenaged Washington: it was a status to be endured because the only path to becoming what he most wanted most to be, a gentleman, ran though thickets of dependency that modern Americans would find bewildering, dense, and oppressive.[1]

Patron-client relationships, and the "sponsored social mobility" that went with them, were central to life in a monarchical culture. They were above all a means of demonstrating and reinforcing the status of the patron, managing upward social mobility in a generational context, and harnessing individual ambition to socially useful purposes while controlling its potentially destructive negative effects. The proper channeling of ambition in particular was crucial to preserve hierarchy, reinforce deference, and prevent the kind of disruptions that would come to be associated with the self-made men of the nineteenth century. Above all, the restraint on ambition was necessary in Virginia, where weak, decentralized governing institutions and a rudimentary educational system coexisted with an honor culture that—within the gentry, at least—placed few restraints on masculine aggression and economic self-aggrandizement. To become a Virginia gentleman, and ultimately to be in a position to assert one's leadership among the gentry, a young man had first to learn how to defer to the older men who would vouch for him—who would, as it was said, "give him a character"—and would introduce him to the wider world of honor and offices.[2]

Ordinarily, a man's first patron was his father, a crucial link between the son and the larger world of social superiors, influence, and power, and the man from whom he learned his first critical lessons in deference. Washington of course was critically disadvantaged in this by the death of his father, Augustine, in 1743, when he was only eleven years old. The fact that his formidable mother, Mary Ball Washington, chose not to remarry made his situation unusually complex, and difficult. His half brother Lawrence did his best to take on a fatherly role, and to some extent did so, but found himself thwarted, at least early on, by Mary's opposition.

Lawrence's patronage connections were solid ones, but did not run directly into the Virginia planter elite so much as around it, into the circle of officers whom the Crown sent to govern Virginia and to defend the empire. His appointment as captain in Gooch's American Foot, the regiment raised by Lieutenant Governor William Gooch in 1740 for the Cartagena expedition, had signified the beginning of a durable tie of influence that extended both to the expedition's army commander, General Thomas Wentworth, and to its naval commander, Admiral Edward Vernon.[3] Lawrence got to know Vernon better than perhaps any other army officer of comparable rank on the expedition when he acted as captain of marines on Vernon's flagship—and came to admire the admiral sufficiently to name his Potomac plantation for him after the war.[4] It was quite likely that his connection with Vernon produced his attempt to procure a midshipman's berth for his fourteen-year-old half brother in the Royal Navy in 1746, an appointment that Mary blocked.

Whether or not George Washington resented his mother's triumph in this dispute over his future, we cannot know, but it is clear that thereafter he gravitated ever more strongly into Lawrence's orbit. He spent as much time as he could at Mount Vernon and made his first enduring patronage connections there, within Lawrence's circle. The most important of these, of course, was to the large and rich Fairfax family, with which Lawrence had allied himself in 1743 when he married Anne Fairfax. Anne ("Nancy") was the daughter of Colonel William Fairfax, who was in turn the cousin and agent of Lord Thomas Fairfax, sixth Baron Cameron and Proprietor of the Northern Neck. It would have been impossible for George, a fatherless boy in an intensely patriarchal society, to do better than to have a connection—even if it was at first an indirect one—to a man who held rights to western lands approximately equal in extent to Wales. When he accompanied Lawrence to Barbados on the trip that ultimately failed to cure his half brother of consumption in 1751–52, the two stayed with a merchant, Gedney Clarke, who was related to Colonel Fairfax's wife *and* who was a business associate of the man tapped to succeed Gooch as Virginia's lieutenant governor, Robert Dinwiddie.[5]

Thus, in effect, Dinwiddie knew the young Washington in all the ways that mattered most even before the two men met at Williamsburg in 1752. Colonel Fairfax, as one of the most important members of the Governor's Council, and Gedney Clark, as a trusted associate, both vouched for him as a worthy young man of good family. Dinwiddie's predecessor, Gooch, had appointed Lawrence as adjutant of the Virginia militia; after Lawrence's death, when Dinwiddie split the militia into geographical districts under regional adjutants, he appointed Lawrence's protégé George as adjutant for one of the new districts. It only made sense to do so: the family connections were strong enough, and young though he was, he had been given a character by Colonel Fairfax, a council member whose opinion and influence mattered greatly to Dinwiddie. When, in the following year, Dinwiddie needed a hardy young man to carry a message warning the French to abandon forthwith the forts they had been building in the Allegheny drainage, it was entirely reasonable to entrust the mission to him. Indeed, it was all the more sensible to make this appointment because, thanks to the patronage of Colonel Fairfax, the young Washington had long been involved in surveying lands from the Northern Neck proprietorship in the Shenandoah Valley and had been named as the official surveyor for Culpeper County in 1749, at just seventeen years of age.[6]

By his late teens, then, Washington was a member in good standing of the Fairfax-Dinwiddie "interest"—a young man rising along channels that should have led to a secure place somewhere in the second tier of the Virginia gentry. This strong position recognized his own brains and skills and ambition, which made him useful to the Fairfaxes as a kind of fictive member of the clan, but he could never have made the connection without Lawrence's influence. When Lawrence died, the Fairfaxes took charge of the young Washington and his future in ways no surviving member of his family could. No matter how admirable the independent-minded Mary Ball Washington might be, she was not rich and she was not a man, and Virginia was no matriarchy. Thus, Colonel William Fairfax continued to look out for George's welfare from his privileged position in the council, while his son George William Fairfax, eight years older than George, became the sounding-board and advisor Lawrence could no longer be.

That George understood his position as a client to the Fairfaxes—and indeed that he understood his family's position as dependent on their goodwill—was evident in the correspondence that he carried on with the colonel and with George William, in which he took pains to offer help in any form they might require, and repeatedly expressed gratitude for their friendship. Such protestations might be dismissed as mere reflections of the ritualized language of polite eighteenth-century social relations, but a letter that he wrote to his younger brother Jack (John Augustine) Washington in May 1755 offers direct evidence of how he understood the relationship. At the time, George was in Winchester, Virginia (a "vile hole"), seeking to make himself useful to another potentially influential patron, General Edward Braddock; Jack was looking after Mount Vernon. The letter contained news and information that Jack was to pass along to the Fairfaxes at their neighboring estate of Belvoir. But George was interested in a good deal more than merely maintaining his usefulness to the Fairfaxes, for he also instructed Jack to do his best to "fish out Colo. [George William] Fairfax's Intention's" concerning who should represent western Fairfax County in the House of Burgesses, in the likely event that county be divided during the current legislative session. If George William had no intention "to offer himself a Candidite" and had no design to support another, George wrote, "I shoud be glad to stand a pole [poll], if I thought my chance tolerably good." This early expression of willingness to act on his political ambition would be enough to make this letter significant, but for our purposes the real interest lies in another paragraph, in which George announced that he would gladly "hear you live in Harmony and good fellowship with the family at Belvoir, as it is in their power to be very serviceable upon many occasion's to us as young beginner's: I woud advise your visiting often as one Step towards the rest[. I]f any more is necessary, your own good sense will sufficient dictate; for to that Family I am under many obligations[,] particularly the old Gentleman."[7]

Here the young Washington described, with less circumspection than he would characteristically show in his later correspondence, what he clearly understood to be a tricky life passage. He needed the goodwill and support of the Fairfaxes (especially old Colonel William), but he longed for the independent standing as a gentleman that membership in the House of Burgesses would signify. If Braddock drove the French from the Forks of the Ohio, as Washington anticipated, then he would be in an excellent position to capitalize on his service as an aide-de-camp to the general, both directly and indirectly: first, by the form of the captain's commission that Braddock had hinted would be his, which in turn would give access to a trans-Atlantic, imperial patronage system; and second, by enhancing his military reputation through participation in a notable victory. Both would boost his stature in Virginia and surely facilitate his election to the House of Burgesses. But those "many obligations" to the Fairfaxes that had put him in a position to gratify his ambition also stood in his way, for he knew that he would imperil the connection by giving even the appearance of a desire to compete with the young colonel, George William, whose intentions he did not know.

Washington did not have to work his way out of the potentially dodgy position in which his ambition had placed him, because Braddock's defeat, six weeks later, plunged the Virginia backcountry into a nightmarish Indian war. With the backing of the old colonel, as well as Lieutenant Governor Dinwiddie, Washington became the colonel of a reconstituted Virginia regiment, responsible for defending the whole three-hundred-mile length of the colony's frontier. Thus, he achieved the status he had coveted with a suddenness he could not have anticipated—and for which he would have been wise not to wish.

In the years that followed, the contradictions and complexities of patronage relations would pose challenges second only to the Indian warriors who raided Virginia's settlements. Washington's position as colonel of the Virginia Regiment gave him considerable stature, but also made him personally accountable for the lives and welfare of the men and officers under his command and, more generally, responsible for the safety of those settlers who chose to fort up in isolated stations along the Shenandoah Valley rather than flee, as most had done, to the safety of the lower counties. That would have been challenge enough for any man, but his job was made vastly more difficult by the fact that his commission and connections made him part of the "Court" interest of the governor and the empire at a time when "Country" politicians—gentlemen disposed by principle and temperament to distrust and oppose the governor—dominated the House of Burgesses.

Suspicion of Dinwiddie, going back to the Pistole Fee Controversy of 1753–54, had blossomed with his attempts to raise monies to support the Virginia Regiment. Powerful burgesses, convinced that Dinwiddie was in fact protecting his own interests as a speculator in western lands, preferred to invest scarce tax revenues in the militia, which could be used to defend against the potential slave uprisings they dreaded far more than Indian depredations on backwoods families beyond the Blue Ridge. From his headquarters in Winchester, Colonel Washington saw only a House of Burgesses whose members had less interest in supporting a regiment raised to defend the frontier against current Indian attacks than in paying militiamen to defend against a phantasmagorical slave insurrection, as well as a governor who seemed unable, or unwilling, to compel them to change their priorities. Over time, the lack of support and supplies—so frustrating to him, and so frequently deadly for his men and for the frontier settlers—drove him to acts that his patron and superior, Dinwiddie, found maddeningly disloyal, and that we have a hard time understanding at all.[8]

Why did Washington behave in the ways he did? In part, it was simply because he had risen too fast. Without an actual father present to restrain, control, and educate him in the arts of deference, he was only partially schooled in the subordination that clientage demanded, at a time when he suddenly found himself with hundreds of dependents—the soldiers of the Virginia Regiment—whom he was obliged to protect. At once naive concerning the political dimensions of patronage and unsupported by any secure relationship to the men and families who dominated the House of Burgesses, he acted rashly and precipitately to defend his regiment and the region. Scarcely in his mid-twenties, with no one on the scene to warn or call him to account, Washington's ambition outran his judgment and intensified his concerns about the personal honor and public reputation that he feared were at risk.

His concern for the regiment and anxiety for his honor emerged in the pleas for support that he made in person to Colonel Fairfax, president of the council, and in writing to John Robinson, speaker of the House of Burgesses—and also in the reckless allegations he made that Dinwiddie was negligent in his responsibilities and hostile to his counsel. "My representations of matters relative to the peace of the Frontiers are disregarded as idle & frivolous," he complained to Robinson in December 1756, "my propositions and measures, as partial & selfish; and all my sincerest endeavours for the service of my Country, perverted to the worst purposes. My Orders are dark, doubtful, and uncertain; *to day approved, tomorrow condemned:* Left to act and proceed at hazard: accountable for the consequence; and blamed, without the Benefit of defence!"[9] Pride and an imperfect control of his temper encouraged him to write in this vein, and he did so without a clear sense of what consequences would ensue if Dinwiddie discovered what Washington had been saying behind his back. Inevitably, of course, Dinwiddie did learn of the correspondence, and accused Washington directly of ingratitude. That charge touched the young colonel to the quick because ingratitude was the worst kind of offense against a patron—and because it came so near the mark. The breach between the two men never healed.

For all the damage that Washington's complaints and appeals did to his standing with Dinwiddie, they succeeded neither in increasing his standing with the Country Party within the House of Burgesses, nor in improving the welfare of his regiment. Distrusted by both Country and Court, Washington became an ever more aggressive promoter of his interest—the welfare of the Virginia Regiment—traveling all the way to New York to petition the Earl of Loudoun, his majesty's commander in chief in North America, to incorporate the Virginia Regiment directly into the British army. Had he succeeded, Washington would have created a direct relationship between himself and Lord Loudoun—a favor that his lordship had no intention of granting to a young provincial officer so lacking in discretion and social credentials. So Loudoun sent Washington packing, fobbing him off with a trivial reward: at Washington's request, he permitted Colonel William Fairfax's feckless son, William Henry ("Billy"), to purchase a regular army commission as an ensign.[10] Billy's commission enabled Washington to do a favor for the Fairfaxes shortly after the old colonel died, but it neither improved the lot of the Virginia Regiment nor satisfied Washington's need to rise in the world. In the end, it only maintained the reciprocity on which patronage relationships turned.

By early 1757, Washington had fulfilled almost none of his personal ambitions. With his prospects for advancement in the imperial hierarchy cut off by Loudoun's refusal to incorporate the Virginia Regiment into the British army, his best hope for advancement lay in resigning his commission, marrying well, and becoming a successful tobacco planter in his own right. That, of course, was exactly what he did, in 1758, when, after the fall of Fort Duquesne, he left the First Virginia Regiment and married the widow Martha Custis—but not before he had experienced yet another significant difficulty in his relationship with a superior officer, Brigadier General John Forbes.

Washington learned a great deal from the campaign of 1758, but only after he had made the very serious mistake of trying to insist that Forbes divert the road he was building across Pennsylvania to the south and connect with Braddock's route of 1755. Ostensibly, this would have sped the progress of the expedition toward Fort Duquesne, but in fact (as Forbes recognized), it would also create a road that would be of enormous benefit to the land speculators of northern Virginia once the French had been driven from the Forks. When Forbes demurred, Washington wrote to Virginia's new governor, Francis Fauquier, and to his old correspondent, Speaker Robinson, to denounce the "P[enn]s[yl]v[ania]n artifice" behind Forbes's choice of route. "See therefore," he wrote, "how our time has been mispent—behold the golden oppertunity lost—& perhaps never [regained]. How is it to be accounted for? can G[enera]l F[orbe]s have Orders for this? Impossible: Will then our Injurd Country pass by such abuses? I hope not. Rather let a full representation of the matter go to His Majesty. Let him know how grossly his [honor] and the Publick money has been prostituted."[11] When Forbes learned of this correspondence, he was understandably furious, and he dressed Washington down for having put the interests of his province over the good of the service—a rebuke as stinging as Dinwiddie's old charge of ingratitude. Chastened, Washington returned to his duty and completed the campaign without occasioning further complaint; but when his service ended in December, he expressed no regret whatever about returning to civilian life.

Washington's problem with Forbes was simple enough: notwithstanding more than four years of bitter experience in war, he had not yet learned to operate under the direct command of another officer. Prior to 1758, Washington had had no military mentors at all—except for the ill-fated General Braddock, who arguably imparted mostly negative lessons. Instead, he learned most of what he knew about command and administration either by reading manuals (like Humphrey Bland's *Complete Treatise of Military Discipline*) and military classics (especially Caesar's *Commentaries on the Gallic and Civil Wars*), or simply by trial and error. Washington became a commander, in effect, without first having mastered the art of being a subordinate—thereby failing to learn the most fundamental principle of life in a regular army. His failure to grasp the importance of military subordination precisely paralleled his earlier failure to grasp the lessons of deference that sponsored mobility afforded those would-be gentlemen who rose through the ranks of civil society in a more leisurely, orderly way than he had been able to do.

And yet, for all the pressured, chaotic quality of Washington's education in arms, his experiences in the Seven Years' War did enable him to master a set of hard lessons about war and human nature, and thus to develop skills and cultivate habits crucial to his later career as commander in chief of the Continental Army. That he developed his ability to defer to authority and expanded his capacity for patience at considerable personal cost made those advances all the more significant. Did Washington's struggles with his own temper, touchy sense of honor, tendency to insubordination, and relentless ambition help him recognize the importance of assisting the men who served under him in the Revolution to govern those same impulses? Did the leadership skills he developed at the head of the Virginia Regiment, and a sense of the reciprocal obligations of power and loyalty that emerged from his uneven experiences as both client and patron, combine to help him become a mentor to Nathanael Greene and Henry Knox and Alexander Hamilton and the other young officers whose careers he nurtured in the Continental Army? The answers are implicit, I think, in the essays in this volume, and I am grateful beyond measure for having had the opportunity to learn from them.

Notes

1. *Oxford English Dictionary,* 2nd ed., s.v. "mentor," "patron," "client." The patron-client relationship mimicked the covenant of protection between sovereign and subject, the basis of monarchical political culture (see Richard L. Bushman, *King and People in Provin-*

cial Massachusetts [Chapel Hill, N.C., 1985], esp. chap. 1). See also Brendan McConville, *The King's Three Faces: The Rise and Fall of Royal America, 1688–1776* (Chapel Hill, N.C., 2006), which addresses the political culture of monarchy from a different perspective and argues that it was an even more pervasive and powerful cultural influence than Bushman suggests.

2. The phrase "sponsored social mobility" originates (I believe) with Gordon Wood. For the concept as applied to the rise of Benjamin Franklin, see Wood, *The Americanization of Benjamin Franklin* (New York, 2004), 25–27.

3. Wentworth secured a half-pay retirement for Lawrence after the expedition ended (see Don Higginbotham, "Young Washington: Ambition, Accomplishment, and Acclaim," in *George Washington Remembers: Reflections on the French and Indian War,* ed. Fred Anderson [Lanham, Md., 2004], 68).

4. Freeman, 1:69.

5. Higginbotham, "Young Washington," 70.

6. Indeed, the appointment made sense on even more grounds than these, for upon Dinwiddie's arrival in the colony he had received a share in the Ohio Company from its members, whom Lawrence had helped organize in 1749 to colonize the lands at the Forks of the Ohio.

7. GW to John Augustine Washington, 28 May 1755, *PGW: Col. Ser.,* 1:289–91.

8. On the political culture of Court and Country, see, especially, John M. Murrin, "The Great Inversion, or Court versus Country: A Comparison of the Revolution Settlements in England (1688–1721) and America (1776–1816)," in *Three British Revolutions: 1641, 1688, 1776,* ed. J. G. A. Pocock (Princeton, N.J., 1980), 368–453; and Pocock, "Political Development," in *Colonial British America: Essays in the New History of the Early Modern Era,* ed. Jack P. Greene and J. R. Pole (Baltimore, 1984), 408–56. The best treatment of the Pistole Fee Controversy is still in Jack P. Greene, *The Quest for Power: The Lower Houses of Assembly in the Southern Royal Colonies, 1689–1776* (Chapel Hill, N.C., 1963), esp. 158–65. The most recent biographical treatment to focus on Washington's early military career and the frustrations he endured as he attempted to defend the Shenandoah frontier is David A. Clary, *George Washington's First War: His Early Military Adventures* (New York, 2011). For a general treatment of these themes and topics, see Fred Anderson, *Crucible of War: The Seven Years' War and the Fate of Empire in British North America, 1754–1766* (New York, 2000), passim.

9. GW to Robinson, 19 December 1756, *PGW: Col. Ser.,* 4:68.

10. Higginbotham, "Young Washington," 82. The outlines and outcome of Washington's solicitations for William Henry Fairfax's commission can be traced in *PGW: Col. Ser.,* 5:17–18 (James Cuninghame to GW, 16 October 1757), 5:70–71 (William Henry Fairfax to GW, 9 December 1757), and 5:136–37 (GW to William Henry Fairfax, 23 April 1758).

11. GW to Robinson, 1 September 1758, *PGW: Col. Ser.,* 5:432–33.

"The Spirit and Ardor of a Veteran Soldier"

George Washington, Daniel Morgan, and the Ideal of Service

L. SCOTT PHILYAW

George Washington knew Daniel Morgan for many more years than any other "son" under consideration in this volume. While the precise date is unknown, it is probable that Washington and Morgan met during the 1750s while at the approximate ages of twenty-five and twenty-one, respectively—roughly the age of a typical graduate or undergraduate student. It is possible that Washington may have heard of Morgan during Braddock's campaign; if so, there is no indication of any relationship beyond the acquaintance of fellow townsmen. Nonetheless, that shared experience would have deepened their understanding of one another when they did meet.[1] Both Washington and Morgan towered over most of their contemporaries by several inches. The general stood at least six feet two inches, while Morgan was six feet or just above. The average height of Revolutionary War–era soldiers was five foot eight.[2]

Their long familiarity did not lead to friendship. Nor did Washington and Morgan enjoy the close relationship that Washington had with some of his other officers. Even during the Revolution, they often fought in different theaters. There is little correspondence between the two men; most of their letters cover relatively routine military matters of orders and reports. All of Washington's letters and most of Morgan's are reserved in tone.[3] Nonetheless, their relationship is instructive, as it illuminates the influence of colonial society on each man, as well as the growth each experienced during the American Revolution. It also illustrates Washington's nuanced consideration as he matched his officers' abilities with their assignments.

An examination of the interactions of Washington and Morgan from the time of Braddock's defeat through the Whiskey Rebellion reveals that, while each man had much in common with the other—connections with the Valley of Virginia and physical prowess, for example—it was their common experiences in the Continental Army that most shaped their American identity. More than most of their fellow Virginians, Washington and Morgan were nationalists. In many respects, their mutual attachment to the new nation does more to explain their relationship than the common elements of their backgrounds.

Although each man cast an imposing figure, Washington and Morgan came from very different circumstances. Their first meeting, whether during Braddock's ill-fated campaign, or afterward, in the backcountry town of Winchester, would have reflected the fundamental inequality of the officer and the wagon driver. Nonetheless, Washington and Morgan each made significant advances above the station of his birth, despite the fact that each also spent the majority of his life as a colonist and as a subject of the British monarch. In that sense, too, they had much in common. While the deferential, hierarchical world of colonial Virginia shaped their respective worldviews and social interactions, that same world placed many barriers between the gentleman and the laborer.[4] Despite their different circumstances, the two men appear to have understood one another well. Morgan was loyal to Washington, just as he was loyal to the new nation and, later, the Constitution. Washington clearly understood Morgan's strengths as a commander, and was often instrumental in ensuring that Morgan's assignments complemented his skills. Washington also sought Morgan's advice on subjects of common interest, such as western lands.

Neither man enjoyed a close relationship with his parents. John E. Ferling argues that Washington was not close to his father, who died when he was only eleven. Washington's mother, Mary Ball Washington, lived until 1789—long enough to witness her son's accomplishments during the Revolution and his inauguration as president. Yet, according to Joseph Ellis, she "never extolled or even acknowledged" her son's "public triumphs." Other scholars agree that Washington did not enjoy an intimate relationship with his mother. In a corrective to this common view, however, Don Higginbotham acknowledges the "tension and friction between a strong-minded, independent mother and a son who shared her characteristics," but he also argues that Mary Ball Washington had a positive influence on her son. We know much less of Morgan's early family life. He grew up in the Delaware River Valley, probably in New Jersey, but perhaps in Pennsylvania. He ran away from home while a teenager.

Morgan rarely spoke of his early family life, only noting that he had to work hard and that he left because of a disagreement with his father.[5]

Both Washington and Morgan had early associations with the town of Winchester, Virginia, a backcountry town of 200–300 inhabitants.[6] Founded in 1745, this newly settled court town was one of a string of small settlements located on the Great Wagon Road that ran from Philadelphia through the Shenandoah Valley to the Carolina Piedmont. Unlike Tidewater Virginia, this second Virginia frontier was settled by an assorted group of European Protestants and settlers from other colonies to the north of Virginia. Most were small farmers who preferred to grow wheat rather than the ubiquitous tobacco of eastern Virginia. These new settlers, together with the many travelers on the Great Wagon Road, soon made Winchester a prosperous market town with many opportunities for surveyors such as Washington and wagoners such as Morgan.[7] Nonetheless, their views of the place differed greatly.

Washington appreciated the potential for great profit in Winchester, its environs, and other western lands—but he rarely appreciated the people of the backcountry. In a 1755 letter to his brother, Washington lamented that he "shou[l]d have been more refreshed from the fatiegues of my journey, and my time wou[l]d have been spent much more agreeably had I halted" before reaching Winchester. In his letter, Washington initially referred to the Valley town as a "vile hole," although he reconsidered and substituted the more neutral term "this place" when revising the letter.[8] Washington had first ventured into the Shenandoah Valley in 1748 at the age of sixteen, when he worked on a survey crew of Lord Thomas Fairfax, North America's only resident peer. Back in the Tidewater, Washington honed his skills, as well as his connections, and soon became a licensed surveyor, an important and often lucrative position in colonial Virginia. He then returned to the Valley, where he spent approximately three years profitably surveying lands west of the Blue Ridge Mountains before returning east and eventually settling at Mount Vernon after Lawrence Washington's death in 1752.[9] Morgan, by contrast, chose to spend the majority of his life in and around Winchester, and spent his final days often associating with a group of veterans from the Quebec campaign called the "Dutch Mess," since all of the men, save Morgan, were German.[10]

In December 1753, Washington passed through Winchester on a perilous journey across the mountains to deliver a message for Virginia's new governor, Robert Dinwiddie. Washington's journey earned international attention after the publication of his journal. His trip was certainly the talk of the town in Winchester, where the young Washington had long been a familiar face.[11] Shortly after his return from the Ohio Country in early 1754, Washington again passed through Winchester, as a major with the Virginia Regiment, a colonial force intended by Governor Dinwiddie to defend Virginia's western claims. Following the untimely death of Joshua Fry, the surveyor and former William and Mary professor who fell from his horse not far from Fort Cumberland, Dinwiddie promoted Washington to colonel. Under Washington's command, the Virginia Regiment won its first battle, a victory marred by the controversial death of the French commander, Joseph Coulon de Jumonville. The regiment's next engagement, the surrender at Fort Necessity, was less controversial. Almost everyone agreed that it was a disaster.

Morgan arrived in Winchester during the spring of 1753. The teenager found work as a laborer in a variety of jobs—clearing land, working in a sawmill, and as a teamster. He saved his wages and soon was able to purchase his own wagon and team. As a young man known to frequent taverns, it is probable that he would have heard many conversations about Washington's exploits. He was in Winchester during the summer of 1754 when word raced through town of Washington's surrender at Fort Necessity—an unexpected setback of great interest to all residents of the community that Governor Dinwiddie described as "the nighest Place . . . which is exposed to the Enemy."[12] Morgan soon joined Virginia's war effort as an independent wagoner delivering supplies to frontier troops—a perilous position in the rapidly deteriorating defenses of the Virginia backcountry.

Virginians rallied the following February when two regiments of British regulars arrived in the Old Dominion under the command of General Edward Braddock. Eight hundred Virginia troops joined Braddock's army at his headquarters in Alexandria.[13] Their enthusiasm soon waned. Many Virginians complained about Braddock's proud attitude. Mystified by the ponderous pace General Braddock set in his slow march westward, Virginia's soldiers nonetheless seemed to share Dinwiddie's "great Hopes" for a British victory—an expectation also held by General Braddock.[14]

Shared confidence of success did not lead to mutual admiration between the British and Virginian troops. The British were often contemptuous of their colonial colleagues. Braddock saw them as "very indifferent Men," whose officers were "very little better." Others believed the colonists to be "languid, spiritless, and unsoldierlike." Worse were charges that the Virginians had "little courage."[15] The British did not limit themselves to words and complaints. They also encouraged the adoption of the regular army's discipline code to better shape the colonial enlistees and conscripts. Soon, Virginians were feeling the pain of the whip—often receiving hundreds of lashes for infractions that had once elicited nothing more than a fine.[16]

British contempt for colonial officers is evident in an anecdote related by Morgan biographer James Graham. One of the British regulars had challenged a captain of the Virginia Regiment to a fight—something scarcely imaginable with a British officer. It was simply unthinkable for a soldier to dare fight an officer. The Englishman—described as "powerful" and "vigorous"—was known to be a "skillful pugilist." The Virginia captain agreed to fight, but Morgan—whose wagon was attached to the company—objected. In Morgan's view, it would be improper for the captain to lower himself to fight such a man. Rather than bring potential humiliation on the entire company (should the captain lose the match), Morgan argued that it would be better if he fought the man. Not surprisingly, the captain agreed. Morgan "at once engaged the bully, and in a very short space of time, gave him so severe a beating that he was unable to rise from the ground." Morgan's decisive victory earned him "high considerations [from] his associates."[17] At another point, while delivering supplies to a garrison along the Virginia frontier, Morgan himself experienced British military discipline. He reportedly struck a British soldier and was sentenced by a drumhead court-martial to receive 400 lashes. According to Morgan, he was keeping count of the number of lashes with the drummer who was delivering the punishment when he realized that his tormenter had miscounted, but as Morgan remembered the tale, he "did not think it worth while to tell him of his mistake and let it go."[18] Whenever Morgan related his story of having cheated King George out of a lash, he reminded his listeners that he was a common man. Unlike the well-born Washington, Morgan had been subject to the same physical punishment of any enlistee or conscript.[19] During the Revolution, Morgan—through his accomplishments and rank—also served as a living embodiment of the idea that merit mattered in the American army.

Morgan's clashes with British authority presaged the actions of the colonists and the regulars during the Battle of the Monongahela—now better known as Braddock's Defeat. Arrogance and European-style tactics were of little use in the forested frontier. The colonists proved to be far better suited to this form of irregular combat. Under Washington's leadership, they prevented the defeat from devolving into a complete catastrophe. Washington's actions earned the praise of his countrymen within the Virginia Regiment and far beyond. His bravery during the battle, his composure during the retreat, and his overall abilities were all on display.[20] Morgan and other wagoners were instrumental to the successful retreat from the field of battle.

Following Braddock's Defeat, both Washington and Morgan saw service in Virginia's backcountry. Washington was promoted to colonel of the re-formed Virginia Regiment, an advancement that indicated as much about his connections as esteem for his relatively limited experience. His assigned responsibilities were challenging enough, but he added to his woes with his extended absences from his troops—often due to his ongoing lobbying efforts to secure a British commission. He may have destroyed any chance he once had to become a British officer when he pressed Brigadier General John Forbes too vigorously on Virginia's behalf regarding the best route to cross the mountains. Washington and other Virginia speculators feared that Pennsylvania would gain the economic and political upper hand in the Ohio Valley if Forbes abandoned Braddock's Road. Forbes, who recognized the colonists' conflicted interests, complained that Washington had shown "weakness in [his] attachment."[21]

It is difficult to re-create Morgan's precise service record during the 1750s. He apparently shifted back and forth between working as a teamster and service with the militia or rangers.[22] Immediately after Braddock's Defeat, Morgan served in Ashby's Ranger Company, a unit plagued with poor leadership. Washington had little good to say about the rangers, which were not part of the Virginia Regiment. In a letter to Governor Dinwiddie, Washington declared the rangers "of no use or benefit to the Country," a belief he thought was shared by the governor, "as well as the Country."[23] As a result of this and other concerns, the ranger units were soon disbanded. Despite the rangers' checkered record, Morgan distinguished himself with his personal bravery. In his 1856 biography of Morgan, James Graham details several of Morgan's noteworthy exploits during this time, including narrowly escaping an ambush, leading a successful counterattack, and other acts that accentuated Morgan's abilities as a soldier and as a leader.[24]

In his role as commander of the Virginia Regiment, Washington was probably aware of Morgan's exploits. Whatever their interactions (if any) during the conflict, they apparently ceased after the fall of Fort Duquesne. Simply put, Morgan was not in Washington's circle. Washington married the wealthy widow Martha Dandridge Custis and devoted himself to managing his lands.

Morgan, again a teamster, was often involved in cards, which sometimes led to fisticuffs. When he took a common-law wife and settled down as a farmer, he, like many other struggling yeomen, was charged with nonpayment of debts. Yet he also enjoyed the trust of the county court, which approved for him several bonds. The court also put him in charge of a section of roads, including the one that ran by Greenway Court, the home of Washington's benefactor, Lord Fairfax.[25] As Morgan aged, he gave up his more rambunctious ways and began to acquire property, including several slaves.

The complex society of the Shenandoah Valley in the mid-eighteenth century offered many ways to make sense of the world. For Morgan, his move to the Valley of Virginia had proven profitable and fulfilling. It was now his home, and the people of the backcountry his friends and neighbors. By contrast, Washington's attitude toward the people of the backcountry hardened during these years. As a surveyor, he clearly understood the promise of western lands. However, first as commander of the Virginia Regiment, and later as an absentee landlord, Washington soon developed a comparatively negative attitude toward the people who had settled the region. As Warren Hofstra notes, the Tidewater environment in which Washington "sought to rise" among the gentry "contrasted sharply" with the Appalachian backcountry, "in which and through which he sought to realize his aspirations."[26] Morgan, by contrast, firmly grounded himself in the backcountry. While Washington often passed through Winchester, he did not live there. Morgan rarely left the region—except during his military service. Washington learned much at the home of Lord Fairfax from men who had served as British officers in far-flung theaters of war. Morgan paid more attention to the wilderness classroom and the world of the yeomen farmer. Each man put his respective skills to good use during the Revolution.

Washington's role during the opening days of the Revolutionary crisis is well known. We know less about Morgan's actions in 1774–75, but they appear to be those of an active and concerned citizen. Morgan was in the Ohio Country as a participant in Lord Dunmore's War against the Shawnee Indians when word arrived about the outbreak of fighting in Massachusetts. As Morgan related it, he and his fellow soldiers pledged to "assist [their] brethren of Boston in case hostilities should commence."[27]

The opportunity for service soon presented itself. New Englanders appreciated any allies, but they were particularly interested in recruiting men skilled with the rifle, as that weapon was rarely used in their region. With the encouragement of John Adams and other New England delegates, Congress voted to raise ten companies of riflemen from Pennsylvania, Maryland, and Virginia. On June 22, the Frederick County Committee of Safety unanimously selected Morgan as captain for that county's company—a distinct honor given that there were several other men available who had more military experience. Morgan soon justified their trust in him, as he quickly raised 96 recruits (well above the 68 men required), accepting only the most able men. Three weeks later, Morgan and his men left Winchester, joining the army at Boston on August 6—a truly blistering pace.[28]

The riflemen soon impressed their fellow colonists with impromptu demonstrations of their weapons' range and accuracy. Inside Boston, the British soon realized that they needed to be more cautious in their movements. Their sentries had become far too casual with their guard duties when faced with only muskets—an oversight that the newly arrived sharpshooters soon corrected with their deadly long-range accuracy. While such harassment demoralized the British, siege operations were not the ideal use of the riflemen. Washington decided to detach three companies—including Morgan's Virginians—to accompany Colonel Benedict Arnold on the ill-fated invasion of Canada. Arnold then selected Morgan to command the three rifle companies. The winter march through northern Maine tested Morgan's wilderness acumen and everyone's stamina. He and the other riflemen served well, and may have inspired some of the farmers and shopkeepers of the New England militia units to rise to the occasion. Even so, the extreme weather, a shortage of supplies, and poor-quality boats led to accidents and disease, as well as to a number of desertions. The remainder of Arnold's command reached the St. Lawrence River on November 8. The rigors of their accomplishment left them too weak for a major assault on the city, but when they were joined by General Richard Montgomery's forces following the capture of Montreal, the combined American army attacked Quebec on the snowy evening of December 30. Morgan and his riflemen distinguished themselves in the assault that followed, but to no avail. The Americans suffered approximately 100 killed and wounded and more than 400 captured—including Morgan. The British, by contrast, lost only 20 men.[29] Impressed with Morgan, the British offered him the rank of colonel if he would join them. He refused—making it clear that his loyalty was not negotiable.[30]

Morgan's meritorious conduct attracted the attention of General Washington, who recommended that the captain be promoted to colonel in command of a regiment of riflemen. In his recommendation, Washington noted Morgan's "conduct as an officer" on the Quebec expedition, "his intrepid behavior in the assault," and "the inflexible attachment he professed to [the American] cause during his imprisonment and which he perserveres in." Washington also noted Morgan's "interest" in and "influence" with the frontiersmen, who were most likely to serve as riflemen. Furthermore, "the States will gain a good and valuable officer for the sort of Troops he is particularly recommended to command."[31] In other words, Washington not only recognized Morgan's skills, but also understood the sort of men who would rally to Morgan's style of leadership. Congress readily agreed, and Morgan was soon serving under Washington during the New Jersey campaign of early 1777. Washington put Morgan and his men to good use keeping a close watch on General William Howe. The riflemen performed well in combat, but Morgan and his men spent much of the summer on the march, as the Americans attempted to determine their adversary's intentions.[32]

Washington clearly appreciated Morgan's reconnaissance, but the rifleman's skills as a light infantry commander were needed farther north, where the situation had become dire. General John Burgoyne, at the head of 9,500 regulars, Hessians, and Native American auxiliaries, had invaded New York, capturing Fort Ticonderoga and several smaller outposts in the process. As Washington noted to John Hancock, even though it was "contrary to [his] wishes," he had "ordered Colo. Morgan to march immediately with his Corps as an additional support" to the northern army. As Washington explained to Morgan, he knew of "no corps so likely to check" Burgoyne's progress "in proportion to its Number as that under your command."[33]

Washington had made a difficult choice in releasing "the best scouts and light infantry in the army" from his own command.[34] To replace Morgan's riflemen, Washington organized a new corps of light infantry. On August 28, he ordered each brigade to furnish "one Field Officer, two captains, six Subalterns, eight Serjeants and 100 Rank & File" to serve in the new corps under the command of Brigadier General William Maxwell.[35] As Washington explained to Congress, he was "sensible to the advantages of Light Troops" and expected this new corps "to be constantly near the Enemy and to give 'em every possible annoyance."[36]

Washington correctly predicted the value of Morgan to General Gates's northern army, as Morgan's corps was instrumental in sealing Burgoyne's fate at the Battle of Saratoga. Much of the fight at Saratoga took place in broken and wooded areas ideally suited for the riflemen. As Burgoyne complained, the American marksmen "hovered upon the flanks in small detachments, and were very expert in securing themselves, and in shifting the ground." Worse, "there was seldom a minute's interval in any part of our line without officers being taken off by single shot."[37] Morgan's men also targeted gunners and Tories—greatly shaking the resolve of the latter. As one British sergeant lamented, this special attention given the loyalists "accelerated their estrangement from our cause and army."[38]

Following Saratoga, Morgan and his men returned to the middle states, where he participated in several skirmishes. Again, he and his troops served as Washington's eyes and ears while the latter was encamped at Valley Forge. One of their tasks was to prevent supplies from reaching the British army in Philadelphia, a task that Morgan accomplished with great sensitivity. While Morgan had little sympathy for those Americans who took up arms on the king's behalf, he believed that civilian loyalists "were misguided and respond best to peaceful persuasion." With civilians, as Higginbotham notes, "Morgan was surprisingly moderate in dealing with Americans who retained their loyalty to the Crown."[39]

Despite these successes, Morgan was unsuccessful in his desired promotion to command the newly formed light infantry. Washington wanted more than a rifle corps for his light infantry. In addition to the skills of a rifleman, Washington sought a corps that could also engage the British in more traditional combat. It is telling that two of the better-known engagements of the American light infantry were their captures of Stony Point on the Hudson in 1779, and of Redoubt No. 10 during the siege of Yorktown. In each case, the battle-hardened Americans attacked with unloaded weapons—relying on their bayonets alone.[40]

Morgan was loyal to General Washington—despite perceived slights over his rank or when grumbling about the boredom of camp life.[41] At Valley Forge, Morgan joined those officers who vehemently asserted their loyalty to Washington during the Conway Cabal. As Higginbotham notes, "Few of his subordinates revered Washington more than Morgan."[42]

Morgan's crowning moments—the battles of Saratoga and Cowpens—shared many characteristics of irregular warfare. His actions in each built on his experience as a frontiersman and as a commander who understood the abilities of his men and knew how to inspire them to do their best, often by appealing to their egalitarian ideals. The latter trait was especially important when working with militias and other volunteers. For example, Morgan successfully persuaded several small parties of Georgia partisans to join him just before Cowpens by appealing to their "character." He noted "the regard" the Georgians had for their "fame," as well as their "love [of] country." He also assured them that he would not ask them "to encounter [any] dangers or difficulties," unless he himself "participate[d] in the" same.[43]

On the eve of the battle of Cowpens, as one soldier reported, Morgan "went among the volunteers, helped them fix their swords, joked with them about their sweethearts, [and] told them to keep in good spirits." Morgan continued "going among the soldiers encouraging them and telling them that the old wagoner would crack his whip over Ben [Tarleton] in the morning, as sure as they lived." The soldier suspected that Morgan had not "slept a wink that night."[44] It is impossible to imagine the famously reserved Washington engaged in similar banter. Instead, Washington advised against being "too familiar" with subordinates. While all men were entitled to civility, they should be kept at a "proper distance."[45]

The Battle of Cowpens was a remarkable success, in large part because Morgan transformed troops who were often considered a liability—militia and partisan volunteers—into the key to his victory. He believed that he had given Tarleton "a devil of a whipping," and that a "more compleat victory never was obtained."[46] In addition to understanding his men, Morgan also correctly read the impetuous Tarleton—to the complete detriment of the latter. Just as Saratoga had turned the tide in the northern theater, Morgan's victory at Cowpens helped to thwart British ambitions in the south. In both battles, Morgan underscored his reputation as an expert with the irregular combat of the frontier.

Regretfully for Morgan, a worsening case of sciatica forced him to take his leave of the army and return to Winchester. There he supervised British prisoners and also coordinated the state's response to the Claypool Rebellion. Under the nominal leadership of John Claypool, a Scotsman, a number of residents of Hampshire County had declared their allegiance to King George. Cornwallis, who had just entered eastern Virginia, had apparently offered commissions to several of the insurgents. Morgan led an army of volunteers from Frederick County westward to the disaffected area. His force arrested several persons and within ten days had crushed the nascent rebellion. Throughout this episode, Morgan was firm yet respectful in his treatment of the would-be rebels, to the extent that Claypool requested Morgan's assistance with his petition for a pardon. Morgan apparently honored Claypool's request.[47] Soon after his return to Winchester, Morgan briefly joined patriot forces in eastern Virginia, but, again, his sciatica prevented his participation in the Battle of Yorktown. In a letter to Washington, he exclaimed that nothing would have provided him "more real pleasure" than to have participated in the "campaign under [Washington's] eye, to have shared the danger . . . and the glory too."[48]

Despite his appreciation for Morgan's military skills, Washington was critical of Morgan on occasion—ironically, for lapses in judgment similar to those he made himself when he oversaw the Virginia Regiment.[49] In 1792, Washington noted that Morgan had been "accused of using improper means to obtain certificates from [his] soldiers."[50] The charge dated from almost a decade earlier, at the end of the Revolution, when Morgan had offered to purchase land certificates from those of his men in need of money. Yet, in 1770, Washington himself had instructed his brother Charles to assist him in the purchase of land bounties as a way to hide his own role in the scheme. As Washington explained to Charles, "Those who may be in want of a little ready money, would gladly sell."[51] Unlike Morgan, Washington feared those willing to sell might expect a greater price if they knew of his role. Even without this knowledge, Washington's officers complained that he had taken advantage of his position to claim "the cream of the country" and "the first choice of it."[52] Upon inspection of the lands in question in 1773, they were "a good deel shagereend" at the relatively poor quality of their bounty lands in comparison to the acreage that Washington had reserved for himself.[53]

Washington's criticisms sprang in part from his lengthier career as an officer. While he and Morgan were nearly the same age, their "professional ages" were different, as Washington had been an officer for much longer. He began his military career in 1753 as a major, not because of his previous experience, but due to his connections. Morgan, by contrast, rose through the ranks and did not attain the rank of colonel until nearly two decades after Washington acquired that honor. As a runaway, Morgan had no connections to advance his cause. Instead, he had to prove himself, through hard work, by besting his peers when they gathered at the neighborhood tavern and on the battlefield. Rather than the intentional self-study for which Washington is famous, Morgan learned the art of command through observation and experience. Washington also learned the value of avoiding any appearance of impropriety—something that the Morgan only slowly came to appreciate.

Washington's criticisms also reflected his life as a gentleman. He and Morgan were products of the colonial era. The four decades they lived as colonists also informed their understanding of social relations.[54] Washington, famous for his reserve, encouraged the use of the British military's harsh techniques of military discipline, including the heavy use of the lash—even though he never lifted his hand against a subordinate. Morgan, on the other hand, deplored the physical punishments common to the eighteenth-century military, in part because he had experienced the lash himself. However, he would readily strike an enlistee when provoked—an acceptable behavior in the rough-and-tumble world of a frontier wagoner.[55] Each man, in other words, demonstrated the behavior expected of a gentleman and a teamster, respectively.

Don Higginbotham notes that "it was European-style warfare that fascinated Washington, not backcountry tactics. . . . Those techniques were used effectively by Gen. Daniel Morgan."[56] Washington himself recognized Morgan's skills as a frontier fighter, as reflected in the duties he assigned the rifleman during the Revolution—the Quebec expedition, Saratoga, and the Carolina backcountry. Yet, in 1792, President Washington dismissed Morgan from consideration as a commander of a new force that was to march west against the Indians northwest of the Ohio. Already two American forces, under Brigadier General Josiah Harmar and Major General Arthur St. Clair, had suffered significant defeats north of the Ohio. St. Clair, who advanced into the Ohio Country with approximately 1,400 troops, lost almost half of his men in a surprise attack. In the wild retreat that followed, the survivors abandoned 1,200 muskets and two cannons on the field of battle. It was one of the worst defeats the U.S. military would ever know.[57]

The situation seemed to call for someone of Morgan's skill and experience. Instead of Morgan, whom Washington declared "intemperate" and "illiterate," the president opted for Anthony Wayne to lead the expedition, although Wayne fared little better in the president's estimation.[58] Washington described the hero of Stony Point as "open to flattery—vain—easily imposed upon," and, like Morgan, "too indulgent . . . to his Officers & men."[59] Other men considered for the command were "addicted to ease & pleasure," or "of inadequate abilities." Some were "infirm: past the vigor of life," or suffered from "delicate health." In several cases, Washington did not know the officer in question well enough, or doubted whether the man would be sufficiently respected at the national level. For example, the president had had "little or no opportunities to form an opinion" of Major General William Moultrie, while Brigadier General Rufus Putnam was "but little known outside his own state."[60] Washington was also well aware of the regional jealousies that had always attended his selection of senior officers—especially if he were to choose a fellow Virginian such as Morgan.

Washington's complex personal history with the Ohio Country, the urgency of securing a victory after losing two armies, the questionable loyalty of many western inhabitants, together with continued presence of British troops on American soil, complicated his decision. At one time, Washington had expressed "full confidence" in Arthur St. Clair.[61] Now, he realized that no single commander could possibly address these interlocking problems. Despite his lack of enthusiasm for Wayne, Washington chose the Pennsylvanian to lead the army against the northwestern Indians. He selected Daniel Morgan to solve a different piece of the western dilemma—the occupation of Pittsburgh following the Whiskey Rebellion.

During the summer of 1792, opposition to the excise tax became much more overt—especially in the western settlements of the young republic. Despite active disaffection throughout most of the frontier regions, Washington soon focused his attention on western Pennsylvania—an area he had known since his first, fateful journey through the region almost four decades earlier. Washington also recognized Pittsburgh's strategic significance as an important supply point for any expeditions against the Ohio Indians. It could serve a similar function if any action were required against the British, who still occupied several posts in the Great Lakes region. Other hotspots of unrest, such as western North Carolina and Kentucky, held less strategic importance, but they also would have presented far greater logistical challenges to federal action.

Already, the Pennsylvania malcontents had indirectly threatened Wayne's army. John Neville, the excise inspector for western Pennsylvania, had rented an office from Captain William Faulkner, an officer serving with that portion of Wayne's army stationed in Pittsburgh. When this became known, a mob of about twenty men ransacked the captain's home, despite the protests of a soldier who was there. At the time, Faulkner was away searching for several deserters. According to Neville, when the rebel group encountered Faulkner on the road, its members "drew a knife on him, threatened to scalp him, tar & feather him, and finally reduce his House and property to ashes if he did not solemnly promise them" to evict Neville's excise office from his home.[62]

Alexander Hamilton strongly urged Washington to take action, and prepared a proclamation "warning all persons to desist from similar" actions and stating his intention to "put the Laws in force against Offenders."[63] Washington agreed that quick action was necessary. On the same day that he received Hamilton's letter, he prepared the proclamation and forwarded it to the secretary of state for his signature. As Washington explained in his cover letter to Thomas Jefferson, resistance to the excise tax in western Pennsylvania had "become too open, violent & serious to be long winked at by the government."[64]

Despite this proclamation, threats and acts of violence continued, to the point that the insurrection also hampered the federal government's ability to support the troops serving under General Wayne. Washington recommended that pay be postponed for these troops, because it would "be too hazardous to send a sum of money by the way of Pittsburgh, thro' counties that are in open rebellion."[65] He believed that he had no choice but to end the rebellion with force. During the fall of 1794, a nationalized militia with Washington at its head began its westward journey. As he noted in his Sixth Annual Address to Congress, his decision "to array citizen against citizen" was an action "too delicate, [and] too closely interwoven with many affecting considerations, to be lightly adopted."[66] As president, he well understood the lesson that he had learned during the fight for Independence—it requires more than military might to defeat a rebellious people.

Whatever his earlier misgivings about Morgan, by August 1794, Washington wrote that he had a "great regard for Genl. Morgan, and respect [for] his military talents, and am persuaded if a fit occasion should occur no one would exert them with more zeal in the service of his country than he would. It is my ardent wish, however, that this Country should remain in Peace as long as the Interest, honour and dignity of it will permit."[67] The "fit occasion" proved to be the occupation of western Pennsylvania in the immediate aftermath of the Whiskey Rebellion.

Why then did Washington believe Morgan best-suited for one position but not the other? Realizing that there would be two military expeditions in 1794, Washington selected Morgan to oversee the more sensitive situation. The expedition ultimately led by General Wayne had one aim—to defeat the Ohio Indians. Wayne also accomplished an important secondary mission—the embarrassment of British officials, who, despite their warm words, refused to come to the aid of the Native Americans during the Battle of Fallen Timbers. The army that would march on Pittsburgh had the more delicate task—to occupy an American town filled with citizens who may or may not have been part of the rebellion. In selecting Wayne as commander of the Legion of the United States, Washington gave serious consideration to how the nation would view his choice. When he selected Morgan to oversee the occupation of Pittsburgh, the president was more concerned with how the citizens of that region would react to his decision.

Washington had many reasons to choose Morgan. The president recognized him as someone familiar with the region and its people. Morgan's style of leadership—friendly, yet firm—and his experience in working with the militia and partisans, also spoke well of his ability to work with civilians. Given Washington's own views of these westerners, he may have considered Morgan's propensity toward common behavior to be an advantageous attribute.[68] Morgan also had strong ties to Pittsburgh. In addition to his frontier service during the Seven Years War and Dunmore's War, he had friends and family there. Even Neville had strong connections to Morgan. Formerly of Winchester and a fellow Revolutionary officer, he had moved to western Pennsylvania in 1781. Two years later, his son Pressley married Morgan's daughter, Nancy. The young couple soon settled in Pittsburgh, where they started a family. Equally important, Morgan was a firm Federalist and strong supporter of the Washington administration.

During the march into western Pennsylvania, Morgan—unlike officers of the right wing of the army—successfully prevented his troops from retaliating against the local population. As commander of the occupying force, he was sensitive and humane in his dealings with the local populace—just as he had been during the Revolution. He was also lenient with the rebels, just as he had been with John Claypool in the Hampshire County insurrection.[69] In a letter praising Morgan's command, Washington now stressed his satisfaction, noting that the "general conduct and character of the Army has been temperate and indulgent; and that [Morgan's] attention to the quiet and comfort of the western inhabitants has been well received by them."[70]

Both Washington and Morgan had an understanding of how the world should work that was firmly grounded in the deferential world of colonial Virginia. Each adapted and grew during the Revolution, but each rejected some of the more radical ideas of the time. The scars on Morgan's back bore clear testimony of his place in colonial society. His achievements and recognition, during and after the American Revolution, indicate the role of merit in the new American republic.[71] Yet Washington achieved unimaginable glory—at least in part because he began his journey with the advantage of birth.

Washington was a nationalist who also had a long history with the western backcountry. Morgan was a man of the Valley and the backcountry who also operated on the national stage. His loyalty to Washington was more personal than intellectual. He initially opposed John Jay's treaty with Spain, for example, at least in part as a result of his many ties to the Ohio Valley. He immediately changed his view upon learning that President Washington favored the treaty, however. From that moment on, he was a steadfast supporter of the unpopular agreement.[72]

Perhaps the greatest compliment that could be paid to Washington and Morgan is that each man accurately assessed the other. Morgan understood the talents that Washington brought to leadership—both as general and as president. Washington certainly understood those circumstances that called for Morgan's talents. While never close, they did respect one another's specific abilities. The former teamster, his back scarred from the British lash, shared with his commander in chief a vision of the United States heavily influenced by their common experience of service with the Continental Army.

The colonial ideal of deference and hierarchy illuminates much of Washington and Morgan's relationship. The Revolutionary ideal of merit informed their understanding of one another. The universal ideal of loyalty—to the army and to the nation—guided them throughout their relationship with one another and with the new nation.

Notes

1. James Graham writes that Morgan's "acquaintance with Washington commenced about this time [1757], and was one of the consequences of his meritorious conduct" (see Graham, *The Life of General Daniel Morgan of the Virginia Line of the Army of the United States, with Portions of his Correspondence; compiled from Authentic Sources* [New York, 1856], 32). The essay's title is taken from Washington's letter to Daniel Morgan, 5 October 1781, ibid., 399.

2. Kenneth L. Sokoloff and Georgia C. Villaflor, "The Early Achievement of Modern Stature in America," *Social Science History* 6 (Autumn 1982): 458–59. Washington certainly was aware of the power of height. For example, when assembling a personal guard for his baggage, Washington ordered that all the soldiers "sh[oul]d look well & be nearly of a size." He further stipulated "that none of the Men may exceed in stature 5 feet 10 inches, nor fall short of 5 feet 9 inches" (see GW to Colonels Alexander Spotswood, Alexander McClanachan, and Abraham Bowman and Lieutenant Colonel Christian Febiger, 30 April 1777, *PGW: Rev. Ser.*, 9:315).

3. Washington, who was very deliberate with the salutation of his letters (using "Sir," "Dear Sir," or "My Dear Sir" as an indication of his closeness to the recipient), only began to address Morgan with the familiar "Dear Sir" in 1784, and never used the more intimate "My Dear Sir" (see Stuart Leibiger, *Founding Friendship: George Washington, James Madison, and the Creation of the American Republic* [Charlottesville, Va., 2001], 2–4).

4. Gordon S. Wood, *The Radicalism of the American Revolution* (New York, 1992), 11–24.

5. John E. Ferling, *The First of Men: A Life of George Washington* (Knoxville, Tenn., 1988), 6–7; Joseph J. Ellis, *His Excellency: George Washington* (New York, 2004), 8; Don Higginbotham, "George Washington and Three Women," in *George Washington's South,* ed. Tamara Harvey and Greg O'Brien (Gainesville, Fla., 2004), 126; Higginbotham, *Daniel Morgan: Revolutionary Rifleman* (Chapel Hill, N.C., 1961), 1–3; Graham, *Life of General Daniel Morgan* (New York, 1856), 19–21.

6. Christopher E. Hendricks, *The Backcountry Towns of Colonial Virginia* (Knoxville, Tenn., 2006), 91.

7. Robert D. Mitchell, "'Over the Hill and Far Away': George Washington and the Changing Virginia Backcountry," in *George Washington and the Virginia Backcountry,* ed. Warren Hofstra (Madison, Wis., 1998), 63–64.

8. GW to John Augustine Washington, 28 May 1755, *PGW: Col. Ser.,* 1:290. For a discussion of Washington's revisions to his letters, see ibid., 1:xvii–xix, and the editorial note "The Letterbook for the Braddock Campaign, 2 March–14 August 1755," 1:236–40.

9. The trustees of the College of William and Mary, a group dominated by Virginia's powerful elite, issued all survey licenses (see Sarah S. Hughes, *Surveyors and Statesmen: Land Measuring in Colonial Virginia* [Richmond, Va., 1979]; and Henry Hartwell, James Blair, and Edward Chilton, *The Present State of Virginia, and the College* [1727], ed. Hunter Dickinson Farish [Williamsburg, Va., 1940], 69). See also "George Washington's Professional Surveys, 22 July 1749–25 October 1752," *PGW: Col. Ser.,* 1:8–19; and Philander D. Chase, "A Stake in the West: George Washington as a Backcountry Surveyor and Landholder," in Hofstra, *George Washington and the Virginia Backcountry,* 159–94.

10. Higginbotham, *Daniel Morgan,* 212.

11. The news of Washington's exploits were spread internationally through the publication of *The Journal of Major George Washington Sent by the Hon. Robert Dinwiddie, Esq; His Majesty's Lieutenant-Governor, and Commander in Chief of Virginia, to the Commandant of the French Forces on Ohio . . .* ([Williamsburgh, Va., 1754]; London, 1754), as reprinted in *PGW: Diaries,* 1:130–61.

12. "Instructions from Robert Dinwiddie" to GW, 14 August 1755, *PGW: Col. Ser.,* 2:5.

13. James Titus, *The Old Dominion at War: Society, Politics, and Warfare in Late Colonial Virginia* (Columbia, S.C., 1991), 65–66.

14. Dinwiddie to the Assembly, 8 July 1755, in *Official Records of Robert Dinwiddie, Lieutenant-Governor of the Colony of Virginia, 1751–1758 . . . in the Collections of the Virginia Historical Society,* ed. Robert Alonzo Brock (Richmond, Va., 1883), 94.

15. Edward Braddock and Robert Orme, as quoted in Titus, *Old Dominion at War,* 66, 170nn79–80.

16. Titus, *Old Dominion at War,* 66–69.

17. Graham, *Life of General Daniel Morgan,* 25.

18. Higginbotham, *Daniel Morgan,* 4–5; Graham, *Life of General Daniel Morgan,* 30. The exact date of this event is unclear, as is the identity and rank of the man Morgan struck down. Some accounts report that Morgan was sentenced to 500 lashes. The only sure evidence of this event are the scars Morgan wore for the rest of his life.

19. Wood, *Radicalism of the American Revolution,* 29.

20. John E. Ferling, "School for Command: Young George Washington and the Virginia Regiment," in Hofstra, *George Washington and the Virginia Backcountry,* 200.

21. Forbes to Colonel Bouquet, 23 September 1758, *Writings of General John Forbes: Relating to his Service in North America,* ed. Alfred Procter James (Menasha, Wis., 1938), 219.

22. Graham, *Life of General Daniel Morgan,* 28.

23. GW to Robert Dinwiddie, [4 August 1756], *PGW: Col. Ser.,* 3:317.

24. Graham, *Life of General Daniel Morgan,* 31–35. See also Higginbotham, *Daniel Morgan,* 7.

25. Higginbotham, *Daniel Morgan,* 14–15. Marriage had a positive effect on both men.

26. Hofstra, "'And Die by Inches': George Washington and the Encounter of Cultures on the Southern Colonial Frontier," in Harvey and O'Brien, *George Washington's South,* 75.

27. Graham, *Life of General Daniel Morgan,* 52.

28. Higginbotham, *Daniel Morgan,* 22–24.

29. Don Higginbotham, *The War of American Independence: Military Attitudes, Policies, and Practice, 1763–1789* (New York, 1971), 108–15; Higginbotham, *Daniel Morgan,* 27–42.

30. Higginbotham, *Daniel Morgan,* 52.

31. GW to John Hancock, 28 September 1776, *PGW: Rev. Ser.,* 6:421.

32. Higginbotham, *Daniel Morgan,* 57–60.

33. GW to Hancock, 17 August 1777, *PGW: Rev. Ser.,* 10:649; GW to Daniel Morgan, 16 August 1777, ibid., 10:641.

34. Edward G. Lengel, *General George Washington: A Military Life* (New York, 2005), 224.

35. GW, "General Orders," 28 August 1777, *PGW: Rev Ser.,* 11:82; GW, "General Orders," 30 August 1777, ibid., 11:91.

36. GW to Hancock, 30 August 1777, ibid., 11:93.

37. Burgoyne, as quoted in Higginbotham, *War of American Independence,* 202n40.

38. Sergeant Roger Lamb, *Memoirs of His Own Life* (Dublin, 1809), 199, as quoted in Higginbotham, *War of American Independence,* 195.

39. Higginbotham, *Daniel Morgan,* 82.

40. Henry P. Johnston, *The Storming of Stony Point on the Hudson, Midnight, July 15, 1779* (New York, 1900), 65–66, 76; Henry P. Johnston, *The Yorktown Campaign and the Surrender of Cornwallis, 1781* (New York, 1881), 145.

41. Higginbotham, *Daniel Morgan,* 95–97.

42. Ibid., 82–83. There is some debate regarding whether Conway's criticisms rose to the level of a conspiracy or cabal (see Lengel, *General George Washington,* 277–78).

43. Higginbotham, *Daniel Morgan,* 125–26.

44. As quoted in Benson Bobrick, *Angel in the Whirlwind: The Triumph of the American Revolution* (New York, 1997), 429.

45. Edmund S. Morgan, *The Genius of George Washington* (New York, 1980), 7.

46. Morgan to William Snickers, as quoted in Higginbotham, *Daniel Morgan,* 142.

47. Graham, *Life of General Daniel Morgan,* 378–81.

48. Morgan to GW, 20 September 1781, as quoted in Higginbotham, *Daniel Morgan,* 168.

49. Higginbotham, *Daniel Morgan,* 98.

50. GW, "Memorandum on General Officers," 9 March 1792, *PGW: Pres. Ser.,* 10:75.

51. GW to Charles Washington, 31 January 1770, *PGW: Col. Ser.,* 8:301.

52. GW to James Ross, 16 June 1794, Fitzpatrick, 33:405.

53. William Crawford to GW, 12 November 1773, *PGW: Col. Ser.,* 9:380; L. Scott Philyaw, *Virginia's Western Visions: Political and Cultural Expansion on an Early American Frontier* (Knoxville, Tenn., 2004), 77–78. Bernhard Knollenberg offers a critical appraisal of this episode in *George Washington: The Virginia Period, 1732–1775* (Durham, N.C., 1964), 91–100.

54. Higginbotham, "Military Education before West Point," in *Thomas Jefferson's Military Academy: Founding West Point,* ed. Robert M. S. McDonald (Charlottesville, Va., 2004), 36.

55. Graham, *Life of General Daniel Morgan,* 199–200; Higginbotham, *Daniel Morgan,* 92–93. See also Elliott J. Gorn, "'Gouge and Bite, Pull Hair and Scratch': The Social Significance of Fighting in the Southern Backcountry," *American Historical Review* 90 (February 1985): 18–43.

56. Higginbotham, "George Washington and Revolutionary Asceticism: The Localist as Nationalist," in Hofstra, *George Washington and the Virginia Backcountry,* 229.

57. Elliott West, "American Frontier," in *The Oxford History of the American West,* ed. Clyde A. Milner II, Carol A. O'Connor, and Martha A. Sandweiss (New York, 1994), 128.

58. GW, "Memorandum on General Officers," 9 March 1792, *PGW: Pres. Ser.,* 10:75. While Washington did note that Morgan would be a suitable brigadier general, he doubted that Morgan would accept the position. As he predicted, Morgan rejected the opportunity to serve in a subservient position.

59. Ibid., 10:74.

60. Ibid., 10:74–76. The officers in question are George Weedon, Charles Scott, Benjamin Lincoln, Otho Holland Williams, William Moultrie, and Rufus Putnam, respectively.

61. GW to St. Clair, 28 March 1792, ibid., 10:163.

62. Thomas P. Slaughter, *The Whiskey Rebellion: Frontier Epilogue to the American Revolution* (New York, 1986), 114–15; John Neville to George Clymer, 23 August 1792, as quoted in *PGW: Pres. Ser.,* 11:61n2.

63. Hamilton to GW, 9 September 1792, *PGW: Pres. Ser.,* 11:94–95.

64. GW to Thomas Jefferson, 15 September 1792, *PGW: Pres. Ser.,* 11:114.

65. GW to the Secretary of the Treasury, 21 August 1794, Fitzpatrick, 33:471.

66. GW to Congress, 19 November 1794, ibid., 34:30.

67. GW to Charles Mynn Thruston, 10 August 1794, ibid., 33:464.

68. Warren R. Hofstra analyzes Washington's infamous antipathy toward the German and Scotch-Irish farmers of Virginia's backcountry and convincingly argues that Washington's early experience in overcoming his personal feelings helped solidify the public virtue and republican values that would serve him well as a national leader (see "'And Die by Inches,'" 69–85). By contrast, Morgan had always felt comfortable with frontier culture. Tellingly, he spent many of his final days socializing with a group of veterans—all

of whom, save Morgan, were Germans. It is scarcely possible to imagine Washington in similar circumstances (see Higginbotham, *Daniel Morgan,* 212).

69. Higginbotham, *Daniel Morgan,* 191–94.

70. GW to Morgan, 27 March 1795, Fitzpatrick, 34:158.

71. Higginbotham, *Daniel Morgan,* 210–11. As Higginbotham notes elsewhere, Morgan's career may have suffered because he, "like Washington, hailed from the Old Dominion" (see Higginbotham, *George Washington and the American Military Tradition* [Athens, Ga., 1985], 92).

72. Higginbotham, *Daniel Morgan,* 199.

Most Loyal but Forgotten Son

Anthony Wayne's Relationship with George Washington

MARY STOCKWELL

When Henry Lee, then the governor of Virginia, learned that his friend George Washington had appointed Anthony Wayne as the commander of the army to be sent west to defeat the Indian confederation formed to halt the advance of the Americans across the Ohio River—a confederation that had already destroyed armies serving under Josiah Harmar in 1790 and Arthur St. Clair in 1791—he was furious at the president, and told him so in no uncertain terms. "You cannot be a stranger," he wrote, "to the extreme disgust which the late appointment to the command of the army excited among all orders in this state." Lee claimed not to be angry because he had not been appointed himself—even though, as he took care to mention, he was qualified for the job.[1]

Standing in the present and knowing what Wayne would achieve across the Ohio River—how he would spend two years training his men to march, ride, shoot, fight, and, above all else, not be afraid—how he would accomplish what the previous armies had failed to accomplish and defeat the confederation led by Little Turtle of the Miami and Bluejacket of the Shawnee—we expect Washington to be as wise as we have come to believe he truly was. Somehow, we expect him to know that Wayne would win a smashing victory at Fallen Timbers on August 20, 1794, and one year later go on to write the Treaty of Greenville, which finally opened Ohio for settlement. If nothing else, we want Washington to acknowledge that he chose the best man for the job—the man with the experience, temperament, and leadership skills necessary to win a great victory for the American people and their future.

But Washington did not say this. Instead, he explained that he had made his decision rationally and with much forethought. After describing how he had chosen the higher-ranking officer, General Wayne, over the lower-ranking one, Colonel Lee, Washington opened up even more to his friend; surely Lee must know the high regard in which he was held. Had President Washington stopped there, his letter would have been almost charming, with its tone of a wise father explaining the ways of the world to his headstrong son. But Washington then went on to disparage the man whom he had appointed. Wayne "has many good points as an Officer," he admitted, "but it is to be hoped, that time, Reflection, good advice, and above all, a due sense of the importance of the trust which is committed to him, will correct his foibles, or cast a shade over them."[2]

It is somewhat surprising that Washington commented on Wayne's foibles when the two men were similar in so many ways. Both were wealthy farmers—Washington by marriage and the work of his slaves, and Wayne through an inheritance from his very successful father. Both men often commented that they wished to return to the life of a farmer, especially as the Revolution dragged on.[3] As a young man, Wayne received a more formal education than Washington—but he chafed against its constraints and left school long before he became the gentleman his father hoped he would be. They each first gained real experience of the world as surveyors, and understood the value of land as opportunity in their very bones. Both also came to feel the lack of education in their lives as they grew older, with Wayne especially reading anything he could get his hands on, from history, to literature, to military tactics, to fill in the gaps in his knowledge. Although neither man was considered an intellectual, each understood the political cause for which he was fighting and each had a keen understanding of how the American experiment in self-government was a true turning point in history. Although both may have denied being a member of a faction or political party, their inclinations were Federalist to the core. As Federalists, they supported the Constitution, in the late 1780s, and came to oppose the political opinions of Thomas Jefferson and his followers, in the 1790s. Their common experience of the near disintegration of the body politic in the worst days of the Revolution confirmed their commitment to a strong national government. Finally, and perhaps most important, they were soldiers who took naturally to army life and endured much in the deep belief that the nation they were building provided an extraordinary chance for the human spirit to soar.

Still, Washington's disparaging remarks may have come from the differences he saw in their personalities, especially the way in which they each handled their deep emotions. Both Washington and Wayne had terrible tempers. One of Washington's greatest outbursts immediately preceded Wayne's appointment to command the army in Ohio. Tobias Lear, Washington's private secretary, recorded the story of what happened when the news arrived in Philadelphia that St. Clair's army had been defeated. The president was at supper when a messenger arrived with the tale of St. Clair's defeat. Washington left the dining room, went out into the hall, where he read the report, and returned to his guests without showing one flicker of emotion. But later, when everyone had gone home, Lear remembered how the president had exploded in a rage, turning red, and at times even weeping. He complained bitterly that he had warned St. Clair to be on guard and not to be surprised—and yet still the army had been surprised and destroyed on the terrible morning of November 4, 1791. St. Clair had lost most of his men and almost all of his officers when the Indians ambushed his unprotected camp. "The army cut to pieces," Washington cried, "hacked, butchered, tomahawked! O God! O God! He's worse than a murderer! He will answer for this to his country!"[4]

Such outbursts were rare for Washington. He had made it a point throughout his life to control his emotions. In contrast, Wayne, who felt just as deeply, had no compunction about appearing to lose control. He was known for swearing better than any general in the Continental Army, and he never flinched from telling his men exactly what he thought of them. He filled his letters to his friends in Philadelphia with colorful epithets—exploding when Congress refused to fund his soldiers in the field, mocking the faithless patriot women who ran after the victorious British, and raging when he thought his motives were questioned.[5] He was just as disciplined as Washington, but he was not as obsessed with appearing to be perfect and always in control. He was unapologetically emotional and imaginative, and must have been annoying to men in an age where reason was still valued as paramount. Only a dozen years younger than Washington, to the degree that he was in tune with the romantic spirit that would burst upon the world in the last decade of the eighteenth century, he was ahead of his time.[6]

If Thomas Jefferson is to be believed, President Washington said even worse things about Wayne to his cabinet than he had written to his friend Henry Lee. Jefferson recalled the cabinet meeting where he, Knox, and Hamilton met with the president to discuss the replacement of Arthur St. Clair. Wayne already had many military accomplishments on his record, including his orderly retreat from the disaster at Three Rivers in Canada at the start of the war; his brave stands at Chadds Ford, Brandywine, and Germantown; his steadfast loyalty to his commander at Valley Forge; his bold "yes" to challenging the British at Monmouth Court House; his "mad" dash up the cliffs to Stony Point; his deliberate actions to stand down the mutiny in the Pennsylvania Line; his harassment of Cornwallis in the lead-up to Yorktown; and his unbelievable endurance in the final Georgia campaign. Nevertheless, Washington had prepared this description of Wayne for his cabinet to review: "More active & enterprizing than judicious & cautious. No oeconomist it is feared. Open to flattery—vain—easily imposed upon—and liable to be drawn into scrapes. Too indulgent (the effect perhaps of some of the causes just mentioned) to his Officers & men. Whether sober—or a little addicted to the bottle, I know not."[7] Jefferson recorded other unflattering charges made during the meeting. Wayne was said to be "brave and nothing else"—a man who "deserves credit for Stony Point, but on another occasion run his head against a wall where success was both impossible and useless."[8]

These comments would have stunned the British, who were watching developments on the Ohio frontier from their posts in Canada and from forts on American soil, such as Detroit and Mackinac, which they refused to surrender after the Revolution. They considered Wayne to be an excellent general and commander—although they, too, thought that his main talents were primarily on the battlefield. George Hammond, the British ambassador to the United States, notified Sir John Graves Simcoe, who had fought Wayne in the Virginia campaign and who was now the governor of Upper Canada, that his old nemesis had just been appointed the commander of the next army heading into Ohio to take on the British-allied Indian confederation. "General Wayne is unquestionably the most active, vigilant, and enterprizing Officer in the American service," explained Hammond. Simcoe, in turn, would keep Sir Henry Clinton apprised of every move Wayne made during the long road to Fallen Timbers. To this day, detailed maps of Wayne's march from Fort Washington to Fallen Timbers can be found among Clinton's papers.[9]

If Wayne had heard the terrible things that Lee, Jefferson, and the British were saying about him, he might have exploded. He had a terrible temper and might at least have hurled a string of curses at them. He probably would have told Lee that in the last year of the Revolution, when Lee's health and sanity broke down while fighting in the Carolina backcountry, Wayne and the rest of the Pennsylvania Line continued the struggle. He probably would have reminded Jefferson of the terrible winter and spring of 1781, when Tidewater

Virginia was aflame with burning tobacco warehouses and refugees fleeing down the country roads. During those awful months, Jefferson had often fled to save his own life, while Wayne stayed in the field day and night in pursuit of the traitor Benedict Arnold, Simcoe's Rangers, and, finally, Lord Cornwallis himself. Along with the Marquis de Lafayette, he had "run his head against the wall" of the redcoats all the way to Yorktown. Wayne might have told the British that there was more to him than soldiering. He clearly understood the principles for which he fought. He knew that the British were being expelled forever so that the people could rule themselves. He could have explained how in the now-forgotten Georgia campaign he had fought to restore civil government in the state. He had worked hand in hand with Governor John Martin to end the "state of nature" into which the people of Georgia had fallen. Finally, he could have told both Jefferson and the British that when it appeared that the nation he had fought to establish was dissolving, he had supported the writing of a new Constitution that would strengthen the Union and give greater powers to the national government. He had even voted for the Constitution as a representative from Chester County at Pennsylvania's ratifying convention.[10]

But if it was still possible for a man like Wayne, who had endured so much—a body tormented with pain and disease from eight years of war (making him, at forty-seven years of age, old before his time), a ruined marriage, a daughter and son who barely remembered him, and a personal estate nearly bankrupt—to have his heart broken, then it surely would have broken if he knew the terrible things that Washington had said of him. From the moment, in the first year of the war, when he was appointed a colonel of one of the four battalions that would become the Pennsylvania Line, he had looked up to General Washington as the perfect commander. If we still have trouble seeing Washington as anything more than a marble statue on a pedestal, then we must acknowledge that Wayne was one of the people who put him there. Every biographer of Wayne who has been through his papers has concluded that there is rarely a criticism against Washington in them.[11]

In fact, there were only three instances when Wayne openly disagreed with his commander. The first came in late 1777 when Wayne urged Washington to continue the campaign against the British. He fretted over Washington's caution, but quickly came to see the wisdom of it as he followed his commander to Valley Forge. The second came after Yorktown when Washington turned down Wayne's request to go home and see his family, who had all but forgotten him. Washington sent him instead, with the rest of the Pennsylvania Line, to the Carolinas to help Nathanael Greene push the British out of the Deep South. Rather than spending the Christmas of 1781 at Waynesborough, his family's estate just outside of Philadelphia near Valley Forge, a tired, wounded, and depressed Anthony Wayne took command of a small group of army regulars and militia, heading into Georgia to oust the British from Savannah and restore order in the state.[12]

The third disagreement came once he had assumed command of the army in Ohio. He had watched Washington send one negotiator after another to the Indian tribes to win peace—knowing all the while that they would never surrender and so war would be inevitable. There were days when he was certain the president and most of the country simply did not understand that the Ohio Indian confederation was linked to the British in Canada. The very commanders who had fought the Americans during the Revolution—men like Simcoe, Allured Clarke (who had opposed Wayne in Georgia), and Sir Guy Carleton (now the governor general of Canada)—had simply moved their operations northward, and were more determined than ever to ruin the young American nation. "This is not a common predatory little war made by a few tribes of Indians," he explained to Governor Charles Scott of Kentucky. "It is a confederated war forming a chain of circumvallation around the frontiers of America."[13] Still, he never questioned a single command that the president sent to him during the entire Ohio campaign.

To understand how deeply Wayne admired Washington, one need only go to Waynesborough. There, Wayne's commission as commander of the army heading into Ohio, signed by Washington himself, is proudly framed on a first-floor wall. Winning this commission from the man he so admired was the highest honor of his life.[14] It was an honor that he made clear he would be willing to receive. As soon as Washington had been elected president, Wayne had written him a congratulatory letter affirming that the nation required "a Washington" at this critical time in its history. The "ardious" nature of the new president's responsibilities, coupled with the "crisis" facing the nation, "tempted" Wayne to "offer my ready & best services, shou'd they be at any time wanted."[15]

Wayne's letter was just one of many that he had written to his commander during and after the Revolution. Most of the letters focused on the business of war, and the responses were similar. They dealt with troop movements and enemy actions, and rarely amounted to more than a few lines in either direction. But other letters written by Wayne to Washington employed a beautifully descriptive and passionate style that went far beyond typical communication. Wayne had a profound imagination that allowed him to see every possible contingency of a future confrontation with the enemy. He could always be counted on to reach into his ancient history books—Caesar's *Commentaries* especially—to pull out some advice for his beloved general.

One of his best letters in this vein came in September 1777 when Washington was less than a week away from making a stand against the British at Brandywine. As Wayne saw it, the Continental Army should not retreat to a defensive position, but should instead attack. "I took the liberty . . . to Suggest the Selecting 2,500 or 3,000 of our best Armed and most Disciplined Troops," he informed Washington, "who should hold themselves in Readiness on the Approach of the Enemy to make a Regular and Vigorous Assault on their Right or Left flank"—or whatever "part of their Army as should then be thought most expedient—and not wait" for "the Attack from them." He assured his commander that "this Sir is no new Idea," for it had "been Often practiced with Success" by many throughout history, including "Caesar at Amiens," who, "when besieged by the Gauls, . . . Sallied out with his Cohorts" and "threw them into the utmost Consternation & Obtained an easy Victory."[16]

Although he seemed never to have realized it himself, there were usually two people he wrote to before and after every battle—George Washington and Polly Wayne. In the letters that he wrote both to his commander and his wife, Wayne revealed himself to be a kind of "cheerleader," buoying the spirits of his general and his spouse. When facing yet another battle, he would resort to the habit of telling Washington how other great generals had been in similar positions and had triumphed. When it was all over and the Continental Army had not triumphed, Washington could usually count on a letter from Wayne telling him that victory could still be salvaged from this latest defeat. A memorable letter in this regard came after Germantown, when Wayne explained that "our people have gained confidence—and have Raised some Doubts in the Minds of the Enemy which will facilitate their total Defeat the Next Tryal." Lest Washington entertain any doubts, Wayne assured him that "you are now in my Hum[b]l[e] Opinion in as good if not a better Situation than you were before this Action."[17]

As a man of emotion, Wayne expressed moodiness in his letters, which often have a rising and falling tone in them. But despite his ever-changing feelings, Wayne could be relied upon to support and defend Washington, especially when members of Congress were calling for Washington's dismissal. In letters to his friends in Philadelphia, Wayne railed against anyone who questioned Washington's authority or competence. Similarly, he reminded his wife, especially early in the war, that he possessed the full "confidence of the General" and could not leave his side.[18] He often counseled Polly—who at first missed him terribly, then resented his absences, and, finally, hated him—to remain steadfast so that the promise of the United States might be fulfilled. "You must endeavor to keep up your spirits as well as possible," he implored her, for "the times require great sacrifices to be made." He reminded her that "the blessings of liberty cannot be purchased at too high a price—the blood & treasure of the choicest & best spirits of the land is but a trifling consideration for such a rich inheritance." He did not ignore the magnitude of the possible sacrifice. As he admitted, "Whether any of the present leaders will live to see it established in this once happy soil depends on Heaven."[19]

What a second to have at one's side. Wayne's relationship with Washington was even more remarkable in that he asked practically nothing in return for his earnestness. Wayne admired Washington and could find no flaw in him. But if we expect Washington to appreciate these sentiments and perhaps to write or dictate letters of equal warmth, then we will be disappointed. Washington rarely wrote more than a few lines to Wayne, even in response to his most passionate missives. Whether responding to Wayne's latest idea for a campaign drawn from the depths of his own imagination and his ancient history books, or to his latest cheerleading session, Washington usually penned only a short note in return. His words, although never cruel or harsh, generally amounted to little more than a simple acknowledgement that Wayne's letters had been received. For example, to Wayne's dramatic endorsement of Washington in 1789 and his offer to serve his commander and his nation, the president merely replied that "your reflections on the arduous nature of the Station in which I am placed correspond exactly with my own. . . . My greatest apprehension, at present, is, that more will be expected from me, than I shall be able to perform."[20]

While Washington did not respond to Wayne with the same level of emotion, he certainly appreciated many of the good qualities that he saw in him. These included Wayne's devotion to his nation and his willingness to take on any task—from the most daring to the most humiliating—for the Revolution. Washington knew that his brigadier was cool under fire, and may even have appreciated the fact that Wayne's first major military action was leading a retreat, not out of the wilds of Pennsylvania and western Virginia, as Washington had done in the French and Indian War, but from the disaster into which St. Clair had led the Continental Army at Three Rivers in Canada in June 1776. Wayne had been willing to endure the isolation and boredom of Ticonderoga before being called to Washington's side to fight with the rest of the Pennsylvania Line in the defense of Philadelphia. Once there, Washington was patient with Wayne as he went from dreaming about fighting—and reciting what Caesar would have done—to actually learning how to fight. Washington recognized him as a good organizer and usually sent him to train new recruits. He did not condemn Wayne when the British massacred his men at Paoli, nor did he believe that Wayne needed to undergo a court-martial to vindicate himself. Washington even sent orders to him on the day the proceedings began, letting Wayne know what he believed the outcome would be. He was just as patient with Wayne when he became confused in the fog at Germantown.[21]

Washington also understood Wayne's acute sense of honor, especially in matters concerning his commander. Wayne could not bear the thought that his "excellency" might think badly of him, and was especially worried about how Washington would react to his handling of the revolt in the Pennsylvania Line in January 1781. "It is with pain I now inform your Excellency of the general mutiny & defection which suddenly took place in the Penn's line between 9 & 10 o'clock last evening," wrote Wayne. He explained that "every possible exertion was used by the officers to suppress it in its rise; but the torrent was too potent to be stemmed." Washington wrote one of his kindest letters on the next day, assuring Wayne that he knew his brigadier had done "everything possible . . . to check the mutiny upon its first appearance."[22] His junior officer's devotion probably caused Washington to realize that Wayne could be counted on to do whatever task was necessary to help him succeed. Whether it was something demeaning, like rounding up cattle in the countryside near Valley Forge or Morristown—a task which won Wayne the title of "Cow Chaser" and the ridicule of the British poet Major John André—or whether it was something insanely daring, like the raid that he planned in order to take Stony Point on the Hudson from the British, Washington knew that Wayne would come to his aid without question.[23]

But if he understood Wayne so well, and used this devotion to his advantage throughout the Revolution, then why would George Washington say such terrible things about Wayne in 1792? Why would he forget the good things he knew about his most loyal "son" and remember only his "foibles"? In part, the answer can be traced to what happened between the two men after Yorktown. Immediately following the stunning victory of the Americans and French over Cornwallis in October 1781, Wayne seemed to wake up from a dream. Since he had joined the Continental Army in 1775, he had rarely been home, and now, six years later, he suddenly realized that his children, Margaretta and Isaac, had grown up without him. He became obsessed with ways to make money, and could be seen about the American camp trying to buy sugar, which he hoped to sell for a quick profit. He was stunned when Washington turned down his request for a leave and ordered him south to the Carolinas to support General Greene.[24]

At first, Washington showed no patience with the string of letters that his brigadier wrote to him begging for a leave. "As a *friend*, I told you that my feelings were hurt, as a *soldier*, I am always ready to submit to difficulties," Wayne complained. "I only requested leave of absence for a short time."[25] Washington was going through a far deeper tragedy himself, with the illness and subsequent death of his stepson, Jack Custis. Washington was also still furious at Admiral de Grasse for refusing to take the army led by Lafayette—with Wayne again as second in command—south to Wilmington, North Carolina. After he had a chance to gain control over his emotions, he relented a bit. Assuming that Wayne's reluctance came from the continuing infighting in the Pennsylvania Line and Wayne's hesitation to serve under St. Clair, Washington agreed to Wayne's request that he be allowed to head south by carriage at his own pace and meet up with the rest of the army later.[26]

From that point forward, Washington no longer received day-to-day communications from Wayne. He tended to remember him thereafter as a devoted young man with big dreams and much daring, who sometimes made critical mistakes. Wayne's new commander, Greene, was a man quite different in temperament from Washington. Yet he came to understand Wayne better than Washington ever had. Greene gave Wayne the unenviable task of leading a small command into Georgia to take back the state. Wayne crossed the Savannah River into Georgia in January 1782 with plans of "opening a wide door" to the many Americans who had gone over to the British side.[27] He also planned to offer inducements to the Hessians to desert from the last British stronghold at Savannah. He was stunned that he would have to accomplish all this with only a handful of soldiers—about 150 cavalry and 300 militiamen—all poorly clad and barely fed. But he would be even more stunned once he inally arrived in Georgia and found that the people there had literally descended into a state of nature. No one would have to describe the horrors of the French Revolution to Wayne in the coming years, for he had seen it all in Georgia. The War for Independence had destroyed all decency and civility. This was a brutal world without law or honor.[28]

With patience and understanding, and the full support of General Greene, Wayne was able to win back most of the Georgians to the patriot cause. But it was not the same with the Indians. Wayne went into Georgia with the certain hope that he could convince the Creeks to stay out of the conflict through careful reasoning. But he soon learned that the Indians could not be cajoled with arguments that made no sense to them. They depended on trade with the British or anyone else who would supply them with guns and other manufactured goods. If Wayne threatened to interrupt that trade, then he was their enemy and could be attacked without any concern for humanity on the battlefield. Even the worst barbarities of the British on the southern frontier could not compare with the horrors of Indian warfare. Americans on that same frontier never forgot and never forgave tribes like the Cherokee for their surprise attacks on settlements in the Carolinas and Georgia. Wayne was nearly killed in a surprise assault led by Creek Indians and their chief, Gustersigo, in June 1782. As a result of this attack, Wayne learned at last never to make up his mind that the enemy would come from only one direction, and so never again would his men be ambushed.[29]

Wayne survived the war on the southern frontier and went on to retake Georgia from the loyalists. He rejoined the rest of the army in South Carolina and helped win that state from the British. While he became a hero in the eyes of many southerners especially, the cost to his own life could hardly be counted. He never fully recovered in mind and body from the trauma of Georgia, and forever remembered that this campaign made him "satiate with this horrid trade of blood." His letters from Georgia, especially to the wife whom he lost emotionally forever in this campaign, are moving, dramatic, and even poetic.[30]

There were days in the last year of the war when, sick from malaria and haunted by depression, Wayne thought he would not live. Greene, his commander and now his friend, pulled him through this darkest time of his life. He sat with him in his tent outside of Charleston, talking of the old days when the war first started and they were both young and idealistic. Wayne's body would always bear the scars of the Georgia campaign. On most mornings, he was in such agony from old wounds and gout that his legs and arms had to be tightly wrapped with flannel to stop the pain—just so he could be lifted onto his horse. When the British finally evacuated Charleston, Greene gave Wayne the high honor of leading the Continental Army into the city. But even with the war finally over, and as close as he had grown to General Greene, he could not board a ship for Philadelphia and head home down the road to Waynesborough until he wrote a twelve-page letter to his beloved commander, Washington, describing the entire Georgia campaign. Washington, still showing little emotion toward Wayne, sent the letter to Congress.[31]

Despite all he had suffered, the Wayne who emerged from the Georgia campaign was in many ways a better man—and certainly a better commander—than the one who had gone into it. He remained just as passionate and ready to serve his nation at a moment's notice. He was as brave as he had been early in the Revolution, but the "mad" daring he had shown at Stony Point was now tempered by an almost obsessive need to protect his men. His ability to imagine every possible contingency in a campaign was still present, but it was now buttressed by careful planning, along with a deepened caution that led him to take far fewer risks. He was also more deeply committed than ever to studying history, war, and military tactics, so that if his country or his beloved commander ever called him again, he would be ready to perform even better than he had before.

Wayne would have to wait nearly a decade before he was summoned to serve his nation. When he finally came home to Pennsylvania, he could do little more than sit and look out over the fields of his farm at Waynesborough. He was even too sick to join his fellow officers at New York City's Fraunces Tavern to say goodbye to Washington. But once he was better, he grew impatient with waiting to resume a more active life in service to his country. The retirement to his family's farm that he had longed for so wistfully while in Georgia now seemed dreadfully dull. He was accustomed to struggle, and he could not bear the calm. His marriage to Polly was strained past repair, and he seemed unable to bridge the distance between himself and his two children. Even worse, at the very moment he should be setting his children up in lives of their own, he found himself with little cash on hand.

He turned to politics as an outlet for his restless spirit and won election to Pennsylvania's general assembly. He soon found himself at odds, however, with younger politicians, who had become too conservative for his taste. He was shocked when they struck down his proposals to end religious tests for office. "What has become of the revolutionary sentiments of this generation?" became his frequent complaint. With people in his home state turning against him, Wayne looked back fondly to Georgia, taking comfort in the memory of how he saved its citizens from the British and the loyalists in the last days of the Revolution. He returned to Georgia and tried to become a rice planter on the Richmond Plantation granted to him as thanks for his services. But all his efforts only sank him deeper into debt. The glories of the War for Independence seemed to fade forever at the nearby plantation of Mulberry Grove, where he sat at the bedside of his dying friend, General Greene.

Wayne seemed to sense that his own troubles reflected the deeper troubles of a nation still sunk in debt and confusion from the Revolution. He supported the writing of the Constitution that would create a stronger national government, and was elected to Pennsylvania's ratification convention as a representative from Chester County. Once the Constitution had been adopted by the states, he wrote not only to Washington, but also to James Madison, a leader in the new House of Representatives, warning of trouble on the frontier and offering his services if Congress ever raised an army against the Spanish and the Indians west of Georgia.[32]

Receiving no positive response from Madison (just as he had received none from Washington), Wayne continued his life as a private citizen, trying to make a success of his rice plantation outside Savannah. He felt overjoyed when news arrived that President Washington would be coming to Georgia in May 1791 on his tour of the southern states. Wayne took charge of the local committee setting up events for the visit. These included a 26-gun salute, a parade, dinner with members of the local Society of the Cincinnati, dances with the best-dressed ladies and gentlemen of Georgia, another dinner with all the citizens of the towns along the Savannah River, a fireworks display, and a visit to the site of the siege of Savannah, where Wayne served as the guide. He also rode with Washington to Mulberry Grove to visit General Greene's widow, Catherine. For him, the visit was a great success, but Washington saw it otherwise, noting in his diary that "Genl Wayne" had accompanied him to the battle site, which now bore no evidence of the terrible siege of 1779, but saying nothing else about Wayne. Later, in letters to Tobias Lear, Washington complained that the visits to Charleston and Savannah had exhausted him. "The continual hurry into which I was thrown by entertainments—visits—and ceremonies," he wrote, "scarcely allowed me a moment that I could call my own."[33]

In the following year, Wayne decided that he could best serve his country by going into national politics. He ran for the House of Representatives from Georgia and won, only to have the election challenged by his opponent, Colonel James Jackson, a militia officer who had served under him during the Revolution. Wayne subsequently lost his seat in the House after Jackson provided evidence to Congress of irregularities in the voting process.[34] It was at this point—with his life in ruins and with no prospect of ever serving his beloved commander or country again—that suddenly "Fortune" showered her favors on him.[35] Washington asked him to lead the army into the western country, granting him the title of "Commander in Chief." It had been nearly three years since Wayne had first offered his services to his nation under the new Constitution.

Wayne knew that many people were saying that Washington only chose him because he could not spare a more valuable man. But he also knew that Washington had turned to him once before in a desperate hour. In the summer of 1779, when Benedict Arnold had gone over to the British after trying to surrender West Point, General Washington had come up with a daring plan to take Stony Point. He seemed to sense that the only man who could handle it was Wayne. Washington later wrote his best letters to Wayne after the successful assault on Stony Point, and even got Congress to give Wayne a medal. If he had known that the situation was desperate in 1777, then how much more so was it in 1792? Wasn't Wayne correct that the British were maneuvering like Caesar at Alisa in 52 BC? By keeping their western forts on the American frontier and allying themselves with all the tribes west of the Appalachians, weren't they putting up a "circumvallation"—or series of fortifications—around the United States? If the nation could not move west, then what would become of the young country, bottled up behind the mountains? Surely it would die on the vine before it had fulfilled its great promise.

Despite the fact that Washington needed Wayne at this moment, the president still remembered his mistakes—especially Paoli—and he feared that Wayne might leave himself unprotected deep in the wilderness, just as St. Clair had done. (He did not know the Wayne who had become far more deliberate and cautious as a result of the Georgia campaign.) Instead, he made sure that Henry Knox, the secretary of war, kept a close eye on him. Knox had been with Wayne in the mad dash up to the British outpost at Stony Point, and he now served as the intermediary between the president and his commander in the field. Knox was patient with Wayne's growing frustration, especially over the government's continuing lack of support for the army. Although the uniforms were better than during the Revolution, the food was not. Wayne railed against Congress and the army contractors for caring so little about the men who were risking their lives for their country. But when he endorsed a petition written by his officers asking Congress to improve the food for the army, Washington lost his temper and ridiculed Wayne for not understanding the political situation of the day—specifically, how much the Madison faction (or, more truly, the Jefferson faction) wanted to dismantle the nation's small army. Contrary to what the president thought, Wayne did understand the rise of party spirit throughout the country, and said so in letters to friends, where he observed that the dissatisfaction of the Republicans seemed to affect not just the nation but also the army as well.[36]

Despite all the scolding, Wayne never once questioned a specific order that came from Washington. He accepted the tight reins his old commander placed on him, respecting his many warnings not to antagonize the Indians and thus instigate a war when negotiations with the tribes were still underway. He did not seem to mind that Washington paid little attention to how he was using his time, to train his men, to move cautiously into Indian territory, building fort after fort as he went, and to wait patiently for a direct command from the president to engage the Indian confederation in battle.

When negotiations between the administration and the Indians finally broke down late in the summer of 1793, the president told Knox to order Wayne and his men north from Fort Washington. The army spent the winter at Fort Greene Ville. In April 1794, when Washington learned that the British had established Fort Miamis on American soil along the Maumee River, it was Stony Point all over again. Wayne was to defeat the Indians somewhere north of Greeneville and, if he got the chance, "dislodge the party at the rapids of the Miami." By August 1794, Wayne had made it to within ten miles of Fort Miamis, at the very moment that Washington was marching from Philadelphia to see the troops off who were heading west to crush the Whiskey Rebellion. Just outside of Carlisle, at a place called "the Trap," an express rider raced up with the news that Wayne had won a smashing victory against the Indians along the Maumee River at a place that would be forever known as Fallen Timbers. Washington took the time to note Wayne's victory in his diary: "At the Trap, late in the evening, we were overtaken by Major Stagg principal Clerk in the Department of War with letters from Genl. Wayne & the Western Army containing official & pleasing accounts of his engagement with the Indians near the British Post at the Rapids of the Miami of the Lake and of his having destroyed all the Indian Settlements on that River in the vicinity of the said Post quite up to the grand Glaize—the quantity not less than 5000 acres."[37] Despite this victory, Washington continued to display little warmth toward Wayne. Wayne remained uncertain whether he had really won a victory over the Indians until a year later, when the Treaty of Greenville was finally signed. When Wayne came back to Philadelphia in 1796 to report on the treaty in person, he was surprised as he approached the city to hear all the church bells ringing. He wondered what the celebration could be about, and was stunned when told that the bells were ringing for him. He actually thought for a moment that all this was part of the president's plan to make him the new secretary of war. But this was not to be. Instead, the commander whom he had admired and served for so many years gave him another arduous task. Although he was even sicker and more exhausted than he had been at the end of the Revolution, Wayne was ordered west by his president to oversee the transfer of all the forts that the British had finally agreed to surrender as a result of Jay's Treaty.

If at this point we expect Washington finally to have the same unquestioning loyalty for Wayne that Wayne had for so long shown to Washington, then we will be disappointed. Washington missed his final chance to avow support for Wayne in the face of James Wilkinson's relentless public and private attacks on Wayne's character and generalship. Wilkinson, who had been Wayne's second in command during the Ohio campaign, and who spent much of his time writing letters complaining about his commander to the Department of War and to anti-administration newspapers in Philadelphia, alleged that Wayne was an incompetent drunkard who listened to the advice of equally incompetent favorites and ignored all overtures of peace from the Indians. Even after Fallen Timbers, the Treaty of Greenville, and now Jay's Treaty, Wayne was stunned to learn the terrible things that Wilkinson had been saying about him. He was even more horrified when Secretary of War James McHenry told him that not only was Wilkinson a backstabber, but also that he might be in the pay of the Spanish government. Wayne was furious that, after giving his all and being totally victorious in the western country, he had been libeled by a traitor.[38]

It was perhaps for the best that Wayne never knew that Washington was not particularly outraged by Wilkinson's allegations. It would have been impossible for Wayne to believe that after giving a lifetime of devotion to his nation and his beloved commander, Washington would not defend him to the hilt. Throughout all the humiliation, Wayne never doubted his country or his president. Even in the last weeks of his life, as he traveled through the western frontier from Niagara to the Maumee River Valley and then on to Detroit, he could not help but worry about the United States. His imagination worked overtime as he feared continuing trouble from the Indians, the Spanish, and, most especially, the British. Once his work in the west was complete, he planned to settle, not in Philadelphia or at Waynesborough, but in Pittsburgh. Still thinking like a surveyor, as he had been trained in his youth, he noted that the distances between Pittsburgh, Cincinnati, and Detroit were equal and made a perfect triangle. If there was trouble in any one corner of the frontier, he could be there in only a matter of days traveling along the edges of the triangle. He would go to Pittsburgh and watch and wait and report any problem to President Washington, the man he had served so diligently for twenty years. But Wayne never made it to Pittsburgh. Instead, he died at Fort Presque Isle—now Erie, Pennsylvania—on December 15, 1796. Not long after, President Washington appointed James Wilkinson as commander of the American army.[39]

There is no explaining the human heart. Why can some people love and serve with such devotion and gain little in return except the chance to love and serve more—even when it seems impossible for them to go on? But that is the story of the relationship between Anthony Wayne and George Washington. When they first met, Washington formed an impression of Wayne as a brash officer, full of enthusiasm and grand plans, who could be called upon in the most desperate situations. After Yorktown, their paths diverged, running parallel in terms of their political convictions, but rarely crossing in a significant way. Washington never came to know Wayne as an older, calmer, and much wiser commander, but thought of him still as the young man who stumbled at Paoli and saved the day at Stony Point. At an even deeper level, he may never have been able to understand a person who lived in his imagination and emotions as completely as Wayne did.

Looking back through so much history, and especially after reading through so many dried and faded letters that lie forgotten and unpublished in archives across America, we cannot help but wish that things could have been different. If nothing else, how wonderful it would be to go back in time and ask Washington to write his letter to Henry Lee once again, but this time noting that, when things became unbearable for Lee in the darkest days of the Revolution and he fled the Carolinas, he had sent Anthony Wayne in Lee's place.

That Wayne had begged him not to be sent—as if he sensed that his life, his marriage, his fortune, his family, and his honor would crumble forever—but that he went nonetheless—to free Savannah and Charleston—giving his all as he had given it at Three Rivers, Ticonderoga, Chadd's Ford, Brandywine, Germantown, Valley Forge, Monmouth Courthouse, Stony Point, the James River, Yorktown, and, finally, Georgia. If only Washington could have noted that although he had not always treated Wayne as respectfully as Wayne had treated him, nor reciprocated his affection, Wayne's personal and patriotic devotion had earned him the high honor of the highest trust.

Notes

1. Henry Lee to GW, 15 June 1792, *PGW: Pres. Ser.*, 10:455.

2. GW to Lee, 30 June 1792, ibid., 10:506.

3. Wayne was especially fond of the poem "The Old Soldier." He quoted it in its entirety in a letter to Polly Wayne dated 5 July 1790, that was written at his plantation in Richmond, Georgia (see the letter in the Bancroft Collection, NYPL, 1:585, 587).

4. John Hyde Preston, *A Gentleman Rebel: Mad Anthony Wayne* (Garden City, N.Y., 1930), 285.

5. Some of his most colorful letters were written to two of his best friends: Sharp Delany and Benjamin Rush.

6. Hugh F. Rankin gave a mocking portrayal of Wayne as an "anachronism" and "a knight errant . . . five hundred years too late to don shining armor" (see Rankin, "Anthony Wayne: Military Romanticist," in *George Washington's Generals and Opponents: Their Exploits and Leadership,* ed. George Billias [New York, 1994], 260). Rankin mistakenly applies romanticism to medieval chivalry rather than to the revolt against reason that swept the world following the American and French Revolutions. When "romanticism" is defined correctly, Wayne is clearly seen as a precursor of the movement.

7. GW, "Memorandum on General Officers," [9 March 1792], in *George Washington's Generals and Opponents,* 74.

8. Thomas Jefferson, *The Complete Anas of Thomas Jefferson,* ed. Franklin V. Sawvel (New York, 1903), 61–62.

9. George Hammond to John Graves Simcoe, 21 April 1792, in *The Correspondence of Lieutenant Governor John Graves Simcoe,* ed. E. A. Cruikshank, 5 vols. (Toronto, 1923–31), 1:131–32. Information on the Clinton Papers can be accessed at http://quod.lib.umich.edu/c/clementsmss/umich-wcl-M-42cli?subview=standard;view=reslist.

10. The first biography of Anthony Wayne that outlined the main story of his life was based on records kept by his son (see Horatio Newton Moore, *Life and Services of Gen. Anthony Wayne: Founded on Documentary and Other Evidence, Furnished by His Son, Col. Isaac Wayne* [Philadelphia, 1859]).

11. Most of Wayne's papers are in the Historical Society of Pennsylvania, located in

Philadelphia. Another important collection is in the Clements Library at the University of Michigan in Ann Arbor. George Bancroft's transcriptions of about five hundred of Wayne's best letters are in the Bancroft Collection at the New York Public Library. Along with Harry Emerson Wildes's *Anthony Wayne: Trouble Shooter of the American Revolution* (New York, 1941), the best biographies of Anthony Wayne are Preston, *A Gentleman Rebel,* and Paul David Nelson, *Anthony Wayne: Soldier of the Early Republic* (Bloomington, Ind., 1985).

12. Nelson, *Anthony Wayne,* 66; Anthony Wayne to GW, 4 November 1781, vol. 14, Anthony Wayne Papers, 1765–1859, Historical Society of Pennsylvania, Philadelphia.

13. Wayne was fascinated by the Battle of Alesia in 52 BC. Julius Caesar besieged the town in Gaul in his campaign against Vercingetorix. Caesar used "circumvallation"—the practice of building fortifications and entrenchments around a walled city—during the siege. For more details, see chapter 7 of "On the Gallic War" in *Caesar's Commentaries: On the Gallic War & On the Civil War,* ed. James H. Ford, trans. W. A. MacDevitt (El Paso, 2005), 133–78; and Wayne to Charles Scott, 5 October 1793, vol. 29, Wayne Papers.

14. Pictures of Waynesborough can be accessed at http://www.philalandmarks.org/wayne.aspx.

15. Wayne to GW, 6 April 1789, *PGW: Pres. Ser.,* 2:36.

16. Wayne to GW, 2 September 1777, *PGW: Rev. Ser.,* 11:131.

17. Wayne to GW, 4 October 1777, ibid., 11:389.

18. Wayne to Polly Wayne, 7 June 1777, Bancroft Collection, NYPL, 1:351.

19. Ibid., 1:353.

20. GW to Wayne, 4 May 1789, *PGW: Pres. Ser.,* 2:209. There is no letter from Washington to Wayne in a collection of his writings (440 documents that are mainly letters) published by the Library of America (see *George Washington: Writings,* ed. John Rhodehamel [New York, 1997]).

21. Although he does not cite the source for this story, Preston notes that Washington liked Wayne on first meeting him in April 1776, stating that the "irrepressible enthusiasm of the young colonel cheered him" (Preston, *A Gentleman Rebel,* 70).

22. Wayne to GW, 2 January 1781, and GW to Wayne, 3 January 1781, in Charles Stillé, *Major-General Anthony Wayne and the Pennsylvania Line in the Continental Army* (1893; repr., Port Washington, N.Y., 1968), 242–43, 251–54.

23. GW to Wayne, 9–12 February 1778, *PGW: Rev. Ser.,* 13:492–93; Nelson, *Anthony Wayne,* 111; Preston, *A Gentleman Rebel,* 196.

24. Wayne to GW, 4 November 1781, vol. 14, Wayne Papers.

25. Wayne wrote a second letter on the same day, immediately after receiving a note from Washington denying his request for a furlough (see Wayne to GW, 4 November 1781, ibid.).

26. Wayne to GW, 20 December 1781, ibid.

27. Wayne to Governor John Martin, 4 January 1782, ibid.

28. Nathanael Greene wrote a memorable letter to Wayne describing the challenges he would face in Georgia (see Nathanael Greene to Wayne, 9 January 1782, ibid.).

29. Wayne to Greene, 24 June 1782, ibid., vol. 17.

30. Wayne to Polly Wayne, 3 March 1782, ibid., vol. 15.

31. Wayne told Washington of his physical breakdown as a result of his participation in the Georgia campaign (Wayne to GW, 17 January 1783, Anthony Wayne Papers, Manuscripts Division, Library of Congress).

32. Wayne to James Madison, 15 July 1789, in *Anthony Wayne and the Ohio Indian Wars: A Collection of Unpublished Letters and Related Articles,* ed. Tony DeRegnaucount and Tom Parker (Arcanum, Ohio, 1995), 10.

33. [12–17 May 1791], *PGW: Diaries,* 6:135–41; GW to Tobias Lear, 1[4] May 1791, *PGW: Pres. Ser.,* 8:183.

34. "Petition of James Jackson to the Speaker and Members of the House of Representatives, 1791," and "Wayne's Notes on the Testimony Regarding Election Irregularities in Georgia," Anthony Wayne Papers, Clements Library.

35. Wayne had an imaginary relationship with Fortune, as if she was truly a woman; one of the first references to Fortune in his letters can be found in Wayne to General William Thompson, 1 September 1776, Bancroft Collection, NYPL, 75, 77.

36. Wayne to Henry Knox, 12 December 1792 and 4 January 1793, vol. 23, Wayne Papers; Knox to Wayne, 22 December 1792, vol. 24, ibid.; Nelson, *Anthony Wayne,* 237.

37. Knox to Wayne, 7 June 1794, vol. 35, Wayne Papers; *PGW: Diaries,* 6:178–79.

38. Nelson, *Anthony Wayne,* 292–96.

39. Wayne to James McHenry, 12 November 1796, vol. 47, Wayne Papers.

"General Washington Did Not Harbor One Principle of Federalism"

Thomas Jefferson Remembers George Washington

BRIAN STEELE

FROM THE EARLIEST DECADE OF THE NINETEENTH CENTURY, Americans have always wanted to have their George Washington and their Thomas Jefferson too. Peter Parish has suggested that the National Mall in Washington, D.C., symbolizes America's "secular trinity": Washington, the Father; Abraham Lincoln, the Son; and Jefferson, the "guiding spirit."[1] But for this analogy to work, Washington and Lincoln have needed to get right, as it were, with the spirit. Lincoln was able to do this actively and more or less consciously, accommodating Jeffersonianism to the Market Revolution and wrenching Jeffersonian antislavery from conditional termination toward the positive liberty that produced the Emancipation Proclamation and the Reconstruction amendments. But, with Washington, such a move was more problematic. By the time the spirit descended, or manifested itself, so to speak, Washington was dead. Worse, while Washington was alive, he had become increasingly estranged from Jefferson, the man, and from a Jeffersonian vision of the national meaning and future. From at least Washington's second administration, then, the father of the nation, if such a thing could be imagined, was at odds with what was to become the national spirit.

Jefferson recognized this as a problem and spent a not inconsiderable amount of energy and thought reconciling Washington to the republicanism that was sweeping the land in his own name after Washington's death. This would involve, Jefferson understood, turning Washington away from the Federalism of his later life—his partisanship—and back into the nonpartisan symbol of American unity that Washington himself embraced. Only, in Jefferson's version, Washington would serve the Republican cause—which, in

Jefferson's view, was a way of rescuing Washington from the grip of partisanship after all.

This project was made much simpler by Washington himself, who consistently worked to shape his own image as beholden to no party, an image that has been compelling to historians for generations. But if we think of Washington in these terms today, it is at least partially due to the largely overlooked fact that Jefferson chose to embrace Washington as a Republican. Jefferson did so partly for partisan purposes—to shape his own image and that of his party as embodying the nation itself. But in the process, ironically, the partisan Jefferson helped transform the partisan Washington into a symbol *transcending* party in a way that made the single greatest symbol of American nationhood safe for the Jeffersonian Republicanism that was becoming the American ideology.

Jefferson was first elected to the House of Burgesses in 1769, where, presumably, he met Washington for the first time. Jefferson was only twenty-five (Washington had been a delegate since 1758), and it took a few years before the two men became confidants. Both also served in the Continental Congress as delegates from Virginia, and during the Revolutionary War remained in close communication, especially when Jefferson served as governor of Virginia from 1779 to 1781. Jefferson, deferential to the older man, developed an "almost filial reverence" for the general during the war, and must have been particularly gratified—in light of the House of Delegates' inquiry into Jefferson's alleged negligence in preparing to meet Benedict Arnold's invasion of Virginia—by Washington's praise of his conduct as governor.[2] The admiration was genuine and mutual. In 1786, Washington told Lafayette that "Mr. Jefferson . . . is a man of whom I early imbibed the highest opinion."[3] He elsewhere expressed a desire for "a continuation of [Jefferson's] friendship and correspondence," and was soon asking Jefferson's advice on a host of topics.[4] In turn, Jefferson, in his *Notes on the State of Virginia,* offered Washington as an example of American excellence. Washington's memory, Jefferson asserted, "will be adored while liberty shall have votaries, his name will triumph over time, and will in future ages assume its just station among the most celebrated worthies of the world."[5]

While Jefferson and Washington's friendship was developing, something was happening to Washington that would complicate nearly all of his relationships from then on. As Jefferson's encomium indicates, over the course of the American Revolution Washington became a symbol of American nationhood and an international hero of the Enlightenment. He began to be celebrated as a man without ambition—a Cincinnatus, above politics and partisanship—with national greatness as his only goal and national service the only calling that could extract him from the pleasures of private life. To some degree, this was merely an intensification of the Virginia ideal of leadership—but an intensification it was. A Washington without personal ambition is the stuff of national mythology rather than history.[6] But what made Washington so compelling to contemporaries was his repeated refusal to abuse whatever power was granted to him. His habit of proving himself trustworthy in spite of remarkable temptations and opportunities to abuse the public's trust simply added to his glory, and rendered most Americans less and less suspicious of whatever power he was able to amass.[7] Washington's fame rested not on lack of ambition, but in his lifelong self-mastery.

Washington's restraint reassured Jefferson to such an extent that his own specific objections to the Constitution were mitigated by the knowledge that Washington would be the first president. Despite his concern—expressed to multiple correspondents—about the "perpetual re-eligibility" of the executive for election, and his hope that such an opening for what amounted to elective monarchy could be corrected prior to ratification, Jefferson withdrew his objection, "during the life of our great leader, whose executive talents are superior to those I believe of any man in the world." Washington, "alone by the authority of his name and the confidence reposed in his perfect integrity," was "fully qualified," Jefferson believed, "to put the government so under way as to secure it against the efforts of opposition."[8] As long as Washington was president, in other words, Jefferson was willing to see the constitutional flaw "uncorrected."[9] Only when "subordinate characters" got into office would Americans need to worry about institutionalizing republicanism. It was more typical of Jefferson to urge institutional reform even while the present holders of office were "perfectly upright," on the theory that it was "better to keep the wolf out of the fold, than to trust to drawing his teeth and talons after he shall have entered."[10] Jefferson's repose in "our great leader," in other words, was altogether uncharacteristic, and speaks to the unique trust he placed in Washington.

For his part, Washington became increasingly obsessive about his reputation and contemplated all his actions in light of how they might affect what people thought about his character and integrity. He also understood his symbolic importance to American unity and began to quite consciously manipulate his symbolism in the service of nationhood.[11] As Washington became understandably concerned with public perceptions of his conduct—even obsessively phobic about appearances of impropriety—he began asking trusted correspondents for advice. Jefferson offered particularly useful counsel, and by 1785, Washington acknowledged that he had "accustomed myself to communicate matters of difficulty to" Jefferson, almost exclusively on matters where Washington's reputation stood in potential conflict with his private inclinations.[12]

Jefferson was a good choice because he fully grasped the significance of Washington's symbolism and seems to have thought a good deal about how best to promote the nation's image by protecting Washington's.[13] It would be difficult to surpass Jefferson's tribute to Washington's centrality to the Revolutionary cause. "The moderation and virtue of a single character," Jefferson wrote in 1784, "has probably prevented this revolution from being closed as most others have been by a subversion of that liberty it was intended to establish."[14] But he also understood that such a reputation was political capital and that the guardian of the Washington symbol could hold the keys to the kingdom. Jefferson took the lead in having busts and statues of Washington constructed by the best artists in Europe for public display and consumption (Jefferson eventually displayed four images of Washington at Monticello).[15] He also had some sense of the value of Washington's reputation to political projects of interest to him. The "popularity of his name," Jefferson told James Madison, made other things possible and would surely "carry" projects Washington endorsed "thro' the assembly."[16] By the time Jefferson took up his position as secretary of state, he understood that his personal relationship with Washington would be bound up with a symbol as well.

Consequently, it was crucial for Jefferson's own conception of national greatness that Washington remain purely republican. This at least partly explains Jefferson's anxiety about Alexander Hamilton's suggestion that the executive "dignity" depended upon the president's setting "a pretty high tone."[17] Washington himself hoped to strike a republican balance, but critics were not wrong to note the Washington "court's" conscious effort to approximate those of European monarchs.[18]

Jefferson later remembered continuing his efforts to preserve Washington's reputation by telling him that "mimicry . . . of royal forms and ceremonies" was "not at all in character with the simplicity of republican government," but looked, instead, “as if wishfully to those of European courts.” Jefferson recalled that these trappings of monarchy had in fact been the “frequent subject of conversation between” Washington and himself.[19]

Jefferson, as is well known, quickly grew disillusioned with Hamilton, but he seems to have long retained a confidence that Washington’s heart was in the right place and needed only the guidance Jefferson had been used to offering. He first wrote Washington of his concerns about a conspiracy to undermine republicanism in May 1792, and he started tattling on Hamilton in September, informing Washington that the treasury secretary was the head of a faction in the government that actually wanted to subvert the Constitution and turn the government into a monarchy. Hamilton’s “system,” Jefferson told Washington, flowed from “principles adverse to liberty, and was calculated to undermine and demolish the republic.”[20] Washington, like a kindly father, seemed to retain faith in both of his protégés, urging them to reconcile over what seemed to him like minor differences over policy.[21] And it is also clear that Washington continued to listen carefully to the opinions of both the secretaries of state and treasury over matters of cabinet-level importance. While Jefferson remained in the administration, it appears, Washington never explicitly agreed with Hamilton’s early public accusation that Jefferson was himself the “head of a party whose politics have constantly aimed at elevating State-power, upon the ruins of National Authority.”[22] But over time, Hamilton’s explanations seem to have become more persuasive to Washington, particularly perhaps because Jefferson’s accusations paralleled and occasionally echoed the incessant and increasingly histrionic criticisms of Washington’s administration that ran in Philip Freneau’s *National Gazette* and, later, in Benjamin Franklin Bache’s *Aurora.*[23]

For his part, Jefferson gradually came to the conclusion that Washington simply did not understand the gravity of the threat Hamilton posed. Jefferson found Washington “really approving the treasury system” and believing that his own [Jefferson’s] “suspicions . . . had been carried a great deal too far.” After all, Washington told him, “there might be *desires,* but he did not believe there were *designs* to change the form of government into a monarchy.”[24]

By that fall, Washington was decrying the “constant . . . News-paper abuse” endured by “the Government and the Officers of it,” and would soon begin to hear scraps of information suggesting that Jefferson was slandering him in private conversations.[25] Washington gave the most generous interpretation to this information.[26] But whatever his personal feelings about Jefferson, he was clearly pursuing, by 1794, policies perceived in Republican circles as dangerously partisan. He described the Whiskey Rebellion as "the first ripe fruit of the Democratic Societies," for example, and, worst of all, he signed the Jay Treaty.[27]

In spite of his increased but still quiet suspicions, Washington continued to seek Jefferson's counsel. Jefferson, for his part, continued to try to wrench Washington away from Hamilton's influence. Toward the end of his tenure as secretary of state, Jefferson attempted once again to appeal to Washington's concern for his image against the prospect that Federalists might use his popularity to divide the nation. In conversation at Mount Vernon in October 1792, Jefferson urged Washington to stay on for a second term as president precisely because "there was no other person who would be thought anything more than the head of a party."[28] This was exactly the language Jefferson used to persuade Washington against attempts to outlaw the Democratic-Republican societies in the fall of 1793. Such an action, Jefferson insisted in one cabinet meeting, would "make the Pres. assume the station of the head of a party instead of the head of the nation."[29] Jefferson assured Washington that "no rational man in the US. suspects you of any other disposition" than that of a nonpartisan republican.[30] But, in spite of Jefferson's efforts, the "great collaboration" of Hamilton and Washington became ever stronger as Jefferson left the administration at the end of 1793.[31]

Although Washington and Jefferson seemed to part on more or less amiable terms, the old truism that "absence makes the heart grow fonder" seems to have not held up in this case.[32] Distance—as well as frequent and alarming reports from the capital from Madison and others—seemed to fuel all manner of suspicion on Jefferson's part about what was happening to Washington. He later suggested that his own resignation left Washington to the wolves: "From the moment . . . of my retiring from the administration, the federalists got unchecked hold of Genl. Washington."[33] Jefferson's letters referring to his fellow Virginian in these years are fairly straightforward: Washington had been turned. He had become a Federalist.[34]

Jefferson and Washington continued to correspond even as Jefferson expressed dismay to others about what was happening to the president. The friendship limped along, at least until one of those letters was published—the infamous one to Philip Mazzei of April 1796.[35] Jefferson's blunt and fairly unguarded explanation of the political scene as he understood it ("an Anglican monarchical, & aristocratical party has sprung up, whose avowed object is to draw over us the substance, as they have already done the forms, of the British government") was published in an Italian newspaper, translated into French, embellished by an editor to look even more pro-French than the original, and finally translated back into English and published in Noah Webster's New York newspaper, the *American Minerva.*[36] Federalists exploded with a combination of barely concealed glee and ostentatious fury.

The key passage for Federalists, which many took as a reference to Washington, was Jefferson's suggestion to Mazzei that "it would give you a fever were I to name to you the apostates who have gone over to these heresies, men who were Samsons in the field & Solomons in the council, but who have had their heads shorn by the harlot England." Jefferson, for his part, seemed mortified that his private correspondence had been published—and mangled—and misrepresented, he said. He worried with Madison over what to do about it, if anything, and finally decided against any public defense.[37] But there is nothing in the Mazzei letter—save the colorful analogy to the story of Samson and Delilah—that Jefferson was not saying to multiple other correspondents about the state of the parties, to be sure, but also about Washington, if "Samson" was indeed Washington at all (which Jefferson denied many years later, though not at the time).

In fact, its veiled reference renders the Mazzei letter much milder (or at least more ambiguous) than other letters Jefferson penned around the same time that contained more-explicit discussions of Washington. He had long been critical of Washington for permitting "himself to be the organ" of a "faction of Monocrats," and for his "habitual concert with the British and Antirepublican party."[38] Less than one week before sending his last letter to Washington, Jefferson denounced what he considered an unrepublican deference to Washington among the people, "who have supported his judgment against their own and that of their representatives."[39] A few weeks later, Jefferson told James Monroe that the Federalists had no support outside of "the colossus of the President's merits with the people, and the moment he retires . . . his successor, if a Monocrat, will be overborne by the republican sense of his constituents," and "if a republican, he will of course give fair play to that sense, and lead things into the channel of harmony between the governors and governed."[40] In other words, Jefferson argued, because Washington's popularity had begun to undermine the government's relationship with public opinion, which alone granted it republican legitimacy, the only thing that could restore this relationship was Washington's retirement—a stunning reversal of Jefferson's early repose in Washington as "our great leader." These letters, both more direct than the one to Mazzei, left little wiggle room: Jefferson believed that Washington had outlived his usefulness to the republic, which would best be served with his removal to Mount Vernon.

Jefferson added insult to injury (again, in private correspondence), describing the way politically savvy Republicans should deal with a Washington who possessed the fragile ego of a prince coddled by sycophants. He told Archibald Stuart that Washington's "mind had been so long used to unlimited applause that it could not brook contradiction, or even advice offered unasked." So the best strategy, Jefferson argued, was "for the republican interest to soothe him by flattery where they could approve his measures, and to be silent where they disapprove, that they may not render him desperate as to their affections, and entirely indifferent to their wishes; in short, to lie on their oars while he remains at the helm, and let the bark drift as his will and a superintending providence shall direct."[41] As he told James Sullivan, once the influence and "preponderant popularity of a particular great character" was "withdrawn," "our countrymen" would once again be "left to the operation of their own unbiased good sense." This, Jefferson had "no doubt," would induce "a pretty rapid return of general harmony, and our citizens moving in phalanx in the paths of regular liberty, order, and a sacro-sanct adherence to the constitution."[42] The implication could not have been more clear: get rid of Washington and the government of the United States would return to its republican (and constitutional) origins. Jefferson was never as pointed or vulgar as Bache—and he never directly attacked Washington's character and integrity—but it is not difficult to read his larger theme in these private letters as consistent with the substance of the *Aurora*'s own vicious farewell to the president upon his retirement: "The name of WASHINGTON from this day ceases to give currency to political iniquity; and to legalize corruption."[43] Jefferson was perhaps fortunate that it was the letter to Mazzei and not those to Monroe, Stuart, and Sullivan that made its way into the newspapers.

While Jefferson believed that Washington had become a Federalist (or at least that he was being manipulated by the Federalists), Washington's reading of Jefferson during these years is more difficult to decipher. He seems not to have connected extreme Republican views with Jefferson himself until well after he left the presidency, though the two never corresponded after August 1797. But Washington's hostility to the Republicans is not to be doubted.

As early as the summer of 1795, he was describing the political conflict as the "difference of conduct between the friends, and foes of order, and good government." Since opposition leaders were "always working, like bees, to distil their poison," he encouraged Federalists to do their part to shape public opinion on the key issues of the day.[44] His Farewell Address condemned partisanship in terms that many historians have rightly seen as a Federalist attack on the Republicans, and Washington began describing a Republican conspiracy to subvert the government that was the mirror image of Jefferson's fears about the Federalists. Lafayette must have been bewildered to hear from Washington that the Republicans formed a party "who oppose the government in all its measures," and were "determined . . . to change the nature of it, and to subvert the Constitution," even as Jefferson's letters to him described the Federalists as "a sect . . . among us, who . . . espoused our new constitution, not as a good & sufficient thing itself, but only as a step to an English constitution."[45]

Jefferson later suggested that his correspondence with Washington ended because "both of us were too much oppressed with letter-writing, to trouble, either the other, with a letter about nothing."[46] In his last letter to Washington (June 19, 1796), Jefferson went out of his way to deny any connection with a recent editorial in the *Aurora* that disclosed privileged information known only to him and certain members of Washington's cabinet. Jefferson also took the opportunity to accuse Henry Lee of "dirtily . . . sifting the conversations of my table" in an effort to sow the seeds of discord between Washington and Jefferson.[47]

Washington's response, the last substantive letter he ever sent Jefferson, seemed an effort to alleviate Jefferson's concerns and diffuse the tension between them.[48] "If I had entertained any suspicions before, that the queries, which have been published in Bache's Paper, proceeded from you, the assurances you have given of the contrary, would have removed them; but the truth is, I harboured none." Since Washington pointed to Edmund Randolph as the culprit, there seems little reason to doubt the sincerity of Washington's reassurance. But, he confirmed, he had indeed heard from Lee that Jefferson's "particular friends and connextions . . . have denounced me, as a person under a dangerous influence; and that, if I would listen *more* to some *other* opinions, all would be well." Of course, Jefferson believed precisely that! But Washington, again, told Jefferson that whenever he heard such rumors, his "answer invariably has been, that I had never discovered any thing in the conduct of Mr. Jefferson to raise suspicions, in my mind, of his insincerity." Washington urged Jefferson to reciprocate: to candidly "retrace" Washington's "public conduct," where he would find "abundant proofs . . . that truth and right decisions, were the sole objects of my pursuit; that there were as many instances within [Jefferson's] own knowledge of my having decided against, as in favor of the opinions of" Hamilton; "and moreover, that I was no believer in the infallibility of the politics, or measures of *any man living.* In short, that I was no party man myself, and the first wish of my heart was, if parties did exist, to reconcile them."[49] Washington thus targeted precisely what was at issue: Was he the father of his country, transcending political dispute in service to the common good, or was he the partisan of a dangerous and anti-republican sect?

Washington eventually did come to doubt Jefferson's sincerity. When John Nicholas wrote him with hints of a dark design on the part of Jefferson's nephew to trick Washington into disclosing useful information, he seems to have read it as a confirmation of all the rumors connecting Jefferson with the vicious attacks in Bache's *Aurora*—and thus of Jefferson's own personal treachery and duplicity.[50] That he needed no independent substantiation of Nicholas's assertions suggests that they were merely the culmination rather than the beginning of Washington's suspicions of Jefferson. "Nothing short of the Evidence you have adduced," he told Nicholas, "corroborative of intimations which I had received long before, through another channel, could have shaken my belief in the sincerity of a friendship, which I had conceived was possessed for me, by the person to whom you allude."[51] If what Nicholas told him was true, Washington informed his nephew Bushrod, then Jefferson's scheme was "a trick so dirty & shabby" that "it would be a pity not to expose him to Public execration."[52] Washington exploded with what can only be described as Federalist vituperative. So Jefferson really was a partisan, as Hamilton had always warned him, and duplicitous to boot! Moreover, the goals of his party were despicable: "to explain away the Constitution, & weaken the Government," and to put "the Affairs of this Country under the influence & controul of a foreign Nation."[53]

The conspiratorial thinking that animated the Republicans had its exact counterpart among Federalists, and now Washington himself jumped fully on board. Suddenly everything made sense to him. He had known for some time that the Republicans had been "moving heaven and earth" to help the French take over the United States.[54] But now he understood that their motivation was not "real affection" for France. Rather, their dark "design" was "subverting their own government."[55] Yes, the Republicans obviously hoped "to disquiet the Public mind with unfounded alarms," with the goal of setting "the People at varience with their Government."[56] The ultimate objective? "Dissolving" the government "and producing a disunion of the States."[57] Washington could only conclude that "the conduct of this Party is systematized; and everything that is opposed to its execution will be sacrificed, without hesitation, or remorse."[58]

Virginia, sad to say, was overrun with "this opposition." It was "an incontrovertible fact, that the principle leaders of the opposition dwell in it." The only way Washington could reconcile Virginians' devotion "to the General Government, and the Union" with their election of Republicans to Congress, was the absence of a clear alternative: "the most respectable, & best qualified characters among us, will not come forward." But in "such a crisis as this, when everything dear & valuable to us is assailed," such unwillingness to enter the fray was dishonorable.[59] Washington himself would not run again, for (among other reasons) he remained "thoroughly convinced I should not draw a *single* vote from the Anti-federal side."[60] But other good Federalists, including Patrick Henry—lately reconciled to the Constitution—*ought* to run for office precisely because ("I am fully persuaded") the "*Leaders* of Opposition . . . are followed by numbers who are unacquainted with their designs, and suspect as little the tendency of their principles."[61] "Let that party set up a broomstick, and call it a true son of Liberty, a Democrat, or give it any other epithet that will suit their purpose, and it will command their votes in toto! . . . Will not the Federalists meet, or rather defend their cause?"[62]

Washington's views essentially became those of a "high" Federalist: encouraging a strengthening of the Alien and Sedition Acts; criticizing John Adams's peaceful overtures to France; and encouraging the commissioning of Federalists to prevent Republicans from filling the officer corps of the expanded army, command of which he accepted only with the provision that Hamilton be named major general under him.[63]

At the time of his death, Washington's feelings about Jefferson were probably reflected most clearly in the reaction of his family to the 1800 presidential campaign. Washington's nephew Bushrod contemplated Jefferson's election with a "God forbid!," and Martha Washington was reported to have declared his election to the presidency "the greatest misfortune our country had ever experienced."[64] The "most painful occurrence of her life," save that of Washington's own death, came, she said, when Jefferson visited Mount Vernon to express his sympathies.[65] She considered him "one of the most detestable of mankind."[66] This was clearly not a family that had heard much good about Jefferson lately. Washington's step-granddaughter, Nelly, noted in 1806 that, despite being in the capital, she had not dined with Jefferson, nor had "the honor to be in that *great mans* good graces." But this was not surprising, she noted, "nor can one who knew so well the *first President*, ever wish to be noticed by the present chief magistrate."[67]

For his part, Jefferson—still the vice president at the time of Washington's death—went out of his way to avoid attending any of the memorial services and ceremonies held in the capital. It seems a fitting, if lamentable, denouement to their relationship.

It is little wonder that many of Jefferson's correspondents who wrote to him about Washington's retirement and death characterized Washington as a Federalist and thus an enemy of the Republic. Thomas Lomax described the image of Washington as the means by which Federalists foisted their policies on an unsuspecting public: "the highest Varnish" the Federalists used "was a *Name*." But, "the Man is now dead, and I sincerely wish that Peace, and Quiet may mingle with his ashes. His Virtues we will imitate, and his Errors, if not buried in the Grave with him, let them be Beacons to avoid the Shoals, and Quicksands on which they ran." Lomax would contribute toward a mausoleum for Washington, he said, only if he could ensure that it would be "an everlasting Sepulchre, for all political Vices & Follies."[68] Joseph Priestley suggested that Washington's death was "seasonable" and "rejoic[ed] more than I can express in the glorious reverse that has taken place, and which has secured your election."[69] Moses Robinson, a former Vermont governor and senator, seemed to wink at Jefferson when he noted that many "had their Eye on your Self as the Successor of Washington, in that they fail[e]d—to Say no more." But Robinson did say more: that the "late Administration" made clear the "Importance of Placing one in the Executive branch of Government whom they were Perswaided Possessed the Same Sentiments that Generally prevaild in 1776."[70]

There was clearly a groundswell of support among Jefferson's base for bidding an explicit "good riddance" to Washington. But Jefferson, always a keen observer of public opinion, also paid attention to other letters wishing his own administration well and praising Washington at the same time.

Many supporters made no distinction between Washington and Jefferson, but encouraged Jefferson to emulate the virtues as he did the "chair" of "the brave General Washington."[71] Others sent copies of eulogies or paintings of Washington, assuming that Jefferson would appreciate remembering his predecessor.[72] Many saw him as a successor to a nonpartisan Washington and encouraged him to "put an end to Party Spirit, & gain Immortal honor & be revered as much as our late father of his Country Washington was, by America at large."[73] Another well-wisher praised without distinction "the Names of Washington Adams and Jefferson."[74] The author of a long poem about Washington even included a stanza predicting that a young Jefferson one day "too shalt be another Washington."[75]

Jefferson was remarkably careful about the way he discussed Washington immediately after his death. He never took the bait offered by some Republicans to exploit the distinction they were clearly making between him and the deceased icon. When he did mention Washington, he took care to praise the man and he avoided the subject of Washington's manipulation by Federalists, which had been a staple of his correspondence in the years before Washington's death.[76]

In retrospect, it seems that Jefferson was already beginning the delicate process of separating Washington from his Federalist admirers. Jefferson praised Samuel Miller's sermon for its "just tribute" to Washington in contrast to other (presumably Federalist) eulogies, "which if they do not border on impiety, yet revolt us by their extravagance, and would have revolted no one more than the great man who was the subject of them."[77] John Adams would also criticize the "impious Idolatry to Washington," but Jefferson clearly was making a careful effort to distinguish the impiety of the idolaters from Washington himself, who, he suggested, would undoubtedly resist deification in death as he did the crown in life.[78]

Because he remained aware of Washington's value as a national icon, Jefferson was already, by 1800, beginning the process of transforming Washington from the partisan he had become late in life. To a French admirer Jefferson noted that it was "a very pleasing thing to Americans to see foreigners so liberally participate in their grief on the loss of their great countryman." He even affected the sentimental, suggesting that "no circumstances can ever efface the memory of those services which had rendered . . . our late most illustrious General Washington . . . so dear to his country; no time can dry their tears."[79] Presidential hopeful Jefferson even contemplated making Bushrod

Washington the chief justice of the Supreme Court, "in consideration" both "of his integrity and science in the laws, and of the services rendered to our country by his illustrious relation." Such a move, Jefferson noted, would be a way to "gratify the living by praising the dead."[80] (And this while Bushrod himself was doing everything possible to ensure Jefferson's defeat![81])

If Washington's reputation for transcending politics was secure only in retirement, it went into the clouds upon his death.[82] This had implications for what Jefferson was later able to do with Washington the symbol. Jefferson had always appreciated Washington's symbolic significance, and even during the 1790s as their relationship deteriorated, he was aware that the Republicans would go nowhere as a party by distancing themselves from Washington. He seemed to intuit what the historian Joseph Ellis later noted: that the "fastest way to commit political suicide in the revolutionary era" was to attack Washington.[83] Even during the 1790s, Jefferson understood that Washington's "popularity" was so great that "the people will support him in whatever he will do, or will not do, without appealing to their own reason or to any thing but their feelings towards him."[84] One reason Jefferson was loathe to come forward with a public defense of his letter to Mazzei, in fact, was precisely that such a defense "would embroil me also with all those with whom his character is still popular, that is to say nine tenths of the people of the US."[85] As long as Washington was alive, Jefferson had a difficult time claiming his imprimatur for his own views—so clearly were they at odds with what Washington himself seemed to encourage, in his second administration particularly. But after Washington's death, the contest for his memory began, and Jefferson was shrewd in his quick efforts to capture it for the Republicans, or at least to neutralize it as part of the iconography of nationhood, which would, he believed, remain firmly republican.

In his First Inaugural Address, Jefferson went out of his way to praise Washington as the "first and greatest revolutionary character, whose preeminent services had entitled him to the first place in his country's love and destined him for the fairest page in the volume of faithful history."[86] In the context of his conciliatory statement that "we are all republicans, we are all federalists," Jefferson's praise of Washington had the effect of rendering the national icon truly national, transcending party politics. Henry Knox, Washington's confidant and secretary of war, noticed this, embracing Jefferson's effort in the inaugural with "heart felt satisfaction." Though he had supported "Mr Adams" in the late campaign, Knox offered his own encouragement of

Jefferson and his hope that "when you chuse to retire, you may receive a richly merited reward, similar to that bestowed by a grateful people on the much loved Washington."[87] Jefferson's rhetorical erasure of the partisan differences he and Washington experienced in life was already beginning to replace politics with an iconography that could reconnect them after Washington's death. Confirming this effect, one supporter rejoiced that in Jefferson, "god has blest us with another Washington."[88]

But others warned Jefferson that true Federalists would never embrace such an identification of their hero with their archenemy, but would, instead, make every effort to sever Washington's image from the republican direction of Jefferson's administration.[89] And, indeed, Federalists had had some success near the end of his life in turning Washington into a partisan symbol; even his memorial commemorations became sharply contested events.[90] Hamilton seems to have cleverly orchestrated Washington's funeral rites in such a way as to enhance the prestige of the new army (which Hamilton now commanded), and he spoke for most Federalists when he publicly distinguished "the virtuous WASHINGTON" from that "Champion of Faction," President Jefferson.[91]

It helped Republicans that, in spite of these efforts, Washington gradually became, as François Furstenberg writes, "emptied of particular partisan connotations" among the general public—a public that had always known him only through his cult image.[92] With Washington dead, Republicans perhaps had to worry less that in celebrating the symbol of American nationhood they would also be endorsing Federalist policies.[93] But among the leadership class—those who had actually known the man—Washington's legacy was still sharply contested, and Jefferson thought a good deal about how to preserve it from Federalist manipulation. From the beginning, Jefferson understood what Walter Jones, a longtime Republican congressman from Virginia writing a history of the parties, told him in 1813: it was a potentially "perilous" matter to both remain "Scrupulously accurate . . . in regard to facts & Inference" and "to bear . . . Genl. washington . . . harmless through the federal Coalition."[94]

As early as 1802, Jefferson began looking for ways to challenge the Federalist memory of Washington, primarily through the encouragement of alternate Republican histories of the 1790s. He offered Joel Barlow complete access to the "public archives" and encouraged him to live in Washington, D.C., mingling with those who knew the truth. "A great deal of the knowledge of things," he explained, "is not on paper, but only within ourselves for verbal communication." The history he wanted Barlow to write, fortified by interviews with Jefferson and Madison, would, he hoped, dissipate the impact of John Marshall's *Life of Washington,* which he believed the chief justice was preparing "principally with a view to electioneering purposes."[95]

Jefferson's concern about the way Americans remembered Washington increasingly directed his attention to the historical record. Republicans, he believed, had "been too careless of our future reputation," which he knew could never be a separate question in the national consciousness from the relationship of Republican leaders to Washington.[96] During his retirement, Jefferson spent a not inconsiderable amount of time and effort both offering his recollections of Washington to reliable historians he hoped would write a Republican history of the 1790s, and compiling and preserving the documentation necessary to write such a work, including the three volumes of memoranda he had gathered during his tenure in Washington's cabinet and which he had re-bound in 1818.[97] To these volumes he added a general preface unifying the various notes, scribbled in haste "on loose scraps of paper, taken out of my pocket in the moment," presenting them years later as a single document of firsthand witness that would, he hoped, recover the truth about the 1790s. The point, Jefferson noted, was to counter Federalist manipulation of the documentary record. Washington's writing could be trusted, for "few men have lived whose opinions were more unbiassed and correct." But not "every thing found among Genl. Washington's papers is to be taken as gospel truth." Washington's genuine views had to be filtered from other documents in his papers, documents from Federalists, who scattered "suspicions . . . rumors . . . & falsehoods" that even the discriminating would find difficult to distinguish. Jefferson described his project of historical recovery as an aid to a dispassionate history of the 1790s, which the "partiality" of Marshall had distorted.[98]

In 1809, by which time he had even more reason to despise the chief justice, Jefferson was still taking notes on Marshall's *Life,* highlighting its "perversions" for Barlow.[99] Marshall's history, Jefferson argued, "pretends to have been compiled from authentic and unpublished documents." But history could "be made to wear any hue, with which the passions of the compiler, royalist or republican, may chuse to tinge it."[100] "History," Jefferson noted, "may distort truth, and will distort it for a time, by the superior efforts at justification of those who are conscious of needing it most."[101] Washington himself could have used such documents to write an account that "would have been a conspicuous monument of the integrity of his mind, the soundness of his judgment, and its powers of discernment between truth & falsehood; principles & pretensions."[102] Jefferson suggested that the documents themselves would reveal the truth: "What a treasure will be found in General Washington's cabinet, when it shall pass into the hands of as candid a friend to truth as he was himself!" For now, Washington's papers were open "to the high priests of federalism only, and garbled to say so much, and no more, as suits their views!"[103] Marshall's "party feeling," for example, had produced a history "as different from what Genl. Washington would have offered, as was the candor of the two characters during the period of the war."[104]

This full-scale assault on the integrity of Marshall's account was consistent with Jefferson's efforts to rescue Washington from the partisanship of his chroniclers. Washington would have told the truth, Jefferson insisted, but only distortion could be expected from Marshall. "Let no man believe that Genl. Washington ever intended that his papers should be used for the suicide of the cause, for which he had lived." Yet Federalist "abuse of these materials" was destroying Washington's fondest hopes, and even the testimony of his character and integrity. Washington had rebuffed many efforts during his lifetime to turn him into something usable by anti-republican characters, Jefferson argued, including efforts to make him a king or to place him at the head of a hereditary aristocracy. To remember Washington as the head of the Federalist faction, as Marshall and other Federalists were doing, would be to replicate posthumously those attempts to enlist his prestige in behalf of views he abhorred. If the source of Washington's greatness was his continual resistance to temptations to abuse his power, then Federalist historians like Marshall, Jefferson argued, were attempting to do for Washington's memory precisely what he always rejected during life.[105] Jefferson's reasoning was absolutely brilliant, if dubious. During an era in which the collective memory of Washington transcended partisan categories, Jefferson castigated Marshall—who had more or less accurately described Washington as a Federalist—for trying to turn Washington into the head of a party.

Marshall, the public figure perhaps closest to Washington in his final years, had some reason to think he understood Washington's mature views.[106] But Jefferson's own history of the 1790s turned Marshall's on its head, fully exonerating Republicans of any significant disagreement with the Father of his Country. Opposition to the "course of [Washington's] administration" was simply an effort to "preserve the legislature pure and independent of the Executive, to restrain the administration to republican forms and principles, and not permit the constitution to be construed into a monarchy, and to be warped in practice into all the principles and pollutions of their favorite English model."[107] The "original objects of the federalists" were "to warp our government more to the form and principles of monarchy" and upset the true balance of federalism called for in the Constitution.[108] Disappointed with the Constitution as ratified in 1789, the Federalists "clung to England as their prototype," which explained both their long-standing (and documented!) preference for England in foreign policy and trade, and their attempts to press monarchical forms upon President Washington. Since the Federalists saw the Constitution as but a "stepping stone to the final establishment of their favorite model," Republicans, devoted to the "present constitution," had never threatened Union and Constitution, as Marshall would have it, but had merely resisted "Anglomany & Monarchy."[109]

A proper understanding of these basic party differences was the key to understanding the relationship between Washington and the Republicans, Jefferson argued. If Federalists were, by definition, monarchists and partisans of England, how could they ever claim the imprimatur of Washington? Since Washington was always "true to the republican charge confided to him" (and who would *dare* deny it?), the Republican opposition to Hamilton's schemes simply could never have been "an opposition to Genl. Washington" himself.[110] "Genl Washington," Jefferson insisted, "did not harbour one principle of federalism. He was neither an Angloman, a monarchist nor a Separatist." So it was "a mere calumny therefore in the Monarchists to associate General Washington with their principles."[111] The Federalists, by "pretending to be the exclusive friends of General Washington," had actually gone some distance toward "sink[ing] his character, by hanging theirs on it, and by representing as the enemy of republicans him, who of all men, is best entitled to the appellation of the father of that republic which they were endeavoring to subvert, and the republicans to maintain."[112] By portraying the *Federalists* as the twisters of Washington's otherwise unsullied reputation—by suggesting that they were tainting his glory with *their* perversions—Jefferson turned Federalist memories on their heads and captured the image of Washington—the Father of the Country—as nonpartisan and republican, both small and, paradoxically, capital "R." For if Washington was a small-"r" republican in his heart, he could not, by Jefferson's definition, be a Federalist. Federalist efforts to "falsify" Washington's "character, by representing him as an enemy to republicans and republican principles, and as exclusively the friend of those who were so," would be thwarted when the record, corrected by Jefferson and the documents, would demonstrate the truth.[113]

But here Jefferson knew he had a small problem: the general drift of Washington's second term and, for those in the know, Washington's clear migration into the Federalist camp after at least 1795. To be sure, Jefferson noted, Washington—generous soul that he was—never quite grasped "the drift, or . . . the effect of Hamilton's schemes."[114] Jefferson's retirement from the cabinet had removed the only voice of opposition, allowing the Federalists to have an "unchecked hold of Genl. Washington."[115] Washington's new cabinet afforded him "no opportunity of hearing both sides of any question." No wonder that "his measures" began to take "more the hue of the party in whose hands he was."[116] Washington's capitulation to their schemes Jefferson explained with reference to physical and mental decline: "His memory was already sensibly impaired by age, the firm tone of mind for which he had been remarkable, was beginning to relax, it's energy was abated; a listlessness of labor, a desire for tranquility had crept on him, and a willingness to let others act and even think for him."[117] Washington, thus, began to acquiesce in measures that Republicans opposed, especially the Jay Treaty. But this was not really Washington's fault, and the Republicans, Jefferson insisted, understanding "his honesty" and "the wiles with which he was encompassed," never "imputed" such measures to him, but, rather, "to the counselors around him."[118]

Washington did, Jefferson admitted somewhat offhandedly, "become alienated from myself personally," but this was due to the "falsehoods" of "a malignant neighbor of mine, who ambitioned to be his correspondent," just as the corrupt cabinet of his second administration had been responsible for Washington's alienation "from the republican body generally of his fellow citizens."[119] Drawing a line between the two men was an essential part of the Federalist project of tearing the first president from the nation, Jefferson believed, and trying to make him the exclusive trademark of their party. Federalists took "great and malignant pains . . . to make him view me as a theorist, holding French principles of government, which would lead infallibly to licentiousness and anarchy." Such efforts, Jefferson reluctantly admitted, had not been "entirely without effect." (Little did he know!) But Republicans understood Washington's plight and soon reconciled themselves to his memory. "I am convinced he is more deeply seated in the love and gratitude of the republicans, than in the Pharisaical homage of the Federal monarchists."[120] Washington's "real friends" had been grieved by his manipulation by the Federalists, but "could not loosen their affections from him." The Republicans, Jefferson avowed, "would not suffer the temporary aberration to weigh against the immeasurable merits of his life; and although they tumbled his seducers from their places, they preserved his memory embalmed in their hearts, with undiminished love and devotion; and there it forever will remain embalmed in entire oblivion of every temporary thing which might cloud the glories of his splendid life."[121]

Washington was "sincerely a friend to the republican principles of our constitution," and the "only point in which he and I ever differed in opinion," Jefferson noted, "was that I had more confidence than he had in the natural integrity and discretion of the people; and in the safety and extent to which they might trust themselves with a controul over their government." Washington, Jefferson reluctantly admitted in one letter, "had not a firm confidence in the durability of our government," and assumed that "we must at length end in something like a British constitution."[122] But he was "no monarchist from the preference of his judgment"; he always stood willing to give the American experiment in republican government "a fair trial," and he would have sacrificed "the last drop of his blood in support of it."[123] He held out the hope, unlike true Federalists, that Americans could govern themselves. It was thus natural for Jefferson to believe that, "had he lived longer," Washington "would have returned to his ancient and unbiased opinions, would have replaced his confidence in those whom the people approved and supported, and would have seen that they were only restoring and acting on the principles of his own first administration."[124]

Jefferson, who knew the man himself, was in a better position than most to know that Washington had not always lived up to his public image as a figure above partisanship. But when it came time to remember Washington, Jefferson described him as untainted with Federalism, largely because he knew that his own political project could hardly do without the indispensable symbol of American nationhood. But recovering Washington for the Republicans, Jefferson understood, would be all the simpler because it would merely require affirmation of the public's embrace of Washington's *nonpartisan* image. If the Federalists had tried to trademark Washington for *party,* the Republicans, who Jefferson simply equated with "the *nation*" itself, could rest content with a Washington transcendent.[125] And a transcendent Washington would, in turn, legitimate the Republicans as Washington's "true friends."

Such manipulation of Washington's image continued the practice of the Revolutionary generation. Adams remembered that the original patriot cause had depended upon the willingness of statesmen from across the Union to "expressly agree . . . to blow the trumpet of panegyric in concert, to cover and dissemble all [of Washington's] faults and errors, to represent every defeat as a victory and every retreat as an advancement, to make that Character popular and fashionable with all parties in all places and with all persons, as a center of union, as the central stone in the geometrical arch."[126] Jefferson could never be so refreshingly candid about Washington's foibles or the mythologies of the Washington cult, precisely because his own national project depended upon a successful appropriation of that very iconography. Accordingly, Jefferson passed along a nonpartisan Washington to the next generation, a Washington with remarkably up-to-date Republican credentials.

But Jefferson's uses of Washington were never cynical, any more than Washington's own professions of nonpartisanship were calculated to serve the ends of party—which they nevertheless did to some extent. The early republic's political culture simply had no language in which statesmen could think of themselves as partisan without shame.[127] In the end, then, Jefferson's project was not all that different from Washington's own: to parlay Washington's reputation into a symbol around which the nation could coalesce. Jefferson's reminiscence of Washington would rescue the man from the partisanship of his old age and convey the image untarnished to the next generation. From Jefferson's perspective, he was rendering Washington a service, allowing him to remain, in death, the national symbol he had generally been in life. In light of Jefferson's own sense that one of the duties of friendship was the preservation of reputations after death—"take care of me when dead," he had asked Madison in his final letter to that best of his political friends—Jefferson's memory of Washington rekindled a friendship long since exhausted. Jefferson had spent a good deal of effort preserving Washington's reputation in the Confederation period, and had attempted the same, less successfully he feared, in the 1790s. Jefferson's later efforts to secure Washington's image were, perhaps, yet another stage in that process. Seen through the long scope of Jefferson's memory, his friendship with Washington had once again grown remarkably close.

Notes

1. Peter Parish, "A Respectful Revisionism: Lincoln and the Jefferson Legacy in the Civil War Era," in *Reason and Republicanism: Thomas Jefferson's Legacy of Liberty,* ed. Gary McDowell (Lanham, Md., 1997), 169.

2. GW to Thomas Jefferson, 8 June 1781, *PTJ,* 6:83; Peter R. Henriques, *Realistic Visionary: A Portrait of George Washington* (Charlottesville, Va., 2006), 107.

3. GW to Lafayette, 10 May 1786, *PGW: Conf. Ser.,* 4:44.

4. GW to Jefferson, 8 June 1781, *PTJ,* 6:83; GW to Jefferson, 25 February 1785, ibid., 8:5. See also GW to Jefferson, 21 January 1790, *PGW: Pres. Ser.,* 5:30; Jefferson, *Autobiography,* in *TJW,* 99; GW to Jefferson, 13 October 1789, *PGW: Pres. Ser.,* 4:174–75; and Jefferson to GW, 15 December 1789, ibid., 4:412–13.

5. Jefferson, *Notes on the State of Virginia* (1787), ed. William Peden (Chapel Hill, 1954), 64. See also Jefferson to GW, 22 January 1783, *PTJ,* 6:222.

6. See John E. Ferling, *The Ascent of George Washington: The Hidden Political Genius of an American Icon* (New York, 2009).

7. Among other works, see especially, Don Higginbotham, *George Washington and the American Military Tradition* (Athens, Ga., 1985); Edmund S. Morgan, *The Genius of George Washington* (New York, 1980); Garry Wills, *Cincinnatus: George Washington and the Enlightenment* (New York, 1984); and Gordon S. Wood, "The Greatness of George Washington," in *George Washington Reconsidered,* ed. Don Higginbotham (Charlottesville, Va., 2001), 309–24.

8. Jefferson to Francis Hopkinson, 13 March 1789, *PTJ,* 14:649–51. But also see Jefferson to Edward Carrington, 27 May 1788, ibid., 13:208–9.

9. Jefferson to David Humphreys, 18 March 1789, ibid., 14:678–79.

10. Jefferson, *Notes on the State of Virginia,* 120–21. On Jefferson's apparent lack of concern with the more militaristic and monarchical aspects of Washington's image as late as 1790, see Kirk Savage, *Monument Wars: Washington, D.C, the National Mall, and the Transformation of the Memorial Landscape* (Berkeley, 2009), 37.

11. Don Higginbotham, *George Washington: Uniting a Nation* (Lanham, Md., 2002).

12. GW to Jefferson, 25 February 1785, *PTJ,* 8:5. For one such occasion, see Ferling, *Ascent of George Washington,* 250–55, and Jefferson to GW, 15 March 1784, *PTJ,* 7:25–27.

13. See Jefferson to GW, 10 July 1785, *PTJ,* 8:280. Perhaps the most famous example is Jefferson's advice concerning Washington's membership in the Society of the Cincinnati, which Jefferson ultimately suggested was an institution incompatible with the spirit of America. On this, see GW to Jefferson, 8 April 1784, ibid., 7:88–89; Jefferson to GW, 16 April 1784, ibid., 105–8; Jefferson to GW, 14 November 1786, ibid., 10:532–533; and "Jefferson's Observations on Demeunier's Manuscript," ibid., 10:49–54 (quotation, 50). For context, see Minor Myers Jr., *Liberty without Anarchy: A History of the Society of the Cincinnati* (Charlottesville, Va., 1983), 48–66.

14. Jefferson to GW, 16 April 1784, *PTJ,* 7:106–7.

15. Wills, *Cincinnatus,* 112.

16. Jefferson to James Madison, 20 February 1784, *PTJ,* 6:548.

17. Alexander Hamilton to GW, 5 May 1789, *PGW: Pres. Ser.*, 2:211; Robert R. Livingston to GW, 2 May 1789, ibid., 2:192–95.

18. GW to John Adams, 10 May 1789, ibid., 2:245–46; Stuart Leibiger, *Founding Friendship: George Washington, James Madison, and the Creation of the American Republic* (Charlottesville, Va., 1999), 112; Ferling, *Ascent of George Washington*, 279; Simon Newman, *Parades and the Politics of the Street: Festive Culture in the Early American Republic* (Philadelphia, 1997), 50.

19. Jefferson to Martin Van Buren, 29 June 1824, *FE*, 12:363–66.

20. Jefferson to GW, 23 May 1792, *PTJ*, 23:535–40; Jefferson to GW, 9 September 1792, ibid., 24:353.

21. GW to Hamilton, 29 July 1792, *PGW: Pres. Ser.*, 10:588–92; GW to Jefferson, 23 August 1792, ibid., 11:28–31; GW to Hamilton, 26 August 1792, ibid., 11:38–39.

22. Hamilton, "American No. 1," *Gazette of the United States* (4 August 1792), *PAH*, 12:163–64; Hamilton to GW, 9 September 1792, ibid., 12:347–50.

23. See *PTJ*, 23:540n.

24. "Notes of a Conversation with George Washington," 10 July 1792, *PTJ*, 24:210–11. See also "Memoranda of Consultations with the President," 9 April 1792, ibid., 23:263.

25. GW to Edmund Randolph, 26 August 1792, *PGW: Pres. Ser.*, 11:45; Henry Lee to GW, 17 August 1794, Fitzpatrick, 33:476–77.

26. GW to Lee, 26 August 1794, Fitzpatrick, 33:476.

27. GW to Burgess Ball, 25 September 1794, ibid., 33:505. See also GW to John Jay, 1 November 1794, ibid., 34:15–18; and GW to J. Adams, 20 August 1795, ibid., 34:280.

28. See "Anas," FE, 1:235.

29. "Notes of a Cabinet Meeting on Edmond Charles Genet," 2 August 1793, *PTJ*, 26:602; Jefferson to Madison, 11 August 1793, ibid., 26:652.

30. Notes on a Conversation with George Washington, 6 August 1793, ibid., 26:628.

31. Henriques, *Realistic Visionary*, 105, 125; Richard B. Morris, "Washington and Hamilton: A Great Collaboration," *Proceedings of the American Philosophical Society* 102 (30 April 1958): 107–16.

32. Don Higginbotham, "Virginia's Trinity of Immortals: Washington, Jefferson, and Henry, and the Story of Their Fractured Relationships," *JER* 23 (Winter 2003): 534.

33. "Anas," FE, 1:183. See also Elizabeth Fleet, ed., "Madison's 'Detached Memoranda,'" *WMQ*, 3rd ser., 3 (October 1946): 541; and Joseph Charles, *The Origins of the American Party System: Three Essays* (New York, 1956), 41–42.

34. On this theme, see Charles, *Origins of the American Party System*, chap. 1, esp. 42–48; Richard Hofstadter, *The Idea of a Party System* (Berkeley, Calif., 1969), esp. 91–102; Leibiger, *Founding Friendship*, 213; Harold W. Bradley, "The Political Thinking of George Washington," *Journal of Southern History* 11 (November 1945): 469–86; Saul K. Padover, "George Washington—Portrait of a True Conservative," *Social Research* 22 (Summer 1955): 199–222; and Marshall Smelser, "George Washington and the Alien and Sedition Acts," *American Historical Review* 59 (January 1954): 322–34.

35. Jefferson to Mazzei, 24 April 1796, *PTJ*, 29:81–83.

36. Ibid., 29:73–88; Dumas Malone, *Jefferson and the Ordeal of Liberty* (Boston, 1962),

302–7; Howard R. Marraro, "The Four Versions of Jefferson's Letter to Mazzei," *WMQ*, 2nd ser., 22 (January 1942): 23–27.

37. Jefferson to Madison, 3 August 1797, *PTJ*, 39:489–91.

38. Jefferson to Madison, 28 December 1794, ibid., 28:228; Jefferson to William Branch Giles, 31 December 1795, ibid., 28:566.

39. Jefferson to James Monroe, 12 June 1796, ibid., 29:124.

40. Jefferson to Monroe, 10 July 1796, ibid., 29:147.

41. Jefferson to Archibald Stuart, 4 January 1797, ibid., 29:252–53.

42. Jefferson to James Sullivan, 9 February 1797, ibid., 29:289–90.

43. *Aurora*, 6 March 1797, cited in James D. Tagg, "Benjamin Franklin Bache's Attack on George Washington," *Pennsylvania Magazine of History and Biography* 100 (April 1976): 224. See also Benjamin Rush to Jefferson, 12 March 1801, *PTJ*, 33:262.

44. GW to Hamilton, 29 July 1795, in *George Washington: A Collection*, ed. W. B. Allen (Indianapolis, 1988), 611–12.

45. GW to Lafayette, 25 December 1798, *PGW: Ret. Ser.*, 3:281–82. See also GW to John Luzac, 2 December 1797, ibid., 1:378; and Jefferson to Lafayette, 16 June 1792, *PTJ*, 24:85.

46. Jefferson to Van Buren, 29 June 1824, FE, 12:369.

47. Jefferson to GW, 19 June 1796, *PTJ*, 29:127–29.

48. On this correspondence, see Jefferson's 1807–8 record (which seems mistaken) in Jefferson to Madison, undated, in *The Republic of Letters: The Correspondence between Thomas Jefferson and James Madison, 1776–1826*, ed. James Morton Smith, 3 vols. (New York, 1995), 3:1558.

49. GW to Jefferson, 6 July 1796, Fitzpatrick, 35:118–19.

50. See John Nicholas to GW, 18 November 1797, *PGW: Ret. Ser.*, 1:475–77; Nicholas to GW, 9 December 1797, ibid., 1:509–11; John Langhorne to GW, 25 September 1797, ibid., 1:273–75; GW to Langhorne, 15 October 1797, ibid., 1:409; and Nicholas to GW, 22 February 1798, ibid., 2:99–102. See also Malone, *Jefferson and the Ordeal of Liberty*, 308–11.

51. GW to Nicholas, 8 March 1798, *PGW: Ret. Ser.*, 2:128.

52. GW to B. Washington, 12 August 1798, ibid., 2:514.

53. GW to Nicholas, 8 March 1798, ibid., 2:128.

54. GW to David Stuart, 8 January 1797, Fitzpatrick, 35:357.

55. GW to Bryan Fairfax, 20 January 1799, *PGW: Ret. Ser.*, 3:324.

56. GW to Patrick Henry, 15 January 1799, ibid., 3:317.

57. GW to Timothy Pickering, 4 August 1799, ibid., 4:222.

58. GW to Nicholas, 8 March 1798, *PGW: Ret. Ser.*, 2:128. See also GW to Bryan Fairfax, 20 January 1799, ibid., 3:324; and GW to B. Washington, 31 December 1798, ibid., 3:303.

59. GW to Henry, 15 January 1799, ibid., 3:317–18.

60. GW to Jonathan Trumbull Jr., 21 July 1799, ibid., 4:202.

61. GW to Henry, 15 January 1799, ibid., 3:319.

62. GW to Trumbull, 21 July 1799, ibid., 4:202. See also GW to John Luzac, 2 December 1797, ibid., 1:378.

63. GW to Pickering, 4 August 1799, ibid., 4:222; GW to James McHenry, 11 August 1799, ibid., 4:238–39; GW to Charles Carroll (of Carrollton), 2 August 1798, ibid., 2:482–83; GW

to William Vans Murray, 26 December 1798, ibid., 3:287; GW to Marshall, 30 December 1798, ibid., 3:297; GW to B. Washington, 31 December 1798, ibid., 3:302–3; GW to Alexander Spotswood Jr., 22 November 1798, ibid., 3:216–17; Smelser, "George Washington and the Alien and Sedition Acts"; GW to McHenry, 4 July 1798, *PGW: Ret. Ser.*, 2:376–82; GW to J. Adams, 25 September 1798, ibid., 3:36–43.

64. B. Washington to Oliver Wolcott, 1 November 1800, *PAH*, 25:250n; Manasseh Cutler, journal entry of 2 January 1802, in William Parker Cutler and Julia Perkins Cutler, *Life, Journals and Correspondence of Rev. Manasseh Cutler*, 2 vols. (Cincinnati, 1888), 2:56.

65. William W. Andrews, *The Correspondence and Miscellanies of the Hon. John Cotton Smith* (New York, 1847), 224–25. Smith noted that Martha seemed to think that Jefferson should have been aware that she "had the evidence of his perfidy."

66. Cutler and Cutler, *Life, Journals, and Correspondence of Rev. Manasseh Cutler*, 2:56–57. Manasseh Cutler—apparently on the same visit with Smith—reported that Martha's "unfriendly feelings toward [Jefferson] were naturally to be expected, from the abuse he has offered to General Washington, while living, and to his memory since his decease." Martha, Cutler noted, was "sometimes very sarcastic on the new order of things and the present administration." See also Higginbotham, "Virginia's Trinity of Immortals," 540–41.

67. Eleanor Parke Custis Lewis to Elizabeth Bordley Gibson, 23 March 1806, in *George Washington's Beautiful Nelly: The Letters of Eleanor Parke Custis Lewis to Elizabeth Bordley Gibson, 1794–1851*, ed. Patricia Brady (Columbia, S.C., 1991), 67, xii. Thanks to Ellen Hickman of the Papers of Thomas Jefferson: Retirement Series for this reference.

68. Thomas Lomax to Jefferson, 2 April 1801, *PTJ*, 33:524.

69. Joseph Priestley to Jefferson, 10 April 1801, ibid., 33:567.

70. Moses Robinson to Jefferson, 3 March 1801, ibid., 33:129–30. For similar expressions, see Robert Livingston to Jefferson, 7 January 1801, ibid., 32:408; David Austin to Jefferson, 16 June 1801, ibid., 34:351; and Hugh Williamson to Jefferson, 6 July 1801, ibid., 34:522.

71. James Kyle Jr. to Jefferson, 5 January 1801, ibid., 32:403.

72. Samuel Kennedy to Jefferson, 11 March 1801, ibid., 33:244–45.

73. George Meade to Jefferson, 17 February 1801, ibid., 33:8. See also Jacob Bayley to Jefferson, 20 January 1802, ibid., 36:397–98.

74. Henry Sheaff to Jefferson, 18 March 1801, ibid., 33:359. See also Joseph Barnes to Jefferson, 4 March 1800, ibid., 31:403; and Seventy-Six Association to Jefferson, in *Papers of Thomas Jefferson: Retirement Series*, 8 vols. to date, ed. J. Jefferson Looney (Princeton, N.J., 2004–), 6:89n.

75. Thomas Northmore, *Washington, or Liberty Restored: A Poem, in Ten Books* (Baltimore, 1809), 135–36.

76. Jefferson to Uzal Ogden, 12 February 1800, *PTJ*, 31:369; Jefferson to Samuel Adams, 26 February 1800, ibid., 31:395.

77. Jefferson to Miller, 25 February 1800, ibid., 31:394. See also J. Adams to Rush, 8 July 1812, in *The Spur of Fame: Dialogues of John Adams and Benjamin Rush, 1805–1813*, ed. John A. Schutz and Douglass Adair (San Marino, Calif., 1966), 229; and J. Adams to Rush, 19 August 1811, ibid., 187.

78. See J. Adams to Jefferson, 2–5 July 1813, in *Papers of Thomas Jefferson: Retirement Series*, 6:259.

79. Jefferson to Auguste Belin, 27 February 1800, *PTJ,* 31:396; Jefferson to Belin, 6 March 1800, ibid., 31:417.

80. Jefferson to Rush, 23 September 1800, ibid., 32:167.

81. B. Washington to Wolcott, 1 November 1800, *PAH,* 25:249–50n. See also William Jackson to Jefferson, 3 February 1801, *PTJ,* 32:541–44; and Jefferson's reply of 18 February 1801, ibid., 33:14.

82. See François Furstenberg, *In the Name of the Father: Washington's Legacy, Slavery, and the Making of a Nation* (New York, 2006), chap. 1; and Barry Schwartz, *George Washington: The Making of an American Symbol* (New York, 1987), chap. 3.

83. Joseph J. Ellis, *Founding Brothers: The Revolutionary Generation* (New York, 2000), 126. See also Madison to Jefferson, 10 January 1801, *PTJ,* 32:436.

84. Jefferson to A. Stuart, 4 January 1797, *PTJ,* 29:252.

85. Jefferson to Madison, 3 August 1797, ibid., 29:490.

86. Jefferson, First Inaugural Address, ibid., 33:151, 147n20.

87. Henry Knox to Jefferson, 16 March 1801, ibid., 33:313.

88. John W. Maddux to Jefferson, 4 August 1801, ibid., 35:21. See also Jean Chas to Jefferson, 1 April 1801, ibid., 33:516–17; Montgomery County, Kentucky, Citizens to Jefferson, 13 April 1801, ibid., 33:583; and "A Kentucky-Citizen" to Jefferson, before 26 June 1801, ibid., 34:455. For a contrary reading by an unconvinced Federalist, see Manasseh Cutler to Ephraim Cutler, 21 March 1801, in Cutler and Cutler, *Life, Journals, and Correspondence of Rev. Manasseh Cutler,* 2:47.

89. Pierce Butler to Jefferson, 26 February 1801, *PTJ,* 33:74.

90. See Newman, *Parades and the Politics of the Street,* 70–73.

91. Gerald E. Kahler, *The Long Farewell: Americans Mourn the Death of George Washington* (Charlottesville, Va., 2008), 45–54; Hamilton, "The Examination" (no. XVIII), *New York Evening Post* (8 April 1802), *PAH,* 25:594. See also *PTJ,* 35:33n.

92. Furstenberg, *In the Name of the Father,* 47. On Washington's cult, see Schwartz, *George Washington,* 9.

93. Newman, *Parades and the Politics of the Street,* 82.

94. Walter Jones to Jefferson, 25 November 1813, in *Papers of Thomas Jefferson: Retirement Series,* 6:643.

95. Jefferson to Joel Barlow, 3 May 1802, FE, 9:370–72, esp. 372.

96. Jefferson to Judge William Johnson, 4 March 1823, ibid., 12:277–78.

97. FE, 1:163–430. On Jefferson's historical project, see Matthew E. Crow, "History, Politics, and the Self: Jefferson's 'Anas' and Autobiography," in *A Companion to Thomas Jefferson,* ed. Francis D. Cogliano (Oxford, U.K., 2011), 477–90; Joanne B. Freeman, *Affairs of Honor: National Politics in the New Republic* (New Haven, Conn., 2001), 63–65; and Herbert Sloan, "Presidents as Historians," in *John Adams and the Founding of the Republic,* ed. R. A. Ryerson (Boston, 2001), 266–83.

98. FE, 1:163–65.

99. Jefferson to Barlow, 8 October 1809, in *Papers of Thomas Jefferson: Retirement Series,* 1:588–89. See also Jefferson's notes on the fifth volume of Marshall's *Life of Washington,* FE, 11:122–23.

100. "Anas," in *Papers of Thomas Jefferson: Retirement Series,* 1:164.

101. Jefferson to Johnson, 12 June 1823, *TJW,* 1471.

102. "Anas," FE, 1:165.

103. Jefferson to Johnson, 12 June 1823, *TJW,* 1471.

104. "Anas," FE, 1:165

105. Ibid., 1:166, 168.

106. See Jean Edward Smith, *John Marshall: Definer of a Nation* (New York, 1996), 328; and Higginbotham, *George Washington: Uniting a Nation,* 68–69.

107. "Anas," FE, 1:178.

108. Jefferson to Johnson, 12 June 1823, *TJW,* 1472.

109. Jefferson to John Melish, 13 January 1813, in *Papers of Thomas Jefferson: Retirement Series,* 5:563–64.

110. "Anas," FE, 1:178.

111. Jefferson to Melish, 13 January 1813, in *Papers of Thomas Jefferson: Retirement Series,* 5:565.

112. Jefferson to Van Buren, 29 June 1824, FE, 12:369.

113. Ibid., 12:371.

114. "Anas," ibid., 1:179.

115. Ibid., 1:183.

116. Jefferson to Van Buren, 29 June 1824, ibid., 12:370.

117. "Anas," ibid., 1:183.

118. Jefferson to Jones, 2 January 1814, in *Papers of Thomas Jefferson: Retirement Series,* 7:102; Jefferson to Van Buren, 29 June 1824, FE, 12:370.

119. "Anas," FE, 1:183.

120. Jefferson to Jones, 2 January 1814, in *Papers of Thomas Jefferson: Retirement Series,* 7:102.

121. Jefferson to Van Buren, 29 June 1824, FE, 12:371.

122. Jefferson to Jones, January 2, 1814, *TJW,* 1320; Jefferson to Melish, 13 January 1813, in *Papers of Thomas Jefferson: Retirement Series,* 5:565. Jefferson's assessment of Washington's views are reaffirmed in Dorothy Twohig, "The Making of George Washington," in *George Washington and the Virginia Backcountry,* ed. Warren R. Hofstra (Madison, Wis., 1998), 25–26.

123. Jefferson to Jones, 2 January 1814, in *Papers of Thomas Jefferson: Retirement Series,* 7:102.

124. Jefferson to Van Buren, 29 June 1824, FE, 12:371.

125. Jefferson to William Duane, 28 March 1811, in *Papers of Thomas Jefferson: Retirement Series,* 3:508.

126. J. Adams to Rush, 19 March 1812, in Schutz and Adair, *Spur of Fame,* 211.

127. See Freeman, *Affairs of Honor;* and Leibiger, *Founding Friendship,* 215.

George Washington and James Monroe

Military Compatriots, Political Adversaries, and Nationalist Visionaries

WILLIAM M. FERRARO

James Monroe, born in Westmoreland County, Virginia, on April 28, 1758, was more than twenty-six years younger than George Washington, who was born in the same county in February 1732. Given Washington's stature in Virginia for his accomplishments as a colonial army officer and his participation in colonial assemblies, it is likely that Monroe knew of him by reputation before seeing, and probably meeting, the older man in the first year of the Revolutionary War, during battles around New York City and in New Jersey. Years later, in 1822, President Monroe pointed toward Washington as "an example to the world for talents as a military commander; for integrity, fortitude, and firmness under the severest trials; for respect to the civil authority and devotion to the rights and liberties of his country, of which neither Rome nor Greece have exhibited the equal. I saw him in my earliest youth, in the retreat through Jersey, at the head of a small band, or rather in its rear, for he was always next to the enemy, and his countenance and manner made an impression on me which time can never efface." Monroe's praise escalated: "A deportment so firm, so dignified, so exalted, but yet so modest and composed, I have never seen in any other person."[1]

While an eighteen-year-old lieutenant in the Continental Army, and then again as president after a long public career, Monroe esteemed Washington. Such admiration, however, was not constant. In fact, it may not be an overstatement to claim that at the time of Washington's death, in December 1799, Monroe, then the newly elected governor of Virginia, hated no man more; Washington felt similarly toward the man for whom he served as erstwhile and subsequent hero. Politics, personalities, and profound differences over the proper means to reach desired ends drove the two men apart. His experience in the cabinet and as president restored Monroe's regard for Washington and their shared vision of an independent and unified nation that acted with integrity and vigor. Firsthand knowledge of a central government overly committed to limited power, wracked with partisan divisions, and clogged by personal ambition or incompetence brought about this result. Neither Washington nor Monroe wanted the United States government to teeter near chaos, impotence, or insignificance.

The relationship between Washington and Monroe has not been a feature of scholarly literature. Students of Monroe have sought primarily to push him from the shadows of more prominent contemporaries and establish his own significance. This was the goal of his first true biographer, who in the early 1880s wanted to "revive" Monroe's memory while drawing "a faithful sketch of an honest and patriotic citizen as he discharged the duties of exalted stations."[2] The same motivation drove early twentieth-century biographers, who sought to demonstrate Monroe's capabilities while fleshing out his career.[3] Underlying these narratives, as well as future accounts, was a desire to undercut Henry Adams, who, in his histories of the presidential administrations of Thomas Jefferson and James Madison, characterized Monroe as a rather bumbling diplomatist and statesman who ascended to the presidency essentially by default.[4] Harry Ammon published in 1971 what remains the best Monroe biography, but its theme of national identity should have given a higher profile to Washington.[5] Still, it is better to have understated Washington's impact on Monroe than to assert, without citation, as does the most recent Monroe biographer, that reading "John Marshall's seminal five-volume work *The Life of George Washington*" during an 1815 summer vacation was an epiphany for the aspiring president, "giving him a commander's rather than a soldier's and citizen's, view of the Revolution for the first time—and a president's rather than a politically partisan congressman's view of government."[6] There is no need to speculate about the crucially important relationship between Washington and Monroe.

Young James Monroe was susceptible to the sway of a mentor. Monroe's father, Spence, prospered enough to send the future president to a distinguished academy, but his death in 1774 orphaned the promising youth, two younger sons, and a daughter. Monroe inherited his father's farm, but he would not control the property until he attained his majority, and he then bore responsibility for the care of his siblings. This task, which he took seriously, became a lengthy trial because neither of the elder Monroe's brothers achieved self-sufficiency in adulthood. James Monroe, on the other hand, benefited greatly from older men. An important mentor was Joseph Jones, a maternal uncle, prominent in Virginia legal circles and government, who provided guidance until his death in 1805. As his nephew's guardian, Jones enrolled Monroe at the College of William and Mary, where the young man began his studies in June 1774. Growing friction between Crown officials and radical Virginia legislators in Williamsburg absorbed Monroe's attention, and he followed calls to protest British policies, participate in military drill, and prepare for war.[7]

Monroe abandoned college in early 1776 and enlisted in the 3rd Virginia Regiment. By the end of the year, he had been commissioned a lieutenant, fought in the battles around New York City, and retreated with the Continental Army remnant across New Jersey to Pennsylvania. With patriot hopes at a low, Monroe rose to a height that surely brought him to Washington's attention. The general's plan to attack the Hessian garrison at Trenton on Christmas night required surprise. Monroe volunteered to serve under Captain William Washington, who commanded a small advance force sent across the Delaware River to block the roads north of Trenton. These troops executed their orders through a snowy night, adding to their number a patriotic doctor who likely saved Monroe's life after he was wounded in the shoulder in a charge. Suffering a severed artery, the young lieutenant would have bled to death if a skilled medical practitioner had not staunched the flow of blood. Captain Washington and Monroe were the only casualties among the officers who shared in this victory. Nearly three months passed before Monroe recovered fully.[8]

Monroe's reward for his valor was a promotion to captain in a new Continental regiment. He returned to Virginia in May 1777 to recruit his company, carrying a letter from General Washington to the surgeon general in Philadelphia requesting medicine for Mount Vernon to address a smallpox outbreak. It is unconfirmed but probable that Monroe completed this errand.[9] Monroe's likely satisfaction at being asked by Washington for a personal favor soon gave way to frustration. Two circuits of the "back Country" only landed a scant fifteen recruits. "I am thoroughly convinc[e]d," Monroe complained, that "we shall not get another man without using those arts wh[ich] I wo[ul]d avoid and which no man of honor should use."[10] Another month proved fruitless, and Monroe rejoined the main army in late August. His uncle Joseph Jones wrote to the general to explain the captain's failure to raise his company.

The letter suggests Monroe's deference toward Washington. Fault, wrote Jones, rested not on Monroe, who had "been diligent," but on "the present disposition of the people of Virginia" to avoid military service or to pocket "the high bounty" offered for local militia duty.[11]

Without a regular field command, Monroe accepted assignment as aide-de-camp to Major General William Alexander, the self-styled Lord Stirling, and saw action in battles around Philadelphia before the winter encampment at Valley Forge. Monroe applauded Washington's decision in the late summer to march his army through Philadelphia with "all the Pomp of military parade" because it "intirely silenc'd" the Tories.[12] His enthusiasm waned after the Continental Army failed to prevent British occupation of the city. Lamenting "that Officers of reputation" frequently departed the service, Monroe believed that "Patriotism, publick spirit and disinterestedness have almost vanis'd; and honor and virtue are em[p]ty names."[13] These thoughts echoed those of Washington and his staff officers, from whom it appears that Monroe derived his views. Monroe became quite friendly with his fellow staff officers. Like many of them, he made social rounds, courted young women, and devoted hours to study.[14]

Such diversions did not suppress Monroe's desire for a field command. After scouting capably in the heat of battle at Monmouth in late June 1778 and in northern New Jersey during the summer and early fall, Monroe decided to address his personal affairs and seek a high commission in the Virginia State Line.[15] His resignation as Stirling's aide-de-camp, dated December 20, 1778, was announced to the army on January 12, 1779.[16] Unhappy over disappointments at home and an inability to visit Europe, Monroe returned in May to the Continental Army's camp at Middlebrook, New Jersey, to obtain a recommendation from Washington.[17] The general obliged, recounting Monroe's service record for Virginia officials before concluding that "in every instance" he "maintained the reputation of a brave active and sensible officer. As we cannot introduce him into the Continental line, it were to be wished the State could do something for him, to enable him to follow the bent of his military inclination and render service to his country. If an event of this kind could take place it would give me particular pleasure, as the esteem I have for him, and a regard to merit conspire to make me earnestly wish to see him provided for in some handsome way."[18] Washington's letter pleased Monroe and materially assisted his appointment late that summer as a lieutenant colonel in the Virginia State Line.

Governor Thomas Jefferson ordered Monroe to Williamsburg to recruit a regiment in anticipation of a British invasion. Recruiting failed, and Monroe found that he spent much of his time reading books from the William and Mary library. Adrift, he contemplated the study of law.[19] Joseph Jones recommended the legal scholar George Wythe for a teacher, but that devoted relative endorsed Jefferson even more warmly.[20] Choosing Jefferson, Monroe followed him from Williamsburg to Richmond in April 1780, when the state capital was shifted to a less-exposed location, and found another mentor who immensely influenced his life's course.

Monroe's studies barely had begun when Jefferson selected him, because of his "great discretion" and "acquaintance with military things," to observe operations in the southern states and send reports. A surviving communication from Monroe conveyed his zeal for this assignment, which lasted about two months.[21] Major General Charles Lee, whom Monroe admired even after his conduct at the Battle of Monmouth led to his court-martial and dismissal, applauded Monroe's appointment. Lee assured his friend that it was best to overcome the "shyness" that concealed his "knowledge and talents," and "only retain a certain degree of recommendatory modesty."[22] Monroe's letter to a friend on Washington's staff offering southern intelligence showed that he perceived this opportunity as an occasion to gain favor with the general, and he likely welcomed the reply indicating that his reports "may be usefull."[23] He probably felt disappointed that his brief assignment to the conflict area restricted his ability to communicate intelligence. No reports from him to army headquarters have been found.

Despite evidence that Monroe fondly remembered Washington, a more signal fact is how quickly he developed a deep emotional reliance on Jefferson. "I feel that whatever I am at present in the opinion of others or whatever I may be in future has greatly arose from your friendship," Monroe gushed on September 9, 1780. His letters to Jefferson over the next months detailed general activities, disappointments in finding an army command, and aspirations to visit Europe, where he could study "on the most liberal plan." More reserve characterized Jefferson's responses, but he liked the younger man and supplied requested assistance.[24]

Monroe's election to the Virginia House of Delegates in early April 1782 shelved his European designs. Jefferson, although burdened by the illness of his wife and infant daughter, which proved fatal to both, commended Monroe upon learning the news.[25] Jefferson's backing, together with a letter of recommendation from Washington, apparently elevated Monroe to the Virginia Executive Council, an eight-member body that advised the governor. Selection to this council, which mandated resignation from the House of Delegates, carried prestige along with tedious work. After a few months, Monroe thanked Washington for the recommendation. "If in the line of my present appointment," Monroe assured him, "fortune sho[ul]d put it in my power to pay attention to or obey in any instance y[ou]r Excellency's commands believe me she co[ul]d not confer a fav[o]r on me I sho[ul]d receive with greater pleasure from her hands." This proffer undoubtedly eased the discomfort Monroe felt in expressing apologies for his failure to raise a regiment and his decision to pursue law.[26] Jefferson, designated a peace commissioner to negotiate a treaty to end the Revolutionary War, asked Monroe to accompany him to Europe as a secretary. Monroe, who felt obligated to accede to the request, was glad when news of a proposed treaty negated the need for his mentor overseas. Instead, the two men journeyed to Annapolis to join the Continental Congress, to which each had been elected.[27]

They took their seats in the Congress on December 13. Monroe shared living quarters with Jefferson, who served on a committee to coordinate Washington's appearance before the Congress to resign as general. A grand entertainment on the evening of December 22 preceded the moving ceremony of the next afternoon, when Washington voluntarily returned his commission and powerfully evoked the principle of military subordination to civil authority. Washington's words and demeanor reportedly reduced many to tears, but, like most witnesses', Monroe's thoughts on the occasion do not survive.[28] That Monroe may have written something praising Washington's action is suggested by the opening of a letter to him from John Marshall, who knew Monroe from their days as students together and was then in Richmond on the Virginia Council: "At length then the military career of the greatest Man on earth is closed. May happiness attend him whereever he goes. May he long enjoy those blessings he has secured to his Country. When I speak or think of that superior Man my full heart overflows with gratitude."[29] Toward the end of his life, Monroe recalled that Washington's resignation was "highly interesting. The manner in which he took his leave and the sentiment expressed in the audience given him by Congress of the conduct through that arduous struggle was such as evinced the high sense entertained of his merit and became the dignity of the body under whom he had so served."[30]

Monroe consistently advocated meaningful central government action as a member of Congress under the Articles of Confederation. Requirements for unanimity among delegates highly attuned to local interests exasperated Monroe as he promoted commerce, white settlement in the Northwest, and navigation of the Mississippi River. Monroe's national orientation commended him to westerners, but he remained current on Virginia attitudes through correspondence with his uncle Joseph Jones and a new friend, James Madison, whose experience ranked his stature near Jefferson's. Monroe's initial overture to Madison went through Jefferson. "The scrupulousness of his honor," Jefferson informed Madison about Monroe, "will make you safe in the most confidential communications. A better man cannot be."[31] The relationship between Monroe and Madison mushroomed, and retained importance for both until their deaths. To preserve confidentiality, Jefferson, Madison, and Monroe concealed in code sensitive portions of their frequent letters on contentious policy matters confronting the Continental Congress.[32]

At various times, Washington received letters from friends mentioning Monroe's efforts to overcome divisions and invigorate the government.[33] Monroe himself wrote to Washington on August 20, 1786, soliciting the retired general's support for the appointment of Jefferson and John Adams to renegotiate John Jay's treaty with Spain that traded free use of the Mississippi River for preferences beneficial to northeastern fisheries. "If in this free communication, I deviate from any of those rules of friendship & respect I have always entertain'd for you, & which I mean this as an evidence of," Monroe averred, "you will attribute it to no motive of that kind since I am not influenc'd by it."[34] The balky machinery of the Articles of Confederation mooted implementation of Jay's treaty, and that no damage had been done to Monroe's cordial relationship with Washington can be seen in the visit of the former to Mount Vernon only two months later, so that he could introduce his new wife, Elizabeth Kortright, the daughter of a New York merchant, to his former commander. Monroe and his wife, traveling with Madison, arrived at Mount Vernon on the evening of October 23. Washington entertained his apparently unexpected company the entire next day, breaking a promise to Martha Washington and her grandchildren to join them at a vacation spot. Washington noted in his diary that the three visitors left after breakfast on Wednesday, October 25.[35]

Washington's next direct communication with Monroe came after the younger man surprised Jefferson, Madison, and probably Washington, by voting against ratification of the Constitution in June 1788 as a member of the Virginia ratifying convention. It was most difficult for Madison, also a delegate to that convention, to fathom how his friend who railed against the defects of the Articles of Confederation could be queasy over the prospect of an aristocratic Senate under the new Constitution, as well as the absence of protections for states and individuals from excessive taxes and an overreaching judiciary. In adopting these views, forcibly voiced during speeches in the convention, Monroe apparently reflected instructions from his Spotsylvania County constituents in equal measure with his own conclusions.[36] Although he stood opposed to his former commanding general on ratification, Monroe advised Jefferson that Washington's conduct "upon this occasion has no doubt been right and meritorious." Monroe observed that for Washington to forsake retirement "and risque the reputation he had so deservedly acquir'd, manifested a zeal for the publick interest, that could after so many and illustrious services, and at this stage of his life, scarcely have been expected from him." He concluded that Washington's influence "carried this government," and that was consoling as he looked ahead. "I have a boundless confidence in him," Monroe wrote, "nor have I any reason to believe he will ever furnish occasion for withdrawing it."[37]

Monroe's pamphlet, *Some Observations on the Constitution,* likely produced in late May 1788, summarized his doubts over the Constitution while still calling for a new government.[38] On February 15, 1789, in the aftermath of his defeat at the hands of Madison for a seat in the first House of Representatives, Monroe sent his pamphlet, never distributed publicly, to Washington. "I am not aware that it contains any thing worthy of attention," a contrite Monroe intoned, and Washington, looking toward his inauguration as president, extended forgiveness. Writing on February 23, Washington acknowledged their differences but praised Monroe for his "candour and liberality." Furthermore, Monroe's "Spirit of unanimity, accom[m]odation and rectitude" promised to facilitate the removal of "any well grounded apprehensions of the possible future ill consequences" that might emanate from the new government.[39] The "liberality and candor" of Washington's response impressed Monroe, and that is how he characterized it many years later.[40]

Monroe's election to the United States Senate on November 9, 1790, to fill a vacancy caused by death, renewed his intense political involvement with Madison, then in the House of Representatives, and Jefferson, then Washington's secretary of state. All three men felt strongly that a monarchical element bent on concentrating power and wealth in the federal government endangered the republican aspirations of the new nation. Alexander Hamilton, Washington's secretary of the treasury, through his advocacy of federal assumption of state debts, a larger standing army, and closer ties with Great Britain, led the anti-republican forces. Developments in France accelerated the split. Hamiltonians, later termed Federalists, saw the French Revolution as an unacceptable threat to the social order, while Jefferson, Madison, Monroe, and their adherents believed the upheaval in France extended the American Revolution by taking the next step toward liberty and freedom.[41] Monroe broadcast his positions in newspaper essays published under the pseudonyms "Aratus" (1791) and "Agricola" (1793). The latter efforts sufficiently shook Edmund Randolph, Washington's second secretary of state, to prompt from him a letter to the president calling for a concerted response.[42]

That Monroe was "Agricola" was not known until the twentieth century, but Monroe's growing distance from Washington and his administration became apparent in more direct ways, such as his vote in the Senate against confirmation of Gouverneur Morris as minister to France, on grounds of that nominee's preference for Great Britain.[43] Upon hearing that Hamilton might be named a special envoy to Great Britain, Monroe wrote to Washington protesting the measure as "injurious to the public interest" and seeking a meeting to explain his opinion. "I *alone* am responsible for a proper nomination," Washington replied the next day, and "it certainly beho[o]ves me to name such an one as in my judgment combines the requisites for a mission so peculiarly interesting to the *peace* & happiness of this country." Washington curtly told Monroe that "any facts or information" damaging to Hamilton could be submitted in writing. Monroe complied, and he condemned in a lengthy letter Hamilton's attachment to Great Britain, "enmity to the French nation & revolution," and general reputation for intrigues. Signs of favor toward Great Britain already had disturbed the French, and further alienation "would be as mortifying as it would be alarming."[44] Washington did not appoint Hamilton, but his selection of John Jay, whom Monroe distrusted as a result of his negotiations with Spain over Mississippi River navigation, certainly gave the senator no comfort.[45]

Striving to placate factions in his own country and to allay suspicions among the French, Washington, on the advice of Secretary of State Randolph, nominated a rather shocked Monroe as minister to France in late May 1794. Initially reluctant, because "he had never contemplated such a trust," held different views from the administration, and "had opposed in the Senate some of the most important measures of the President," as he remembered late in his life, Monroe yielded to the pressing nomination after a quick consultation with Madison and after having received expressions of Washington's belief in his "upright and honorable motives." As a sign of Washington's favor, Monroe later recalled, this appointment pleased him tremendously.[46] It would be "the highest gratification," Monroe assured Washington in his formal letter accepting his commission, "to have it in my power to promote by my mission the interest of my country & the honor & credit of your administration which I deem inseperably connected with it."[47]

Monroe apparently forgot this promise once in Paris, where he flamboyantly—and contrary to his instructions—pronounced the fundamental alignment between the interests of the United States and the French Republic when presenting his credentials.[48] After digesting Monroe's words, Washington communicated his dismay to Jay, observing "that considering the place in which they were delivered, and the neutral policy this country had resolved to pursue, it was a measure that does not appear to have been well devised by our Minister."[49] News of Jay successfully negotiating a commercial treaty with Great Britain in the early months of 1795 greatly complicated Monroe's relationship with French officials. He stalled while trying to obtain details of the agreement and authorization to share its confidential terms with the French, who saw it as an abrogation of their 1778 treaty of alliance with the United States.[50]

In a June letter to Madison, Monroe probed his predicament. He expanded upon his concerns the following month in another letter to Madison, written largely in cipher.[51] Finally seeing the terms of Jay's Treaty in the public prints during the late summer, Monroe wailed to Madison: "In examining therefore this project from the beginning to the end & impartially, I do not find one single stipulation in our favor, or which certainly improves our condition from what it was before: whilst on the other hand it most certainly contains a series of stipulations, many of which are extremely unfavorable & disgraceful, and others at best indifferent."[52] Monroe sounded a similar note several weeks later. "We are in the deepest concern respecting the treaty of Mr. Jay," he wrote. "If it is ratified, it may be deemed one of the most afflicting events that ever befell our country." The next day, he added that "I most sincerely hope the President has not & will not ratify this treaty, for if he does, I greatly fear the consequences here."[53]

Ratification of Jay's Treaty, which occurred on June 24, 1795, heightened

Monroe's distress, and he intimated to French officials that the administration had acted against the true sentiments of the American people. Indiscreet communications with partisan friends and newspapers, and perceived embellishments in letters to the state department, already had compromised Monroe in the eyes of Washington and the new secretary of state, Timothy Pickering. Other than Monroe, few were stunned by his recall, finally determined upon in August 1796.[54] Morose over his ouster, he dallied with his family for several months before returning to the United States in early summer 1797.[55]

It is noteworthy that Monroe retained a high regard for Washington even as his relationship with the presidential administration became impossibly strained and his official standing plummeted. He aired these sentiments to Madison over the latter months of 1795 and into 1796, writing in cipher at one point that "Washington is an honest man" and could not be blamed for the mistaken American policy toward France. Even as his frustration grew over his treatment at the hands of the people around Washington, he could not bring himself to condemn the president. "Poor Washington into what hands has he fallen," he bemoaned in cipher to Madison. Monroe revealed his deep devotion to his early mentor when, despite the "unprecedented outrage" of his recall, he confessed to Madison that "I have still some tenderness towards General Washington."[56]

Monroe's rancor increased, however, possibly because of a confrontation with Alexander Hamilton, Washington's persistent favorite. A newspaper report had alleged a financial scandal from Hamilton's time as secretary of the treasury. Monroe, then a senator, was among a small group who interviewed Hamilton and learned that the money in question was not the government's, but Hamilton's—and had been transferred to buy silence after an affair with another man's wife. Deeming the matter a private rather than a public indiscretion, the investigators agreed to secrecy. When the "Reynolds Affair" became known in 1797, Hamilton confronted Monroe, almost immediately after the latter's return to the United States, and demanded a public statement of exoneration. When Monroe delayed, Hamilton erupted, charging Monroe with dishonorable duplicity and challenging him to a duel. Tensions mounted through exchanges of missives until Hamilton's public acknowledgement of his inappropriate intimacy, with sordid details, shifted focus from Monroe. The two men dropped arrangements for a duel after trading final, lukewarm sentiments, but Monroe undoubtedly felt tremendous anxiety for the future of the nation under the reign of men like Hamilton.[57]

Disgusted by what he perceived as the vitriolic attacks and misguided notions of the Federalists, and still seething with anger and embarrassment from his recall as minister to France, Monroe decided to justify his actions in a written assault on Washington's administration and its foreign policy. After months of labor, in 1797 Monroe published *A View of the Conduct of the Executive, in the Foreign Affairs of the United States, Connected with the Mission to the French Republic, During the Years 1794, 5, & 6 . . .*, a work provocative not only for its criticisms but also for the inclusion of sensitive communications that flaunted conventions of confidentiality.[58] Both Jefferson and Madison, who believed the production beneficial to Republicans in their struggle against the Federalists, provided encouragement and support, most tangibly when Jefferson supplied financing to print the pamphlet, which scarcely warranted that designation at more than four hundred pages of introduction and documents. Extreme cold that froze shipping channels slowed distribution, and the collaborators lamented how delay reduced its influence on vital state legislative sessions.[59]

The impact of Monroe's *View* on the relative strength of the contending parties may be debated, but Washington, then in retirement at Mount Vernon, took notice. While waiting, in January 1798, for a copy, Washington wrote to a friend that "Mr. Monroe, I am told, appears in a voluminous work!" "What," he then asked, "is said of it?" He addressed the same inquiry to others.[60] The replies undoubtedly pleased Washington: "Monroe's publication . . . is considered by every one whom I have heard speak of it, as his own condemnation," reported Timothy Pickering. "Mr[.] Munroe's book is a wicked representation of facts; his conduct is detested by all *good* men," surmised Oliver Wolcott Jr. "Munroe's memoir has been little read and has made no converts to his party," observed James McHenry. "He has I think sunk in public opinion."[61]

Finally receiving a copy, Washington recorded his thoughts in marginal notes, which, in the words of his modern editors, "comprise the most extended, unremitting, and pointed use of taunts and jibes, sarcasm, and scathing criticism in all of his writings." To Monroe's observation that he had opposed "measures of the administration, particularly . . . the mission of Mr. Morris to France, and of Mr. Jay to London," Washington retorted: "Unpardonable, to app[oin]t these men to Office, altho' of acknowledged first rate abilities—when they were of different political Sentiments from Mr[.] Monroe—whose judgm[en]t one w[oul]d presume must be infallible."[62] Washington never publicized his cutting comments, preferring "the observations of others," which he wanted "to hear with the most unreserved frankness."[63] Monroe evidently pondered a private explanation to Washington. The tone and blasts that he weighed—for instance, "the labours of y[ou]r more early life contributed to promote the liberties of y[ou]r country; but those of y[ou]r latter days to enthral[l] & enslave it"—indicate why Monroe retained that letter as a heavily emended draft.[64]

Washington's animosity toward Monroe surfaced again during the final hours of his life. Taking cold after being outside for much of an inclement day, Washington rested in the evening by reading newspapers and commenting on various items. After his wife retired, he continued perusing the newspapers with his secretary, Tobias Lear, who read a report of Madison's nomination speech for Monroe as governor of Virginia. The account, Lear recalled in his diary, caused the sick man to appear "much affected," and he "spoke with some degree of asperity on the subject." Lear tried "to moderate" Washington's anger, as he "always did on such occasions."[65] Becoming seriously ill, and dying the next day, December 14, 1799, it is almost certain that Washington's final statement on public affairs was to curse James Monroe!

In the wave of encomiums that washed over Washington's memory after his death, nothing was heard from Monroe. His silence, suggestive of his intense hostility toward the deceased, is particularly striking given the tributes for Washington penned by Jefferson and spoken by Madison.[66] Late in his life, Monroe wrote that he had intended to restore friendly relations with Washington after being elected governor of Virginia had redeemed his public character. He learned of Washington's death, which surprised and disturbed him, while riding to Richmond to begin his term, and this plan was ruined.[67] The absence of any sorrowful or acclamatory sentiments in late 1799 or early 1800, however, mark Monroe's claim of a desire for a reconciliation as probably disingenuous.

Monroe remained a stalwart within the Republican Party during Jefferson's presidential administration, and like Jefferson, he gained an appreciation for the use of executive power beyond a strict construction of the Constitution. As a diplomat, Monroe negotiated the Louisiana Purchase, vital to an expansion of the nation's commerce and prestige. He also negotiated a commercial treaty with Great Britain that drew denunciations from Jefferson and Madison, then secretary of state. Monroe resented this treatment, and it contributed to his willingness to stand against Madison for the presidential nomination in 1808. Iciness between the two men did not thaw until President Madison reached out through Jefferson to see whether Monroe would accept a cabinet portfolio.[68] Monroe's ambition and old ties overcame his grievances, and he joined Madison's cabinet as secretary of state in March 1811, just in time for the anxieties and indignities of the War of 1812. Chief among these moments were the surrender of Detroit without a fight in August 1812—"this most mortifying & humiliating event," Monroe wrote to Senator Henry Clay—and the British burning of the White House in September 1814.[69] Monroe displayed resolve during both disasters—seeking command of the western army after the first, and working heroically to coordinate the defense and eventual evacuation of the capital during the second. From these experiences he learned the insufficiency of a national government dependent on state governments for money, troops, and supplies.

"History records no example, of so glorious a victory, obtained, with so little bloodshed, on the part of the victorious," Monroe replied to Andrew Jackson on hearing news of the general's rout of the British at New Orleans in January 1815.[70] Rejuvenated by this success, Monroe began his presidency in March 1817 with an apparent determination to follow the example of Washington, who had made the most of earlier opportunities to conciliate disaffected elements.[71] The Federalists—an opposition element akin to Tories during the Revolution and the Anti-Federalists during the ratification period—had collapsed, and an opportunity for national harmony seemed at hand. Monroe's tours of the states mimicked Washington's and sought the same goal of greater unity. In foreign policy, Washington's neutrality proclamation of April 1793 announced the autonomy of the United States in world affairs. Monroe underscored the same point when his annual message of December 1823 declared the primacy of the United States in the western hemisphere, an enduring policy now known as the Monroe Doctrine. Both Monroe and Washington, however, ran afoul of policy disagreements, personal rifts, and newspaper perfidy. In particular for Monroe, the debate over slavery that resulted in the Missouri Compromise assumed a life beyond his control.[72] In the end, Monroe, like Washington, departed the presidency with more dejection than elation. No wonder he thought more of Washington in 1825 than he did in 1800.[73]

Monroe certainly aroused emotions among his contemporaries. John Armstrong Jr., a fellow Revolutionary War veteran who had served with him in important government positions, such as President Madison's cabinet during the War of 1812, developed an inveterate enmity for Monroe.[74] A "slowness of comprehension, and want of penetration in Col. Monroe, have been conspicuous throughout his political life," spat Armstrong in a pamphlet denouncing his target's attempt to secure nomination for the presidency. After asserting that Monroe invariably botched his diplomatic assignments, Armstrong concluded that the potential nominee "has no title to rank with the first characters of America. But thus ordinarily gifted, Col. Monroe has furnished unequivocal evidence that his lust for power is insatiable."[75] Even after Monroe's death, Armstrong hurled sarcasm. A favorite strategy was upholding Washington at Monroe's expense, as in a condemnation of the latter's "repeated efforts" while minister to France "to divert Washington from that system of *neutrality,* which he had so wisely adopted—and by a strict adherence to which he had been able like a second Moses, to lead his people safely through the Red Sea of crime and misery, connected with the French Revolution."[76] Aaron Burr, once a military and political friend, later rivaled Armstrong's animosity. Thinking over Monroe's nomination for president in a private letter, Burr railed that Monroe "is one of the Most improper & incompetent that could have been selected—Naturally dull & stupid—extremely illiterate—indecisive to a degree that would be incredible to one who did not know him—pusillanimous & of course hypocritical—has no opinion on any subject [and] will be always under the Govt. of the worst Men—pretends as I am told, to some Knowledge of Military Matters, but never commanded a platoon nor was ever fit to command one."[77]

Many, however, liked Monroe, and he enjoyed stout support from friends and acquaintances. When Monroe found himself in financial straits near the end of his life and sought payment from the federal government for unsettled claims related to his official activities, especially those related to his diplomatic postings, citizens of Albemarle County, Virginia, where Monroe had resided for much of his adulthood, vouched for his merits in a memorial to Congress. The memorialists praised Monroe as a "patriot" who had devoted "himself with unwearied zeal to the service of his country" and selflessly sacrificed "fifty years of his life, and a large portion of his property, to the promotion of her welfare."[78] Kind words from Chief Justice John Marshall, a friend from youth who remained cordial despite political differences, surely pleased Monroe. "While I take the liberty to express my personal regrets that your retirement approaches so nearly," wrote Marshall near the close of Monroe's second presidential term, "I may be permitted to congratulate you on the auspicious circumstances which have attended your course as chief Magistrate of the United States, and which crown its termination."[79] Another friend, John Quincy Adams, Monroe's secretary of state, who followed him into the presidency, eulogized the departed as a "pure and gallant spirit" of "distinguished ability" who secured a "well-earned fame."[80] In this eulogy, Adams also alluded to Washington frequently, praising him as "the great military leader" who embodied "the cause of American independence."[81] Adams downplayed friction between the two men in a celebration of their virtuous characters, extraordinary services to their country, and mutual desire for national unity and integrity.

Monroe would have approved the views of Adams. His own assessment of Washington's presidency, penned a few years before his death, on July 4, 1831, embraced the same almost reverential tone. After eight years in office, despite "the novelty of the station, the divisions among ourselves, and the convulsed state of the world at that important epoch," Washington "had the peculiar felicity to enjoy to the end of his services and of his life the undiminished confidence of his country." Unlike other Revolutionary patriots whom Monroe believed harbored monarchical tendencies, Washington's "devotion to the rights and liberties of his country and incorruptible integrity had been too fully proved by his long, very eminent and very faithful services to admit any doubt on that point." Striving for pithiness, Monroe concluded that "no person was ever called to a trust of greater delicacy and difficulty than was our first Chief Magistrate. His greater dread was that of disunion, but it proceeded solely from a disinterested regard for the public welfare."[82] These thoughts echoed ideas that Monroe had expressed at a dinner given in his honor at Richmond in June 1826. "He remarked," wrote a reporter, "that the American People were making a grand Experiment for the benefit of the World at large; that he fervently trusted this experiment for the support of free Institutions would be prosecuted with the greatest enthusiasm and with every advantage of which it was susceptible; and that our fellow-citizens would unite and stand together as much as possible for the support of our rights and our liberties."[83]

The same idea animated an August 1828 letter written to John C. Calhoun, who had served as secretary of war in Monroe's cabinet. "As to the Union," Monroe warned upon learning of southern disagreement with tariffs meant to promote manufactures, "all movements which menace, or even suggest the least danger to it, cannot fail to have an ill effect. . . . Hostility and Wars would be inevitable, whereby our free system of Government would be overwhelmed. . . . It is my candid opinion if there is any portion of the Union which ought to feel peculiar solicitude for its preservation, it is those States, as it likewise is, that they should promote, the connection and dependance of the several parts on each other, by intercourse, commerce, & every *practicable* means tending to obliterate local distinctions, diffuse a common feeling, and bind the Union by the strongest ties of interest & affection, more closely together."[84] At bottom, both Washington and Monroe believed in the potential unity and strength of a national government based on the sovereign people acting through duly elected leaders.

Notes

1. James Monroe, "Views of the President of the United States on the Subject of Internal Improvements," in James D. Richardson, comp., *A Compilation of the Messages and Papers of the Presidents, 1789–1902,* 10 vols., rev. and enl. (Washington, D.C., 1903), 2:181.

2. Daniel C. Gilman, *James Monroe: In His Relations to the Public Service during Half a Century, 1776 to 1826* (1883; repr., Boston, 1895), 2, 4.

3. See George Morgan, *The Life of James Monroe* (Boston, 1921); Arthur Styron, *The Last of the Cocked Hats: James Monroe and the Virginia Dynasty* (Norman, Okla., 1945); and W. P. Cresson, *James Monroe* (Chapel Hill, N.C., 1946).

4. Henry Adams, *History of the United States of America during the Administrations of Thomas Jefferson* (1889–91; repr., New York, 1986), esp. 221, 508, 630–31, 886–87, 1015; Henry Adams, *History of the United States of America during the Administrations of James Madison* (1889–91; repr., New York, 1986), esp. 1017, 1266. For analyses of Monroe in the same vein as that of Adams, see George Dangerfield, *The Era of Good Feelings* (New York, 1952); and Dangerfield, *Chancellor Robert R. Livingston of New York, 1746–1813* (New York, 1960).

5. Harry Ammon, *James Monroe: The Quest for National Identity* (New York, 1971). For a distillation of Ammon's thinking on Monroe, see his "Executive Leadership in the Monroe Administration," in *America, The Middle Period: Essays in Honor of Bernard Mayo,* ed. John B. Boles (Charlottesville, Va., 1973), 111–31.

6. Harlow Giles Unger, *The Last Founding Father: James Monroe and a Nation's Call to Greatness* (Philadelphia, 2009), 257–58. For a more measured recent biography, see Gary Hart, *James Monroe* (New York, 2005). An accessible and useful assessment of Monroe as president is Noble E. Cunningham, *The Presidency of James Monroe* (Lawrence, Kan., 1996), but also see the pertinent portions of Daniel Walker Howe, *What Hath God Wrought: The Transformation of America, 1815–1848* (New York, 2007).

7. Ammon, *James Monroe,* 2–7.

8. *The Autobiography of James Monroe,* ed. Stuart Gerry Brown (Syracuse, N.Y., 1959),

22–26; Ammon, *James Monroe,* 8–14. One account inaccurately reported Monroe as "slightly wounded" at Trenton (see *Memoir of Lieut. Col. Tench Tilghman,* ed. S. A. Harrison [1876; repr., New York, 1971], 148–49).

9. GW to William Shippen Jr., 3 May 1777, *PGW: Rev. Ser.,* 9:340.

10. James Monroe to Lt. Col. John Thornton, 3 July 1777, in *The Papers of James Monroe,* ed. Daniel Preston et al., 3 vols. to date (Westport, Conn., 2003–), 2:4.

11. Joseph Jones to GW, 11 August 1777, *PGW: Rev. Ser.,* 10:586.

12. Monroe to Lt. Col. John Thornton, 25 August 1777, *Papers of James Monroe,* 2:5–6.

13. Ibid., 2:6–7.

14. Monroe to Peter Duponceau, 11 April and 7 May 1778, *Papers of James Monroe,* 2:8–9; Monroe to Theodosia Prevost, 8 November 1778, ibid., 2:11–12; Monroe to Brig. Gen. William Woodford, September 1779, ibid., 2:14–15.

15. Monroe to GW, 28 June 1778, *PGW: Rev. Ser.,* 15:580; Maj. Gen. Stirling to GW, 9 and 21 October 1778, ibid., 17:324, 515.

16. General Orders, 12 January 1779, ibid., 18:621.

17. Monroe to Charles Lee, 13 June 1779, *Papers of James Monroe,* 2:14.

18. GW to Archibald Cary, ca. 22 May 1779, *PGW: Rev. Ser.,* 20:574–75. See also Monroe to Brig. Gen. William Woodford, 26 May 1779, *Papers of James Monroe,* 2:13.

19. Monroe to Brig. Gen. William Woodford, September 1779, ibid., 2:14–15.

20. Joseph Jones to Monroe, 1 March 1780, ibid., 2:16–17.

21. Thomas Jefferson to Monroe, 10 and 16 June 1780, *PTJ,* 3:431–32, 451–52; Monroe to Jefferson, 26 June 1780, ibid., 3:464–67. See also *Papers of James Monroe,* 2:22.

22. Charles Lee to Monroe, 18 July 1780, *Papers of James Monroe,* 2:25–26.

23. Richard Kidder Meade to Monroe, 3 July 1780, ibid., 2:23–25.

24. Monroe to Jefferson, 9 September 1780, *PTJ,* 3:621–23; Jefferson to Monroe, 15 May 1781, ibid., 5:655; Monroe to Jefferson, 18 June 1781, ibid., 6:95–96; Monroe to Jefferson, 1 October 1781, ibid., 6:124–25; Jefferson to Monroe, 5 October 1781, ibid., 6:126–28; Jefferson to Benjamin Franklin, John Adams, and John Jay, 5 October 1781, ibid., 6:126. See also Monroe to Lafayette, 27 September 1781, *Papers of James Monroe,* 2:30.

25. Monroe to Jefferson, 6 May 1782, *PTJ,* 6:178–79; Monroe to Jefferson, 11 May 1782, ibid., 6:183; Jefferson to Monroe, 20 May 1782, ibid., 6:184–87; Monroe to Jefferson, 28 June 1782, ibid., 6:192–93.

26. Monroe to GW, 15 August 1782, *Papers of James Monroe,* 2:44. See also Monroe to Maj. Gen. Stirling, 10 September 1782, ibid., 2:45–46.

27. Monroe to Jefferson, 8 February 1783, *PTJ,* 6:233; Monroe to John Francis Mercer, 14 March and 16 May 1783, *Papers of James Monroe,* 2:55–58.

28. "George Washington's Resignation as Commander-in-Chief" (editorial essay), *PTJ,* 6:402–14; Freeman, 5:473–77.

29. John Marshall to Monroe, 3 January 1784, in *The Papers of John Marshall,* ed. Herbert A. Johnson et al., 12 vols. (Chapel Hill, N.C., 1974–2006), 1:113–14.

30. *Autobiography of James Monroe,* 34.

31. Jefferson to James Madison, 8 May 1784, *PTJ,* 7:234.

32. For partly encoded letters, see, e.g., Monroe to Jefferson, 25 May, 1 June, and 1 November 1784, ibid., 7:290–92, 299–300, and 459–62. See also Monroe to Madison, 7 No-

vember 1784, in *The Papers of James Madison: Congressional Series,* ed. William T. Hutchinson and Robert A. Rutland et al., 17 vols. (Chicago and Charlottesville, Va., 1962–91), 8:125–27.

33. Richard Henry Lee to GW, 20 November 1784, *PGW: Conf. Ser.,* 2:142–43; William Grayson to GW, ca. 4–8 May 1785, ibid., 2:535–38; Lee to GW, 11 October 1785, ibid., 3:303–4; Henry Hill Jr. to GW, 1 October 1786, ibid., 4:280–81.

34. Monroe to GW, 20 August 1786, ibid., 4:223–25.

35. GW, 23–25 October 1786, *PGW: Diaries,* 5:56–57. Monroe's marriage was long and happy. For praise of his wife, see *Autobiography of James Monroe,* 49.

36. *The Documentary History of the Ratification of the Constitution,* ed. John P. Kaminski et al., 23 vols. to date (Madison, Wis., 1976–), 9:611–12, 1103–15, 1139–42, 10:1229–35, 1371–73, 1469, 1518–19.

37. Monroe to Jefferson, 12 July 1788, *PTJ,* 13:351–53.

38. For a transcription of this rare pamphlet, with annotation, see *Documentary History of the Ratification of the Constitution,* 9:844–77.

39. Monroe to GW, 15 February 1789, *PGW: Pres. Ser.,* 1:310–11; GW to Monroe, 23 February 1789, ibid., 1:337.

40. *Autobiography of James Monroe,* 50.

41. For Monroe's mature thoughts on how the French Revolution "excited in a high degree party feeling," see *Autobiography of James Monroe,* 54.

42. Edmund Randolph to GW, 10 November 1793, *PGW: Pres. Ser.,* 14:356–57.

43. Ammon, *James Monroe,* 89–90.

44. Monroe to GW, 8 and 11 April 1794, *PGW: Pres. Ser.,* 15:548, 568–71; GW to Monroe, 9 April 1794, ibid., 15:551–52. See also Edmund Randolph to GW, 9 April 1794, ibid., 15:552–54.

45. See Monroe to Jefferson, 4 May 1794, *PTJ,* 28:69–71.

46. *Autobiography of James Monroe,* 57–58; Monroe to Madison, 26 May 1794, *Papers of James Madison: Congressional Series,* 15:338–39; Ammon, *James Monroe,* 112–15.

47. Monroe to GW, 1 June 1794, James Monroe Papers, Manuscripts Division, Library of Congress.

48. For Monroe's lengthy and somewhat disingenuous subsequent account of this event, see *Autobiography of James Monroe,* 59–66, 88.

49. GW to John Jay, 18 December 1794, John Jay Papers, Columbia University Rare Book and Manuscript Library, New York.

50. *Autobiography of James Monroe,* 83–85, 91–97.

51. Monroe to Madison, 13 June and ca. 23 July 1795, *Papers of James Madison: Congressional Series,* 16:16–19, 37–40.

52. Monroe to Madison, 8 September 1795, ibid., 16:77–85. See also *Autobiography of James Monroe,* 103–7.

53. Monroe to Madison, 23 and 24 October 1795, *Papers of James Madison: Congressional Series,* 16:105–7, 109–12.

54. For Monroe's unflagging belief in the propriety of his course as minister to France under Washington's administration, see *Autobiography of James Monroe,* 89, 91, 124–42.

55. For a detailed analysis of Monroe's course as minister to France in the context of the Washington administration, see Stanley Elkins and Eric McKitrick, *The Age of Federal-*

ism (New York, 1993), 497–513. For assessments largely critical of Monroe, see Alexander DeConde, *Entangling Alliance: Politics and Diplomacy under George Washington* (Durham, N.C., 1958), 347–87; Louis Martin Sears, *George Washington and the French Revolution* (Detroit, Mich., 1960), 211–13, 230–31, 260–68; Ammon, *James Monroe,* 116–56; and Richard Norton Smith, *Patriarch: George Washington and the New American Nation* (Boston, 1993), 205–7, 270–81.

56. Monroe to Madison, 29 October, 8 November, 20 December 1795, 7 June, 5 July, 1 August, 1 and 29 September, and 15 November 1796, *Papers of James Madison: Congressional Series,* 16:114–17, 123–25, 168–71, 368–70, 374–80, 383–90, 392–93, 403–5, 412–14.

57. Treatments of the "Reynolds Affair" are standard in the pertinent secondary literature. For important presentations of the documentary record, see *PAH,* 10:376–79, 13:115–16, 291, 330, 339, 344, 21:121–48, 159–62, 176–87, 192–93, 200–202, 204–12, 316–20, 346; and *Political Correspondence and Public Papers of Aaron Burr,* ed. Mary-Jo Kline et al., 2 vols. (Princeton, N.J., 1983), 1:306–14.

58. On this point, Washington wrote to John Nicholas on 8 March 1798: "As to the propriety of exposing to public view his private Instructions, and correspondence with his own Government, nothing need be said; for I should suppose that the measure must be reprobated by the well informed and intelligent of *all Nations;* and not less so by his abettors in this Country; if they were not blinded by Party views, and determined at all hazards to catch at any thing, that, in their opinion, will promote them" (*PGW: Ret. Ser.,* 2:128–29).

59. Jefferson to John Barnes, 8 October 1797, *PTJ,* 29:544–45; Monroe to Jefferson, [22] October 1797, ibid., 29:562–63; Jefferson to Monroe, 25 October [1797], ibid., 29:564–65; Monroe to Jefferson, [November 1797], ibid., 29:576; Jefferson to Monroe, 27 December 1797, ibid., 29:593–95; Jefferson to Madison, 3 January 1798, ibid., 30:9–12; Jefferson to Madison, 8 February 1798, ibid., 30:87–89; Madison to Jefferson, 21 January 1798, ibid., 30:40–41; Monroe to Jefferson, 27 January 1798, ibid., 30:57–58; Jefferson to Monroe, 8 February 1798, ibid., 30:89–90; Monroe to Madison, 24 September 1797, *Papers of James Madison: Congressional Series,* 17:48–49; Ammon, *James Monroe,* 165–69; Richard R. Beeman, *The Old Dominion and the New Nation, 1788–1801* (Lexington, Ky., 1972), 173–74. For a convincing argument that Monroe actively helped to establish the Republican Party, see Noble E. Cunningham, *The Jeffersonian Republicans: The Formation of Party Organization, 1789–1801* (Chapel Hill, N.C., 1957).

60. GW to Timothy Pickering, 12 January 1798, *PGW: Ret. Ser.,* 2:20–21; GW to Oliver Wolcott Jr., 22 January 1798, ibid., 2:39; GW to James McHenry, 28 January 1798, ibid., 2:54–55.

61. Pickering to GW, 20 January 1798, *PGW: Ret. Ser.,* 2:31–32; Wolcott to GW, 30 January 1798, ibid., 2:61–62; McHenry to GW, 1 February 1798, ibid., 2:66.

62. GW to Pickering, 6 February 1798, *PGW: Ret. Ser.,* 2:76–77; "Comments on Monroe's *A View of the Conduct of the Executive of the United States,*" ca. March 1798, ibid., 2:169–217.

63. GW to Alexander White, 1 March 1798, *PGW: Ret. Ser.,* 2:113–14.

64. Monroe to GW, "James Monroe: Notes on Government," undated but likely 1798, Gratz Collection, Historical Society of Pennsylvania, Philadelphia. For Monroe's later thoughts on publishing his *View,* see *Autobiography of James Monroe,* 145–47.

65. Tobias Lear's "Diary Account," [14 December 1799], *PGW: Ret. Ser.*, 4:547–52.

66. For tributes to Washington by Jefferson and Madison, see Jefferson to Uzal Ogden, 12 February 1800, *PTJ*, 31:369; Jefferson to Samuel Miller, 25 February 1800, ibid., 31:394; Jefferson to Auguste Belin, 27 February 1800, ibid., 31:396; and Jefferson to Auguste Belin, 6 March 1800, ibid., 31:417. For Madison's remarks, see *Papers of James Madison: Congressional Series*, 17:295.

67. *Autobiography of James Monroe*, 150.

68. See "Jefferson's Conversation with James Monroe" (editorial essay), in *Papers of Thomas Jefferson: Retirement Series*, 2:42–46.

69. Monroe to Henry Clay, 28 August 1812, in *The Papers of Henry Clay*, ed. James F. Hopkins et al., 11 vols. (Lexington, Ky., 1959–92), 1:722–23.

70. Monroe to Andrew Jackson, 5 February 1815, in *The Papers of Andrew Jackson*, ed. Sam B. Smith, Harold D. Moser, and Daniel Feller et al., 6 vols. to date (Knoxville, Tenn., 1980–), 3:271–72.

71. Thanks to David Mattern, senior associate editor of the Papers of James Madison, University of Virginia, for suggesting that Monroe modeled his presidency on Washington's.

72. For an account that credits Monroe with strong leadership throughout this crisis over slavery extension, which I find unpersuasive, see Robert Pierce Forbes, *The Missouri Compromise and Its Aftermath: Slavery and the Meaning of America* (Chapel Hill, N.C., 2007).

73. Monroe's autobiography, written after his presidency, is replete with fond Washington recollections. For instance, upon remembering his return to Trenton in fall 1784 for a session of the Confederation Congress, Monroe considered it "natural" that he felt "with great sensibility" the importance "of the action which had occurred there on the 26th of December 1776, both in relation to his country and himself, since it formed a very interesting epoch in our revolutionary struggle, being the first step to the new and imposing attitude which was assumed immediately afterwards by our Commander-in-chief towards the enemy, and which he sustained in every subsequent stage of the contest" (*Autobiography of James Monroe*, 41).

74. See C. Edward Skeen, "Monroe and Armstrong: A Study in Political Rivalry," *New-York Historical Society Quarterly* 57 (April 1973): 121–47; and Skeen, *John Armstrong, Jr., 1758–1843: A Biography* (Syracuse, N.Y., 1981).

75. *Exposition of Motives for Opposing the Nomination of Mr[.] Monroe for the Office of President of the United States* (Washington, D.C., 1816), 11. For Charles Pinckney's vigorous response to Armstrong's attack, see *Observations to Shew the Propriety of the Nomination of Colonel James Monroe, to the Presidency of the United States by the Caucus at Washington . . .* (Charleston, S.C., 1816).

76. *Notice of Mr. Adams' Eulogium on the Life and Character of James Monroe* (Washington, D.C., 1832), 23.

77. Aaron Burr to Joseph Alston, 15 November 1815, *Papers of Aaron Burr*, 2:1165–66.

78. "Memorial of the Citizens of Albemarle County, in Virginia . . . ," [ca. January 1829], 20th Cong., 2d sess., H. Doc. 94. Monroe's attempts to secure payment for claims on the federal government troubled his final years. For an unsympathetic analysis, see Lucius

Wilmerding Jr., *James Monroe: Public Claimant* (New Brunswick, N.J., 1960). Monroe systematically presented his own case in *The Memoir of James Monroe, Esq., Relating to His Unsettled Claims upon the People and Government of the United States* (Charlottesville, Va., 1828), but also see "Letter from James Monroe, Late President of the United States, Upon the subject of his claim upon the General Government," 20 November 1830, 21st Cong., 2d sess., H. Doc. 6. "I have always cherished the highest respect for his memory," wrote Monroe of Washington in his *Memoir,* "and admired his great virtues and talents" (6).

79. Marshall to Monroe, 13 December 1824, *Papers of John Marshall,* 10:134–35; see also Marshall to Monroe, 7 March 1825, and Monroe to Marshall, 10 March 1825, ibid., 10:151, 153.

80. John Quincy Adams, *The Lives of James Madison and James Monroe, Fourth and Fifth Presidents of the United States* (Buffalo, N.Y., 1851), 252, 269.

81. Adams, *Lives of Madison and Monroe,* 213–14.

82. *Autobiography of James Monroe,* 51–52. Amid his praise, however, Monroe does blame Washington for promoting party divisions by overwhelmingly selecting Federalists for positions of trust (see ibid., 53–54).

83. *Richmond Enquirer,* 27 June 1826.

84. Monroe to John C. Calhoun, 4 August 1828, in *The Papers of John C. Calhoun,* ed. Robert L. Meriwether, W. Edwin Hemphill, and Clyde N. Wilson et al., 28 vols. (Columbia, S.C., 1959–2003), 10:408–10.

Guns of the Revolution

Henry Knox, George Washington, and the War of American Independence

MARK THOMPSON

On July 6, 1775, Washington for the first time looked upon the army that Congress had recently adopted and placed under his command. What he saw this day must have caused him to pause at the enormity of the task before him. The new Continental Army, the primary means by which he was supposed to counter superior British regulars, was a motley collection of inexperienced and unprepared citizens turned soldiers. The troops were undisciplined and ill-trained, arms and supplies were insufficient, and defenses were inadequate. Washington confessed that these problems made his life "one continued round of a[nnoyance] & f[at]igue."[1]

Despite his dismay, Washington did find skilled and reliable individuals. Among the men who caught his eye that first day was Henry Knox, a young local volunteer who had been directing construction of the fortifications south of Boston. His work on the Roxbury defenses in particular drew the Continental commander's attention. With a sense of excitement and pride, Knox explained to his wife, "Yesterday as I was going to Cambridge I met the Generals [Washington and Charles Lee] who beg[ge]d me to return to [R]oxbury again which I did. When they viewed the works they express[e]d the greatest pleasure and surprize at their situation and apparent utility to say nothing of the plan which did not escape their praise."[2] This fortuitous meeting began Knox's rapid ascent through the ranks. Promoted to colonel within a few months, he earned a place in Washington's inner circle, or "family," and eventually came to lead the Continental artillery, a role he performed until war's end. His personal and professional relationship with Washington continued in the postwar years. The two men maintained a regular correspondence, and

Knox served as secretary of the War Department during the Confederation period and Washington's first administration.

In some ways, Washington's support for Knox in 1775 might have seemed a risky move, if not a foolish one. After all, the enthusiastic Bostonian was not quite twenty-five years of age when the two first met. Furthermore, before the war, he had been a modest book peddler by trade and, despite membership in the local peacetime militia, had not a single day of combat experience to his credit. The closest he had come to battle was in street fights among Bostonians and in a hunting accident, during which an exploding gun blew off two fingers from his left hand. Also worth noting, the position of artillery commander promised to be a very demanding one, especially considering that the American colonies lacked a gunnery tradition and that the Continental establishment had almost no artillery. With these points in mind, what thoughtful person would have placed Knox on a "short list" of candidates, or even a long one? As unlikely a selection as the Bostonian might have been, Washington's faith in him proved to be well founded. Despite his youth, Knox proved to be not only one of Washington's key military subordinates, but also a loyal lieutenant, close confidant, and friend. Theirs was a relationship born in war, forged by eight years of service together, and lasting until Washington's death nearly a quarter of a century later.

The Continental commander proved himself to be a shrewd judge of men, and if he saw a spark of talent in the young Bostonian on that July day of 1775, he had ample opportunity to see in the ensuing weeks if that hunch would hold true. The pressures of war demanded that he find soldiers of ability, but it also created extraordinary opportunities for individuals to be tested and to display those abilities. Throughout the summer and early fall of 1775, Knox distinguished himself by working on the fortifications of the Continental Army that sought to encircle the British troops in Boston. When Congress sent a committee of conference to the Cambridge camp in October, Washington complained to its members about the desperate need for capable engineers and secured their recommendation to Congress that Knox be appointed an assistant engineer with the rank of lieutenant colonel.[3]

Shortly thereafter, in November 1775, Washington gave the young volunteer his most significant challenge to date. The shortage of artillery posed a serious obstacle for patriot forces trying to conduct a siege of Boston. To address that deficiency, Washington sent Knox to find and retrieve whatever field and garrison guns were available in New York, including any available from recently captured Fort Ticonderoga. During the ensuing nine weeks, Knox's team transported nearly 60 tons of artillery over a distance of three hundred miles through the New York backcountry, along waterways and gullied roads, across ice and snow, and despite innumerable difficulties along the way. It was an extraordinary feat that had significant consequences. The expedition demonstrated the young artillerist's "strength of body and fortitude of mind."[4] If the assignment was Washington's way of testing Knox, as one historian speculates, then the young volunteer surely passed with flying colors.[5] However, the experience might have served another valuable purpose that aided the fortunes of Washington's Continental Army. The transport of the guns likely contributed to Knox's growing conviction—an important one for the fortunes of the Continental Army—that artillery could be made mobile, even in the frozen wilderness and difficult terrain of North America. In addition, and perhaps most importantly for the current campaign, this "Cohorn Caravan" allowed Washington in March 1776 to evict the British soldiers from Boston.

Upon Knox's return to Cambridge, Washington fed Knox additional challenges. After the arrival of Fort Ticonderoga's guns, patriot forces finally had the firepower to level a blow against the British army in Boston. The Continental commander, therefore, ordered troops, under the cover of darkness, to occupy and place batteries atop Dorchester Heights, the unoccupied high ground to the south of Boston that offered a commanding view of the city and the enemy. Knox, along with Israel Putnam and Richard Gridley, was given the task of laying out rebel positions there, a task executed with extraordinary success despite the difficult conditions.[6] Compromised by Washington's move, the British forces evacuated Boston. With that immediate threat removed, Knox tackled other assignments. In April, he inspected the coastal defenses of New London, Connecticut, and Newport, Rhode Island, and proposed improvements.[7] At the same time, Washington gave him the complex logistical assignment of moving the artillery, ammunition, and ordnance stores to New York for the upcoming campaign.[8] Once there, he had to help plan and prepare defensive fortifications to counter the Redcoats' expected attack. And, after the enemy arrived and the commander of the British forces offered a flag of truce, Knox and Adjutant General Joseph Reed were sent to meet his representative.[9] When Washington and Knox had first met, in early July 1775, the latter was only three months removed from his life as a book merchant and part-time militiamen. During the following year, he performed an impressive series of military tasks and shouldered burdens on a scale well beyond anything he, or his peers, for that matter, had previously attempted. That must have been heady stuff for a young man who was still a few weeks away from his twenty-sixth birthday.

Throughout the war, Washington demonstrated his support for young officers, and certainly for Knox. Three weeks after he had recommended the Boston volunteer be made an assistant engineer, he wrote John Hancock, president of the Continental Congress, urging him to commission Knox a colonel in the Continental establishment, with command of its lone artillery regiment. Then, the following year, he pressed Congress to expand the Continental artillery to four regiments, as Knox had recommended, and to promote Knox to brigadier general, thereby giving him command of all of them. In 1781, Washington requested that his artillery chief be promoted to major general, which, as in the other cases, Congress did, this time making Knox the youngest American officer to hold that rank.

Washington showed his loyalty in other ways, even standing by Knox in controversy. When, in 1777, a French officer, Philippe du Coudray, tried to lay claim to the command of Continental artillery, as promised to him by a U.S. agent, Washington intervened. Always reluctant to tread upon Congress's authority, he nevertheless warned that body against such an action, claiming it would have "the most injurious consequences." Knox, he explained, "who has deservedly acquired the character of One of the most valuable Officers in the service, and who combating almost innumerable difficulties in the department he fills, has placed the Artillery upon a footing, that does him the greatest Honor." The appointment of the Frenchman would cause the loss of the American, and "there would be too much reason to apprehend a train of ills, and such as might convulse and unhinge this Important Department."[10]

The support and loyalty shown by Washington to Knox was reciprocated. The two men ultimately knew each other for more than two dozen years, and virtually none of their correspondence betrays any ill will by one toward the other. They demonstrated a professional respect, and even a personal fondness, for each other. The basis for that connection is not made clear by their correspondence, but they shared common experiences and interests that might have drawn them together. While mere boys, both men had lost their fathers, with Washington's dying and Knox's abandoning the family for the West Indies, never to return. Washington found guidance and a role model in his older brother, Lawrence, while Knox had to leave school at the age of nine to serve as an apprentice and help support his mother and younger brother. It is conceivable that, for Knox, Continental service provided him the paternal figure he had lacked through most of his youth. Both of these fatherless boys grew to be ambitious young men who ardently sought success and upward mobility. And both were drawn to things military, read widely on the art of warfare, and desired martial careers in an age when such opportunities were few and far between. Therefore, in addition to mutual respect, they had much in common. Knox became a frequent guest at Washington's dinner table, and his wife, Lucy, a regular companion of Martha Washington when in camp. The personal connection they developed is demonstrated by the fact that Henry, along with his wife Lucy, made the commander in chief of the Continental forces the godfather of one of their children and the namesake of another.[11]

That Washington had created a coterie of young officers, and that Knox had joined it, was a fact not lost on others, especially those who did not have Washington's ear or were critical of him. Thomas Mifflin, the general's former aide-de-camp and a member of the Board of War, complained in 1777 of the army's failures under Washington, and of the "deep rooted System of Favoritism" that had emerged in it.[12] That charge was echoed by disgruntled officers within the Continental ranks. Thomas Conway, the Frenchman and Continental brigadier general who Washington feared was part of a cabal to unseat him, resented the preferential treatment that he felt was shown at headquarters, and charged that the Revolutionary cause was threatened by a "weak General and bad Councellors."[13] Henry Laurens acknowledged the rumors that the commander in chief was under the "pernicious influence of two General Officers," Nathanael Greene and Henry Knox, but denied that Washington blindly followed them.[14] Whether friend or foe, few would have refuted that Knox had assumed a prominent place in Washington's military family.

If Washington and Knox had mutual respect and fondness for each other, the key to the wartime relationship that they developed is that it, quite simply, worked. Both were military conservatives who, prior to the Revolutionary War's first shots at Lexington and Concord, had read extensively the literature on warfare, studied British practices, and drew inspiration from what European writers and soldiers wrote about armies and battle. Both men believed that to win the war, American rebels needed, in part, an army that reflected the sort of professionalism achieved by the Europeans, as well as strategies grounded in the practices of European armies. Their guide to success in the conflict was what had worked in the past—the European past. In their pursuit of military victory, Knox proved to be a valuable subordinate to Washington, especially after the disastrous battles in and around New York during 1776 that left the Continental Army on the verge of dissolution and the Revolution imperiled. The campaigns that followed demonstrate not only Knox's sophisticated understanding of warfare but also his impressive use of artillery to support Washington's broader strategic goals. His success, in part, was his ability to tap into current European practices, and even recent developments, and apply them to the needs of the Continental artillery and Washington's army.[15]

European warfare during this era was shaped by the general intellectual climate. The Age of Reason was a time when the prevailing belief in superstition or the mysterious hand of God was giving way to reasoned inquiry and the quest for knowledge, at least among European intellectuals. These philosophes were inspired by the notion that their world was not shaped simply by forces unknown to all but God. Instead, they insisted, immutable, identifiable, and quantifiable natural laws created and guided a rational universe that operated with machine-like efficiency and predictability. They drew inspiration from the conviction that humans, with their superior minds and analytical skills, could not only uncover the mysteries of the world, but they could also understand that world, and perhaps even become masters of it. Enlightenment thinkers therefore displayed an insatiable desire for education and experimentation, and saw these pursuits as the primary means by which to uplift society and expedite the inexorable process of civilization.

That mode of thinking extended beyond scientific investigation. War and war-making also felt the Enlightenment's effects, and the result was a style of warfare that served the needs of Knox, Washington, and other soldiers of the Revolutionary War. Just as intellectuals reveled in the natural harmony and mechanistic nature of the cosmos, so too did military commanders try to create order and precision in their armies. And just as the philosophes sought to identify rational forces shaping the universe, so too did many military thinkers hope to isolate and codify the rules of war—rules they thought expressed universal truths and would guarantee victory to those generals who mastered and employed them.[16]

Knox, much like Washington and his British counterparts, drew heavily upon the works of seventeenth-century writers and reformers who helped impose a greater degree of regularity, order, and professionalism on warfare in the next century.[17] When the bookish John Adams asked his fellow Bay colonist for a reading list on the art of war, Knox compiled a list of favored authors. Among them was Sébastien Le Presle, sieur de Vauban, who had systematized fortification and siegecraft.[18] However, the soldier and writer whom Knox admired most was Arminius Maurice, the comte de Saxe and marshal general of the French army. Among the European theorists of war, Knox ranked Saxe as the most important, and claimed that he "stalked a God in war."[19] Saxe established himself as a prominent military commander and theorist by the mid-eighteenth century. In *My Reveries Upon the Art of War*, which reflected the rationalism of the age, he bemoaned warfare's lack of precision and order:

> War is a science covered with shadows in whose obscurity we cannot move with an assured step. Routine and prejudice, the natural result of ignorance, are its foundation and support.
>
> All sciences have principles and rules; war has none. The great captains who have written of it give us none. . . . [T]hey have attempted rather to be interesting than instructive, since the mechanics of war is dry and tedious.[20]

He intended for this great tome to fill that void in military knowledge, and it consequently reads like a manual or handbook, highlighting the fundamental rules of war and offering instructions for fielding an army and engaging it in combat. It was Saxe, Knox explained, "who has done more towards reducing war to fix[e]d principles than perhaps any other man of the age."[21] Vauban's and Saxe's works were in crowded company. During the Enlightenment, with its emphasis upon education and instruction, military publications proliferated as theorists sought to identify the elements of war and systematize the organization and deployment of armed forces.[22]

The Enlightenment also inspired political and military leaders to reduce the brutality and bloodshed that had characterized earlier conflicts. If humankind was to be uplifted and civilized by its growing knowledge, people could no longer wage war in such a barbarous and destructive fashion. They became convinced that intellectual, scientific, and technological developments would enable them to ameliorate war's harsher aspects and its more gruesome consequences. Vauban, for instance, emphasized and refined siege warfare because it offered greater rewards at lower costs in blood than did pitched battles between armies in the open field. In his distillation of the rules of war, Saxe showed a similar aversion to the climactic confrontation. "I do not favor pitched battles," he wrote, "especially at the beginning of a war, and I am convinced that a skillful general could make war all his life without being forced into one. Nothing so reduces the enemy to absurdity as this method; nothing advances affairs better. Frequent small engagements will dissipate the enemy until he is forced to hide from you."[23] If wars were inevitably going to be fought, then humans had an obligation to wage them in a relatively bloodless and civilized manner.

Knox shared the Enlightenment's penchant for order, regularity, and rational inquiry.[24] The same principles that promoted Knox's quest for an ordered world also shaped his approach to battle and his view of war along the lines countenanced by Enlightenment thinkers. Like Saxe or Vauban, he invariably contemplated campaign prospects with the reasoning of a mathematician or an engineer. In 1777, for instance, he urged Washington against an attempt to recapture Philadelphia, explaining that it is "an invariable principle in War that it cannot be [in] the interest at the same time of both parties to engage." War, in its most rational form, thereby became an exercise in cost–benefit analysis. From this perspective, he reasoned, the plan to assault Philadelphia was clearly a losing proposition, for the British army enjoyed advantages in strength, skill, and position (battle was said always to favor the defender).[25] On the other hand, Knox later explained to his commander in chief in 1780, New York should be the primary focus of their forces, "because the chances of success will be greater than of a failure and more beneficial, than the latter will probably be distressing."[26] Throughout the war, he sought guidance from maxims that were as fundamental to war as natural laws were to the universe.

The young artillery chief also shared the European predilection for limiting and "civilizing" armed conflict. During the New York campaign of 1776, he lamented to his wife Great Britain's brutish treatment of captured patriot soldiers and its repeated refusal to exchange prisoners: "I dislike the mode of making war like Savages—War has horrors enough which are inseperable from its nature—We ought by every means in our power to endevor to soften its rough visage."[27] For that very reason, he later explained, "civilized nations" imposed laws regulating the behavior of combatants. "And if that law is *refused,* when *demanded,* upon the supposition of its not being *expedient,* the Law is *violated*[.] And by violating one Law of War, every Cruelty will become allowable, and War [will] be carried on not by *Men* but by *Monsters.*"[28]

With his emphasis on minimizing the cost and brutality of war, Knox quite logically revealed little fascination with battle. Napoleon, at the turn of the century, would make the clash of arms the raison d'être of his armies and the principal method of resolving war, but Knox was firmly committed to the eighteenth-century notion that battle was merely one of many means, and perhaps one of the least desirable means, by which to secure military success.[29] If Continental forces could outlast the enemy without being drawn into costly engagements, then so much the better. He further recognized that, even if fighting became necessary, victory on the battlefield was not essential to securing American interests. For example, after Nathanael Greene took command of the Southern Department's ailing and nearly nonexistent army in late 1780, Knox marveled at his friend's skill. While often avoiding battle, and even while losing the unavoidable ones, Greene managed to prevent his opponents' subjugation of the Carolinas by making British battlefield "victories" too costly to enjoy. "Indeed," as Knox phrased it, "it may be said he has conquer[e]d by being defeated."[30] Greene's brilliance lays not so much in his role as a leader of men, but in his ability to recognize the crucial elements that connected military operations to political results, and the most effective ways to secure those results with the various tools at hand. Battle, therefore, was a means and not an end in itself. "He has fought where necessary," Knox explained, in language reminiscent of Saxe, and "he has run when occasion demanded it."[31] With this rational, or "civilized," approach to war, enlightened peoples could make the pursuit of victory consonant with the pursuit of liberty and republican principles.

How then did "civilized" battles in Europe develop during the century leading up to the American Revolution? Henry Guerlac wrote that seventeenth- and eighteenth-century European warfare "often appears to us as nothing but an interminable succession of sieges."[32] If he exaggerated the primacy of the siege, clearly it was a regular feature of the military landscape during this period. With an emphasis on territorial rewards, generals often opted for the relatively profitable, safe, and low-cost siege. Artillery played a key role, as attacking armies slowly and methodically crept toward their targets before hauling forward the ponderous siege guns by which they intended to reduce the enemy position and force its surrender. If not in formal sieges, battling armies also met in open-field engagements. Opposing forces often paraded onto the battlefield and maneuvered for favorable position. If conditions appeared fortuitous, then one or the other of the opposing forces would usually proceed through a series of predictable rituals. The artillery would be laboriously dragged onto the field, carefully positioned, and then fired to weaken the enemy lines. Then the primary burden of deciding the battle shifted to infantry and cavalry.[33]

When Knox, Washington, and others sought to fight a European-style war against Great Britain and its allies, they consequently could draw from a foreign military heritage that emphasized the territorial rewards gained from battle, the benefits of static siege warfare, and the wisdom of maneuvering to avoid costly field engagements. The first two lessons held limited appeal to the American commander in chief.[34] Washington defined victory in terms of destroying Britain's willingness to prosecute the war, not by how much land he lost or gained. Even had he been inclined to fight for control of territory, his perennial shortage of men and materiel prevented it. The merits of siege warfare also held limited relevance to the American cause. Although the Revolutionary War began with a siege (at Boston) and for all practical purposes ended with a siege (at Yorktown), the major conflicts were primarily open-field battles. It was rather in the European emphasis on maneuver and the avoidance of the climactic battle that Americans could find the most inspiration and guidance.

After the fiascoes of the New York campaign of 1776, Washington often sought to avoid the main British army, despite his aggressive spirit and his determination to demonstrate it to Congress and critics. The previous engagements revealed that his soldiers' inexperience, lack of discipline, and short periods of enlistment, along with the young republic's political and financial weaknesses, would prevent him from matching the enemy's military prowess anytime soon. With the success of the Revolution riding on the continued existence of the Continental Army, he refused to allow the king's forces to draw him into a climactic confrontation. Instead, he pursued a strategy of attrition, maintaining a defensive posture in which he only occasionally gave battle, and did so when favorable conditions prevailed.[35] With limited human and material resources at his disposal, Washington could not prevent the enemy from seizing important ground, which was largely a defining purpose of war in seventeenth- and eighteenth-century Europe. Defending territory required him to fight wherever and whenever British commanders chose. Instead, he focused on the preservation of his own forces and the incremental destruction of the enemy's—primarily through quick strikes upon detachments, rather than the main body, of the opposing army.[36] The resulting protracted war, he hoped, would destroy Great Britain's willingness to continue the struggle.[37]

Knox clearly understood the wisdom of Washington's strategic approach and did not hesitate to remind him of its necessity. When the Continental commander queried his war council about the wisdom of taking the offensive in 1779, Knox expounded upon the merits of a Fabian strategy and the folly of risking so much in a direct confrontation with a superior foe.[38] In drafting his sentiments, he offered a concise description of the strategy employed by the main Continental Army over the preceding two and a half years: "The General principles of the War, being known to be defensive, and having been found by our own experience, and the concurrent opinion of our Enemies, and all Europe, to be the proper line by which we are to conduct ourselves we are still to pursue the same measures, and the end must be crown[e]d with success—That is That there can scarcely be a combination of events so exceedingly unfavorable which will warrant our fighting general actions with the Enemy, with the ballance of chances against us—But we are to be very watchful for all detachments and upon every favorable opportunity ende[a]vor to strike."[39] Considering European military lessons and the needs of American Revolutionaries, then, a war of maneuver appeared to Knox as the most viable alternative to a climactic confrontation. Considering the historical limitations of artillery, however, a strategy dependent upon speed and mobility put extraordinary demands on the artillery chief and his corps.

How then could Knox develop and deploy the artillery to complement this broad strategy? From what body of knowledge could this inexperienced soldier draw for inspiration and guidance? Again, European military history and practices provided him valuable lessons. Despite being an ocean away from Europe in an age of poor transportation and communication, Knox familiarized himself with modern developments in warfare. Napoleon, whom Knox would come to admire late in life, ushered in what most historians would agree was a military revolution at the turn of the century.[40] Yet the transformation of warfare did not occur overnight.[41] Some of the pivotal elements of Napoleonic warfare were made possible by related transformations in strategy and technology that began long before the earliest days of the French Revolution and were available to Knox and his contemporaries. Among the more significant modifications were those concerning artillery, and those ongoing changes had extraordinary implications for the War of American Independence and the Continental artillery.

During the seventeenth and eighteenth centuries, the performance and the value of siege and field guns gradually changed in a way that greatly aided Knox's task of supporting Washington's strategic inclinations. Artillery in its early stages of development was extremely heavy, cumbersome, virtually immobile, and of limited use, especially for armies on the move. After an initial cannonade, field guns often fell silent, and proved inconsequential in the outcome of fighting.[42] Artillery of this sort was of limited use to Knox, considering Washington's emphasis on mobility and maneuverability.

Fortunately for Knox's corps, the seventeenth and eighteenth centuries brought important if uneven changes that greatly increased the mobility and effectiveness of all artillery, but especially field guns. Sweden's Gustavus Adolphus transformed the artillery into an integrated military branch and fostered technological developments that resulted in improved metallurgy, shorter gun tubes, pre-measured charges, smaller (and thus lighter) calibers, and more effective coordination between gunners and foot soldiers.[43] The Dutch enhanced casting techniques that made gun barrels stronger, thinner, and lighter, and therefore more mobile than older designs. John Muller, of England's Royal Military Academy, helped increase the field gun's power, despite its reduced weight. Benjamin Robins carried out the first modern study of ballistics, giving artillery a precision it had theretofore lacked.[44] These developments, among others, contributed to the growing prominence of artillery in European warfare. By the last half of the eighteenth century, soldiers witnessed field guns that no longer opened battles only to sit idle as the fighting shifted. Artillerists, with their light and mobile pieces, now found it possible to keep pace with the ebb and flow of battle.[45] Even Frederick the Great, who glorified infantrymen and built his armies around them, had to concede the importance of this trend: "Cannister kills a six-footer as effectively as a man who measures five foot seven. Artillery does everything, and the infantry can no longer come to grips with cold steel."[46]

Knox appreciated and drew from these prevailing theories and practices. Since the siege, in which artillery had long played its most important role, had limited relevance to American designs, his greatest contribution was to draw from these recent European developments in artillery to bring maneuverability and mobility to the artillery branch so that it could support Washington's strategy of attrition and keep pace with the infantry's quick strikes against the enemy. He promoted the Continental Army's use of smaller and lighter field guns (three-, four-, and six-pounders) and artillery's focus on the opposing infantry rather than enemy fortifications. In addition, Knox placed great emphasis not only on drill for his men, but on education in the technical aspects of gunnery. In late 1778, while Washington's main army established winter quarters at Middlebrook, New Jersey, Knox set up the "Academy" at nearby Pluckemin.[47] There, Knox ordered officers to confront the specialized complexities of artillery and warfare. They attended lectures on a variety of topics—such as tactics, gunnery, and mathematics—in order to master basic military principles that they could apply to combat. The United States Military Academy would not be established for another quarter century, but an informal and rudimentary version of it existed at Knox's artillery park.[48]

The result of Knox's efforts was an artillery branch that became increasingly proficient and that contributed substantially to the successes of the Continental Army following its demoralizing losses in New York and retreat through New Jersey into Pennsylvania at the end of 1776. With those disasters at hand and the end of the campaign near, Washington sought to strike back by using speed and mobility against the Hessian garrison at Trenton. On December 24, he met with Knox and the general officers in camp, where a "hardy design was form[e]d of attacking the Town by storm."[49] The plan ultimately called for a three-pronged offensive against the king's forces, with Washington leading 2,400 men across the Delaware River at McKonkey's Ferry and two smaller forces crossing below and above Trenton. Despite freezing rain, snow, and unexpected delays, the main body crossed the Delaware River and trudged the nine miles southward to attack the unsuspecting Hessians.[50] The role of Knox's regiment was a prominent one. Even with the emphasis on speed and stealth, artillery accompanied Washington's force in numbers beyond even those traditionally employed in European armies.[51] By eight o'clock in the morning, the American army pushed past the advance guards and entered the town simultaneously from the south and north, with surprised Hessian forces scurrying to stave off the rebel attack. Although inclement weather rendered many American muskets useless, the artillery wheeled into place at the heads of King and Queen Streets and sent a withering fire into the scrambling enemy. Knox's men then helped silence two enemy guns and, as he later recounted, "in the twinkling of an eye cleared the streets."[52] American troops charged down the two main streets, creating greater confusion among the Hessians. Trenton's commander, Colonel Johann Rall, tried to rally his remaining troops for a counterattack, but fell from his horse, fatally wounded by two shots to the torso. Leaderless and surrounded, the Hessians gave up the fight less than an hour after the Americans had first stormed the town. The patriot cause received a much-needed boost.[53]

On December 30, just four days after the defeat of Rall's forces, Knox accompanied Washington's army back to New Jersey and reoccupied Trenton, only to learn that they faced possible destruction by a rapidly approaching 5,000-man army under Lord Charles Cornwallis. American pickets, however, managed to hold off the advancing enemy while the rest of the army withdrew across Assunpink Creek. Knox's artillery, perched on the high ground commanding Trenton from the south, then "saluted them with great vociferation and some execution," and thereby forestalled Cornwallis's "vigorous" assault, which the British commander decided to suspend until the following morning.[54] Realizing that his army could be pinned against the Delaware, Washington decided that his best option was to decamp quietly, exploit the cover of darkness, and attack the British position at Princeton, a trek nearly twelve miles to the rear of Cornwallis's army. At approximately one o'clock on the morning of January 3—with campfires blazing and a relatively small contingent of men left behind to create the illusion of an entrenching army—rebel forces abandoned their camp and headed toward Princeton.[55] Knox's regiment managed again to keep pace and provide support for the marching infantry, despite the fact that a cold front turned the muddy roads to ice. Outside of Princeton, they collided with Redcoats of the 17th and 55th Regiments, who were as "astonish[e]d as if the [American] Army had drop[pe]d perpendicularly upon them."[56] As the two sides raced toward Princeton, they clashed in an orchard northeast of the Quaker meetinghouse, where British troops seemed to turn the tide and push back rebel forces in disarray. However, Washington bravely rallied his battered infantry, and a company of Knox's artillery helped slow the enemy's advance. They eventually routed the British, as General John Sullivan led the Continentals' right wing into Princeton, where it easily dislodged, scattered, and captured the remaining British army. Less than a week after the startling blow at Trenton, Washington's men thus secured a second critical victory, with the artillery again providing important support.

The two battles demonstrated the benefits of speed, maneuver, and surprise for Washington's army, and the potential of Knox's gunners.[57] The lesson could not have been lost on the commander in chief, who commended his artillery officer in terms "strong and polite," and then urged Congress to promote him to the rank of brigadier general with command of all Continental artillery.[58] For the remainder of the war, Washington continued to assign an artillery company (usually wielding two small field pieces) to each infantry brigade, reflecting his faith in Knox's ability to provide important support to Continental forces in the field and indicating the artillery's integral role in the protean American military system.[59] Furthermore, Congress greatly expanded Knox's command when it significantly increased his corps during 1777 from a single regiment to four.[60]

The development of the Continental Army and its artillery branch continued during the campaign of 1777. Knox accompanied Washington and the main army, which focused on stopping the British advance on Philadelphia. In September, the two forces clashed along Brandywine Creek, twenty miles southeast of the rebel capital. There, Americans were stretched across a three-mile front and prepared to meet the oncoming army of Sir William Howe. One of Howe's two grand divisions marched directly toward the center of Washington's line and tried to push its way across the Brandywine. Knox's artillery and Greene's infantry provided a fierce and steady fire that kept the British at bay for nearly two hours. Then the momentum shifted. Washington, after receiving conflicting intelligence reports all morning, discovered that Howe's other grand division had outflanked him and threatened to roll up his entire right wing. He quickly shifted infantry and artillery to slow that advance, but also faced a renewed attack to the front of his army. Disaster, once again, loomed. The result, however, was different than what had occurred in the New York campaign. An "incessant cannonade" by both sides helped to slow the British attack and spilled considerable blood into the Brandywine. The artillery duel eventually created so much smoke that rebel troops could not detect or stop enemy movements across the river, and consequently were forced to join the army's general retreat to Chester, over a dozen miles to the east.[61] Although Washington suffered yet another defeat, his soldiers' tenacious fighting, the reserves' rapid deployment, and the artillery's mobility and firepower staved off catastrophe and left Continental troops surprisingly upbeat about their performance. "My corps did me great honor," Knox boasted to his wife, for "they behav[e]d like men—contending for every thing that[']s valuable." The subsequent loss of Philadelphia, he explained, was no more than a blow to the Continental Army that could be rectified "when expedient."[62]

Two weeks later, Continental troops executed one of the more ambitious and complicated assaults of the war. With the main British army in Philadelphia, Washington targeted a portion of it positioned in the vicinity of Germantown. His plan was reminiscent of the attack on Trenton, only on a larger scale. Under the cover of darkness, his army would march twelve miles before attacking in four converging columns what they hoped would be unsuspecting enemy troops. Knox's artillery would be deployed with the infantry in each of the four columns. As had been the case at Trenton and Princeton, speed, maneuverability, and surprise were critical to success. On the morning of October 4, the battle unfolded as planned. American Continentals and militia attacked, according to Knox, with "an impetuousity that would have done honor to old soldiers."[63] They made rapid and dramatic gains, sweeping across two to three miles of enemy ground before Howe could begin to re-form his beleaguered Redcoats. Artillery, as had been the case in previous campaigns, moved with the flow of battle. Victory seemed nearly at hand—so much so that Washington even prepared to order a general advance of his army to finish off its reeling foe. To see his army move with such alacrity and success must have been gratifying for him. Then, as quickly as success had come, the tide shifted in the other direction.[64]

The Americans' initial rapid advance and the Redcoats' desultory retreat took place in the midst of a dense fog—a fog made all the thicker by smoke from burning fields and the fire of cannon and musketry. The heavy blanket limited combatants' vision to as little as 20 yards.[65] According to one officer, the fog and smoke "made such a midnight darkness, that [for a] great part of the time there was no discovering friend from foe but by the direction of the shot, and no other object but the flash of the gun."[66] While the heavy fog aided the Americans' stealth and covered their movement over open ground and through various obstructions, it also prevented them from recognizing the extent of their success, the vulnerability of their opponents, and their own dispositions relative to each other. In short, it quite likely helped turn advance into retreat. Two additional factors contributed to the reversal. One involved Knox directly, the other indirectly. The initial American advance was so rapid that it bypassed pockets of resistance. One of those areas included Cliveden, a large stone-walled house recently abandoned by Judge Benjamin Chew. There, remnants of the 40th British Regiment hid behind the building's thick walls and became a thorn in Washington's side.[67] He quickly formed a council to discuss the problem. The officers debated the issue until Knox argued that a maxim in war was to never leave a "castle" to an army's rear. Washington apparently agreed, for they wasted a full hour and over a hundred American lives futilely bouncing cannon balls off Cliveden's stone walls until abandoning the scheme.[68] In the midst of the fog and the firing upon the Chew house, one of the four converging columns veered unwittingly into another, with the result that Americans fired upon Americans. These three problems conspired to stall Washington's assault and give Howe time to regroup his men for a counterattack that soon sent Continental forces in full retreat, with Knox's artillery providing the necessary cover. The outcome produced a growing criticism of Washington, but morale among his soldiers remained high.[69] Knox reported that "our troops are in prodigious Spirits," and Washington explained that the battle "serv[e]d to convince our people that when they make an Attack, they can confuse and Rout even the Flower of the British Army with the greatest Ease and that they are not that Invincible Body of Men which many suppose them to be."[70] Despite the lack of success at Brandywine Creek and Germantown, Continental forces, including the artillery, displayed a growing proficiency while avoiding crippling defeats.

The 1778 campaign provided another challenge for Washington and Knox. By the spring of that year, after France signed an alliance with the United States, the British government determined that the occupation of Philadelphia was too burdensome and Royal forces ought to be consolidated in the vicinity of New York. Meanwhile, Continental troops regrouped and received additional months of training, this time under the guidance of Baron Friedrich Wilhelm von Steuben, the new inspector general of the army. As a result, when the Redcoats abandoned Philadelphia, Washington was ready to strike. He ordered a sizeable force under Major General Charles Lee, only recently released from British captivity, to strike the vulnerable enemy army as it marched toward New York City. The assault on the enemy rearguard began on June 28 and quickly unraveled as American forces retreated in the face of a British counterattack. Knox rode onto the battlefield, perhaps sent forward by Washington for an appraisal of Lee's situation, and accompanied American forces as they fell back. Washington soon followed and angrily seized control of the situation. He established a line of defense while Lee organized his men's retreat. Knox used his artillery to slow the British advance and provide cover for the infantry. The battle became a slugfest in stifling summer heat. Knox helped position his guns as the British brought up theirs, and infantry tried to break the deadlock. For hours, attackers and defenders battered each other in what a Boston newspaper described as the "severest cannonade . . . that is thought ever happened in America."[71] By six o'clock that evening, the two sides disengaged and beleaguered British forces resumed their trek to New York. "Upon the whole it is very splendid," Knox reflected with obvious satisfaction.[72] The battle served to "convince the enemy & the world that nothing but a 'good constitution' keeps our army from being as good as any." The key role of the artillery in the battle was not lost on its commander or Washington. Knox bragged to his brother that "the Corps of Artillery have their full proportion of the Glory of the day. His Excellency the General has done them & me the honor to notice us in General orders in very pointed & flattering terms."[73] Since the decisive losses in New York two years before, the Continental Army had found increasing success, and the artillery had played a key role in acquiring it.

If the artillery had proved effective in open-field engagements, it also displayed its skill in more-formal sieges. The war essentially had begun with a siege at Boston, and would effectively end with one at Yorktown, Virginia. Following the success at Monmouth, Washington focused on driving the British from New York City, but never had the financial, material, and military support to do so. Nevertheless, the opportunity to end the war came in the southern theater. There, Lord Charles Cornwallis's army perched itself precariously on the peninsula between the York and James Rivers. American forces, along with the French infantry navy, converged on Yorktown and began a methodical siege of British troops there. In customary fashion for a siege, artillery played a vital role. Allied forces dug a series of trenches that allowed them in relative safety to approach Cornwallis's army and then to haul up the heavy siege guns to bombard it. Knox's artillery arrived at the end of September, 1781, and began a heavy, two-day barrage on October 9. On the 11th, the allies opened a second line of trenches, moving their firepower 300 yards closer to British lines and precipitating a vicious artillery exchange between the two sides. A Hessian soldier recorded that American and French ordnance fired 3,600 shells over the previous twenty-four hours that killed and maimed British troops, silenced their guns, destroyed buildings, and chipped away at their morale.[74] In the wake of the devastating barrage, Cornwallis, on October 15, advised his superior not to bother sending relief, and, two days later, proposed a cease-fire.[75] Two days after that, following a furious barrage from the allies' batteries, the British commander proposed a cease-fire to settle upon the terms of his capitulation. And two days after that, he and his 7,000-man army laid down their arms and surrendered to Franco-American forces.

Combatants on both sides of the battlefield acknowledged the artillery's critical contributions to the dramatic American victory, as well as its high degree of professionalism and proficiency. Washington reported to Congress following the Yorktown victory and singled out the important contributions made by the engineering and artillery branches of the Continental Army. Of Knox, he wrote that "the Resources of his Genius have supplied, on this and many other interesting Occasions, the Defect of Means: his distinguished Talents, and Services equally important and indefatigable entitle him the same Marks of Approbation from Congress, as they may be pleased to grant to the chief Engineer."[76] Nathanael Greene concurred, explaining to his close friend that he had heard about Knox's important role in the victory and that Knox was the "genius" behind it.[77] Greene perhaps overstated that importance, but the victory did prompt Congress to consider promoting Knox to the rank of major general, based on his "special merit" and "good conduct" at the siege of Yorktown.[78] Praise of Knox and the Continental artillery also came from the French ranks. The Chevalier de Chastellux, a French writer and soldier, claimed that he and his fellow countrymen were impressed by the "extraordinary progress" of the Continental artillery. It was "extremely well served" by its commander, whose "intelligence and activity" one could not too much admire.[79] Cornwallis similarly gave credit to French and American gunners, "who brought an immense train of heavy artillery, most amply furnished with ammunition and perfectly well manned." The allies' batteries, he explained to Clinton, virtually destroyed his defenses, which exhausted his men as they tried to rebuild them and left his lines exposed to the impending enemy assault that was avoided only by his surrender.[80]

The Continental artillery's record of effectiveness throughout the war established a mutual respect and deep trust between the two men that was created in and sustained throughout the eight-year war and beyond. Washington repeatedly demonstrated his support of Knox, and Knox proved a loyal subordinate.

The end of hostilities predictably weakened wartime connections between military veterans, but the Washington-Knox relationship continued for virtually the remainder of their professional and personal lives. In the immediate postwar years, they conferred in writing over a variety of political and military issues: the business of the Society of the Cincinnati, problems in the western states and territories, the dangers of Shays's Rebellion, the proper establishment for peacetime defense, the dire need for a constitutional convention, the importance of Washington's role in it, and the prospects of the Constitution's ratification, among others. And after the new government was formed and Washington was elected president, he turned once more to Knox, this time to head the War Department, a position the latter had held during the Confederation period. Together again, they addressed, in an increasingly tense and partisan environment, the military problems and needs of the new nation, including militia reform, Indian policy, western conflicts, and foreign threats.[81] On the last day of 1794, nearly twenty years after the two men first met, the Secretary of War retired and thereby ended their long professional relationship. Washington wrote to him, "My personal knowledge of your exertions, while it authorizes me to hold this language, justifies the sincere friendship which I have ever borne for you, and which will accompany you in every situation of life."[82] Several years later, they discussed rekindling their partnership a third time and, in doing so, created the first significant challenge to the trust and friendship they had long shared.

Military crisis had brought Washington and Knox together in 1775, and again in 1789, and it threatened to drive them apart in 1798. By that time, Washington had retired to private life, rancorous political battles between the Federalist and Jeffersonian Republican parties threatened national unity, and the nation sat on the precipice of war with France. To prepare for the possible conflict, Congress authorized the establishment of a Provisional Army, which heightened political differences between Federalists, who loathed revolutionary France, and Jeffersonians, who were averse to a larger army. President John Adams hoped to unify the divided public by asking Washington, still very popular among most Americans, to leave Mount Vernon and resume command of U.S. forces. He agreed, but with specific stipulations, including that he would not actually join the army until circumstances required it, and that he could select the three major generals, as authorized by Congress, and their hierarchy. He selected Alexander Hamilton, from the mid-Atlantic states; C. C. Pinckney, a southerner; and Henry Knox, the New Englander, in that order.[83]

Anticipating that the order of commissions might not be "perfectly agreeable" to Knox, Washington wrote his old artillery chief on July 16, 1798, tendered the offer, conveyed some of the reasons for his decision,[84] and expressed hope that the problems would be not "insurmountable." He explained in somewhat vague and disingenuous terms that his second in command, "in the public estimation as declared to me," would be Hamilton, though the selection really came at Washington's insistence. Further, he wrote, an expected

French invasion in the southern states necessitated that Pinckney, a native son, be next in line. That left Knox with the remaining commission, making him subordinate to two men who had held lesser ranks in the Revolutionary War.[85] In his reply, Knox expressed "astonishment," and left no doubt that he saw it as a personal betrayal: "Conscious myself of entertaining for you a sincere, active, and invariable friendship, I easily beleived it was reciprocal. Nay more, I flattered myself with your esteem and respect in a military point of view. But I find that others greatly my juniors in rank, have been, upon a scale of comparison, preferred before me." He bluntly challenged Washington's reference to the "public estimation," declared he would not accept a commission on the terms presented, and professed a desire to serve, but in a role less degrading to himself.[86] Washington tried in his return letter to explain the logic of Hamilton's appointment, and he offered another sincere expression of his affection for Knox, who would have none of it. Knox continued to question the propriety and legal basis for the ranks, though he volunteered to serve as Washington's aide.[87] When Washington expressed surprise to Knox that he was still tormented by the issue, any chance of their professional relationship being renewed quickly disappeared.[88] Knox responded with a brief missive, declaring, "The possibility being suggested by you of my harbouring any secret 'gnawings' upon the subject of rank, precludes decisively my having the satisfaction proposed of sharing your fate in the field."[89]

The rank controversy of 1798 created the most serious strain between the two longtime friends, but not an irreconcilable rift. The closeness of their relationship made likely the personal pain of the rank controversy, but that enduring wartime bond was not easily broken. While Washington insisted on Hamilton as his second in command, he also explained to Adams his devotion to Knox: "With respect to General Knox, I can say with truth, there is no man in the United States with whom I have been in habits of greater intimacy; no one whom I have loved more sincerely; nor any for whom I have had a greater friendship."[90] In the following year, each wrote the other, neither mentioning the unhappy events of the previous fall, and both closing with their usual avowals of affection for the other.[91] Washington's unexpected death in 1799 prevented them from further demonstrating their mutual loyalty.

Nearly a quarter of a century before, they had first met along the outskirts of Boston. Washington then had seen something of promise in the young military enthusiast—perhaps his erudition or resourcefulness or determination—that led him to place so much trust and responsibility in him. And it was an investment well made. Despite Knox's youth and limited experience, he proved to be one of Washington's most effective lieutenants, and their wartime relationship one of Washington's most important. Their professional partnership was resurrected during Washington's presidency, but their friendship, despite the tensions of 1798, was a long, uninterrupted, and enduring one.

Notes

1. GW to Richard Henry Lee, 29 August 1775, *PGW: Rev. Ser.,* 1:375.

2. Henry Knox to Lucy Knox, 6 July 1775, Henry Knox Papers, Gilder Lehrman Collection at the New-York Historical Society. See also Thomas J. Fleming, *Now We Are Enemies: The Story of Bunker Hill* (New York, 1960), 168. The quotation is also in Noah Brooks, *Henry Knox: A Soldier of the Revolution* (1900; New York, 1974), 32. Brooks makes the connection between "Generals" and Washington and Lee.

3. In preparation for his meeting with the committee, Washington prepared questions and answers, and he later recorded minutes of conference deliberations (see "Questions for the Committee," ca. 18 October 1775, and "Minutes of the Conference," 18–24 October 1775, *PGW: Rev. Ser.,* 2:185–205, esp. 186, 189, and 201 for references to Knox).

4. The quotation comes from a letter by Joseph Peirce to Knox, 19 February 1776, Knox Papers.

5. William L. Browne, *Ye Cohorn Caravan* (Schuylerville, N.Y., 1975), 7, 11.

6. See Washington's order for the operation in his letter to Artemas Ward, 3 March 1776, *PGW: Rev. Ser.,* 3:409–10. The fortification of Dorchester Heights on the night of March 4–5 was in itself an extraordinary feat. According to Rufus Putnam, he developed, along with Knox and Richard Gridley, the plan to occupy and fortify Dorchester Heights (see the entry in Putnam's memoirs, in *Engineers of Independence: A Documentary History of the Army Engineers in the American Revolution, 1775–1783,* ed. Paul H. Walker [Washington, D.C., 1981], 66–67). Jeduthan Baldwin, who served during the Siege of Boston and became an engineer in the Continental ranks, described the difficult conditions in *The Revolutionary Journal of Col. Jeduthan Baldwin, 1775–1778,* ed. Thomas William Baldwin (New York, 1971), 23–25. A British perspective on the operation is in John Barker, *The British in Boston: Being the Diary of Lieutenant John Barker of the King's Own Regiment from November 15, 1774 to May 31, 1776,* ed. Elizabeth Ellery Dana (Cambridge, Mass., 1924), 69–70.

7. Robert Hanson Harrison to Knox, 20 April 1776, Knox Papers; Nicolas Cooke to GW, 23 April 1776, *PGW: Rev. Ser.,* 4:110–11.

8. GW to Knox, 3 April 1776, *PGW: Rev. Ser.,* 4:23–25.

9. Knox describes the meeting in a letter to Lucy Knox dated July 22, 1776 (see Knox Papers). Joseph Reed penned a fuller description on July 20, 1776 (*PGW: Rev. Ser.,* 5:398–403).

10. GW to John Hancock, 31 May 1777, *PGW: Rev. Ser.,* 9:569.

11. Knox to GW, 10 September 1782 and 15 January 1797, Knox Papers.

12. Thomas Mifflin to Horatio Gates, 17 November 1777, in *Letters of Delegates to Congress, 1774–1789,* ed. Paul H. Smith (Washington, D.C., 1981), 8:314–15.

13. Conway's criticism was made in a letter to Horatio Gates but conveyed indirectly to Washington by William Alexander, Lord Stirling. The "bad Councellors" to whom Conway alluded are likely Knox and Nathanael Greene (see John E. Ferling, *The First of Men: A Life of George Washington* [New York, 2010], 224–30).

14. Henry Laurens to Benjamin Huger, 15 November 1777, in *Letters of Delegates to Congress,* 8:269–71; Freeman, 4:587.

15. Don Higginbotham examines the sources and nature of American military education in the Revolutionary period, and its connection to European thinkers, in "Military Education before West Point," in *Thomas Jefferson's Military Academy: Founding West Point,* ed. Robert M. S. McDonald (Charlottesville, Va., 2004), 23–53. For a discussion of the European influence on George Washington, see ibid., 30–39.

16. For lengthy discussions of war and military thinking in the Age of Reason or the Enlightenment, see Christopher Duffy, *The Military Experience in the Age of Reason* (New York, 1987); Azar Gat, *The Origins of Military Thought: From the Enlightenment to Clausewitz* (Oxford, U.K., 1989); Henry Guerlac, "Vauban: The Impact of Science on War," in *Makers of Modern Strategy: Military Thought from Machiavelli to the Nuclear Age,* ed. Peter Paret, Gordon A. Craig, and Felix Gilbert (Princeton, N.J., 1986), 64–90; and Russell F. Weigley, *The Age of Battles: The Quest for Decisive Warfare from Breitenfeld to Waterloo* (Bloomington, Ind., 1981), esp. 54, 194–95, 265–67.

17. Ira D. Gruber has written extensively on the military literature of the age, including *Books and the British Army in the Age of the American Revolution* (Chapel Hill, N.C., 2010). Knox's reading list reflects what British officers commonly read, including their affinity for French authors.

18. Guerlac, "Vauban," 64–90; Weigley, *Age of Battles,* 53–58.

19. In his response to John Adams's query about the study of war, Knox compiled a brief list of recommended reading on the "military art." Saxe received Knox's unwavering praise. Vauban's name also appeared on the list of books that were, in Knox's opinion, "more Scientific" but "essentially necessary" to Americans' future military operations (see Knox to John Adams, 16 May 1776, in *The Papers of John Adams: Series III, General Correspondence and Other Papers of the Adams Statesmen,* ed. Robert J. Taylor et al., 15 vols. to date [Cambridge, Mass., 1977–], 4:190).

20. Saxe, *My Reveries Upon the Art of War,* in *Roots of Strategy: A Collection of Military Classics,* ed. Thomas R. Phillips, (Harrisburg, Pa., 1955), 189.

21. Knox to John Adams, 16 May 1776, *Papers of John Adams,* 4:190.

22. See Gruber, *Books and the British Army;* and Gat, *Origins of Military Thought,* 25–29.

23. Saxe, *My Reveries Upon the Art of War,* 298.

24. For a general discussion of the American colonists' affinity for limited wars, see Reginald C. Stuart, *War and American Thought: From the Revolution to the Monroe Doctrine* (Kent, Ohio, 1982), 2–16. Other historians emphasize the trend among the colonists of British North America away from limited conflicts. They instead argue that as Europeans adopted a relatively mild form of battle, the colonists waged war with much greater ferocity and less restraint. See, e.g., John Shy, "The American Military Experience: History

and Learning," in *A People Numerous and Armed: Reflections on the Military Struggle for American Independence* (New York, 1976), 227–54; and Russell F. Weigley, *The American Way of War: A History of United States Military Strategy and Policy* (New York, 1973), chaps. 18–20. Knox's quotation is taken from Alan Taylor, *Liberty Men and Great Proprietors: The Revolutionary Settlement on the Maine Frontier, 1760–1820* (Chapel Hill, N.C., 1990), 37. In this study of Maine's land speculators, Taylor offers a critical assessment of Knox and his character. Knox, by Taylor's account, was driven by his unending pursuit of financial wealth and his obsessive quest for control (see, e.g., 37–57, and also Taylor, "From Fathers to Friends of the People: Political Personas in the Early Republic," *JER* 11 [Winter 1991]: 465–91).

25. Knox to GW, 26 November 1777, *PGW: Rev. Ser.*, 12:415.

26. Knox to GW, 23 May 1780, Knox Papers. For other examples, see Knox to George Washington, 18 June 1778 and 2 September 1778, ibid.

27. Knox to Lucy Knox, 7 September 1776, ibid.

28. Knox to unknown recipient, [1782], Morristown National Historical Park Collection, Manuscripts Division, Library of Congress.

29. Gruber argues that eighteenth-century writers from the Continent, especially France, showed a predilection for limiting battle, minimizing the impact of war, and, when possible, avoiding unnecessary conflicts (see Gruber, *Books and the British Army*, 50–53).

30. Knox to William Knox, 5 August 1781, Knox Papers.

31. Ibid.

32. Guerlac, "Vauban," 72.

33. Ibid., 72–80.

34. Finding the relevance of European military practices to war in the wilderness of North America proved troublesome even for British military leaders. They were repeatedly stymied and frustrated by the unusual circumstances—unusual for Europeans—of fighting in an extremely vast theater of operations and suffering all the related problems for command, communication, and logistical support. Daniel J. Beattie discusses the problems for British commanders in adapting Old World experience to a New World setting in "The Adaptation of the British Army to Wilderness Warfare, 1755–1763" (in *Adapting to Conditions: War and Society in the Eighteenth Century*, ed. Maarten Ultee [University, Ala., 1986], 56–83).

35. In his definitive study of the Trenton and Princeton campaign, David Hackett Fischer outlined Washington's strategic options (see Fischer, *Washington's Crossing* [New York, 2004], 370–79).

36. In late 1776, Washington facilitated the army's maneuverability and adaptability to the changing face of battle by shifting organizational emphasis from the regiment to the smaller brigade, and by attaching artillery companies directly to those brigades. These changes were partly fostered by the Continental Army's eroding numbers. Whatever the cause, they gave the army the important ability to adapt more easily to changing circumstances. Washington's innovation was a key to American victory in the war, argues Robert K. Wright Jr., in *The Continental Army* (Washington D.C., 1983), 97–98.

37. Russell F. Weigley, "American Strategy: A Call for a Critical Strategic History," in *Re-*

considerations on the Revolutionary War, ed. Don Higginbotham (Westport, Conn., 1978), 32–53; Weigley, *The American Way of War,* chap. 1. For a discussion of Washington's strategy, see Dave Richard Palmer, *The Way of the Fox: American Strategy in the War for America, 1775–1783* (Westport, Conn., 1975); and Weigley's critical response in "American Strategy," 47–53. John Ferling emphasizes Washington's aggressive, offensive-minded approach to the war, which, he argues, was the product of the general's pride and vanity: "To imagine Washington thinking any other way is to fail to understand the man, for the personality style that shaped his inescapable quest for esteem also structured the decisions he made in this war" (see Ferling, "George Washington and the American Victory," in *The World Turned Upside Down: The American Victory in the War of Independence,* ed. John Ferling [Westport, Conn., 1988], 53–70 (quotation, 63).

38. "Fabian strategy" derives its name from Quintus Fabius Maximus, a Roman dictator and general who, in the third century BC, gained victory over Hannibal's superior army by avoiding decisive battles and employing a strategy of attrition.

39. Knox to GW, 27 July 1779, Knox Papers.

40. Knox to David Cobb, 12 November 1796, David Cobb Papers, Massachusetts Historical Society, Boston.

41. John A. Lynn explains that the Gribeauval artillery system that was so crucial to Napoleonic warfare was not as innovative as some argue: "To be sure, his [Gribeauval's] reforms constituted more an important refinement than a radical transformation of artillery technology, which would not be truly revolutionized until the introduction of rifled and breech-loading pieces in the mid-nineteenth century" (see Lynn, "En avant! The Origins of the Revolutionary Attack," in *Tools of War: Instruments, Ideas, and Institutions of Warfare,* ed. John A. Lynn [Urbana, Ill., 1990], 157). Owen Connelly argues the evolutionary nature of artillery in his study of Napoleonic warfare, *Blundering to Glory: Napoleon's Military Campaigns* (rev. ed., Wilmington, Del., 1999). Connelly argues that Napoleon did not use artillery in greater number or concentration than eighteenth-century commanders, but merely followed the lead of the innovative Frederick the Great: "Napoleon's genius lay in using everything better than anyone before" (ibid., 3).

42. O. F. G. Hogg, *Artillery: Its Origin, Heyday, and Decline* (Hamden, Conn., 1970), 18–25, 100.

43. Robert L. O'Connell, *Of Arms and Men: A History of War, Weapons, and Aggression* (New York, 1989), 144–47; Hogg, *Artillery,* 27, 57–58, 98–103; Duffy, *Military Experience,* 216–18, 230–33; Weigley, *Age of Battles,* 270–73.

44. Duffy, *Military Experience,* 230–33; Weigley, *Age of Battles,* 270–73; Hogg, *Artillery,* 18–103.

45. Palmer, "Frederick," in Paret, Craig, and Gilbert, *Makers of Modern Strategy,* 100–101; Wright, *The Continental Army,* 4–5.

46. The quotation, from Frederick's *Testament politique,* appears in Duffy, *Military Experience,* 231.

47. A contemporary description of the Artillery Park at Pluckemin appeared in the *Pennsylvania Packet,* 6 March 1779. It noted that the "academy" ("fifty feet by thirty") was where "lectures are read on tactics and gunnery." John Lewis Seidel provides a lengthier discussion of Knox's "Academy" in "The Archaeology of the American Revolution: A

Reappraisal and Case Study at the Continental Artillery Cantonment of 1778–1779, Pluckemin, New Jersey" (PhD diss., University of Pennsylvania, 1987).

48. Wright, *The Continental Army,* 103; Seidel, "Archaeology of the American Revolution," 685.

49. Knox to Lucy Knox, 28 December 1776, Knox Papers.

50. Fischer describes the difficult river crossing and march to Trenton in *Washington's Crossing,* 206–33.

51. Jac Weller, "Guns of Destiny: Field Artillery in the Trenton-Princeton Campaign," *Military Affairs* 20 (Spring 1956): 1–2, 7–8; Fischer, *Washington's Crossing,* appendix M, 404. Fischer notes the atypically heavy emphasis on field guns, but also explains that transportation of the artillery slowed the army's progress in crossing the Delaware River and marching to Trenton (ibid., 223–25).

52. Knox to Lucy Knox, 28 December 1776, Knox Papers; Fischer, *Washington's Crossing,* 239, 245.

53. Fischer, *Washington's Crossing,* 234–62; Alfred Hoyt Bill, *The Campaign of Princeton* (Princeton, N.J., 1948), 50–57; Christopher Ward, *The War of the Revolution,* 2 vols. (New York, 1952), 1:291–305; William S. Stryker, *The Battles of Trenton and Princeton* (1898; repr., Spartanburg, S.C., 1967), esp. chaps. 9–11.

54. Knox to Lucy Knox, 7 January 1777, Knox Papers.

55. Ibid.

56. Ibid.

57. Ibid. See also Stryker, *Battles of Trenton and Princeton,* 254–57; Ward, *War of the Revolution,* 1:312–16; and Fischer, *Washington's Crossing,* 330–40.

58. The quotation is from Knox's account of Washington's praise (see Knox to Lucy Knox, 28 December 1776, Knox Papers). Washington's support of Knox's promotion can be found in *Journals of the Continental Congress,* ed. Worthington C. Ford, 34 vols. (Washington, D.C., 1904–37), 6:1043.

59. GW to John Hancock, 13 December 1776, *PGW: Rev. Ser.,* 7:324; Robert K. Wright Jr., "'Nor Is Their Standing Army to Be Despised': The Emergence of the Continental Army as a Military Institution," in *Arms and Independence: The Military Character of the American Revolution,* ed. Ronald Hoffman and Peter J. Albert (Charlottesville, Va., 1984), 57; Wright, *The Continental Army,* 97–98.

60. These military reforms are discussed in Wright, "'Nor Is Their Standing Army to Be Despised,'" 50–57; and in Wright, *The Continental Army,* chap. 5.

61. See Stephen Jarvis's passage quoted in George F. Scheer and Hugh F. Rankin, *Rebels and Redcoats: The Living Story of the American Revolution* (New York, 1957), 237. Knox's official account is in Brooks, *Henry Knox,* 268–69.

62. Knox to Lucy Knox, 24 September 1777, Knox Papers.

63. Knox to Lucy Knox, 6 October 1777, ibid.

64. Freeman, 4:510. See also John S. Pancake, *1777: Year of the Hangman* (Tuscaloosa, Ala., 1977), 192–98; Paul David Nelson, *Anthony Wayne: Soldier of the Early Republic* (Bloomington, Ind., 1985), 58–64; Harry M. Ward, *Major General Adam Stephen and the Cause of American Liberty* (Charlottesville, Va., 1989), 184–96; and *The Papers of General Nathanael Greene,* ed. Richard K. Showman et al., 13 vols. to date (Chapel Hill, N.C., 1976–), 2:171–77n1.

65. Knox gave that estimate in a letter to his wife (see Knox to Lucy Knox, 6 October 1777, Knox Papers). Reports of visibility vary widely, however, probably reflecting both the inexact estimates and the varying thickness of the fog from place to place. Washington claimed that the range of sight was 30 yards, while other sources indicated it to be as much as 50 or 60 yards (see Freeman, 4:507n108).

66. Unknown author, "Extract of a letter from an officer in Gen. Washington's Army," *Boston Gazette and Country Journal,* 20 October 1777, 2.

67. Walter Stewart estimated that 500 British soldiers and four artillery pieces occupied the Chew house (see his letter to Horatio Gates, 12 October 1777, Knox Papers). In his biography of Knox, Noah Brooks listed the number of men to be considerably fewer—200 (see Brooks, *Henry Knox,* 108). Timothy Pickering wrote that these Redcoats "killed and wounded a great many of our officers and men" (see his journal entry printed in Octavius Pickering, *Timothy Pickering,* 4 vols. [Boston, 1867], 1:168–69).

68. Freeman, 4:507–8, 515. Timothy Pickering was a member of the debate and one who recommended bypassing the Chew house. His detailed account of, and commentary on, the incident are recorded in his letter of August 23, 1826, to the *North American Review* (vol. 23 [October 1826]: 425–30), and in a journal entry (see Octavius Pickering, *Timothy Pickering,* 1:168–69). See also *Papers of General Nathanael Greene,* 2:174–75; and Brooks, *Henry Knox,* 108.

69. For a discussion of the growing criticism of Washington and the increased civil-military tensions in 1777–78, see Don Higginbotham, *The War of American Independence: Military Attitudes, Policies, and Practice, 1763–1789* (New York, 1971), 206–22.

70. Knox to Lucy Knox, 6 October 1777, Knox Papers; GW to Israel Putnam, 8 October 1777, *PGW: Rev. Ser.,* 11:447.

71. *Boston Gazette and Country Journal,* 20 July 1778.

72. Knox to Lucy Knox, 29 June 1778, Knox Papers.

73. Knox to William Knox, 3 July 1778, ibid.

74. Johann Conrad Döhla, *A Hessian Diary of the American Revolution,* ed. Bruce E. Burgoyne (Norman, Okla., 1990), 166–69. See similar comments by British officer Banastre Tarleton, in Lieutenant-General Tarleton, *A History of the Campaigns of 1780 and 1781 in the Southern Provinces of North America* (1787; repr., New York, 1968), 385; and by Ebenezer Denny, an American who served as a Continental officer in the Pennsylvania line, in *Military Journal of Ebenezer Denny: An Officer in the Revolutionary and Indian Wars,* ed. William H. Denny (Philadelphia, 1860), 242–48.

75. Theodore Thayer, *Yorktown: Campaign of Strategic Options* (Philadelphia, 1975), 126.

76. GW to the President of Congress, 31 October 1781, Fitzpatrick, 23:307–8.

77. Nathanael Greene to Knox, 10 December 1781, Knox Papers.

78. The promotion, when finally bestowed, made Knox the Continental Army's youngest officer of that rank (see *Journals of the Continental Congress,* 21:1120–21, 22:105, 143–46; and North Callahan, *Henry Knox: General Washington's General* [New York, 1958], 194).

79. François Jean, Marquis de Chastellux, *Travels in North America,* 2 vols. (Chapel Hill, N.C., 1963), 1:282.

80. Cornwallis to Clinton, 20 October 1781, in *Documents of the American Revolution, 1770–1783,* ed. K. G. Davies, 21 vols. (Shannon, Ireland, 1972–81), 20:245–46. Cornwallis's

principal biographers, Franklin and Mary Wickwire, refer to Knox as the "most brilliant artilleryman in either army" (see Franklin B. Wickwire and Mary Wickwire, *Cornwallis and the War of Independence* [London, 1971], 111).

81. For an overview of these military policies and debates, see Richard H. Kohn, *Eagle and Sword: The Federalists and the Creation of the Military Establishment in America, 1783–1802* (New York, 1975), esp. pt. 2; and Lawrence D. Cress, *Citizens in Arms: The Army and Militia in American Society to the War of 1812* (Chapel Hill, NC, 1982), chaps. 5–7.

82. GW to Knox, 30 December 1794, Knox Papers.

83. GW to John Adams, *PGW: Ret. Ser.,* 2:403–4; GW to Alexander Hamilton, ibid., 2:407–9. For a summary of Washington's correspondence concerning the order of the major generals, see the editor's comments, ibid., 2:409–12n5.

84. Washington had tried to remain above partisan divisions during his presidency, but during his retirement, fearing the Jeffersonians' growing power and political agenda, he openly sided with Federalists. According to John E. Ferling, he saw the crisis with France as an opportunity to set the nation on a Federalist course since the veteran officers appointed to save the country would come from his party's ranks. Washington saw Hamilton as the Federalists' best hope for the future, and therefore insisted he serve as second in command. For Washington, the Provisional Army and preparation for war with France was as much a political issue as a military one (see Ferling, *First of Men,* 497–99).

85. GW to Knox, 16 July 1798, *PGW: Ret. Ser.,* 2:423–25.

86. Knox to GW, 29 July 1798, ibid., 2:469–72. Knox contended that the placement of Pinckney over him, and Hamilton over both him and Pinckney, violated a measure passed by Congress during the Revolutionary War. This legal issue caused concern for Washington and advocates for Hamilton. Secretary of State Timothy Pickering, one of those strong supporters of Hamilton, explained the point to Washington and offered counters to it (see Pickering to Washington, 1 September 1798, ibid., 2:573–77).

87. Knox to GW, 26 August 1798, ibid., 2:562–63.

88. GW to Knox, 21 October 1798, ibid., 1:122–23.

89. Knox to GW, 4 November 1798, ibid., 3:178.

90. GW to John Adams, 25 September 1798, ibid., 3:42.

91. GW to Knox, 22 May 1799, Fitzpatrick, 37:212–13; Knox to GW, 22 December 1799, Knox Papers. Knox wrote his letter after Washington had died, but news of the death had not yet reached him.

"My Favorite Officer"

George Washington's Apprentice, Nathanael Greene

JOHN W. HALL

George Washington might have considered November 16, 1776, the worst day in what had already been a very bad year. Happy memories of American victories around Boston faded in late summer and early autumn as British forces embarrassed the Americans on Long Island and then outmaneuvered them on Manhattan, turning the Continentals out of one position after another and compelling the abandonment of New York City. By late October, Washington ceded the rest of the island save a single post that bore his name. With its mate, Fort Lee on the Jersey shore, Fort Washington ostensibly commanded the Hudson River, and the Continental Congress regarded its preservation a matter of national interest. Washington harbored doubts about both the tenability and utility of the post—especially after several British ships successfully ran the gauntlet in early November. Although he favored abandoning the post, Washington left the decision to the local commander who, despite his relative inexperience, had become one of Washington's closest advisors. Drawing on all of his eighteen months of active military service, this subordinate used the discretion granted him to reinforce Fort Washington—only to watch it fall to the British on November 16.

It was the worst defeat the Continental Army had suffered since the beginning of the war, and it would not be surpassed until the fall of Charleston nearly four years later. Although casualties were relatively light (54 killed and twice as many wounded), the surviving garrison of nearly 3,000 men marched off to British prisons—incubators for disease from which only a third of them would ever emerge.[1] The effects on morale were nearly as devastating as the loss of these precious troops, and Major General Charles

Lee aptly characterized the debacle as "a cursed affair." In a characteristically blunt letter to Washington, Lee wailed, "Oh, General, why would you be over-persuaded by men of inferiour judgment to your own?"[2] Lee did not need to be more specific. Clearly, the inferior judgment of which he wrote belonged to Washington's eager apprentice, Nathanael Greene.

Lee's ulterior motives aside, the question deserves serious consideration, for it sheds light on one of the most important personal relationships of the American Revolution. The fiasco at Fort Washington might well have ended Greene's brief but promising military career were it not for the reciprocal loyalty of two men upon whom the fate of the Revolution rested. Jealous or casual observers mistook the true nature of this relationship, charging Greene with sycophancy and supposing that Washington was too insecure to make his own decisions. Although uncharitable, such allegations were perhaps inevitable given the extent to which the two men depended upon one another. But what some perceived as an unhealthy relationship in 1776 and 1777, ultimately proved essential to the patriot cause. Indeed, Washington and Greene were as indispensible to one another as they were to American independence.

Unfulfilled by his Quaker upbringing, Greene yearned for martial accomplishment, and he found in Washington an icon and mentor able to provide the affirmation he craved. In return, Greene provided Washington with the ideal lieutenant: he was competent, loyal, and—critically—less experienced than the commander in chief. In the Revolutionary milieu, these last two characteristics were inextricably connected. Typically, Washington's staunchest critics were those who measured a man's military worth by his experience (as Washington's was fairly limited), and his most ardent supporters were those tyros likely to resent experience. Not coincidentally, Washington surrounded himself with men of the latter sort, most notably the Marquis de Lafayette, Henry Knox, and Greene. These men, whom Lee denigrated as "dirty earwigs," looked up to their commanding general when Lee and others would not.[3] In the desperate and uncertain moments of the Revolution, Washington needed these loyal "sons" as much as they needed him. Hence, while Washington did not conceal Greene's role in the "unfortunate affair" at Fort Washington, neither did he throw his loyal lieutenant to the baying critics.[4] Instead, Washington continued to place Greene in positions of immense importance, culminating in his appointment to two of the army's most critical posts: quartermaster general and command of the Southern Department. Subsequent events vindicated Washington's faith in Greene, who proved not only a masterful logistician and operational commander, but arguably a strategist superior to Washington himself.

Washington could not have recognized this potential in Greene when the two first met outside of Boston on July 4, 1775. Two months earlier, Greene had been an anchorsmith and militia private who, because of a stiff right knee, marched awkwardly. His meteoric rise to command all of Rhode Island's troops and ensuing commission as the Continental Army's junior brigadier general bespoke the poverty of military experience in America. A veteran of the French and Indian War, Washington was one of the few native-born patriots who could lay claim to any substantial military experience, albeit most of it tactical and administrative in nature. In an army full of novices, Greene was exceptional only for his lofty rank and the relatively superior discipline of his Rhode Island troops. "Though raw, irregular, and undisciplined," Washington observed, they were "under much better government than any around Boston."[5] Faint praise, perhaps, but it was the best Washington could muster for the otherwise "dirty & nasty" New Englanders who formed the nucleus of his Continental Army.[6] While he disapproved of their egalitarian sentiments and lack of respect for military authority, the New Englanders resented the Virginian's haughty pretentions, and generally reciprocated his disdain.

But Greene was another case altogether, and his exuberance appears to have blinded him to the prevalent sentiment among his fellow New Englanders. Describing Washington's arrival in camp to Rhode Island's congressional delegate, Greene exclaimed that "joy was visible on every countenance and it seemed as if the spirit of conquest breathed through the whole army." But if we may doubt the accuracy of Greene's report, there is no reason to question the sincerity of his praise: "I hope we shall be taught to copy his example and to prefer the Love of Liberty . . . to all the soft pleasures of domestic Life. . . . And I doubt not under the General[']s wise direction we shall establish such excellent order and stricktness of Discipline as to invite Victory to attend him where ever he goes."[7] Greene's enthusiasm for his new commander was not confined to the public sphere, as seven months after writing this letter, Greene's wife Catherine gave birth to the couple's first child, George Washington Greene. A daughter, Martha Washington Greene, joined the family only thirteen months later.

But there was more to Nathanael Greene than adulation. Although only ten years Washington's junior, Greene was nevertheless at the very beginning of his military career, and Washington might have seen much of himself in the ambitious New Englander.[8] Both men had lost a parent at the age of eleven, and although they came from the esteemed classes of their respective colonies, neither man had the benefit of a formal education. They were both painfully conscious of this disadvantage, which contributed to similarly sensitive conceptions of pride and honor. If, by 1775, Washington no longer took offense as easily or threatened to resign as often as Greene would in the years ahead, he could still sympathize with his prideful and sometimes peevish understudy.

Thanks to the influence of his half brother Lawrence, who mentored George after their father's death, Washington had developed an affinity for and access to a military career quite early in life.[9] Greene, who had instead lost his mother, remained under the influence of a father committed to the Quaker traditions of pacifism, hard work, and adherence to Scripture. While Greene's paternal relations were cordial, he resented his father's prejudice against education, which consigned him to a life of "dig[g]ing into the Bowels of the Earth after wealth."[10] Following his father's death in 1770, Greene strayed from his Quaker roots, and by July 1773 had been suspended from the Society of Friends for patronizing a "Publick Resort" where he "had No Proper Business."[11] Thus freed from his confining influences, and with war on the horizon, Greene turned his attention to military affairs, which better suited both his literary and professional tastes.[12] With the help of the Boston bookseller Henry Knox, Greene dedicated himself to learning his new calling's principles, which he later cited in his correspondence, even as he violated them in his conduct. Indeed, it might be said that Greene's fairly superficial understanding of the art of war eventually worked to his advantage as he gained experience and exhibited a willingness to rely on his own judgment more than convention. But in 1775 Greene was yet a simple apprentice in search of a master. In Washington, he found everything that he hoped he could become.

Washington, meanwhile, wondered whether he would be equal to the challenge confronting him. Not only did he doubt his own qualifications for command, but the army waiting for him in Massachusetts inspired little confidence. Throughout his career, Washington endeavored to build, train, and maintain professional military forces on a European model, and the rabble that was the Continental Army of 1775 appeared woefully incapable of taking on one of the best armies in the world. In Greene, Washington found a loyal subordinate who at once exuded confidence in the commanding general and shared his convictions about the sort of soldiers and institutions required to win the war. Neither man suffered illusions about the supposed superiority of the American citizen at arms. In nearly identical language, each averred that militiamen, "coming from home with all the tender feelings of domestic life," were incapable of confronting the ardor and horror of combat.[13] Their mutual solution to the problem—long-term enlistments of men subjected to the training and discipline of regular troops—required much more than personal convictions. On the basis of his experience defending the Virginia frontier during the French and Indian War, Washington realized that building the sort of army that he envisioned would require the solicitude of Congress, which he worked diligently throughout the war to foster. Here, too, Greene followed his master's lead, maintaining parallel communications with purported allies in Congress and lobbying on behalf of his commander.[14]

Over the course of 1775 and 1776, Greene rose in Washington's esteem and became, along with artillery chief Henry Knox, one of the commander in chief's most-trusted subordinates. The bonds between these men were strengthened in no small way by their spouses. Throughout the war, the wives of senior American officers joined their husbands when the army settled into winter quarters. Among the most regular visitors were Martha Washington, Lucy Knox, and Catherine Greene.[15] It did not take long for the pretty, vivacious "Caty" to endear herself to the Washingtons—and to most of the men who made her acquaintance. Indeed, rumors of infidelity followed Caty (who was more than twelve years younger than her husband) for much of the war, but she nevertheless proved a most welcome addition to Washington's camp family, in which the Greenes enjoyed a special station.

Yet Caty's charm would have mattered little had Nathanael not established himself as one of the most competent and reliable officers at Washington's disposal. Despite his lack of combat experience, Greene's shrewd judgment and organizational abilities earned Washington's trust. Following the British evacuation of Boston, Washington briefly designated Greene the military commander of that city, before rushing him off to New York to take responsibility for the crucial (yet doomed) defense of Long Island. According to Washington's biographer Douglas Southall Freeman, "Greene had developed more in Washington's fourteen months of command than had almost any other subordinate officer. He was of all of them the man who probably could get the utmost in wholehearted defence from the troops allotted him."[16] A surprising selection for brigadier general the previous year, by the summer of 1776 Greene appeared favorably positioned to win a promotion to major general in an expanding army. He left nothing to chance, however, and sent a supplicating letter to Washington, pleading for "your Excellency[']s protection."[17] Greene had less reason to worry about his promotion than about his health. Six days after John Hancock signed his commission as a major general, Greene informed Washington that he was "confined to . . . Bed with a raging Fever."[18] As a consequence, he missed the Battle of Long Island, which went badly for his successor, Israel Putnam. It is unlikely that Greene would have fared much better, and his illness probably preserved a reputation and influence that—despite Greene's inexperience—continued to grow.

Washington's aide, Tench Tilghman, referred to Greene as "a first-rate military genius, and one in whose opinions the General places the utmost confidence." His correspondent agreed: "I am much mistaken if he is not possest of the Heaven born Genius which is necessary to constitute a great General."[19] Washington thought so as well, and as soon as Greene recovered, he assumed command of New Jersey's defenses—a crucial responsibility that entailed the protection of Philadelphia from landward attack. Greene also exerted a powerful influence in Washington's councils of war, albeit not to the extent that he could overrule the majority. This much was clear in early September, when Washington weighed his options for defending Manhattan. Greene was perhaps the most outspoken advocate of abandoning (and, indeed, burning) New York City. "Tis our business to study to avoid any considerable misfortune," Greene advised, "and to take post where the Enemy will be obliged to fight us and not we them."[20] Privately, Washington agreed with Greene, but he bent to the majority opinion of his senior officers and what he perceived to be the wishes of Congress.[21] Dividing his forces between the northern and southern ends of Manhattan, Washington invited disaster, which nearly came on September 15 when the British landed 4,000 men at Kips Bay and nearly cut the island in two. Chastened, Washington would think twice before again discounting Greene's advice. By mid-October, Washington had, at Greene's urging, abandoned all of Manhattan save Fort Washington.[22] As a consequence, Greene assumed responsibility for the post that might have ended his military career.

As already addressed, Washington seriously questioned the tenability of this post—particularly as it had failed to perform the function for which it was designed.[23] But every officer with a hand in building or defending the fort was adamant that it could withstand a British assault. None of these was more influential than Greene, who considered Fort Washington as an ideal place to replicate the Americans' earlier success at the Battle of Bunker Hill. Washington gave his subordinate the discretion to use his judgment, but was nevertheless alarmed to discover that Greene had reinforced rather than withdrawn Fort Washington's garrison. As Washington later confessed, he struggled to reconcile his own instincts with Greene's decision.[24] According to Washington's aide, Joseph Reed, the commander in chief "hesitated more than I ever knew him on any other occasion."[25] Critics subsequently pointed to this episode as evidence of indecisiveness on Washington's part, but it revealed more about his tremendous regard for Greene. On this singular occasion, the apprentice betrayed his master's trust.[26]

Yet the master remained loyal. Although Washington made clear in his report to Congress that the decision to reinforce Fort Washington belonged to Greene, his tone was sympathetic, and he afterward refused to blame Greene for the disaster. As he explained to Joseph Reed nearly three years later, "I shall never attempt to paliate my own faults by exposing those of another." Only then, and in the confidence of a mutual friend, did Washington place the blame at Greene's feet.[27] This was no news to Reed, who—although close to Greene—shared the view of many officers that Washington was too much under the influence of a precocious, yet inexperienced, advisor. The harshest criticism came, not surprisingly, from Charles Lee, who accused Greene of partiality toward "his connections and townsmen, to the prejudice of men of manifestly superiour merit."[28] But Washington could see through Lee's lectures and recognize them for what they really were: thinly veiled assaults on Washington himself. Lee, who was never short on patronizing advice, resented not so much that Greene had the commanding general's ear, but that this ear was not attached to Lee's head. In the wake of the Fort Washington debacle, Greene endured his fair share of criticism, but he also absorbed slings and arrows aimed a bit higher. It would not be the last time that Greene rendered Washington such service.

But in the winter of 1776–77—the very "times that try men's souls" immortalized by Thomas Paine—Washington needed more than a stalking horse, and he could ill afford to dispense with Greene's services on the basis of a single mistake (however large it was). After all, Washington's seminal military experiences in the Ohio Country were hardly worthy of celebration, yet indispensible to his subsequent maturation as a military officer.[29] Presumably, Greene also would learn from his error. But more to the point, Greene remained one of the most talented and loyal officers of Washington's command. Much to the younger man's relief, Washington stood by Greene, assigning him critical roles at Trenton and Princeton while retaining his services as aide. "I am exceeding happy in the full confidence of his Excellency General Washington," Greene wrote Caty in late January 1777, "and I found [that confidence] to increase every hour, the more [difficult] and distressing our affairs grew."[30] According to one of Greene's recent biographers, "His regard for Washington bordered on worshipful . . . [and] he seemed like a schoolboy proud to have won the approval of his teacher."[31] His full restoration to Washington's confidence became clearer yet in March, when Washington sent Greene to Philadelphia to communicate concerns about the state of the army to Congress. Providing Greene little guidance, Washington explained to Congress that "this Gentleman is so much in my confidence—so intimately acquainted with my ideas—with our strength, and our weaknesses—with everything respecting the Army, that I have thought it unnecessary to particularize or prescribe any certain line of duty or enquiries for him."[32]

Washington could depend on Greene to reflect the commander's views on issues of administration and politics because they were virtually of the same mind on such matters. But in terms of strategy, Washington was, in truth, as much of a neophyte as Greene, and he relied increasingly on the younger man's advice as the war progressed. Already Greene had displayed an independence of thought that made him invaluable to Washington. Whereas Washington had spent his younger years emulating the British army and trying to cast his Virginia provincials in the mold of a proper European force, Greene had spent several years reading military theory as a dilettante, and less than two years adapting this theoretical knowledge to practice. Greene looked up to Washington as the proper model of a general officer, and he shared most of his hero's convictions regarding military policy and administration. And yet, while neither man surrendered the ideal of a well-trained force of regulars, Greene did a better job of reconciling this ideal to the realities of circumstance. While Washington depended on the militia for reinforcements and to conduct local defense, he sought symmetrical contests throughout the war—looking for propitious moments to launch offensive operations with like organizations employing similar tactics.[33] Although less experienced than Washington, Greene needed only the harsh lesson of Fort Washington to realize that the Revolutionary War was not a contest between peers. Perhaps more deserving of the label "Fabian" than his commander,

Greene recognized that winning the war would require more than picking the right spots for a "brilliant stroke"; it demanded mastery of the sort of irregular war that Washington wished to overcome.[34]

Between common characterizations of Washington as either a Fabian practitioner of protracted war or a thoroughly conventional product of an era of "limited warfare," it is easy to overlook Washington's commitment to offensive action.[35] Meanwhile, some biographers have imparted to Greene an audacious or even imprudent streak without reconciling it with his remarkable operational patience. Rather than risk battle under unfavorable conditions, he displayed a willingness to suffer public scorn. While Washington always looked for opportunities to go on the attack, Greene persistently urged caution. But these were hardly virtues in the eyes of untutored congressmen or designing army officers, whom Washington accused of desiring to make names for themselves whatever the consequences.[36] In April 1777, while William Howe's British army loitered menacingly about Brunswick, New Jersey, Washington asked Greene to devise a plan of attack. Greene did so, but placed its prospects for success at no better than even, and he voted against it once it was submitted to a council of war.[37] Even the most casual of observers could not fail to notice the extent to which Washington depended upon Greene's advice. For the jealous, it seemed as though Greene exerted an excessive, restraining influence on his commander.

Nevertheless, Greene basked in his role as Washington's courtier. After returning from a special mission in the Hudson Highlands (in which Washington had charged Greene with reviewing and altering the region's fortifications as he saw fit), Greene wrote his wife Caty to convey his regrets that he would not be coming home to Rhode Island. "The General keeps me constantly upon the go," he explained with as much pleasure as grief. "The love and friendship he has for me and the respect and kindness he shows me goes a great way to alleviate my pains." Dutifully, he added, "I am as well [loved] and respected in the Army as I can wish; but notwithstanding the honnors of War and the love and respect of [men] I feel a blank in my Heart which nothing but your presence can fill up."[38] Whether Greene's reputation within the army was so favorable is uncertain, but it would not endure the balance of the year.

On July 8, 1777, British forces in New Jersey boarded ships and invited nearly two months of conjecture about their destination. The most likely candidates were Philadelphia or the Hudson Highlands, where Howe's main British force could support General John Burgoyne's ongoing invasion from

Canada. Uncertainty prevented Washington from taking positive measures to prepare for either event, but in Greene's eyes this was not entirely unfortunate. He had learned a sharp lesson in positional warfare at Fort Washington, and he came to view fixed fortifications as more "prejudicial, than useful" to the patriot cause. Although he realized that preserving the loyalty of the citizenry sometimes required the defense of fixed positions, he also grasped that siege warfare played to the asymmetric strengths of their powerful foes. Rather than securing terrain, American forts provided the British lush prizes waiting to be picked.[39]

Washington generally concurred. On August 25, William Howe finally showed his hand by landing forces at the head of the Chesapeake Bay, with the obvious intent of marching against Philadelphia. Washington was obligated to defend the city, but he chose to do so by opportunistic attacks along the enemy's route of march. Unfortunately, the Americans were no more capable of waging mobile warfare than they were of holding fixed fortifications, and in the span of two weeks Howe dealt them a pair of embarrassing defeats, at Brandywine and Paoli, before marching into Philadelphia on September 26, 1777. On October 4, Washington tried to reprise his success at Trenton by attacking Howe's main camp at Germantown—only to watch his complex plan disintegrate in an ominous fog that blanketed the battlefield.

Neither Washington nor his men regarded the Battle of Germantown as a defeat, but it certainly paled in comparison to Horatio Gates's almost simultaneous victory over Burgoyne at Saratoga. Although his army's morale remained relatively high, its lackluster performance in September and early October 1777 emboldened Washington's critics.[40] As Washington's troops marched off to winter quarters at Valley Forge, congressmen such as John Adams and James Lovell wondered aloud whether they had entrusted the Continental Army to the right commander. Yet they had to proceed with caution. His reverses notwithstanding, Washington remained a veritable icon of the Revolution itself, and to criticize him directly suggested irreverence bordering on blasphemy. But the general's disciples—Knox and Greene in particular—were another matter. Already the notion that Washington relied excessively on the counsel of a few had wide currency, even among some of his most steadfast supporters.[41] Moreover, it was common knowledge that Washington took most of his advice from the man rumored to be the commanding general's chosen successor.[42] With so much influence and yet so little experience, Greene became the obvious proxy through which Washington's enemies launched their attacks. Already, the loss of Fort Washington stained Greene's escutcheon, and now some blamed him for the loss of Philadelphia and the lost opportunity at Germantown. The claims were almost entirely without merit; Greene had saved the Continental Army from calamity at the Battle of Brandywine, and if his performance at Germantown was unexceptional, neither was it worthy of censure. Nevertheless, Greene's critics charged him with governing Washington's conduct and dampening "the spirit of enterprise."[43] Dr. Benjamin Rush went further still, describing Greene as "a sycophant to the general, timid, speculative, [and] without enterprise."[44]

This interpretation almost certainly originated with Thomas Mifflin, a former aide to Washington and, until his resignation in October 1778, quartermaster general of the army. Although a fellow apostate Quaker, Mifflin had never cared for Greene, considering him as an unwise and dangerous influence on Washington. In truth, Mifflin probably resented that Washington placed so much stock in Greene while failing to show Mifflin the deference he thought he deserved. A native Philadelphian, he also accused the Rhode Islander of indifference regarding the fate of the capital and of influencing Washington in a manner that contributed to its loss.[45] Throughout, Mifflin professed loyalty to Washington himself, but the commanding general's political foes found in the Mifflin-Greene feud the space that they needed to undermine Washington's support in Congress. Writing to Gates, a veteran of the British army who some favored over Washington, Congressman James Lovell reported gleefully that "by the Winter the middle Army will be divided into Greenites and Mifflineans, if Things do not take a great Turn from their present Situation."[46] Most historians from Bernard Knollenberg forward have concluded that the movement to replace Washington with Gates enjoyed precious little support, and that Gates himself was not party to any such scheme.[47] But this realization in hindsight meant little to Washington or Greene during that trying winter at Valley Forge. Congress certainly did not appear to be extending Washington a vote of confidence when it resurrected a board of war to provide external oversight of his conduct. Particularly troubling were the appointments of none other than Gates, Mifflin, and the infamous Thomas Conway as the board's president, secretary, and inspector general, respectively.

Having preferred the role of intriguer to that of logistician, Mifflin left Washington to serve as his own quartermaster until March 1778, when he reluctantly shifted this thankless yet crucial burden to Greene.[48] The department Greene inherited was in absolute disarray—its horses, wagons, and teamsters far flung and its purchasing agents lacking the power or currency to procure supplies. Although these challenges played to Greene's strengths as an organizational leader and represented something of a poetic triumph over his nemesis Mifflin, the new quartermaster did not relish the assignment. Just before accepting the post, he complained to Knox that "His Excellency . . . presses it upon me exceedingly," and he subsequently reminded Washington that "I engag'd in this business as well out of compas[s]ion to your Excellency as from a regard to the public."[49] Greene's principal objection to the job was that it removed him from "the Line of splendor," but it also subjected the hypersensitive general to increased public scrutiny. Nevertheless, Greene threw himself fully into the task of reforming a quartermaster department reeling from Mifflin's neglect and Congress's suspicion of concentrated power. The plot to supplant Washington with Gates (if it may be called such) melted with the snow at Valley Forge, but the disaffected Mifflin fired a parting shot by insinuating that Greene had accepted the post of quartermaster general to remove himself from the dangers of the battlefield.[50] Greene proved otherwise at the Battle of Monmouth Court House in June, but he recognized the true basis of Mifflin's invective. "The partiallity that His Excellency General Washington has always shewn to my advice when supported with the strongest reasons," Greene apprised his cousin, "has created me a great many jealous friends and some deadly enemies."[51] So long as Greene enjoyed a privileged station in Washington's heart and headquarters, he could endure such assaults on his character.

But while Washington was liberal in his esteem for Greene, he was parsimonious when it came to praise. He had more pressing matters to attend, but his neglect for Greene's feelings reached a head in late July 1778 as the army approached its summer camp near White Plains, New York. When Washington, who had urgent business for Greene but had seen no one from the quartermaster department for several days, complained of neglect, the younger officer could bear no more. "Your Excellency has made me very unhappy," he opened a pettish letter to his commander and hero. He went on to vent a year's worth of pent-up frustrations. Could Washington not appreciate that all of Greene's exertions and sacrifices had been made for his commander's reputation rather than his own? All Greene sought in return was Washington's approbation. Was this too much to ask? In particular, Greene wished to know why he had been deprived of praise following the Battle of Brandywine. And surely Washington knew that only his affection could have induced Greene to assume the thankless chores of quartermaster general. "Your influence brought me in," he stated plainly, "and the want of your approbation will induce me to go out."[52]

For an officer of the Revolutionary era to threaten resignation over injured pride was hardly novel. As a younger man, Washington had done the same, and only the previous summer, several of his major generals—including Greene—occasioned a minor crisis in civil-military relations when they impertinently protested the contemplated promotion of a French officer to their disadvantage. Disgusted by such displays, John Adams complained that army officers "worry one another like mastiffs, scrambling for rank and pay like apes for nuts."[53] Washington, too, found this tendency among his subordinates "truly alarming," but he could at least sympathize with their eighteenth-century notions of military honor.[54]

But more than honor was at stake in Greene's case, and Washington knew it. As a younger man, Greene had never shared his father's notions of achievement and seemed almost indifferent to his father's approval. From the moment Greene met Washington in 1775, however, the eager apprentice sought not only his master's approval, but also his affection. Only ten years separated the two, but at the time of their meeting Greene was in some sense thirty-three going on thirteen. Those who derided Greene as a sycophant missed the fact that he genuinely looked up to Washington as a father figure.[55] Their relationship over the ensuing three years was so intimate that Washington must have realized this, but by nature and habit he exuded the aloofness and stoicism of a Roman senator. It was quite possibly beyond Washington to provide what Greene wanted, and Washington's written response was characteristically reserved. While assuring Greene that his affection, loyalty, and esteem were secure, he also acknowledged a reluctance to praise Greene publicly—albeit without written explanation.[56] According to Greene's grandson-biographer, Washington verbally assured Greene that "You, sir, are considered my favorite officer," and explained that he had to be wary of charges of favoritism.[57] While no surviving correspondence substantiates the statement, the circumstances do. Shortly after receiving Washington's letter (and, presumably, this verbal assurance), Greene's spirits recovered considerably. Afterward, he confided to a friend that Washington withheld praise because "I was thought to be one of his favorites."[58] For his part, Washington soon afterward wrote a letter to Congress in which he lauded Greene's "judicious management and active exertions" as quartermaster.[59] Overdue and insufficient, it was all of the public praise that Washington was willing to offer, and it had to suffice. Subsequently, Greene resigned himself to the fact that his hero valued "the public weal" over "private friendship."[60]

But private regard for Washington was the only thing binding Greene to the quartermaster department, where he served for twenty-eight months. Holding such a demanding job for so long would have strained the endurance of most men, and Greene's task was made more demanding by Washington's dependency. Washington had hesitated to recommend Greene for the post for fear of losing his most-trusted advisor and one of his ablest fighting generals. When opportunities arose (as at Monmouth, Newport, and Springfield), Washington permitted Greene to rejoin the "line of splendor," but he dared not make a habit of it for fear of exciting the jealousies of other officers. When it came to accepting Greene's counsel, however, Washington showed no reservations. By the autumn of 1778, Washington finally stopped convening councils of war and instead relied exclusively on the guidance of his most-trusted confidants—Lafayette, Knox, and Greene—the very band of "dirty earwigs" that Lee railed against when court-martialed for disrespecting Washington during the Battle of Monmouth Court House.[61] By the fall of 1778, Washington had silenced his most powerful critics and vanquished his most powerful foes within the army. All of them had cited his excessive reliance on Greene's judgment to press their claims, ultimately to no avail. Ironically, Washington *did* rely on Greene's counsel to the extent that their enemies alleged. But the quality of Greene's advice was far superior than any of them had supposed or admitted, and it had helped Washington to navigate the most treacherous years of the Revolution. Had Washington responded directly to Lee's insolent question after the fall of Fort Washington—"Oh, General, why would you be over-persuaded by men of inferiour judgment to your own?"—the commanding general might simply have challenged the assumption on which it was based. Far from inferior, Greene's judgment was, even at that early juncture, as sound as Washington's, and it steadily improved as the war progressed.

Indeed, from the summer of 1778 forward, Greene revealed himself to be far more than Washington's pet. As he settled into his duties as quartermaster general, Greene passed from apprentice to journeyman. He still attracted a fair amount of criticism, but it dealt with his independent actions as quartermaster rather than his influence over Washington. Realizing that Congress would have to be part of any solution to the army's overwhelming logistical problems, Greene cultivated a collaborative relationship with that body's "committee at camp" and lobbied for increased congressional prerogative to provide for the common defense. Although his proposals were sound, some in Congress resented his intrusion into affairs properly belonging to civilian officials. But most of the criticism Greene endured centered on the fact that he and his purchasing agents earned commissions off of their many public transactions. Greene never denied that the job flattered his personal finances, but these were far less important to him than his public reputation and honor. And as he ruefully explained to the man who recommended him for the job, "No body ever heard of a quarter Master in History as such or in relateing to any brilliant Action."[62]

Within a year of assuming his duties, Greene grew disillusioned with the Continental Congress's impotence and considered resigning the post of quartermaster. He stayed on only out of loyalty to Washington, who sympathized with Greene and made no effort to sway his mind on the matter. To the contrary, Washington assured Greene that, were Congress to ask, he would recommend Greene to succeed Benjamin Lincoln as the commander of the Southern Army.[63] But Congress did not ask, bequeathing that post to the suspected intriguer Horatio Gates and threatening to cashier Greene for his contemptuous attitude toward the legislature. With uncharacteristic bluntness, Washington leapt to his apprentice's defense, but Congress's ire against the quartermaster had largely blown over by the time his letter arrived.[64] Moreover, any lingering suspicion that Gates was Washington's better disintegrated with the Southern Army's left flank at the Battle of Camden. With Gates's reputation no less savaged than his army, Congress finally permitted Washington to designate a successor.

No one was surprised when, in October 1780, he selected Greene for this vital command. When informing Greene of his appointment, Washington offered "no particular instructions," instead leaving his former apprentice "to govern yourself intirely."[65] Although Washington asked that Greene keep him apprised of affairs in the South, the state of communications essentially rendered Greene's new post an independent command. The beneficiary of invaluable experience and a relatively distant theater of war, Greene conducted operations as he saw fit, with more autonomy than Washington had ever enjoyed around New York or Philadelphia. Dependent upon local militia for manpower and facing desperate circumstances, Greene waged an effective partisan war against the British and became, in the words of Don Higginbotham, "the only American army commander who deliberately assumed the part of a guerrilla."[66] Like other successful practitioners of this brand of warfare, Greene scarcely ever won a tactical engagement. Yet he drove Cornwallis out of the Carolinas and then reduced the British army's hold on the South one post at a time until, in December 1782, the British at last evacuated Charleston.

Whether the more conventional Washington would have been capable of such a feat is uncertain. Nor is it warranted to claim that Greene learned all he knew from his commander in chief. Indeed, Washington was arguably better at identifying talent than he was at developing it—but his importance to Greene's career is difficult to overstate. Greene's meteoric rise from a militia private to the operational commander of the war's most active theater in the span of six years was the product of Greene's natural talent and ambition, invaluable experience gained in the North, and—crucially—the patronage of George Washington. Eulogizing Greene after his untimely death in 1786, Alexander Hamilton traced Greene's ascendance to his early days in camp outside Boston, where "the discerning eye of the American Fabius marked him out as the object of his confidence. . . . His abilities entitled him to a preeminent share in the councils of his chief. He gained it, and he preserved it amidst all the *checkered varieties* of military vicissitude, and in defiance of all the intrigues of jealous and aspiring rivals."[67] In the end, the Rhode Island anchorsmith was much more than his mentor's protégé. Nathanael Greene had become his own master.

Notes

1. *The Papers of General Nathanael Greene,* ed. Richard K. Showman et al., 13 vols. to date (Chapel Hill, N.C., 1976–), 1:354n.

2. Charles Lee to GW, 19 November 1776, in *Collections of the New-York Historical Society for the Years 1871–74: The Lee Papers,* 4 vols. (New York, 1872–75), 2:288 [hereafter cited as *Lee Papers*].

3. *Lee Papers,* 4:309. John Ferling has argued that Washington's insecurity caused him to surround himself with sycophants, but the argument does not do credit to men who proved of inestimable value to the Continental Army (see John E. Ferling, "George Wash-

ington and the American Victory," in *The World Turned Upside Down: The American Victory in the War of Independence,* ed. John E. Ferling [New York, 1988], 64–67).

4. GW to John Augustine Washington, 6[–19] November 1776, *PGW: Rev. Ser.,* 7:103.

5. Quoted in Theodore Thayer, *Nathanael Greene: Strategist of the American Revolution* (New York, 1960), 67.

6. *PGW: Rev. Ser.,* 1:336.

7. Greene to Samuel Ward Sr., 14 July 1775, *Papers of General Nathanael Greene,* 1:99.

8. Terry Golway, *Washington's General: Nathanael Greene and the Triumph of the American Revolution* (New York, 2006), 58; Spencer Tucker, *Rise and Fight Again: The Life of Nathanael Greene* (Wilmington, Del., 2009), 28.

9. Edward G. Lengel, *General George Washington: A Military Life* (New York, 2005), 14–18.

10. Greene to Samuel Ward Jr., 9 October 1772, *Papers of General Nathanael Greene,* 1:48.

11. Quoted in ibid., 69n.

12. Thayer, *Nathanael Greene,* 24, 40.

13. Greene to Jacob Greene[?], 28 September 1776, *Papers of General Nathanael Greene,* 1:303. Cf. Washington's reference to "men just dragged from the tender Scenes of domestick life" (GW to John Hancock, 25 September 1776, *PGW: Rev. Ser.,* 6:396).

14. Greene corresponded principally with Massachusetts's Samuel Ward Sr. (until he died of smallpox) and John Adams (until a falling-out over the potential promotion of the Frenchman de Coudray to a senior major generalcy).

15. Holly A. Mayer, *Belonging to the Army: Camp Followers and Community during the American Revolution* (Columbia, S.C., 1996).

16. Freeman, 4:152.

17. Greene to GW, 21 May 1776, *Papers of General Nathanael Greene,* 1:216–17.

18. Greene to GW, 15 August 1776, ibid., 1:288.

19. Quoted in Thayer, *Nathanael Greene,* 112.

20. Greene to GW, 5 September 1776, *Papers of General Nathanael Greene,* 1:294–95.

21. GW to Hancock, 8 September 1776, *PGW: Rev. Ser.,* 6:248–54.

22. Greene further recommended burning New York City to the ground. Washington concurred, but Congress did not (see Greene to GW, 5 September 1776, *Papers of General Nathanael Greene,* 1:295).

23. GW to Greene, 8 November 1776, ibid., 1:342–43.

24. GW to Joseph Reed, 22 August 1779, in Fitzpatrick, 16:151–52.

25. Joseph Reed, *Life and Correspondence of Joseph Reed: Military Secretary of Washington, at Cambridge, Adjutant-General of the Continental Army, Member of the Congress of the United States, and President of the Executive Council of the State of Pennsylvania,* ed. William B. Reed, 2 vols. (Philadelphia, 1847), 1:262.

26. GW to Hancock, 16 November 1776, *PGW: Rev. Ser.,* 7:162–65.

27. GW to Reed, 22 August 1779, Fitzpatrick, 16:151–52. According to Bernard Knollenberg, Washington's reluctance to expose others diminished with age. Responding to a letter from Rev. William Gordon in 1785, Washington blamed Congress's restrictive guidance and Greene's decision to reinforce Fort Washington. In this telling, Congress and Greene had tied Washington's hands. But as Knollenberg argues, Congress's guidance was not

binding and Washington still had time to evacuate Fort Washington (see Bernhard Knollenberg, *Washington and the Revolution, a Reappraisal: Gates, Conway, and the Continental Congress* [New York, 1941], 129–39).

28. Lee represented these accusations as the views of his officers and "unbiased persons," but he clearly shared their sentiments (see Lee to GW, 19 November 1776, *Lee Papers,* 2:287).

29. See, especially, John E. Ferling, "School for Command: Young George Washington and the Virginia Regiment," in *George Washington and the Virginia Backcountry,* ed. Warren R. Hofstra (Madison, Wis., 1998).

30. Greene to Catherine Greene, 20 January 1777, *Papers of General Nathanael Greene,* 2:7.

31. Golway, *Washington's General,* 118.

32. GW to Hancock, 18 March 1777, *PGW: Rev. Ser.,* 8:597.

33. For Washington's use of the militia, see Mark V. Kwasny, *Washington's Partisan War, 1775–1783* (Kent, Ohio, 1996).

34. GW to Hancock, 8 September 1776, *PGW: Rev. Ser.,* 6:251. For comparisons of Washington and Greene in this regard, see Russell F. Weigley, *The American Way of War: A History of United States Military Strategy and Policy* (1973; repr., Bloomington, Ind., 1977), 36; and John Morgan Dederer, *Making Bricks without Straw: Nathanael Greene's Southern Campaign and Mao Tse-Tung's Mobile War* (Manhattan, Kan., 1983), 12–17.

35. Edward Lengel, in particular, has challenged the widely held view that Washington was a Fabian at heart (see Lengel, *General George Washington,* 149–50). Russell Weigley has written that Greene was more willing to assume the offensive than Washington, but this argument overlooks Greene's persistently cautious counsel while working closely with Washington and the unique circumstances of the southern theater. Greene urged offensive action when he believed that the balance of forces was favorable (as at Monmouth), but he and Washington were of a very similar mind in this regard. Once Greene assumed command of the Southern Department, he used the geography and the clever dispersal of his forces to create favorable conditions for the offensive. If it is unlikely that Washington would have integrated militia and regular units as peers (as Greene did), it must also be admitted that neither Washington nor Greene considered it appropriate to wage a "partisan war" in the North, where the Americans needed to maintain a massed Continental Army as both a psychological center of gravity for the patriot cause and to maintain the ability to strike a decisive blow against the main British force.

36. Both men maintained an active correspondence with Congress, and they wrote in perfect consonance about the administrative and logistical woes of the army as well as the appropriateness of their "Fabian" strategy (see Greene to John Adams, 3 March 1777, *Papers of General Nathanael Greene,* 2:28–29; and GW to Joseph Reed, 23 June 1777, quoted in Freeman, 4:435–36).

37. Greene to GW, April 1777, and Proceedings of Council of General Officers, 2 May 1777, *Papers of General Nathanael Greene,* 2:61–64.

38. Greene to Catherine Greene, 20 May 1777, ibid., 2:85.

39. Maj. Gen. Greene's Opinion, ca. 7 August 1777, *PGW: Rev. Ser.,* 10:528.

40. *Papers of General Nathanael Greene,* 2:176–77n.

41. Perhaps Washington's most ardent congressional champion, Henry Laurens con-

fided to his son that Washington paid too much heed to "the opinion of some who have no superior claim." Incongruously, Anthony Wayne supported both Washington and his friend Greene, yet wrote to Horatio Gates, "I don't yet despair . . . if our worthy general will but follow his own good judgment without listening too much to some counsel" (quoted in Thomas J. Fleming, *Washington's Secret War: The Hidden History of Valley Forge* [New York, 2005], 102).

42. Major John Clark Jr. to Greene, 10 January 1778, *Papers of General Nathanael Greene,* 2:250; George Washington Greene, *The Life of Nathanael Greene, Major-General in the Army of the Revolution,* 3 vols. (1867–71; repr., Freeport, N.Y., 1972), 2:32–33.

43. Greene to Alexander McDougall, 25 January 1778, *Papers of General Nathanael Greene,* 2:260.

44. Quoted in ibid., 2:230n.

45. Kenneth R. Rossman, *Thomas Mifflin and the Politics of the American Revolution* (Chapel Hill, N.C., 1952), 96–98.

46. Lovell to Gates, 5 October 1777, quoted in ibid., 98.

47. Knollenberg, *Washington and the Revolution,* 73–77; Don Higginbotham, *The War of American Independence: Military Attitudes, Policies, and Practice, 1763–1789* (New York, 1971), 218–21; John E. Ferling, *The Ascent of George Washington: The Hidden Political Genius of an American Icon* (New York, 2009), 157.

48. Recently, Thomas Fleming has suggested that Greene had been Washington's first choice for quartermaster from the beginning, but Dennis Showman argues convincingly that Washington was reluctant to remove his most-trusted field commander from the line (see Fleming, *Washington's Secret War,* 197–98; and *Papers of General Nathanael Greene,* 2:310n).

49. Greene to Henry Knox, 26 February 1778, *Papers of General Nathanael Greene,* 2:294; Greene to GW, 24 April 1779, ibid., 3:427.

50. George Lux to Greene, 26 May 1778, ibid., 2:410.

51. Greene to Griffin Greene, 25 May 1778, ibid., 2:405.

52. Greene to GW, 21 July 1778, ibid., 2:461–63.

53. John Adams to Abigail Adams, 22 May 1777, in Abigail Adams and John Adams, *Familiar Letters of John Adams and His Wife Abigail Adams, during the Revolution,* ed. Charles Francis Adams (New York, 1876), 276.

54. Washington to Major Isaac Beall, 31 March 1778, *PGW: Rev. Ser.,* 14:363.

55. Golway, *Washington's General,* 58.

56. GW to Greene, 21 July 1778, *Papers of General Nathanael Greene,* 2:464.

57. Greene, *Life of Nathanael Greene,* 1:457. The author acknowledges the exchange as anecdotal and places it immediately following the Battle of Brandywine. Based upon extant correspondence, it seems more likely that Washington offered such an explanation as a complement to his letter of July 21, 1778. Washington's desire to avoid charges of favoritism was much older. Commanding Virginia's forces in the Seven Years' War in 1756, Washington pledged that "partiality shall never bias my conduct, nor shall prejudice injure any" (Orders, 8 January 1756, *PGW: Col. Ser.,* 2:257).

58. Greene to Henry Marchant, 25[?] July 1778, *Papers of General Nathanael Greene,* 2:471.

59. Ibid., 2:464n; GW to Henry Laurens, 3[–4] August 1778, *PGW: Rev. Ser.*, 16:238.

60. Greene to Samuel H. Parsons, 11 April 1779, *Papers of General Nathanael Greene,* 3:395.

61. Lee, *Lee Papers,* 4:309.

62. Greene to GW, 24 April 1779, *Papers of General Nathanael Greene,* 3:427.

63. GW to Greene, 24 April 1779, ibid., 3:429.

64. James Thomas Flexner, *George Washington,* 4 vols. (New York, 1965–72), 2:368; GW to Joseph Jones, 13 August 1780, Fitzpatrick, 19:355–68.

65. GW to Greene, 22 October 1780, Fitzpatrick, 20:238–40.

66. Don Higginbotham, "Reflections on the War of Independence, Modern Guerrilla Warfare, and the War in Vietnam," in *Arms and Independence: The Military Character of the American Revolution,* ed. Ronald Hoffman and Peter J. Albert (Charlottesville, Va., 1984), 23.

67. Quoted in Greene, *Life of Nathanael Greene,* 2:417.

Gouverneur Morris and George Washington

Prodigal Son and Patient Father

MARY-JO KLINE

WHAT UNLIKELY CANDIDATES FOR FRIENDSHIP: GEORGE WASHington, the model of a Virginia gentleman, famed in his time and ours for faultless rectitude and reserved behavior, and Gouverneur Morris, a cosmopolitan New Yorker twenty years Washington's junior, an irrepressible jokester with a reputation that led Richard Brookhiser, one of his most recent biographers, to subtitle his study *The Rake Who Wrote the Constitution.*[1]

The unlikely nature of that friendship accounts for the persistence of one of the best-known (although thoroughly discredited) apocryphal stories of the early republic. The story gained credence when Max Farrand included it in an appendix of "Anecdotes" in the last volume of his *Records of the Federal Convention of 1787:*

> When the Convention to form a Constitution was sitting in Philadelphia in 1787, of which General Washington was president, he had stated evenings to receive the calls of his friends. At an interview between Hamilton, the Morrises and others, the former remarked that Washington was reserved and aristocratic even to his intimate friends, and allowed no one to be familiar with him. Gouverneur *Morris* said that was a mere fancy, and he could be as familiar with Washington as with any of his other friends. Hamilton replied, "If you will, at the next reception evenings, gently slap him on the shoulder and say, 'My dear General, how happy I am to see you look so well!' a supper and wine shall be provided for you and a dozen of your friends." The challenge was accepted. On the evening appointed, a large number attended;

> and at an early hour Gouverneur *Morris* entered, bowed, shook hands, laid his left hand on Washington's shoulder, and said, "My dear General, I am very happy to see you look so well!" Washington withdrew his hand, stepped suddenly back, fixed his eye on Morris for several minutes with an angry frown, until the latter retreated abashed, and sought refuge in the crowd. The company looked on in silence. At the supper, which was provided by Hamilton, Morris said, "I have won the bet, but paid dearly for it, and nothing could induce me to repeat it."[2]

Farrand borrowed the story (without attribution) from an appendix to Martin Van Buren's posthumously published *Inquiry into the Origin and Course of the Political Parties in the United States,* where it appeared in an 1857 letter from a New York judge who had heard the story five years earlier in Cincinnati. There, the source was Jacob Burnet, a distinguished Ohio pioneer who claimed to have heard the account from Hamilton himself before young Burnet left Philadelphia nearly sixty years earlier.[3] Another version of the story, which placed the incident in Philadelphia during Washington's presidency (a period when Morris was on the other side of the Atlantic) appeared in W. T. Read's 1870 *Life and Correspondence of George Read.* The source for this retelling of the tale was ninety-year-old Susan Read Eckerd, who claimed to have heard it from her father at some time before his death a half century earlier.[4] A third version of the story has Morris slapping Baron von Steuben, not Washington.[5]

No biographer of Morris in the past six decades has given credence to the anecdote, of course, but it lingers on. Indeed, Richard Brookhiser shared the remarks of an unnamed "academic historian," who told him that "he loved the Washington/Morris/Hamilton version because it was so characteristic of all three men."[6] In truth, the story's persistence says a great deal about ourselves and our own misconceptions of the founders' personalities.

Perhaps nothing more effectively disproves some of those misconceptions than the bond between Morris and Washington. Despite apparent contrasts in attitude and temperament, they were true friends, and their friendship, like most such relationships, grew from the fact that they learned that their shared experiences and common values outweighed any differences.

Even their childhoods boasted marked similarities. Both were the sons of the second marriages of middle-aged widowers. Both lost their fathers at an early age and found themselves with heavy responsibilities in families that included hostile older children of their fathers' first marriages. The story of Washington's early years is well known, but it may be helpful to summarize the facts of Morris's youth. Born in 1752, he was the third child and only son born to "Judge" Lewis Morris, lord of the manor of Morrisania (then in Westchester, now part of the Bronx), and his second wife, Sarah Gouverneur. At the time of this second marriage, Lewis Morris had four adult children by his first wife, who was, not incidentally, his second wife's aunt. The older Morris children, three sons and a daughter, did not welcome their cousin as a stepmother.[7]

Gouverneur was only ten when his father died, a student at a boarding school in Philadelphia. Lewis Morris's will gave his widow a life interest in part of the manor of Morrisania, with instructions that she focus her attention on providing their son with the best education to be found in America. That life interest also guaranteed friction with the "first" children, who would have to wait decades to realize anything from this portion of their father's estate.

On graduation from King's College, when he was only sixteen, Morris was apprenticed in a legal office. At twenty, he was ready to face the world, but lamented, "I have somehow or other been so hurried through the different scenes of childhood and youth, that I have still some time left to pause before I tread the great stage of life."[8] He was dissuaded from his dream of spending a year in London and settled down to practicing law in Manhattan.

"Settled down" is not, perhaps, the most accurate description of his years as a young lawyer. He quickly earned a reputation for dissipation and riotous living. In 1772, when Morris complained of "melancholy," an older cousin in New Jersey commented that "I did not suspect you of it while there was Youth Beauty C[laret] Wine and Company to be had in New York."[9] His image as a scalawag and pursuer of the fair sex would follow Morris for the rest of his life, and his avowed disinterest in politics—the Morrises' "family failing" for three generations—did little to make family and friends take him seriously.[10] Inevitably, however, he succumbed to the passions of the anti-imperial ferment in New York. Throughout 1774, he was an interested observer and commentator. In the spring of 1775, he had no choice but to become a participant.

Many may have wondered which side he would take. His mother as well as two of his sisters and their husbands were recognized as pro-Crown. The anti-imperial wing of his family included his third sister and her husband, his uncles, and two of his three half brothers. In May 1775, only weeks after the engagement at Lexington, Morris won a seat in the extralegal first Provincial Congress.

It was in this capacity that he met George Washington and their remarkable friendship was born. Their first encounter, on June 25, was probably brief. Morris was a member of a congressional committee that journeyed to Newark to confer with Washington on the best approach for his troops to Manhattan. Washington found the committee's advice sound, and his meeting the next day with the Provincial Congress was a cordial one.[11] Washington and his army moved north, and the two apparently had no contact for another ten months.

The commander and the congressman probably had no time or inclination to pursue a personal acquaintance at the first meeting. Still, they must have recognized one significant trait they shared: both were tall men, well over six feet, near giants in a day when most of their civilian and military colleagues were no taller than five feet eight inches. Both also were well built, muscular outdoorsmen. Indeed, the similarity in their physiques was so strong that the sculptor Houdon persuaded Morris to sit as his model for Washington's torso when he completed his famed statue of the bare-chested first president nearly fifteen years later.[12]

A letter from Morris to Washington in late April 1776 hints that they had already established some degree of cordiality. Morris writes with obvious reluctance on behalf of John Tudor, the owner of Montressor's Island, which Washington had identified as the site for an army hospital.[13] In their next meetings, they would have time to discover more in common than their height. On May 19, the New York Provincial Congress named Morris to the committee that would act as liaison with Washington as he prepared Manhattan's defenses. The two worked together closely through the summer, with Morris riding back and forth from the army's headquarters to the Congress, shuttling reports of Tory plots and forwarding Washington's desperate requests for help.

In those same weeks, the Provincial Congress debated action on independence. Now Morris revealed another bond that linked him with Washington—a passionate, romantic, nationalist fervor. In Morris's draft of an "Oration on the necessity of declaring Independence," he envisioned a new nation that would not only support a "flourishing Economy" and an "increase in population," but also offer "an asylum from Oppression for all nations," a "great Garden" for all mankind.[14] Washington indulged in no such high-flown sentiments at the time, but his own life was testimony to his nationalism. As one scholar observes, "He seems to have seen himself as an American from the moment of his appointment as Continental Commander in 1775, if not before."[15]

The British advance forced Morris and Washington to part at the close of the summer. Washington led his retreating army across the Hudson to New Jersey. With New York City now in British hands, Morris and other members of the new government of the "state" of New York fled up the Hudson, finally settling in Kingston, where a state constitution was adopted in the summer of 1777.

That winter, Washington's army camped at Valley Forge. Morris, newly elected to the Continental Congress, and the commander now embarked on another chapter in their public and private partnership. Only a few hours after taking his seat in Congress, Morris was added to the committee named to confer with Washington at his winter camp. Six weeks earlier, Washington had appealed to Congress for a complete reorganization of the army, and Morris's committee was faced immediately with the both short- and long-term problems of the military.[16] Indeed, the general had learned that conferences at camp were an extremely useful method of convincing congressmen that the army's problems demanded immediate attention. Delegates who viewed conditions at the camp were far readier to listen to Washington's suggestions than those who managed to avoid tours of Valley Forge and its population of cold and hungry Continental soldiers.[17] Washington never found a more receptive student, nor the army a more sympathetic witness than Gouverneur Morris.

"Heu miseres! The Skelton of an Army presents itself to our eyes in naked, starving Condition, out of Health, out of Spirits," Morris wrote his friend John Jay shortly after reaching Valley Forge.[18] He immediately set to work to review the detailed plan for reform that Washington had in readiness. Reorganization of army supply came first, and Morris, the scion of Dutch and French merchants, put his accountant's eye to the lengthy returns to prepare tables for the committee's report to Congress for immediate action. Other matters would have to await Morris's return to Congress, where he and Francis Dana assumed responsibility for seeing Washington's measures through to adoption. Reorganization of regiments was won. But Washington's pet project, "half pay" pensions for officers and their widows, proved more troublesome. Washington had convinced Morris of the need for the measure—and it would remain a mutual cause for years to come.

Washington soon learned that Morris was not always the most useful political lieutenant of whom a man could boast. The younger man always seemed on the verge of some dangerous blunder through his outspokenness or irreverence. Another member of the New York delegation in Congress described him as "like the Elephant in War—after-times more destructive to his Friends than his Antagonists."[19]

Still, Morris more than redeemed himself in Washington's eyes through his letters. For three years, Washington had been accustomed to the dull, unimaginative prose of official letters from Congress. Now he enjoyed reports that were well-written, forthright—even funny.

As Morris commented acidly in April 1778, "Every Man of Business knows that Words are of great Weight and we receive Reports from the Board of War every Day. I need say no more except that it is not always possible to weigh Sentences with that Accuracy in a public Assembly which is practicable in the Closet."[20] In May, he forecast that "you will perhaps get Something like an Army by September—How happy are we that even our Negligence cannot ruin us."[21]

By the spring of 1779, Morris felt secure in his personal relationship and closed one letter: "Forgive the length & Idleness of this Letter and believe me with all the Sincerity of private Friendship superadded to publick Esteem Affectionately Your Friend & Humble Servant."[22]

Indeed, by the fall of 1779, Washington had gone so far as to respond to one witticism with another. In a postscript to a letter of October 21, Morris wrote: "I recollect that it is long since I received a Letter from you recommending Union in Congress. I could not answer it then as I wished for I could [not] *truly* say it existed or was like to exist. . . . At length let me congratulate your *virtuous Moderation* (I do not compliment) that we are united as much as is safe for the Public." Washington replied drolly: "I am exceedingly happy in your postscript; for I am a great friend to harmony at all times, and especially in public Councils."[23]

Morris left Congress at the end of 1779 and retired for a time from public life, practicing law in Philadelphia and enjoying that city's social life. He contributed to the local newspapers the essays of "An American," denouncing Congress's fiscal irresponsibility. Any chance that he would soon return to public life ended in May when he was injured in a carriage accident and had to undergo the amputation of his shattered left leg. Recuperation from the surgery was complicated by recovery from a serious case of unrequited love for his companion in the disaster, Eliza Plater, the wife of a Maryland congressman.[24] As the year drew to a close, however, Morris felt his family's genetic urge for politics. He offered Washington unsolicited advice on military affairs and sharp comments on state politics to friends back in New York at the close of November.[25]

The New Year, 1781, brought a new opportunity for Morris and Washington to collaborate in public fashion. Congress hammered out the resolutions and compromises that formed executive departments for the Continental government, and these included the post of superintendant of finance, a position designed for Gouverneur's friend, Robert Morris. Although it would be July 6 before Gouverneur was officially named Robert's "Assistant," he began working for the Finance Office—and the United States of America—months earlier, as an unpaid advisor-of-all-trades, lawyer, deputy, and literary craftsman.[26] For the rest of the summer, the Morrises put together a program that actually kept the army in the field—generally if not always paid, reasonably well fed, and content. There are no letters of appreciation or support between the Finance Office and Washington, yet none were needed. All concerned were united in a mission to maintain the momentum of the summer campaign.

The most poignant symbol of this collaboration came at the end of August, when the Morrises learned that the French fleet was expected momentarily with plans in the works for a joint Franco-American campaign. Less than a week later, Washington wrote, begging for a month's pay to ensure that Benjamin Lincoln's troops would remain in the field, putting an end to their threat to halt their march south in Philadelphia if they received no money. The Finance Office was penniless, but the French admitted reluctantly that de Grasse's fleet carried precious livres from the royal treasury. The money could be released, however, only with the approval of the army *intendant,* then in Maryland. Robert and Gouverneur Morris immediately saddled their horses to ride south to obtain that authorization. On the road, they learned that permission had already been given.

As the two Morrises turned their horses to return to Philadelphia, they were blocked by the last division of the French army marching south to meet Cornwallis in Virginia. A crippled lawyer from New York and a stout, middle-aged Philadelphia merchant stood at the roadside, knowing that they, too, played an integral role in the historic military campaign that had just begun.[27]

With the British surrender at Yorktown, the financier and his assistant could turn their attention to goals broader than supplying an army in the field. In the winter of 1781–82, the Morrises embarked with allies like Alexander Hamilton on a campaign to put Continental finances in order and to create a sense of nationalism. Hindsight gives us the wisdom to wonder how they could have believed this was possible, but in the months after Yorktown, there seemed to be realistic hope that their plans might succeed.

"With Money," Gouverneur Morris wrote John Jay on January 20, 1782, "we can do every Thing."[28] The money, they expected, would come from America's Bourbon allies. Spain and France, according to this scenario, would continue their war with England—but continue it at sea, probably in the Caribbean. This war would cost the United States nothing in terms of men, money, or materiel, and it would bring profits to the North American merchants and ship owners and farmers who supplied their allies in the continuing war with Britain.

Alas for the Morrises, the tides of war and European public opinion were against them. The conflict did not drag on as they had anticipated. By the end of May 1782, all hope for a continuing naval war was gone. Spain had retaken the Floridas and captured Barbados and was not disposed to press further. The French fleet under de Grasse suffered a humiliating defeat at the battle of the "Saints" in April. News from Britain was even more discouraging. In March, Gouverneur Morris joined Henry Knox for conferences with the British on the subject of prisoner exchange. In the process, he learned that William Petty, the Earl of Shelburne, had won the prime ministry—and the pro-American leader would almost certainly open peace negotiations.[29]

Summer brought even worse news. In August, word reached Philadelphia that Jay was on his way from Madrid to Paris to lend his hand to peace talks. "I am well convinced of two Things," Morris wrote gloomily, "one that a Peace will not easily be made and another that it is not much for the Interest of America that it should be made at present." He saw "only a continuance of the War" as a means to his ends of national unity and sound finance.[30]

The Morrises did not ignore Washington in their campaign. Gouverneur drafted the letter that Robert Morris sent the commander in chief on October 16: "War is more likely than Peace to produce Funds for the Public Debts, Increase of Authority to Congress, and Vigor to the Administration as well of the Union as of its component Parts."[31]

Until the fall of 1782, however, the Morrises scrupulously refrained from using military claims to advance their causes. Events at the close of the year changed this prudent strategy. On January 1, 1783, Gouverneur Morris revealed a new and more ruthless view of American affairs: "The Army have Swords in their Hands, and you know enough of the History of Mankind to know much more than I have said and possible much more than they themselves yet think of."[32] Unrest among army officers at the encampment at West Point in October 1782 opened the chain of events that led to the Newburgh addresses five months later. The role of the Morrises in that episode has been the subject of debate among historians for decades.[33] What is certain is that they and Hamilton overstepped the bounds of common sense in encouraging that discontent. They ignored the curt responses of men like Washington and Knox when hints were dropped to them. Washington disarmed the Newburgh conspirators at the legendary meeting of March 15, 1783, and a grateful Congress passed a half-pay measure—without providing for its funding, of course.

Washington viewed the machinations of the "continentalists" in Philadelphia with alarm and anger. He may have felt special disappointment—even betrayal—at Gouverneur Morris's part in the murky affair. Four and a half years earlier, on learning of the angry petition of disgruntled army officers, Congressman Morris had told the commander: "I considered myself in some Degree as an Advocate for the Army[.] I loved them from an Acquaintance with some Individuals and for the Sufferings which as a Body they had bravely and patiently endured; and therefore I could not but suffer when I found them taking Steps which In my Opinion cannot do them Honor."[34]

In 1778, Morris confessed, "What chiefly affected me was that this Meeting of Delegates from Brigades in a Mixture of civil and military Capacity carries with it the Air of deeper Design than I believe is in the Bosoms of those who were immediately concerned." He reminded Washington of the dire historical precedents: "It was by Proceedures such as these that the good Fairfax made Way for a crafty Cromwell and that he dismissed a tedious Wrangling Parliament and established a military Despotism." Morris went on to state: "Thinking on this Subject as I do it did and does appear to me my Duty as a good Citizen thoroughly to discountenance every Measure of this Kind particularly when it is ushered as the first Mention of this Affair was to me by an Observation that the Army had it in their Power to do themselves Justice."[35]

It was May 29 before Robert Morris could complete a lame letter of explanation of his role to Washington.[36] The general failed to rise to the bait Morris offered for him to take a public stand on the measures of the Finance Office. Instead, he wrote, "Before I retire from public life, I shall with the greatest freedom give my sentiments to the States on several political subjects, amongst those will be comprehended the particular object you recommend to my attention."[37]

For the next two years, Morris and Washington seem to have suspended their friendship. There were no outward expressions of hostility, but neither was there any contact or correspondence. Morris spent more and more of his time as a corporate attorney for Robert Morris's private business interests, work that brought him again into Washington's personal sphere.

The court hearings regarding Robert Morris's incredibly complicated relationship with the French tobacco monopoly took Gouverneur to Virginia in the summer of 1785, when he spent three days at Mount Vernon. Whatever explanations or apologies were needed to restore friendship were made. When Morris left the estate, Washington rode with him as far as Alexandria to extend their time together.[38] Morris resumed his correspondence with the general, cheerfully executing errands to the north for the Washington family and writing lighthearted letters as a family friend.

Less than a month after his July visit, Morris reported the success of his shopping expedition for Frances Bassett, fiancée of Washington's nephew, George Augustine Washington. "I write this Letter as a Companion for some Shoes of Miss Bassett and if it is addressed to you rather than to her," he began lightheartedly, "you must for that Trouble as well as many others accuse that Celebrity which you had no little Trouble in acquiring." Continuing with his banter, he cautioned Washington: "But you must tell the Lady that I am far from thinking that she ought not be as much celebrated as any General among you. Indeed between ourselves I think she will probably be entitled to the civic Crown as soon as the Modes and Forms of the World will permit a free Use of the Means. Not perhaps like a roman Soldier for a Citizen saved but like a good American Wife for a Citizen born." A bit more seriously, he closed with this easy and graceful wish for the young couple: "That this Praise may be speedily and frequently carried and long enjoyed is my sincere Wish and I know not of any better Epithalamium tho I have read some more pleasant."[39]

Washington and Morris reestablished their personal and public partnership just in time for what may be the most lastingly productive part of their collaborations: the Philadelphia Convention of 1787. To no one's surprise, Washington was elected as a delegate from Virginia. To the surprise of almost everyone, Morris was returned as a delegate from his newly adopted state of

Pennsylvania. Washington was elected president of the convention when sessions opened on May 25, and Morris assumed an unofficial role as advocate of the "continental," "nationalist," and "American" programs they both longed to see in the new system of government.

They carried their partnership outside the walls of the convention hall as well. Washington's diary records two joint fishing trips during the summer, with one in Montgomery County, Pennsylvania, on the borders of Valley Forge. One afternoon, while Morris fished, Washington rode to the old cantonment—his first visit since 1779. He did not, alas, leave a record of his reflections that day, or of his conversations with Morris that evening in the boardinghouse of the widow Jane Moore.[40]

On the convention floor, Morris inevitably focused on the powers that would be given to the executive. One of his recent biographers has remarked that "more than anyone else, he helped to mold the office into a strong counterforce to the legislative branch."[41] He was, of course, creating an office that George Washington would be willing to accept. For Morris, as for most Americans, there could be no other first president of a new United States. Unlike most other Americans, however, Morris knew what Washington would want and need to accept this role.

Washington quietly acknowledged the depth of his partnership with Morris in the diary entry recording his departure from Philadelphia. As he prepared to leave for Mount Vernon after the convention's close, he wrote, "I took leave of those families in w[hi]ch I had been most intimate." The last of those "intimates" to bid farewell were Robert and Gouverneur Morris, who shared an early dinner with the general and then rode with him to Gray's Ferry.[42]

In the fall of 1788, just as the process for putting the new federal government into operation began, Gouverneur Morris announced his decision to leave the country. The needs of Robert Morris's far-flung business commitments demanded his presence in Europe. Moreover, he felt that he left America in good hands. He bade farewell to Washington in a letter that combined a tribute to their friendship, ribald barnyard humor, and patriotic sentiment. Nothing could have been more characteristic.

Morris opened by reminding Washington of his promise to execute any errands needed in Europe: "When I desire to be favored with your Commands it is not the meer ceremonious Form of Words which you every Day meet from every Man you meet and which you know better than any Man to estimate at its true Value. Whether I can be useful to you in any Way I know not but this I know that you may command my best Endeavours."[43]

Next, there was the troublesome tradition of letters of introduction that travelers carried with them. "You will oblige me," he began, "I once ment[ione]d to you my Wish not to be encumbered with the Letters introductory of the many who are prone to give them. I think them a Kind of Paper Money which is not only of little Value but which is not always a reputable tho perhaps a legal Tender. I solicit yours as an undoubted Bill of Exchange which is Gold wherever it goes. Permit me however to pursue the mercantile Phrase (or Metaphor) and honestly to request that you do not give me Credit for more than I am worth lest proving a Bankrupt you be called on by my Creditors." Mindful of his reputation as a humorist, Morris continued with an anecdote of interest to two determined agriculturists: "I promised you some Chinese Piggs A Promise which I can perform only by Halves for my Boar being much addicted to Gallantry hung himself in Pursuit of meer common Sows And his Consort to asswage her Melancholy (for what alas can helpless Widows do) took up with a Paramour of Vulgar Race and thus her grunting Progeny have jowls and Bellies less big by Half than their Dam." Still, he promised: "Such however as I have such send I unto you And to piece and patch the Matter as well as I may In Company with the Piggs shall be sent a Pair of Chinese Geese Which are really the foolishest Geese I ever beheld for they chuse all Times for Sitting but the Spring And one of them is now actually engaged in that Business."[44]

Of course, he could not close without referring to the matter that occupied them both: "It would be too degrading to the Noble Race of Man should I introduce Politics after Hogs and Geese. This is a tolerable Excuse for saying Nothing but the Truth is I have Nothing to say I am of the Breed of Optimists and beleive that all will go well for you will certainly be seated in the Presidents Chair and will I am certain when there greatly Labor to prevent Things from going ill As to the Rest I heartily agree in the Text that the Wisdom of Man is Foolishness with God having seen both Fools and Folly succeed in a most surprising Manner."[45]

Washington's reply demanded an immediate response, for he had not only obliged with letters of introduction and a request that Morris procure for him a gold watch, but also expressed a heartfelt wish that he not be chosen president. On the eve of sailing, Morris replied: "I have ever thought, and said that you *must* be the President. No other Man can *fill* that Office. No other Man can draw forth the Abilities of our Country into the various Departments of civil Life. You alone can awe the Insolence of opposing Factions, & the greater Insolence of assuming Adherents. I say Nothing of foreign Powers, nor of their Ministers."[46]

"You will become," Morris predicted, "the Father to more than three Millions of Children. And while your Bosom glows with parental tenderness, in theirs (or at least in a Majority of them) you will excite the dutious Sentiments of filial Affection. This, I repeat it, is what I firmly expect; and my Views are not directed by that Enthusiasm which your public Character has impressed on the public Mind. Enthusiasm is generally shortsighted and too often blind." Rather, Morris concluded, "I form my Conclusions from those Talents and Virtues which the World *beleives* and which your Friends *know* you possess. That they may long continue a rich Treasure in the Hands of our Country is the sincere Wish of your affectionate Friend & *obedient Servant.*"[47]

Morris was to spend ten years abroad. Between 1789 and 1794, he represented the American government in London and Paris as well as securing Robert Morris's precarious financial situation. His nominations for those diplomatic posts and his performance in those capitals forced Washington again and again to defend his younger friend against political enemies.

When Morris was first suggested as America's unofficial agent at the British Court in October 1789, Washington had to chair a lively debate among Hamilton, Jay, and Madison, three men who had recently been happily allied as contributors to *The Federalist.* The new president noted that Madison "thought if the necessity did not press it would be better to wait the arrival of Mr. Jefferson who might be able to give the information wanted on this head—and with me thought, that if Mr. Gouvr. Morris was employed in this business it would be a commitment for his appointment as Minister if one should be sent to that Court or wanted at Versailles in place of Mr. Jefferson—and Moreover if either of these was his Wish whether his representations might not be made with an eye to it." Hamilton and Jay agreed with Madison that "Mr. Morris is a man of superior talents." Jay and Madison, however, cautioned that "his imagination sometimes runs a head of his judgment," and that "his Manners before he is known and where known are oftentimes disgusting." These traits, and his sometimes "immoral & loose expressions had created opinions of himself that were not favourable to him and which he did not merit."[48]

In the two years that followed, Hamilton's policies in the Treasury and events in France sharpened partisan lines in America. By December 1791, when Washington submitted Morris's nomination as minister in Paris to the Senate, the New Yorker's enemies had increased in number and vehemence. Although Morris's residence abroad had relieved him from taking a formal stand on such domestic issues as assumption of the debt, no follower of Jefferson or Madison doubted for a moment that he supported Hamilton's fiscal programs. There was even less room for doubt about Morris's views on French politics. Both his public and private letters from Europe made clear his alarm at the growing excesses of French revolutionaries. In the Senate, James Monroe expressed the views of many when he called Morris "a monarchy man." It took more than two weeks before the Senate confirmed Morris's appointment—and then by the narrow vote of 16 to 11.[49]

The rancor over Morris's nomination so disturbed Washington that he thought it necessary to give his friend a brutally frank picture of the opposition to his appointment. The president's letter of January 28, 1792, was a private one, but he asked Jefferson to review his initial draft. The secretary of state, hardly counted among Morris's staunchest supporters, was so alarmed by the sharpness of the president's language that he returned the draft with penciled revisions "softening some expressions lest they should be too much felt by mister Morris."[50]

Even with Jefferson's "softening," the letter was a remarkable warning to Morris: "You were charged . . . with levity, and imprudence of conversation and conduct. It was urged, that your habit of expression, indicated a hauteur disgusting to those who happen to differ from you in sentiment; and among a people who study civility and politeness more than any other nation, it must be displeasing." Morris's behavior in Europe had merely given his enemies more ammunition against him, including the charge "That in France you were considered as a favourer of Aristocracy, & unfriendly to its Revolution—(I suppose they meant Constitution)."[51]

Washington tried to pinpoint the arguments of Morris's adversaries: "The promptitude with w[hi]ch your brilliant, & lively imagination is displayed, allows too little time for deliberation, and correction; and is the primary cause of those sallies which too often offend, and of that ridicule of characters which begets enmity not easy to be forgotten, but which might easily be avoided if it was under the control of more caution and prudence." Diplomats, in other words, should be diplomatic: "It is indispensably necessary that more circumspection should be observed by our Representatives abroad than they conceive you are disposed to adopt."[52]

Washington assured Morris that, "in this statement you have the pros & the cons; by reciting them, I give you a proof of my friendship, if I give none of my policy or judgment. I do it on the presumption, that a mind conscious of its own rectitude, fears not what is said of it; but will bid defiance to and dispise shafts that are not barbed with accusations against honor or integrity." His correction continued with assurance that, "because I have the fullest confidence (supposing the alligations to be founded in whole or part) that you would find no difficulty, being apprised of the exceptionable light in which they are received, and considering yourself as the representative of this Country, to effect a change; and thereby silence, in the most unequivocal and satisfactory manner, your political opponents. Of my good opinion, & of my friendship & regard, you may be assured."[53]

Morris took the president's criticisms as they had been intended. "Beleive me," he wrote in reply, "I know how to value the friendship by which they were dictated. I have always thought that the Counsel of our Enemies is wholesome, tho bitter, if we can but turn it to good Account & In order that I may not fail to do so on the present Occasion *I now promise you* that Circumspection of Conduct which has hitherto I acknowlege formed no Part of my Character. And I make the *Promise* that my Sense of Integrity may enforce what my Sense of Propriety dictates."[54]

Morris was not a brilliant success as American minister to the French Republic, but no one could have been. In two and a half years in the post, he dealt with seven different heads of France's Department of Foreign Affairs—men representing five distinct shifts in government. As early as March 1792, Morris remarked that the "Ministerial Seats resemble electrical Chairs which give every Occupant a kick in the Breeches."[55] For nine months, he functioned without any instructions from Secretary of State Jefferson, while Morris himself provided the government with regular reports that even his modern critics agree were models of accuracy and fairness.[56] Inevitably, his recall came, and in the summer of 1794, he happily surrendered his position to his successor, Monroe, whom he described as "a person of mediocrity in every respect."[57]

Washington himself came to share this opinion. In marginal comments on Monroe's *View of the Conduct of the Executive of the United States,* he wrote: "Whatever may have been his [Morris's] political Sentiments, he pursued steadily the honor & Interest of his C[oun]try with zeal and ability, & with respectful firmness asserted its rights. Had Mr Monroe done the same, we should not have been in the situation we now are."[58]

Morris returned to America in December 1798. He found a nation dealing with the undeclared "Quasi-War" with France that had called Washington out of retirement as commander of an army that never saw the field. Adams's administration had passed the Alien and Sedition Acts and new tax measures that, within two months, would foment a rebellion among Pennsylvania farmers. Jefferson, the vice president, only bided his time to unseat Adams in the next election. Hamilton, Morris soon learned, was ready to split the Federalist Party to ensure Adams's refusal to be a candidate in 1800. For Morris, there was only one solution: Washington's return to office.

On December 9, 1799, Morris wrote his old chief: "You must be convinced (however painful the Conviction) that should you decline no Man will be chosen whom you would wish to see in that high Office. Beleiving then that the dearest Interests of our Country are at Stake, I beg Leave to speak with you freely." Morris conceded that Washington had compelling reasons for refusing to serve: "No reasonable Man can doubt that after a Life of glorious Labor you must wish for Repose." But, he asked, "is Retirement, in the strict Sense of the Word, a possible Thing? And is the Half-Retirement which you may attain to more peaceful than public Life? Nay, has it not the Disadvantage of leaving you involved in Measures you can neither direct nor control?" Morris even suggested that presiding over the government from the new capital on the Potomac would be less onerous than it had been in Philadelphia: "Will you not when the Seat of Government is in your Neighbourhood, enjoy more Retirement as President of the United States than as a General of the Army?"[59]

Desperately, Morris appealed to "a more important Consideration" by asking, "Shall the vast Treasure of your Fame be committed to the Uncertainty of events, be exposed to the Attempts of Envy, and subject to the Spoliation of Slander? From Envy and Slander no Retreat is safe but the Grave, And you must not yet hide you behind that Bulwark."[60]

With growing urgency, he appealed now to Washington's concern for his legacy, his reputation in history: "As to the Influence of Events, if there be a human Being who may look them fairly in the Face you are the Man. Recollect Sir," he reminded the Virginian, "that each Occasion which has brought you back on the public Stage has been to you the Means of new and greater Glory. If General Washington had not become Member of the Convention he would have been considered only as the Defender and not as the Legislator of his Country. And if the President of the Convention had not become

President of the United States he would not have added the Character of a Statesman to those of a Patriot and a Hero. Your Modesty may repel these Titles," Morris conceded, "but Europe has conferred them and the World will set its Seal of Approbation when in these tempestuous Times your Country shall have again confided the Helm of her Affairs to your steady Hand."[61]

Finally, Morris appealed to Washington's sense of honor and duty: "But you may perhaps say that you stand indirectly pledged to private Life. Surely Sir you neither gave nor meant to give such Pledge to the Extent of possible Contingencies. The Acceptance of your present Office proves that you did not." Morris used Washington's reluctant return to public life to command forces during the Quasi-War to bolster his argument that he must again seek the presidency to save their nation. "Nay, you stand pledged by all your former Conduct that when Circumstances arise which may require it you will act again. Those Circumstances seem to be now imminent, and it is meet that you consider them on the broad Ground of your extensive Information. Ponder them I pray: and whatever may be the Decision pardon my Freedom and beleive me truly yours."[62]

Washington died before the letter reached Mount Vernon. Morris was left to deliver his eulogy at St. Paul's Chapel on the last day of the year. In his diary, he noted sadly: "Pronounced my oration badly."[63] The day was cold and blustery, and Morris may have referred to the effects of a hoarse voice and not the quality of his tribute. When printed copies of the address were available, he proudly sent copies to friends at home and abroad.[64] To modern readers, the address seems stilted and formal—a hallmark of funeral orations of the time—and it certainly did no justice to Morris's feelings for his departed leader or the facts of their remarkable relationship.

Washington and Morris were joined in a friendship based on shared opinions on public affairs and a mutual regard for each other's merits. With the exception of Morris's headstrong behavior relating to army claims in 1783, Washington never had reason to question his motives or stand back when Morris required a defense. The older man said it best in his comment on one of Monroe's attacks: "Mr Morris was known to be a man of first rate abilities; and his integrity & honor had never been impeached."[65]

For his part, Morris summarized his opinion of Washington in a letter to the president himself in 1793. Reflecting upon affairs in France, he wrote that there, "the different Parties pass away like the Shadows in a Magic Lanthorn, & to be well with any one of them would in a short Period become Cause of unquencheable Hatred with the others." By contrast, Morris saw "Happy Happy America governd by Reason, by Law, by the Man whom she loves, whom she almost adores. It is the Pride of my Life to consider that Man as my Friend and I hope long to be honor'd with that Title."[66]

And honored with that title he was until the day Washington died.

Notes

1. Richard Brookhiser, *Gentleman Revolutionary: Gouverneur Morris, the Rake Who Wrote the Constitution* (New York, 2003).

2. Max Farrand, ed., *The Records of the Federal Convention of 1787,* 3 vols. (New Haven, Conn., 1911), 3:85.

3. Martin Van Buren, *Inquiry into the Origin and Course of the Political Parties in the United States,* ed. His Sons (New York, 1867), 105–6.

4. William Thompson Read, *Life and Correspondence of George Read: A Signer of the Declaration of Independence, with Notices of Some of His Contemporaries* (Philadelphia, 1870), 441n.

5. Brookhiser, *Gentleman Revolutionary,* 26.

6. Ibid., 225n28.

7. For Morris's early life and family background I have relied on chapters 1 and 2 of my own study, *Gouverneur Morris and the New Nation, 1775–1788* (New York, 1978), and on the first chapters of Brookhiser, *Gentleman Revolutionary,* and William Howard Adams, *Gouverneur Morris: An Independent Life* (New Haven, Conn., 2003).

8. Gouverneur Morris to William Smith, 20 February 1772, in *The Life of Gouverneur Morris, with Selections from His Correspondence and Miscellaneous Papers,* ed. Jared Sparks, 3 vols. (Boston, 1832), 1:17.

9. Robert Morris to G. Morris, 3 May 1772, Robert Morris Papers, Rutgers University, New Brunswick, N.J.

10. R. Morris to William Sydney, 14 February 1772, ibid.

11. *PGW: Rev. Ser.,* 1:32–33, 40.

12. Melanie Randolph Miller, *Envoy to the Terror: Gouverneur Morris and the French Revolution* (Dulles, Va., 2005), 21–22.

13. G. Morris to GW, 26 April 1776, *PGW: Rev. Ser.,* 4:96–98.

14. "Oration on the necessity of declaring Independence," [ante 4 July 1776], Gouverneur Morris Papers, Columbia University, New York.

15. Don Higginbotham, *George Washington: Uniting a Nation* (Lanham, Md., 2002), 8.

16. For Morris's first year in the Continental Congress, see Kline, *Gouverneur Morris and the New Nation,* 94–139.

17. Freeman, 4:561–63.

18. G. Morris to John Jay, 1 February 1778, John Jay Papers, Columbia University, New York.

19. William Duer to Robert R. Livingston, 10 March 1778, Robert R. Livingston Papers, New-York Historical Society.

20. G. Morris to GW, 18 April 1778, *PGW: Rev. Ser.,* 14:551.

21. G. Morris to GW, 15 May 1778, ibid., 15:128.

22. G. Morris to GW, 26 April 1779, WPLC.

23. G. Morris to GW, 21 October 1779, ibid.; GW to G. Morris, 6 November 1779, ibid.

24. Kline, *Gouverneur Morris and the New Nation,* 170–79.

25. G. Morris to GW, 28 November 1780, WPLC; GW to G. Morris, 10 December 1780, ibid.; Kline, *Gouverneur Morris and the New Nation,* 184.

26. Kline, *Gouverneur Morris and the New Nation,* 184–91.

27. Ibid., 203–4.

28. G. Morris to Jay, 20 January 1782, Gouverneur Morris Papers, Columbia University.

29. Kline, *Gouverneur Morris and the New Nation,* 205–37.

30. G. Morris to Matthew Ridley, 6 August 1782, Ridley Papers, Massachusetts Historical Society, Boston.

31. R. Morris to GW, 16 October 1782, Robert Morris Papers, Huntington Library, San Marino, Calif.

32. G. Morris to Jay, 1 January 1783, Gouverneur Morris Papers, Columbia University.

33. I still have a fondness for the arguments advanced forty years ago by Richard H. Kohn in "The Inside History of the Newburgh Conspiracy: America and the Coup D'Etat" (*WMQ,* 3rd ser., 27 [April 1970]: 187–220), and attacked, counterattacked, and debated again over the next four years in the pages of the same journal. For a summary of the ensuing arguments, see C. Edward Skeen and Richard H. Kohn, "The Newburgh Conspiracy Reconsidered," *WMQ,* 3rd ser., 31 (April 1974): 273–98.

34. G. Morris to GW, 26 October 1778, *PGW: Rev. Ser.,* 17:586.

35. Ibid.

36. R. Morris to GW, 29 May 1783, WPLC.

37. GW to R. Morris, 3 June 1783, ibid.

38. GW, [7 July 1785], *PGW: Diaries,* 4:160–61.

39. G. Morris to GW, 1 August 1785, *PGW: Conf. Ser.,* 3:168–69. See also GW to Tench Tilghman, 17 July 1785, ibid., 3:134.

40. GW, [30 July 1787], *PGW: Diaries,* 5:178–80.

41. Adams, *Gouverneur Morris,* 155.

42. GW, [18 September 1787], *PGW: Diaries,* 5:186.

43. G. Morris to GW, 12 November 1788, *PGW: Pres. Ser.,* 1:103–4.

44. Ibid.

45. Ibid.

46. GW to G. Morris, 6 December 1788, ibid., 1:165–66.

47. Ibid.

48. GW, [8 October 1789], *PGW: Diaries,* 5:456.

49. Brookhiser, *Gentleman Revolutionary,* 128–29; Miller, *Envoy to the Terror,* 93–96.

50. *PGW: Pres. Ser.,* 9:515n1.

51. GW to G. Morris, 28 January 1792, ibid., 9:515–17.

52. Ibid.

53. Ibid.

54. G. Morris to GW, 6 April 1792, ibid., 10:223.

55. G. Morris to William Short, 22 March 1792, in Gouverneur Morris, *A Diary of the French Revolution,* ed. Beatrix Cary Davenport, 2 vols. (Boston, 1939), 2:391.

56. Miller, *Envoy to the Terror,* 167, 198.

57. *The Diary and Letters of Gouverneur Morris,* ed. Anne Cary Morris, 2 vols. (New York, 1888), 2:437.

58. GW, Comments on Monroe's *A View of the Conduct of the Executive of the United States,* [ca. March 1798], *PGW: Ret. Ser.,* 2:196.

59. G. Morris to GW, 9 December 1799, ibid., 4:452–53.

60. Ibid.

61. Ibid.

62. Ibid.

63. G. Morris diary entry, 31 December 1799, Gouverneur Morris Papers, Manuscripts Division, Library of Congress.

64. See, e.g., his covering letters for copies of the pamphlet in early 1800: G. Morris to M. Ogden, 12 February 1800, Gouverneur Morris Papers, Columbia University; G. Morris to the Duke of Montrose, 1 April 1800, and G. Morris to the Princess de la Tour, 1800, Private Letterbooks, Gouverneur Morris Papers, Manuscripts Division, Library of Congress; and G. Morris to Richard Harison, 1 January 1800, and G. Morris to R. Morris and to John Parish, 7 April 1800, Commercial Letterbooks, ibid.

65. GW, Comments on Monroe's *A View of the Conduct of the Executive of the United States,* [ca. March 1798], *PGW: Ret. Ser.,* 2:171.

66. G. Morris to GW, 14 February 1793, *PGW: Pres. Ser.,* 12:143.

The Great Collaboration

The Increasingly Close Relationship between George Washington and Alexander Hamilton

PETER R. HENRIQUES

In every relation, which you have borne to me, I have found that my confidence in your talents, exertions and integrity, has been well placed.

—George Washington to Alexander Hamilton, February 2, 1795

Alexander Hamilton is unique even among the inner circle of the six most famous and renowned Founding Fathers. George Washington lived until he was sixty-seven, and the others—Benjamin Franklin, Thomas Jefferson, James Madison, and John Adams—all lived into their eighties or beyond (Adams was ninety). Hamilton was dead before his fiftieth birthday. All of the other founders were native-born Americans. Hamilton was born on the tiny British island of Nevis in the Caribbean. None had such a stigmatized childhood to overcome. He was the illegitimate son of Rachel Lavein (a woman imprisoned for "whoring" by her vengeful husband), and her paramour, a wayward Scot of noble lineage by the name of James Hamilton. His father later deserted the family. His mother died in early 1768, and her vengeful husband made sure neither of her two illegitimate sons, "born into whoredom," received a penny of inheritance.[1]

All of the founders engendered a certain amount of controversy, but none proved to be (or remains) as divisive a figure as Hamilton. He was the bête noire of Jefferson, and the Jeffersonian image of Hamilton has had remarkable staying power, especially in view of the paucity of evidence to support it. In that rendering, Hamilton emerges as the dark side of the American picture: the champion of the rich and well born, an elitist distrustful and disdainful of ordinary people, a proponent of a dangerously powerful national government threatening the rights of the states and the liberties of the people. His character was as dangerous as his philosophy. He was a Machiavellian intriguer with a Napoleonic complex.[2] Perhaps the most scathing comments come from Adams, who came to despise the man whom he called "a bastard brat of a Scotch peddler," a man who lived his life in a "delirium of Ambition."[3] Adams thought he knew the source of Hamilton's ambition. It was from "a superabundance of secretions which he could not find whores enough to draw off."[4] Even in the era of "shock jock" radio shows, that is hard to surpass.[5] Adams's wife, Abigail, was not much kinder: "I have read his heart in his wicked eyes. . . . They are lasciviousness itself."[6] How a man who generated such vituperative comments became Washington's most significant and influential advisor is one of the most interesting and important stories in America's founding.

To historians of the early national period, the term "the great collaboration," the title of an important book by Adrienne Koch, normally refers to the remarkably productive relationship between Jefferson and Madison, the subjects of Koch's study. Viewed as the founding fathers of the democratic movement in America, these two great men have received the lion's share of the praise and attention.[7] As my chapter title indicates, there was another "great collaboration." Indeed, one might argue that it was an even greater collaboration than the one between Jefferson and Madison. The remarkably productive alliance between Washington, the Father of the Country, and Hamilton, the Father of American Government (and the Father of American Capitalism), did more than anything else to bring about the modern United States of America. As George Will expressed it, if you want to see Hamilton's memorial, look around America.[8] Their relationship was not only extremely productive and important, but it is also fascinating, with ups and downs that reveal interesting aspects of both men's character.

Washington was old enough to be Hamilton's father. (And it was later falsely rumored that he was in fact his father.) By the time the two men first met, in 1776, Washington was the commander in chief of the Continental Army and the most famous man in America. Hamilton was a young twenty-one-year-old captain of New York artillery. (There is a controversy among historians about whether Hamilton was born in 1755 or 1757.) Considering his background, it is amazing that he was in a position of even that much influence. Hamilton had been able to escape his fate as a "groveling" clerk on the island of St. Croix, partly because of his great talents and partly because his generous employer and others recognized his talents and sent him to the mainland to obtain an education. He attended King's College (now Columbia), got caught up in the fervor of the coming of the American Revolution, and soon produced pamphlets so sophisticated that people assumed they had been written by one of the mature leaders of the protest movement, certainly not by a teenager. This vignette points to an essential fact in assessing Hamilton. One can scarcely overstate the brilliance and power of his intellect. Later, John Marshall testified that "Hamilton's reach of thought was so far beyond" his that, compared to Hamilton's, it was like a candle "before the sun at noonday."[9] Even his adversary, Jefferson, described him as "really a colossus . . . without numbers, he is a host within himself."[10]

Hamilton's great mental acuity was matched by a desire for fame that seems to have been every bit as great as Washington's. Undoubtedly, Hamilton's unusually intense ambition was part of his innate personality, but it may well have been augmented by a desire to overcome his stigmatized childhood. In the words of one scholar, "The real debt Hamilton owed his father he could never have acknowledged. The stain of illegitimacy and poverty that James Hamilton had left on the family name could be effaced only by illustrious achievement, and Hamilton from boyhood on was an overachiever, one who found it necessary to more than compensate for his feelings of inadequacy."[11] This led to a capacity for productive work that has been unsurpassed by any American statesman.

Another central aspect of Hamilton's personality, again undoubtedly a combination of his innate personality and the effects of slights he endured as a child, was his extreme sensitivity involving issues of honor. In the words of his eulogist (Fisher Ames), no man, "not the Roman Cato himself, was more inflexible on every point that touched, or seemed to touch, integrity and honor."[12] This supersensitivity to any perceived slight led Hamilton to be involved in *ten* "affairs of honor" during his life—prior to his fatal encounter with Aaron Burr. It appeared that his sense of honor inclined him toward open encounters.[13] "For all of his superlative mental gifts," according to Ron Chernow, the author of the best-selling biography, *Hamilton,* "he was afflicted with a touchy ego that made him querulous and fatally combative." He was in a constant battle to control his own emotions, a battle he often lost.[14]

Early in 1777, Hamilton officially joined Washington's "family" (as the general himself called it), a group of remarkably talented young men (ultimately becoming thirty-two in number over the course of the war) who served as His Excellency's personal aides. In so doing, Hamilton inadvertently stumbled upon the crowning enterprise of his life: the creation of a powerful new country. A born fighter, walking a high wire of self-creation, he sensed that the importance of the Revolution and his connection to Washington were his ticket to fame and glory.[15] In yet another testament to Hamilton's remarkable ability, in the space of less than a year, and despite his youth, he became, as Washington later described him, his "principal & most confidential aid."[16]

The harried commander in chief wanted, in his words, "persons that can think for me, as well as execute orders," and Hamilton's affinity for the way Washington thought was unequaled.[17] Viewing things the same way, Hamilton was soon able to compose Washington's letters for him, putting into words what Washington wanted to say—and doing it more eloquently than he could. In the words of Ron Chernow, his aide was "able to project himself into Washington's mind and intuit what the general wanted to say, writing it up with instinctive tact and deft diplomatic skills. It was an inspired piece of ventriloquism: Washington gave a few general hints, and presto, out popped Hamilton's letter in record time."[18] It is easy to understand how delighted the overburdened general would be on discovering someone with this skill.

The young aide, however, was much more than simply a superb secretary. Washington, clearly seeing something special and understanding Hamilton's unique abilities, quickly placed him in situations where his talents could be developed and used. His Excellency sent him on very sensitive and important missions. For example, in late November of 1777 he sent Hamilton, who had been his aide for less than a year, to General Horatio Gates, the hero (whether deservedly or not) of the Saratoga campaign, with orders to extract from his command a thousand soldiers needed by Washington. The errand was an indication of the commander's great trust in Hamilton, for the task was a delicate one, requiring ingenuity, tact, and skill.[19] He performed a similar task with General Israel Putnam, ruffling some feathers in the process but maintaining Washington's confidence and support. The young lieutenant colonel's description of General Putnam indicates his frankness and tendency to use pungent and caustic language, a tendency he never lost: "Every part of this Gentleman's conduct is marked with blunder and negligence, and gives general disgust."[20] Another quality that made Hamilton invaluable was his complete fluency in French, which aided Washington's dealing with France and that ally's many generals and officers.

One might reasonably expect that Hamilton would be delighted to find himself in such an important position, but the facts do not support such a supposition. Hamilton's personality was not that of an aide, even the most important aide of the commander in chief of the American forces. His inclination ran strongly to command and to execute, not to carrying out the orders of another, and his personality ensured there would be some friction between himself and his commander. There is no doubt that the relationship between the two men was strong and tenacious. What its exact nature was is much harder to say. Young Hamilton was clearly ambivalent and conflicted in his feelings about Washington, torn between his desire to defer to him and to please His Excellency (as he regularly addressed him), and his apparent need to resist being dependent on him. It would have been almost impossible for two such strong characters to be in constant contact without a certain amount of friction. Hating any sense of dependency, Hamilton tended to hold himself aloof from his commanding general. If one is willing to venture into psychohistory, it seems plausible to speculate that such a course of action would also guard against his deep-seated fear of abandonment and disappointment. Perhaps, having been abandoned by his birth father, Hamilton feared allowing himself to get too close to a substitute father, lest he be abandoned again.[21]

Then, too, Hamilton's strongest desire was for military glory and fame. Youthful fantasies of performing illustrious deeds in battle still had a strong hold on him. (In his first surviving letter, as a very young teenager, he wished for a war, with its attendant opportunity for fame and honor.) Yearning for military glory, resenting his dependence on Washington, increasingly frustrated by the general's seeming indifference to his plight, Hamilton felt trapped. Many of his letters, especially those to his closest friend, Colonel John Laurens, show signs of depression. "I hate Congress—I hate the Army—I hate the world—I hate myself—the whole is a mass of fools and knaves."[22] He later bitterly declared that "three fourths of them [members of Congress] are mortal enemies [to talent] . . . and three fourths of the other fourth have . . . contempt [for integrity]." In the same letter, he seemed suicidal: "I am disgusted with every thing in this world . . . I have no other wish than as soon as possible to make a brilliant exit."[23]

Being so desirous of fame, the Little Lion (Hamilton's nickname by his fellow aides because of his short stature and commanding personality) could not avoid being jealous of all the fame General Washington garnered. As the sociologist Barry Schwartz demonstrates, the crisis and collective fervor of the Revolution propelled Washington's image far beyond the realm of any normal reputation, however sterling. The people desperately needed a symbol that would unite their varying and fractious regions and stand for something of which all could be proud. His Excellency filled the bill, and the result was an adoration of General Washington almost approaching idolatry.[24] Such excessive praise did not sit well with Hamilton. "Being brilliant and coldly critical," working intimately with the general, Hamilton detected numerous flaws in Washington less visible to others. To his eye, the commander was not what he appeared to be on first impression. Rather, Hamilton saw him as demanding and moody, with an uneven and explosive temper, and given to periodic outbursts at his aides. And Washington was selfish, keeping Hamilton chained to a desk he despised, seeming to offer release but never fulfilling his promise.[25]

The elements for a rupture were all falling into place. "I explained to you," Hamilton wrote plaintively in 1779, "my feelings with regard to military reputation, and how much it was my object to act a conspicuous part by some enterprise that might raise my character as a soldier above mediocrity. You were so good as to say you would be glad to furnish me an occasion."[26] But the time never seemed right to Washington. How valuable he considered Hamilton's help is clear from his reiterated efforts to keep his hold on the young prodigy. In Washington's mind, the time for Hamilton's departure was always "not yet."

The break finally came in February 1781, hastened by two developments in 1780. The first was the execution of Major John André, the top aide of the British commander in chief, Henry Clinton, as a spy for André's role in the infamous treason of Benedict Arnold. Hamilton was completely won over by the dashing André, who demonstrated the type of character, courage, wit, and sophistication that Hamilton desired for himself. André, realizing that his fate was sealed, desired only to be shot like a soldier and not hanged like a thief. Hamilton strongly pleaded his case, but Washington would not budge, and André was hanged. Hamilton was stunned by what he took as Washington's callousness in refusing André's wish to die with honor like a soldier. (And perhaps he connected it with how Washington kept him from an honorable life as a soldier.) Never before had His Excellency appeared to Hamilton in so unfavorable a light: stern, obstinate, and insensitive to the finer feelings of a gentleman.[27] Commenting on the event to his fiancée, Hamilton wrote, "Some people are only sensible to motives of policy, and from a narrow disposition mistake it."[28] Washington seemed to the young colonel to almost have a heart of stone.

The second event was Hamilton's marriage in December of 1780 to Eliza Schuyler, the daughter of General Philip Schuyler, one of the wealthiest and most important men in the state of New York. Before his marriage, if Hamilton had walked away from headquarters, he would have had no support system. But now he had a powerful and enthralled father-in-law. (Despite Hamilton's shaky pedigree, General Schuyler sincerely welcomed him into the family and viewed him as a rare gem who could do no wrong.) This new security apparently made Hamilton ready to seek a break at the first opportunity.

It came on February 16, 1781, and from our perspective, seems surprisingly trivial. His Excellency met his aide at the top of the stairwell and asked to see him. Hamilton indicated he had to deliver a message to another aide but would be with Washington shortly. Meeting his friend Lafayette on the way back, Hamilton was slightly delayed (in his telling, no more than a minute or so). When he reached the general, he was met with a curt rebuke: "You have kept me waiting at the head of the stairs these ten minutes. I must tell you, sir, that you treat me with disrespect." Hamilton rejoined that he was not aware of doing so, but "since you have thought it necessary to tell me so, we part."[29]

That was it! And within an hour, the general sent another aide and Hamilton's friend, Tench Tilghman, bearing an olive branch, with instructions to smooth out the quarrel and set up an interview between the two men. Hamilton would have none of it. He asked to be excused from even discussing the incident with Washington, further requested the general not to say anything to anyone about the quarrel, and promised to stay on as if nothing had happened until other aides returned and took up the slack.

Hamilton sought to justify his actions in a long, much revised letter to his father-in-law, in which he made a rather astonishing confession: "For the past three years, I have felt no friendship for him and have professed none." He further indicated that he could reveal much that was negative about the general, but would hold his pen until the end of the war, since, he admitted, Washington was useful to the cause.[30] Hamilton succinctly expressed his view of the quarrel in a letter to another aide and friend. "The Great Man and I have come to an open rupture," he wrote to James McHenry. "Without a shadow of reason and on the slightest of ground, he charged me in the most affrontive manner with treating him with disrespect . . . proposals of accommodation have been made on his part but rejected. I pledge my honor to you that he will find me inflexible. He shall for once at least repent his ill-humor."[31] It is worth noting that, although the two men agreed to keep the incident a secret, Hamilton then conveyed his version of the quarrel to a number of key mutual friends. Washington, who "religiously" remained silent, was hurt when he found out that Hamilton had not done what he had asked him to do.

One might logically assume that the aftermath of the incident would write finis to the relationship between Washington and Hamilton, much as the publication of Jefferson's 1796 letter to Philip Mazzei would lead Washington to sever his relationship with his former secretary of state. A brash aide keeps his harried commander in chief waiting, responds to a relatively minor rebuke by quitting on the spot, refuses a genuine offer at reconciliation or even to speak to the general about it, and then shares his side of the story with friends while denying Washington the same opportunity. For such effrontery, one might expect that Washington would simply consign Hamilton to historical oblivion, keep him away from the center of power, or, more importantly, from any chance to find the military glory that Hamilton so desperately sought.

Instead, Washington responded to Hamilton's request and found a military command for him, allowing him to lead the assault on Redoubt No. 10 at Yorktown, one of the climactic moments of the campaign leading to the surrender of Cornwallis and the virtual end of the war. On one level, Washington's forbearance seems almost supernatural. We will never know exactly why he acted as he did, but I think there were likely several factors at work. Washington saw much of himself as a young warrior in the French and Indian War in the young Colonel Hamilton of the American Revolution. Both young men were brash, impulsive, quick-tempered, overly ambitious, and possessed with a burning desire for military glory. This empathy helps explain his toleration of Hamilton's antics.[32] And, of course, Hamilton possessed many positive qualities. Washington had earlier written about him and declared that no one "is more firmly engaged in the cause, or exceeds him in probity and sterling virtue."[33] Finally, Washington was inherently a very fair man. He had, perhaps selfishly, perhaps unfairly (even if understandably), kept Hamilton on as an aide for longer than he should have. Hamilton had more than paid his dues and performed yeoman service for the commander in chief and for the new country. The general might well have concluded it would simply be wrong to deny him his chance for military glory. Interestingly, in accommodating Hamilton's wishes, Washington, whether with specific intent or not, left the door open for the relationship to continue into the future. It would not be quite the same kind of relationship that they had as general and aide. The break allowed for the emergence of a new one, one of a senior partner to a junior partner, but a partnership nevertheless.

During these years, General Washington was never personally close to Hamilton in the way he was to Lafayette, who really appears to be almost a surrogate son (a role Lafayette, unlike Hamilton, was eager to play). Nevertheless, one senses affection for Hamilton in addition to deep respect for his remarkable talents and contributions. As Lafayette tried to reassure Hamilton, "I know the General's friendship and gratitude for you, My Dear Hamilton, both are greater than you perhaps imagine."[34] And despite the harsh words written in anger, there was much in Washington that Hamilton admired. In his words, the general was a "very honest" man, a true patriot who would "never yield to any dishonorable or disloyal plans into which he might be called . . . he would sooner suffer himself to be cut to pieces."[35] Shortly after watching Washington rally the Continental forces at the Battle of Monmouth, Hamilton declared: "I never saw the general to so much advantage. His coolness and firmness were admirable. . . . America owes a great deal to General Washington for this day's work." (And he was a second for his friend John Laurens in a duel with General Charles Lee when the latter criticized Washington.)[36]

Hamilton was too cocksure and critical to ever act in a fawning manner toward Washington, as Lafayette did. Yet he knew the character of the man well enough to write Washington two months after resigning his post to request His Excellency's help in securing a military command. It was done with the expectation that Washington would in fact help him. Almost in the manner of a recalcitrant son who takes parental forbearance for granted, Hamilton apparently believed it was in character for Washington to reward fractious aides. In his case, he was correct.[37]

There is no indication of any type of special and close relationship between the two men in the time between Yorktown and Washington's inauguration as the nation's first president. In the events leading up to the famous incident known as the Newburgh Conspiracy, Washington had been somewhat alarmed at Hamilton's willingness to use the army to pressure Congress into reform, and he warned him that the army was a dangerous instrument to play with. When Washington made Hamilton a brevet colonel at the end of the war, there apparently was no friendly thank-you letter from Hamilton.

There is no evidence Hamilton joined the weeping officers at Fraunces Tavern in New York City as they bid a fond farewell to their commander, or that he made any effort to see the general on his visit to the city. Their correspondence in the years immediately after the war was meager and perfunctory.

If America had prospered under the Articles of Confederation, it is unlikely that Washington and Hamilton would have had any more significant contact. But it did not prosper, and the desire to preserve and strengthen the American union once again brought these men back into a working relationship. The bond between them was not so much one of personal intimacy as one of shared views and common goals for the country they both loved. "By dint of his youth, foreign birth, and cosmopolitan outlook," Chernow suggests, Hamilton "was spared prewar entanglements in provincial state politics, making him a natural spokesman for a new American nationalism."[38] As much as any man, Hamilton was the brainchild of the Constitutional Convention. Washington's reluctant decision to attend ensured the gathering would be the last best effort to strengthen the central government and give it sufficient power to keep the "United States" united as one country. Hamilton's views on how to change the government were more extreme than any of his colleagues at Philadelphia, and it is interesting that he and Washington did not discuss his ideas before Hamilton left for an extended period in the middle of the convention. Washington did write that he was sorry Hamilton had left and wished he would return.[39]

With the ratification of the Constitution in the summer of 1788, it was a foregone conclusion to everyone (with the possible exception of Washington himself) that only the man who was viewed as the savior of American liberty should be its first president. Hamilton was among those who wrote and forcefully argued that Washington, whatever his personal desires, *must* be president. Hamilton was surprisingly blunt, basically arguing that in attending the Constitutional Convention, Washington implicitly committed himself to accepting the presidency, and to refuse would be going back on his unspoken pledge.[40] Hamilton later explained why he was so outspoken: "I trust that the greatest frankness has always marked and will mark every step of my conduct towards you."[41] Washington responded favorably. While Hamilton possessed a devastating candor that sometimes got him in trouble, his frankness appealed to Washington, who admired Hamilton's transparency and straightforward approach (which, incidentally, was quite different from the approach used by Jefferson).

After Robert Morris, the financial wizard of the American Revolution, declined the president's request to be his secretary of the treasury, Washington next asked his brilliant and financially savvy former aide to take the post. It turned out to be perhaps the most important decision that Washington made as president of the United States. Washington's determination to secure the Union defined his presidency. The success of his administration largely hinged on the adaptation of fiscal policies that would revive confidence in the fledging nation, for the country seemed to be drowning in a debt it could not pay off. (The nation's entire income under the Articles of Confederation was less than the interest on the debt.) President Washington knew a great deal about foreign affairs and about issues involving war with Native Americans and trade, but he knew little about the intricacies of high finance. Lacking that type of financial knowledge, Washington in effect told Hamilton that the Department of Treasury was his bailiwick. He left the way open, and Hamilton, always eager to seize control, quickly filled the vacuum.

It is not an exaggeration to say that Hamilton was much more than merely Washington's secretary of the treasury. Concerning himself with every phase of public policy, he was in many ways Washington's prime minister, and in at least one famous letter he attacked critics of "me and my administration." His complicated financial plans involved funding the debt and paying the full amount to whoever currently held the certificates of debt (often to the great benefit of speculators and to the detriment of original holders of the certificates). His plans for the federal government to assume the war debt for all the states, for the establishment of a new powerful national bank, new excise taxes, and government encouragement of manufacturing were audacious, very controversial, and amazingly successful in putting the credit of the United States on a sound economic footing.[42] In Ron Chernow's telling phrase, Hamilton was "a messenger from the future that we now inhabit." No one else "articulated such a clear and prescient vision of America's future political, military and economic strength."[43] He was an early promoter of what later was called high-tech capitalism (he set up the legal framework for capitalism) and championed the development of a world-class military force. Basically, all of his endeavors were directed toward establishing the United States as a formidable nation.

His far-reaching program engendered great controversy and intense opposition. It led to the central fact of Washington's first administration: the bitter split between his two top advisors and the beginning of what ultimately led to the creation of our modern political parties. Beginning a tendency that continues to the present day, the historian James Roger Sharp reminds us, the opposing sides both "surveyed the political landscape as if looking through hideously distorting spectacles, seeing grotesque and tormenting shapes and figures that were products of intense and deeply felt fears."[44] As Jefferson and Madison saw it, Hamilton was creating a vast system of special privilege that enriched the few at the expense of the many, encouraged an unhealthy speculative spirit among the people, upset the balance of property in society, and corrupted the national legislature. In the Hamiltonian insistence on a loose construction of the Constitution, Jefferson espied a dangerous trend to aggrandize the powers of the central government at the expense of the authority of the states and the liberties of the people.[45] Under Hamilton's diabolical leadership, the secretary of state feared the United States would re-create the very political and economic institutions that hopefully had been destroyed by the American Revolution. In 1792, Jefferson explicitly warned the president that Hamilton hoped to "change . . . the present republican form of government to that of a monarchy."[46]

Hamilton, of course, saw it very differently. In his words: "I assure you on my *private faith and honor* as a man that there is not . . . a shadow of foundation of it. . . . I am *affectionately* attached to the Republican theory. . . . The only enemy which republicanism has to fear in this Country is the spirit of faction and anarchy" which would not let government work effectively and thus would set the stage for disaster.[47] Ron Chernow emphasizes the positive aspects of his program: "Hamilton promoted a forward looking agenda of a modern nation-state with a market economy and an affirmative view of central government. His meritocratic vision allowed greater scope in the economic sphere for the individual liberties that Jefferson defended so eloquently in the political sphere."[48]

Over time, the hatred between the two departmental heads became palpable, and the president, despite his very best efforts, could not heal the breach—or even paper over the differences. Certainly, Hamilton was partly to blame. He was incapable of the forbearance His Excellency requested. A captive of his emotions, Hamilton revealed an irrepressible need to respond to attacks and never knew when to stop. That is one of the very significant differences between Washington and Hamilton. The mature Washington managed, with few exceptions, to control his emotions and passions. Hamilton never did, and while he would function brilliantly under Washington's calming influence, without it, he was likely to go off the deep end and make major errors of judgment.

Jefferson's hostility toward Hamilton came out most clearly in his outburst to Washington, one Virginia planter to another, about the immigrant interloper. He declared he could no longer stand to have his reputation "beclouded by the slanders of a man whose history, from the moment at which history can stoop to notice him, is a tissue of machinations against the liberty of the country which has not only received and given him bread, but heaped it's honors upon his head."[49] In the words of one Hamilton scholar, "At bottom, Thomas Jefferson could not countenance the fact that an immigrant upstart without pedigree had dared challenge him."[50] Landed aristocrat though he was, Washington did not allow such statements to cloud his confidence or his trust in the brilliant West Indian. Indeed, I think it is significant that Washington was obviously more impressed by Hamilton's defense of his conduct in office than by Jefferson's criticism of it. For Washington sent Jefferson's critique to Hamilton for his rejoinder (pretending the criticism came from someone else), but never communicated to Jefferson the substance of Hamilton's reply so that he might respond. In short, Hamilton's rejoinder satisfied the president.

Another incident bolsters this interpretation. On October 1, 1792, responding to Jefferson's charges that Hamilton was a monarchist, Washington lectured Jefferson that, "as to the idea of transforming this government into a monarchy, he did not believe there were ten men in the United States whose opinions were worth attention who entertained such a thought."[51] There is no record that Washington *ever* spoke or wrote to Hamilton in this curt, condescending tone. Given that Washington was the soul of tact and diplomacy, this blunt rebuke is highly revealing. It is almost as if the president is telling his secretary of state that he has fallen victim to a crackpot conspiracy theory.

Jefferson, who recorded the conversation in his personal notes, apparently interpreted the comments differently. He could never accept the fact that Washington might agree with Hamilton on the merits of the argument, and he looked for other explanations, such as the president's general decline due to aging and Hamilton's skill as a manipulator. Ron Chernow is on target. Hamilton, he writes, "gained incomparable power under Washington because the President approved of the agenda that he promoted with such tireless brilliance."[52] Jefferson was wrong when he charged that Hamilton manipulated the president. Despite how often the charge is made, and it is still made regularly, the idea that Washington was essentially Hamilton's puppet simply does not reflect reality. In areas he considered his province and responsibility, Washington was, among human beings, one of those most unwilling to be led. On fundamental political matters, Washington was simply more in tune with his secretary of treasury than he was with his secretary of state. They shared an intense nationalism, belief in a strong central government, and a relentlessly realistic view of human nature. As Washington once expressed it, "The motives which predominate most in human affairs is self-love and self-interest."[53] The basic fact is that, for better or for worse, Washington was more of a Hamiltonian than he was a Jeffersonian.

Hamilton resigned his position in 1795 to return to private practice and to care for his growing family (he and Eliza had eight children). It should be noted that Hamilton remained a relatively poor man throughout his years of public service, despite the opportunities for achieving great wealth. He conducted his affairs at the Treasury Department with such probity that his many enemies, try as they might, could never prove any personal malfeasance in his position. (It is now clear that Jefferson was behind the failed Giles Resolutions that called for Hamilton's ouster for misappropriation of public funds.)[54] His critics failed because he lived up to his pledge: "It shall never be said, with any color of truth, that my ambition or interest has stood in the way of the public good."[55] Hamilton expressed his approach on the way a public official should act when a friend suggested an action which, while legal, might appear improper: "You remember the saying with regard to Caesar's wife. I think the spirit of it applicable to every man in the administration of finances in the country." (Caesar's wife was not only to be pure—she must *appear* to be pure as well.)[56] As to why he worked so hard, suffered extreme criticism, and sacrificed financially for as many years as he did, Hamilton made two revealing comments: "There must be some public fools who sacrifice private to public interest."[57] Or again, writing to his fascinating sister-in-law, Angelica Church: "You will ask why I do not quit this disagreeable trade. How can I? What is to become of my fame and glory?"[58]

When Hamilton resigned, the president wrote a letter which indicates how closely and effectively they had worked together: "In every relation, which you have borne to me, I have found that my confidence in your talents, exertions and integrity, has been well placed. I the more freely render this testimony of my approbation because I speak from opportunities . . . w[hi]ch cannot deceive me." The treasury secretary was also impressed. He described the president as "modest and sage." Facing complicated issues, Washington "consulted much, pondered much, resolved slowly, resolved surely."[59] Hamilton's resignation by no means ended his relationship with Washington. He remained the president's unofficial but most trusted advisor, and he played a key role in trying to win support for the controversial Jay Treaty, being stoned by an angry mob in the process. The two men, now exchanging notes marked "private," closely cooperated in producing one of the great documents in American history, "Washington's Farewell Address." While Hamilton was the major wordsmith, the ideas and the spirit were Washington's. As Richard Norton Smith concludes, "The Farewell Address became, like the administration it capped, an intellectual alliance between two like-minded nationalists."[60]

Washington's genuine affection for Hamilton, as well as his exquisite tact, is best illustrated in the aftermath of the Maria Reynolds scandal that broke shortly after Washington left office. It was the first great sex scandal in American history, and it captivated Americans' attention then as the Monica Lewinsky scandal did in the 1990s. In briefest essence, Hamilton carried on a fairly lengthy adulterous affair with the seductive Maria Reynolds, apparently with the encouragement of her husband, James, who then blackmailed the secretary of the treasury. The tryst became public knowledge in 1797 as a result of an article by the scandalmonger James Callender, who also claimed that Hamilton had helped James Reynolds by giving him inside information from the Department of Treasury. (Ironically, Callender would later be the first to publish the charges linking Hamilton's nemesis, Jefferson, to his slave, Sally Hemings.) The charge of public malfeasance led Hamilton to do something that hurt his family, shocked his friends, and titillated the nation. He published an unprecedented ninety-seven-page confession, laying out in excruciating detail the specifics of the affair. Why did he do it? Perhaps there was some deep psychological need for self-flagellation, but the main reason was to prove that while he had been guilty of a private sin, he was not guilty of a dereliction of his trust as a public official. So important was his public image and his need for a spotless official reputation that Hamilton was willing to risk destroying his marriage and humiliating his colleagues by publicly admitting to a sordid affair which included many meetings in his own home while his wife was away.[61]

In the midst of the crisis, but without making any reference to it, Washington sent Hamilton a valuable wine cooler that had sat on his desk when he was president, "as a token of my sincere regard and friendship for you, and as a remembrance of me." In the brief letter, which he began with the salutation "My dear Sir," a salutation Washington used only with those with whom he was very friendly, he twice assured Hamilton that he was his *"sincere"* friend, and also sent his wife's regards (Martha and Eliza were close friends).[62] The letter was notable for what it did not say as well as what it did say. The most famous and revered man in the country was expressing his solidarity with a friend in a time of great personal crisis—and doing it with great sensitivity. Hamilton was moved by the gesture: "The token of your regard which it announces, is very precious to me, and will always be remembered."[63] The wine cooler in fact became one of the family's most treasured possessions, along with a Gilbert Stuart portrait of Washington that was given as a gift at another time. Washington ended another letter that year with strong words that he rarely employed: "I would wish you to believe, that with great truth and sincerity, I am *always Your Affectionate friend.*"[64]

Another example of their friendship is that, after leaving office, Washington wrote to Hamilton and asked him to aid Lafayette's son in his effort to return to France. (Both men were fond of Lafayette, which further strengthened their relationship.) Washington requested Hamilton to advance the young Lafayette $300 on his, Washington's, behalf, a request Hamilton honored. Other events dealing with France soon pulled the two men back into direct face-to-face contact. Washington's dream of a peaceful, undisturbed retirement was shattered by the crisis with France that seemed likely to lead to war in the aftermath of the XYZ Affair in 1798, during which a French official sought bribes from American diplomats before agreeing to meet with them. Once again, in the midst of crisis, the nation turned its gaze to the master of Mount Vernon.[65]

The aging general, enjoying retirement, was called upon to be the commander in chief of the American forces raised to meet the impending struggle as France and America engaged in an undeclared war. Washington, while professing his typical reservations, agreed to take on the onerous responsibility, but only if Hamilton were made his second in command. In this case, second in command would be particularly important, as Washington declared he would take to the field only in the unlikely case of an actual invasion by

French troops. Washington essentially forced President John Adams (who, as we have seen, despised Hamilton) to accept his choice by threatening resignation unless he did so. (One wonders how President Washington would have responded if someone had treated him in the heavy-handed manner that he treated his successor.)

The choice of Hamilton as his second in command also temporarily ruptured the close friendship between Washington and General Henry Knox, one of the few men whom Washington declared that he "loved."[66] Knox was deeply hurt and offended by Washington's action of ranking Hamilton, a colonel in the past war, ahead of him, who had been a major general. As a sign of just how close Washington had become with Hamilton, he confidentially shared Knox's angry letter with his second in command "as a proof of my frankness and friendship."[67] Hamilton showed the same type of candor in sharing with Washington his negative assessment of James McHenry, the secretary of war: "My friend McHenry is wholly insufficient for his place, with the additional misfortune of not having himself the least suspicion of the fact."[68]

Of course, the threatened war did not materialize (thanks in large part to Adams's courageous diplomacy). It was a frustrating experience for the former president, who may have become concerned with Hamilton's plans to perhaps use the crisis for causes other than the defense of the country against France. Joseph Ellis argues that Hamilton wanted to use the new army, officered completely by Federalists, to awe Virginia into better submission to the national government. For this, or for some other reason or reasons, the final letters between the two men lacked the closeness and intimacy of those at the beginning of their final partnership.[69]

Washington's sudden death, on December 14, 1799, shocked the entire nation. It was certainly a terrible blow to Hamilton on several levels. While Hamilton's correspondence focused on Washington's death primarily in political terms, he was undoubtedly touched by personal grief as well, as indicated by his comment, "Tis only for me to mingle my tears with those of my fellow soldiers."[70] In his condolence letter to the president's widow, Hamilton referred to "the numerous and distinguished marks of confidence and friendship of which you have yourself been a witness."[71] To a friend, he asserted, "Perhaps no friend of his has more cause to lament, on personal account, than my self."[72] His best known—and most controversial—comment was to

Washington's personal secretary, Tobias Lear: "I have been much indebted to the kindness of the General, and he was an Aegis very essential to me."[73] Critics have interpreted the term "aegis" in a very negative way. They utilize it as proof that Hamilton "used" Washington to achieve his goals.[74] Personally, I don't believe Hamilton intended it in that fashion. Hamilton knew how much Lear loved Washington, and would not have written him a letter emphasizing how he used him. Rather, in employing the word "aegis," I believe Hamilton meant to acknowledge what a "protector" Washington was, as opposed to an instrument (a shield) that was to be wielded by him. There is a subtle but significant difference.

The final example of how close the men had become is revealed by Hamilton's concern as to what would happen to the many confidential letters that they had shared (we know that Hamilton had used a simple code in some of them).[75] Lear acknowledged the problem, admitting there were "many which every public and private consideration should withhold from further inspection."[76] Apparently, they were destroyed, as no letters from Hamilton to Washington employing any code have been found. Perhaps those letters would have enabled us to flesh out in even more detail the relationship between them, but the evidence is clear that while Washington broke with Jefferson, Madison, and Monroe (all Hamilton's opponents as well), he remained friendly and close to Hamilton until his own death. Some dispute the amount of affection between the two men, noting, for example, that Hamilton never visited Mount Vernon, but they ignore the fact that Washington sincerely invited him to come and that Hamilton rarely traveled beyond New York City and Albany.[77]

Washington's death ended perhaps the most productive collaboration in American history. Certainly, Washington was the senior partner and the superior man in terms of overall character. But Hamilton, despite his many flaws (even his eulogist, Gouverneur Morris, privately conceded he was vain, opinionated, and indiscreet), also had numerous admirable and likable characteristics (courage, intellect, charm, wit, personal probity, and deep patriotism) that earned the affection of Washington.[78] George Washington is the "Indispensable Man" in the founding of America. But could he have achieved his goals for a strong and economically powerful nation without the ideas and skillful administration of his secretary of the treasury? The answer is, almost certainly, "No." Thus, it is fair to conclude that Alexander Hamilton was the indispensable man to the "Indispensable Man."

Notes

This essay is adapted from chapter 7 of Peter R. Henriques, *Realistic Visionary: A Portrait of George Washington* (Charlottesville, Va., 2006).

1. By far the most detailed and thorough examination of Hamilton's youth appears in the first two chapters of Ron Chernow's *Alexander Hamilton* (New York, 2004).

2. Joseph Charles's *The Origins of the American Party System* (New York, 1961) is one example of a portrayal of a Machiavellian Hamilton controlling a rather dimwitted Washington.

3. Quoted, among other places, in Stephen F. Knott, *Alexander Hamilton and the Persistence of Myth* (Lawrence, Kans., 2002), 11.

4. Quoted, among other places, in John C. Miller, *Alexander Hamilton: Portrait in Paradox* (New York, 1959), 523.

5. I am indebted to Rick Brookhiser for this analogy.

6. Quoted in Jacob E. Cooke, *Alexander Hamilton* (New York, 1982), 266n44.

7. See Adrienne Koch, *Jefferson and Madison: The Great Collaboration* (New York, 1950).

8. George Will, quoted in Knott, *Alexander Hamilton and the Persistence of Myth,* 6.

9. Quoted in Chernow, *Alexander Hamilton,* 189–90.

10. Thomas Jefferson to James Madison, quoted in ibid., 496.

11. Richard B. Morris, *Seven Who Shaped Our Destiny* (New York, 1976), 223.

12. Quoted in Chernow, *Alexander Hamilton,* 308.

13. Joanne B. Freeman, *Affairs of Honor: National Politics in the Early Republic* (New Haven, Conn., 2001), 167.

14. Chernow, *Alexander Hamilton,* 5.

15. Freeman, *Affairs of Honor,* 161.

16. GW to John Adams, 25 September 1798, *PGW: Ret. Ser.,* 3:41.

17. GW to Joseph Reed, 23 January 1776, *PGW: Rev. Ser.,* 3:173.

18. Chernow, *Alexander Hamilton,* 89.

19. Hamilton's difficult dealings with Gates are recounted in Chernow, *Alexander Hamilton,* 100–106.

20. Hamilton to GW, 12 November 1777, *PGW: Rev. Ser.,* 12:225.

21. This point is taken from Cooke, *Alexander Hamilton,* 27.

22. Hamilton to John Laurens, 12 September 1780, *PAH,* 2:428.

23. Hamilton to Laurens, 8 January 1780, ibid., 2:254–55.

24. Barry Schwartz, *George Washington: The Making of an American Symbol* (New York, 1987), 88.

25. Chernow, *Alexander Hamilton,* 89.

26. Hamilton to GW, 22 November 1780, *PAH,* 2:509.

27. This point is taken from Miller, *Alexander Hamilton,* 71.

28. Hamilton to Eliza Schuyler, 2 October 1780, *PAH,* 2:448.

29. Hamilton to Philip Schuyler, 18 February 1781, ibid., 2:564.

30. Hamilton to P. Schuyler, 18 February 1781, ibid., 2:566.

31. Hamilton to James McHenry, 18 February 1781, ibid., 2:569.

32. I am indebted to Dorothy Twohig for this insight.

33. GW to John Sullivan, 4 February 1781, Fitzpatrick, 21:181.

34. Lafayette to Hamilton, 28 November 1780, *PAH,* 2:517.

35. Madison's notes of a discussion with Hamilton on 13 February 1783, ibid., 3:264.

36. Hamilton to Elias Boudinot, 5 July 1778, ibid., 1:512.

37. This point is taken from Cooke, *Alexander Hamilton,* 28.

38. Chernow, *Alexander Hamilton,* 157.

39. GW wrote to Hamilton on July 3, 1787: "Not having compared ideas with you, Sir, I cannot judge how far our sentiments agreed" (*PGW: Conf. Ser.,* 5:245).

40. Hamilton to GW, 13 August 1788, ibid., 6:444.

41. Hamilton to GW, 9 September 1792, *PGW: Pres. Ser.,* 11:92.

42. Hamilton to Edward Carrington, 26 May 1792, *PAH,* 11:429.

43. Chernow, *Alexander Hamilton,* 6.

44. James Roger Sharp, *American Politics in the Early Republic: The New Nation in Crisis* (New Haven, Conn., 1993), 49.

45. These points are drawn from an unpublished talk by Eugene R. Sheridan, "Thomas Jefferson and the American Presidency," in the possession of the author.

46. Jefferson to GW, 23 May 1792, *PGW: Pres. Ser.,* 11:104.

47. Hamilton to Carrington, 26 May 1792, *PAH,* 11:443–44 (emphasis added).

48. Chernow, *Alexander Hamilton,* 628.

49. Jefferson to GW, 9 September 1792, *PGW: Pres. Ser.,* 11:104.

50. Knott, *Alexander Hamilton and the Persistence of Myth,* 11.

51. Jefferson, Notes of a Conversation with George Washington, 1 October 1792, *PTJ,* 24:435.

52. Chernow, *Alexander Hamilton,* 290.

53. GW to Madison, 3 December 1784, *PGW: Conf. Ser.,* 2:166.

54. Eugene R. Sheridan, "Thomas Jefferson and the Giles Resolutions," *WMQ,* 3rd ser., 49 (July 1992): 589–608.

55. Hamilton to GW, 29 July (and 1 August) 1798, *PGW: Ret. Ser.,* 2:467.

56. Miller, *Alexander Hamilton,* 244.

57. Hamilton to Robert Troup, 13 April 1795, *PAH,* 18:329.

58. Hamilton to Angelica Church, quoted in Chernow, *Alexander Hamilton,* 457.

59. *Letter From Alexander Hamilton, Concerning the Public Conduct & Character of John Adams, Esq. President of the United States,* 24 October 1800, *PAH,* 25:214.

60. Richard Norton Smith, *Patriarch: George Washington and the New American Nation* (New York, 1993), 280. Chapter 4 of Joseph J. Ellis's *Founding Brothers: The Revolutionary Generation* (New York, 2000) has an excellent section on this topic.

61. This fascinating chapter of Hamilton's life is sympathetically but not uncritically presented in Chernow, *Alexander Hamilton,* especially chapters 21 and 30.

62. GW to Hamilton, 21 August 1797, *PGW: Ret. Ser.,* 1:313. I am indebted to Rick Brookhiser for the insight about how this incident reflects Washington's tact and sensitivity.

63. Hamilton to GW, 28 August 1797, *PGW: Ret. Ser.,* 1:322.

64. GW to Hamilton, 27 May 1798, ibid., 2:297 (emphasis added).

65. GW to Hamilton, 8 October 1797, ibid., 1:388.

66. GW to Henry Knox, 2 March 1797, Fitzpatrick, 35:409.

67. GW to Hamilton, 9 August 1798, *PGW: Ret. Ser.*, 2:500.

68. Hamilton to GW, 29 July–1 August 1798, ibid., 2:467.

69. Joseph J. Ellis, *His Excellency: George Washington* (New York, 2004), 250–52.

70. General Orders, December 1799, *PAH,* 24:112.

71. Hamilton to Martha Washington, 12 January 1800, ibid., 24:184.

72. Hamilton to Charles C. Pinckney, 22 December 1799, ibid., 24:116.

73. Hamilton to Tobias Lear, 2 January 1800, ibid., 24:155.

74. Joseph Charles is a good example of an historian who has done this.

75. Hamilton to Lear, 2 January 1800, *PAH,* 24:155. Hamilton wrote to Washington on February 16, 1799, and made reference to using codes (see *PGW: Ret. Ser.*, 3:383).

76. Lear to Hamilton, 16 January 1800, *PAH,* 24:198.

77. For GW's invitation, see GW to Hamilton, 26 August 1792, *PGW: Pres. Ser.*, 11:39. On Hamilton not venturing far, see Chernow, *Alexander Hamilton,* 332.

78. Gouverneur Morris, *Diary,* 13 July 1800, quoted in *PAH,* 26:324n3.

George Washington and Lafayette

Father and Son of the Revolution

STUART LEIBIGER

Virtually all historical works on George Washington and the Marquis de Lafayette affirm the existence of a father-son relationship between the two men. Most of these works do not, however, probe the nature of this association very deeply. Instead, most take it for granted, and some romanticize it. For example, David A. Clary's *Adopted Son: Washington, Lafayette, and the Friendship that Saved the Revolution* offers a starry-eyed, idealistic interpretation, describing the relationship as love at first sight for both men, and declaring that Washington "had no other confidential friend." A picture caption in Douglass Southall Freeman's monumental biography of the Virginian claims that "never during the Revolution was there so speedy and complete a conquest of the heart of Washington" as that performed by the Frenchman. An unusual exception to the general interpretation is James R. Gaines's *For Liberty and Glory: Washington, Lafayette and Their Revolutions,* which takes a much more realistic, down-to-earth view of the association.[1]

The father-son claim is based on the writings of both Lafayette and a few of his contemporaries. He described the commander in chief as his father, and himself as a son, in letters to Washington and others. Many firsthand observers also described the association in these terms. Interestingly, however, Washington himself did not—at least not in writing. He often expressed deep affection, even love, for his friend, but his letters never reciprocated the filial language. This circumstance raises interesting questions about the relationship: Did the older man view it the same way as Lafayette and many of his contemporaries, and as historians have ever since? Was it "love at first sight" for either or both men? Did the relationship change over time, and, if so, then how? How unusual was the friendship for Washington? How typical, or atypical, was it for the time period?

A careful analysis reveals that the Washington-Lafayette friendship began not as love at first sight, but instead as a marriage of convenience based on mutual interest, and that it then gradually grew and developed into an intimate friendship. In addition, while it may have seemed a father-son relationship to Lafayette, it may not have served as one for Washington. Over time, he certainly grew to love Lafayette, but ultimately the Frenchman was perhaps more of an intimate friend than the son Washington never had. Was Lafayette Washington's closest friend? Almost definitely not.

As a teenage aristocrat in 1770s France, Lafayette probably first learned about Washington and the American Revolution at Masonic meetings and at aristocratic social functions. In Paris he and several other French officers were recruited to fight for America by the diplomat Silas Deane, who promised them general's commissions in the Continental Army. Against the orders of his own government (then at peace with Great Britain), the nineteen-year-old sailed for the United States in the spring of 1777 in his own ship. For him, the Revolution was an opportunity to gain personal glory, but he also believed in the ideology of the Declaration of Independence. To his wife, Adrienne, Lafayette wrote that "the welfare of America is intimately connected with the happiness of all mankind; she will become the respectable and safe asylum of virtue, integrity, tolerance, equality, and a peaceful liberty."[2]

Deane, as well as Benjamin Franklin, the American minister to France, urged Congress to receive Lafayette warmly. "The Civilities and Respect that may be shown to him will be serviceable to our Affairs here," wrote the two diplomats, "as pleasing, not only to his powerfull Relations & to the Court, but to the whole French Nation." Deane advised Robert Morris that "a generous reception of [him] will do Us infinite Service," and that if "well managed it will greatly help us."[3]

Lafayette's influential relatives insisted that Deane and Franklin place him under a watchful eye. "I assured them I would recommend him to the Care & oversight of one who would be as a Father to him on every Occasion," Deane explained to Morris. "All he seeks is Glory." Knowing that Lafayette would sooner or later end up with the Continental Army, the commissioners wrote a similar letter to Washington, although no evidence exists that the commander in chief ever received it. "Favour him with your Counsels," they pleaded. "Advise him if necessary, with a friendly Affection, and Secure him from too much Imposition." The intended recipient hardly needed this advice.[4]

When Lafayette arrived in Philadelphia in July 1777, General Washington had already become fed up by having French officers, who had been promised high rank, thrust upon him. The two men met at a public dinner at the City Tavern. At forty-five years old, Washington was the same age that Lafayette's father would have been had he still been alive. Lafayette, whose father died when he was two, had grown up fatherless.

The young adventurer, who could only speak broken English, found himself awed by Washington's physicality and demeanor (not an unusual reaction). The American commander, in turn, also experienced the typical reaction—he was charmed by the enthusiastic Frenchman, who described the encounter in his memoir (referring to himself in the third person, as was his usual bent). Although Washington, he wrote, "was surrounded by officers and citizens, the majesty of his figure and his height were unmistakable. His affable and noble welcome to M. de Lafayette was no less distinguished. . . . It was with such simplicity that two friends were united whose attachment and confidence were cemented by the greatest of all causes." French officer Chevalier Dubuysson attested that "General Washington . . . paid him a thousand compliments."[5]

In 1828, Lafayette described the climactic moment to the historian Jared Sparks: "When they were about to separate, Washington took Lafayette aside, spoke to him very kindly, complimented him on the noble spirit he had shown and the sacrifices he had made in favor of the American cause, and then told him, that he should be pleased if he would make the quarters of the Commander-in-chief his home . . . and consider himself at all times as one of his family; adding, in a tone of pleasantry, that he could not promise him the luxuries of a court, or even the conveniences . . . but, since he had become an American soldier, he would doubtless . . . accommodate himself . . . with a good grace to the customs, manners, and privations of a republican army." And so, in spite of his frustration with the French, Washington invited the would-be warrior to join his "military family" as an aide on the headquarters staff.[6]

On the very same day that the two met, Congress resolved "that in consideration of his zeal, illustrious family and connexions," Lafayette should "have the rank and commission of major general" in the Continental Army. It was an honorary appointment, with no pay and no troops. Congressman Henry Laurens noted that "the honour of fighting near General Washington & having rank in the Army was all he coveted. . . . This illustrious Stranger . . . will have a Short Campaign & then probably return to France & Secure to us the powerful Interest of his high & extensive connections."[7]

When the new recruit arrived in camp resplendent in his fancy uniform, Washington may well have wondered what he had gotten himself into. To his dismay, he discovered that Lafayette expected not an honorary post, but to command an actual division in the army. Even worse, he expected the Virginian to lobby Congress to get it for him. Privately, Washington complained to Congressman Benjamin Harrison: "What the designs of Congress respecting this Gentn. were and what line of Conduct I am to pursue, to comply with their design, and his expectations, I know no more than the Child unborn and beg to be instructed. If Congress meant, that this Rank should be unaccompanied by Command I wish it had been sufficiently explain'd to him. If on the other hand, it was intended to vest him with all powers of a Major General, why have I been led into a Contrary belief, and left in the dark?" Harrison confirmed that Congress never meant for Lafayette to have anything more than an honorary command.[8]

David Clary's *Adopted Son* suggests that the two men almost immediately fell in love with each other as the father and son each never had. Yet there is a problem with this interpretation of a "love-at-first-sight" instant mutual father-son relationship. The relationship seems to have developed by degrees, especially on Washington's end. His connections rarely, if ever, were love at first sight. Instead, they started as marriages of convenience and then only gradually became intimate. "Select the most deserving only for your friendships," Washington once wrote, "and before this becomes intimate, weight their dispositions and character *well*. True friendship is a plant of slow growth; to be sincere, there must be a congeniality of temper and pursuits."[9]

If this relationship began as a marriage of convenience, then what was in it for each man? Lafayette sought fame and saw the American commander as his avenue to achieve it. He hoped that if he attached his star to Washington's, it would lead to glory. For Lafayette, the friendship, in short, was the means to an end. His own writings show that his admiration for his commander took hold only gradually. He often wrote things like, "I have come to venerate [him] as I know him better," or that Washington's "affectionate interest in me soon won my heart," and that "I admire him more each day."[10]

Washington's letters make the exact same point. A couple of years after they met, he informed Lafayette that "your strict & uniform friendship for *me*, has ripened the first impressions of esteem . . . into perfect love & gratitude that neither time nor absence can impair." For him, too, the friendship needed to ripen over time. Here, again, he used his horticultural metaphor, likening the development of a friendship to the slow growth of a delicate plant.[11]

What was in the friendship for Washington? The general shrewdly cultivated the aristocrat, hoping to gain French support in the war—perhaps even to obtain a French alliance. He also recognized a potentially powerful personal ally who could help fend off his American critics. This relationship was thus a typical marriage of convenience, born of self-interest, that grew and evolved over time into intimacy. As Clary argues, however, Washington became intimate with Lafayette more quickly than he did with other people. Relatively speaking, this friendship grew very fast, as these men came to admire each other remarkably quickly.

Lafayette no longer had a father, and Washington didn't have a biological son. At twenty-six years apart, they were the right age for a father-son relationship. Moreover, the American saw in the Frenchman a lot of himself as a young man, especially his irrepressible ambition. One nevertheless wonders, could Washington really have been influenced by the effusive and obsequious letters that Lafayette wrote to him? Improbable as it might seem, this was the eighteenth century, and the Virginian understood the importance of a patron and the language of patronage. Having himself written such letters as a young man to British generals during the French and Indian War, he was not put off by flattery. But it is also worth noting that as the patron, he did not reciprocate with equally effusive terminology. Lafayette's letters began to call Washington his "adopted father," but Washington's letters never refer to Lafayette as an "adopted son." His replies call the young man "a friend," but never "a son."[12]

Lafayette got his first taste of battle at Brandywine on September 11, 1777. He began the battle as an observer but ended up as a participant, rallying retreating troops before getting shot in the left calf. As far as the Frenchman was concerned, Brandywine was significant for two reasons. First, he won Washington's respect by proving his personal bravery. Time and again, the older man had exhibited incredible personal bravery under enemy fire, and he respected it when he saw it in others. Second, the twenty-year-old Lafayette did at Brandywine exactly the same thing that the twenty-three-year-old Washington had done at General Edward Braddock's defeat during the French and Indian War in 1755. He began the battle as a volunteer observer and he ended it as a participant, rallying the troops. The commander in chief could not have missed how similar the young general's performance was to his own behavior twenty-two years earlier.[13]

Lafayette later claimed that, as he was carried from the field, Washington instructed the surgeon "to care for me as though I were his son, for he loved me in the same way." This story is perhaps either an exaggeration or an outright fabrication, but Brandywine was a milestone in their growing friendship nevertheless.[14]

In October, Lafayette wrote to Washington seeking support and advice in obtaining command of a division. "Give me leave, dear general, to speack to you about my own business with all the confidence of a son, of a friend, as you favoured me with those two so precious titles. . . . Advise me, dear general, for what I am to do." Why, Lafayette asked, should he "stay in a country where I could not find the occasions of distinguishing myself." He promised to "conduct myself entirely by your advices."[15]

Rather than discourage Lafayette's pretensions, Washington instead wrote to Congress supporting the request: "I feel myself in a delicate situation with respect to the Marquis Le Fayette. He is extremely solicitous of having a Command equal to his Rank, and possesses very different Ideas as to the purposes of his appointment, from those Congress have mentioned to me. He certainly did not understand them. . . . It appears to me, from a consideration of his illustrious and important connections, the attachment which he has manifested to our cause, and the consequences, which his return in disgust, might produce, that it will be adviseable to gratify him in his wishes, and the more so, as several Gentlemen from France, who came over under some assurances, have gone back disappointed in their expectations." Washington's reason for backing the appointment is very revealing: the United States could not afford to let Lafayette go back to France in disappointment and disgust. He wanted his young officer promoted because it could help bring the French into the war. "Besides," the commander in chief added, "he is sensible, discreet in his Manner has made great proficiency in our Language and from the disposition he discovered at the Battle of Brandy Wine, possesses a large share of bravery and Military ardor."[16]

On November 25, 1777, General Nathanael Greene sent about 400 Continentals under Lafayette to Gloucester, New Jersey. The American force attacked and routed over 300 British and Hessians under General Earl Cornwallis, killing 20, wounding 20, and taking 14 prisoners. To his commander in chief, Lafayette praised the conduct of his troops, adding, "I wish *that this little succes of ours* may please you."[17]

Duly impressed, Washington the next day tried to persuade Congress to grant Lafayette a command. As always, he emphasized the positive effect the young soldier's advancement would have in France, with whom the United States hoped to ally. To refuse his "applications for a Command," Washington warned, "will not only induce him to return in disgust [to France], but may involve some unfavorable circumstances. There are now some vacant Divisions in the Army, to one of which he may be appointed. . . . He went to Jersey with Genl. Greene and I find he has not been inactive there." In December, Congress complied with the request. Given a division of Virginians, Lafayette outfitted them at his own personal expense.[18]

During much of the winter at Valley Forge, the two men saw one another on an almost daily basis. Lafayette wrote uninhibited letters to his commander, in which he expressed affection, sought favors, gave advice, and even disagreed. He typically addressed the correspondence to "My most dear and beloved general." He gave written suggestions (sometimes on his own, sometimes in reply to requests issued to all the officers) on the location of the winter encampment, on the feasibility of conducting a winter campaign, on uniforms, on handling French soldiers, on the need for a quartermaster general, and on courts-martial. In January 1778, he promised to take "the liberty you gave me of telling freely every idea of mine which could strike me as not being useless to a better order of things." According to Lafayette's memoir, Washington remarked at a council of war that "'we should be embarrassed . . . to show ourselves to an officer who has just left the French army.'" "'I am here to learn, and not to teach,' replied M. de Lafayatte, and that tone produced a good effect, because it was unusual for a European."[19]

Washington's letters to his young subordinate began with the salutation "My Dear Marqs.," and closed with the term "Affectionately." These words are extremely significant. Washington always addressed letters to remote acquaintances with "Sir," and letters to familiar acquaintances with "Dear Sir," but he reserved "My Dear Sir" only for intimate friends. Moreover, only to intimates did he end his letters with the term "Affectionately." Remarkably, Washington's earliest surviving letter to Lafayette, written in late December 1777, only five months after the two men met, begins with "My Dear Marquis" and closes with "affectionate" regards.[20]

To Congressman Gouverneur Morris, Washington wrote that "I do most devoutly wish that we had not a single Foreigner among us, except the Marquis de la Fayette, who acts upon very different principles than those which govern the rest." Yet it is difficult to evaluate this friendship, because Lafayette's writings consistently exaggerated it. Then, and later, he claimed that the commander depended upon him for advice. The truth is just the opposite—Lafayette needed Washington's advice and craved his approval, which the Virginian steadfastly provided. The older man enjoyed mentoring his young friend, but he also did it to keep him happy and out of trouble.[21]

It was during the Valley Forge winter that the so-called Conway Cabal, a critical episode in their friendship, took place. Contrary to myth, the Conway Cabal was not a full-blown conspiracy to replace the commander in chief. But there were grumblings in Congress about Washington's lack of military success. A few officers, including Thomas Conway (from France), Horatio Gates, and Thomas Mifflin, also expressed dissatisfaction with his leadership. Hearing rumors of this criticism, Washington magnified this molehill into a mountain, seeing a conspiracy where there was none. When Conway sent ingratiating letters to Lafayette, the naive young Frenchman unsuspectingly replied with equally ingratiating letters. Eventually, though, it finally dawned on Lafayette that Conway doubted Washington's abilities. He immediately became panic-stricken that he, too, would seem a conspirator, which would doom his military career.

He rushed to headquarters to plead his innocence in person, but the commander refused to see him. By now completely overcome with anxiety, Lafayette wrote an anguished letter, confessing that he had been duped by Conway but that his love and loyalty belonged irrevocably to Washington. "I went yesterday morning to Head Quarters with an intention of Speaking to Your Excellency But you were too Buzy and I Shall lay down in this letter What I Wished to Say," wrote the anguished young man. "I wish you could know as well as myself, what difference there is Between you and any other man Upon the continent. . . . You Shall See very plainly that if you were lost for America, there is nobody who could keep the army and the Revolution for six months. . . . [Y]ou, my dear general, who have been indulgent enough to permit me to look on you as a friend," must "know the confession of my sentiment." Although Conway "had engaged me by entertaining my head with ideas of glory and shining projects, and I must confess for my shame that it is a too certain way of deceiving me," Lafayette affirmed that "I am now fixed to your fate and I shall follow it and sustain it as well by my sword as by all means in my power."[22]

The letter convinced Washington that Lafayette was sincere. "My Dear Marquis, Your favour of Yesterday conveyed to me fresh proof of that friendship and attachment which I have happily experienced since the first of our acquaintance, and for which I entertain sentiments of the purest affection," soothed Washington. "It will ever constitute part of my happiness to know that I stand well in your opinion, because I am satisfied that you can have no views to answer by throwing out false colours, and that you possess a Mind too exalted to condescend to dirty arts and low intrigues to acquire a reputation." Once these misfortunes blow over and the war is won, Washington continued, "I hope My Dear Marqis . . . you will give me your Company in Virginia, [where] we will laugh at our past difficulties and the folly of others; where I will endeavor, by every civility in my power, to shew you how much and how sincerely, I am, Your Affectionate and obedient servant."[23]

In the end, the Conway Cabal perfected their friendship and sealed their intimacy. Lafayette's memoir states that "General Washington's confidence in other people always had limits, but for M. de Lafayette it had no bounds, because it came from the heart. . . . M. de Lafayette was attached to the general . . . and he did not waver. Despite the flatteries of the other party, he remained faithful to the one whose ruin was predicted. He saw his friend every day and wrote to him often to discuss . . . his personal situation."[24]

Knowing that Washington's demise would also spell disaster for himself, the devoted young officer defended his general to Americans and foreigners alike. To his father-in-law, the duc d'Ayen, he pronounced him indispensable to the cause: "Our general is a man truly made for this revolution, which could not succeed without him. I am closer to him than anyone else, and I find him worthy of his country's veneration. His warm friendship and his complete confidence in me regarding all military and political matters, great and small, put me in a position to know all that he has to do, to reconcile, and to overcome." Lafayette emphasized that his admiration had developed gradually over time. "I admire him more each day for the beauty of his character and his spirit. . . . His name will be revered down through the centuries by all those who love liberty and humanity. . . . I believe the role that he plays gives me the right to make known how much I admire and respect him."[25]

To Baron von Steuben, Lafayette enthused that "this great man has no enemies but those of his own country, and yet every noble and sensitive soul must love the excellent qualities of his heart. I think I know him as well as anyone. . . . His honesty, his candor, his sensitivity, his virtue in the full sense of the word are above all praise . . . his opinion in the [military] counsil always seemed to me to be the best, though his modesty sometimes kept him from sustaining it, and his predictions have always been fulfilled." As Washington had anticipated from the beginning, Lafayette had become one of his most valuable weapons against criticism, real and imagined.[26]

To Henry Laurens, president of Congress, Lafayette, who shared his commander's conspiratorial outlook, demanded to know "by what chance so little regard is pay'd to General Washington" in creating a Board of War featuring so many of the Virginian's enemies, including Mifflin and Gates. Laurens's reply, meant to be conveyed to Washington, assured that nine of ten delegates firmly supported the commander in chief, and that Congress would never replace him against his will.[27]

To his wife, Adrienne, Lafayette explained both his need to stay in America and his value to Washington: "My presence is more necessary to the American cause at this moment than you could imagine. So many foreigners who have not received commissions . . . have made powerful cabals. They have tried all sorts of tricks to disgust me both with this revolution and the one who leads it." The British, too, had tried to spread rumors damaging to Washington's reputation. "I cannot in good conscience prove all these people to be right. If I depart, many Frenchmen who are useful here will follow my example. General Washington will be truly unhappy if I speak to him of leaving. His confidence in me is greater than my age allows me to admit. In his position, he is surrounded by flatterers and secret enemies. He finds in me a trustworthy friend to whom he can open his heart, and who always tells him the truth. Not a day passes that he does not have long conversations with me or write me long letters, and he likes to consult me about the most important matters." Referring to the Conway Cabal, Lafayette added that "at this very moment there is a particular matter in which my presence is of some use to him."[28]

In January 1778, Congress authorized a winter invasion of Canada, targeted at Montreal, to be led by Lafayette with Conway as second in command. The expedition would not take its orders from Washington, but directly from Congress and the Board of War, headed by Gates. Ignoring orders to proceed to Albany to take charge of American forces assembling there, the Frenchman went to York, Pennsylvania, to lobby Congress to place the operation under the commander in chief. Indeed, he informed Congress that "his first condition for accepting the position was not to be independent of General Washington."[29] "I dare hope," he wrote to Laurens, "that Congress will permit me to look upon myself only as a detachment of General Washington's army, and an officer under his immediate command. . . . I Confess [to] you that love and friendship have alwais been my duties. This last sentiment I feel to the most perfect degree for General Washington." Moreover, Lafayette simply could not tolerate working with a man he believed to be an enemy of Washington's. Of "all the men who could be sent under me, Mr. Connway [*sic*] is the most disagreable to me and the most prejudiciable to the cause," he explained. "How can I support the society of a man who has spocken of my friend in the most insolent and abusive terms, who has done, and does every day all in his power to ruin him. . . . I am very certain that everyone who can find one single reason of refusing due respect and love to Gal. Washington will find thousand ones of hating me."[30]

Once in York, Lafayette found "General Gates . . . dining with several of Washington's opponents. A toast was drunk to the United States and to Congress, and people began to rise from the table. 'You have forgotten to drink to the health of General Washington,'" reminded the Frenchman. The officers performed the requested ritual, "but not with much exuberance of feeling." Lafayette's "purpose was answered, however, which was to let them see at the outset the tone and tendency of his sentiments." According to his memoir, "When the toast had been drunk, Lafayette very openly declared his sentiments to Gates, concerning the command which had been given him. He told him that if his military duties should require him to correspond directly with the Board of War, he would only send them copies of letters addressed . . . to General Washington, whom he always regarded as his commander in chief." Congress, Lafayette triumphantly noted, "granted everything he required."[31]

In Albany, he found few men and no supplies, forcing the abandonment of the proposed invasion. Washington had warned him to expect disappointment and broken promises, but he was shocked at the "blunders of madness or treachery (God knows what)" that he encountered. Lafayette complained of "my distressing ridiculous, foolish, and indeed nameless situation. I am sent with a great noise at the head of an army for doing great things" with the world watching. With nothing accomplished, "I will become very ridiculous and laughed at. . . . I confess, my dear general, that I find myself of very quick feelings whenever my reputation and glory are concerned. . . . I schould be very happy if you was here to give me some advices."[32]

Washington, who also obsessed over his reputation, assured Lafayette that the abortive Canadian expedition had not damaged his image. On the contrary, "It will be no disadvantage to you, to have it known in Europe, that you had received so manifest a proof of the good opinion and confidence of Congress as an important detached Command." Upon being summoned back to headquarters at Valley Forge, a relieved Lafayette explained that he had originally wanted to serve under Washington out of "respect for your excellency's name and reputation," but now wanted to serve "out of mere love for General Washington himself."[33]

Lafayette demonstrated the robust health of their friendship in May 1778 when word of the French Alliance arrived in camp. Overjoyed at the news, he supposedly hugged and kissed Washington on both cheeks. The commander in chief's high esteem for the Frenchman can be seen in the growing responsibilities he gave him. In May, Lafayette received his first independent command (2,200 troops), with orders to scout the enemy in Philadelphia and to discover whether the British planned to abandon the city. Making his way along the west bank of the Schuylkill River, Lafayette lingered so long at Barren Hill that the British detected him and sent a force of 5,000 men under General Henry Clinton to apprehend him. Only a brilliant escape along the river prevented his capture.[34]

Having acquitted himself well overall, Lafayette received even more responsibility. In June 1778, Washington learned that the Redcoats had abandoned Philadelphia and had begun marching across New Jersey toward New York. A majority of Washington's officers, led by General Charles Lee, argued against attacking the enemy's line of march. A minority, including Greene, Steuben, Anthony Wayne, and Lafayette, wanted to fight. The commander in chief compromised by sending forward only 1,500 troops to harass the enemy's rear. Lafayette received the command after Lee turned it down. Since his own inclination was to fight, Washington then increased the force from 1,500 to 4,000 men. The main army would follow close behind the advance party to provide support as needed. On June 25–26, as Lafayette closed in on the British, he exchanged nine letters with Washington in an attempt to coordinate their movements. Now that the detachment had grown in size and importance, Lee decided that he wanted to command it after all. Lafayette helped Washington out of an embarrassing dilemma by voluntarily stepping aside in favor of Lee.[35]

On June 28, 1778, at Monmouth Court House, Lee attacked and then retreated. Washington, arriving on the field in the midst of the retreat, demanded an explanation from Lee. According to some eyewitness accounts, Washington's volcanic temper got the better of him and he swore "till the leaves shook on the trees." He assumed personal command, rallied the troops, and halted the retreat. Although the Americans held their own against the British regulars, he and Lafayette believed that a golden opportunity to win a significant victory had been lost. After the battle, Greene found both men side by side, asleep under a tree, lying on Washington's cloak.[36]

In July 1778, Washington ordered Lafayette to march two Continental brigades to Providence, Rhode Island, and to place himself under the command of General John Sullivan, who would lead a Franco-American attack against enemy forces in that state. Lafayette readily complied with Washington's order to divide his Continentals with General Greene. Once again, Lafayette's willingness to accept a lesser command, wrote Washington, "obviated every difficulty, and gave me singular pleasure." The young Frenchman, however, allowed himself to be drawn into, rather than to assuage, friction between American and French officers over the French fleet's departure for Boston to repair storm damage. Washington nevertheless thanked Lafayette for his efforts in Rhode Island.[37]

To Congress, Washington endorsed his friend's request for a furlough to return to France, though he confessed "a reluctance to part with an Officer, who unites all the military fire of youth, [with] an uncommon maturity of judgment." Congress granted the furlough, to which it added a letter of praise to King Louis XVI.[38]

Late in November, near army headquarters in New York, Lafayette fell victim to an "inflammatory illness" that threatened his life. "General Washington came every day to ask for news of his friend," wrote Lafayette in his memoir. "But, fearing to disturb him, he spoke only with the doctor and returned to his camp with a heavy heart and tears in his eyes." After recovering sufficiently to travel, Lafayette bid Washington "a tender and painful farewell" and continued on to Boston, where he fully regained his health. Just before his ship sailed, on January 11, 1779, he wrote a final good bye: "Farewell, my most beloved General, it is not without emotion I tell you this last adieu before so long a seperation. Do'nt forget an absent friend. . . . Adieu; my dear and for ever belov'd friend, adieu."[39]

Back in France, Lafayette found himself a celebrity, not only because of his own exploits, but also because of his friendship with Washington. He relentlessly lobbied the French government for the loans, ships, and troops the

Continental Army desperately needed. France not only promised to send an army to America, but agreed that Washington would be the supreme commander of allied forces. Thus, the French general Compte de Rochambeau would be subordinate to the American commander in chief.[40]

From France, Lafayette wrote how much he missed his general, and when his first son was born, he named him George Washington Lafayette. "There never was a friend, my dear General, so tenderly Belov'd, as I do love and Respect you," he wrote. "I had taken such an habit of being inseparable from you, that I can't now get the use of absence and am more and more afflicted of that distance which keeps me so far from my dearest friend." Recognizing that Washington was the Indispensable Man (as historians have termed it), Lafayette reminded Washington that the success of the Revolution depended on his survival. "I can't express you how uneasy I feel on account of your health, and the dangers you perhaps in this moment are exposing yourself to. Those you may possibl[y] laugh at and call woman-like considerations, but . . . any sentiment of my heart I never could . . . Conceal." The Frenchman pleaded for Washington to gratify the curiosity of Europe by making a personal visit there after the war. Most of all, Lafayette begged for letters from Washington. "For God's sake, write me frequent and long letters and speak most chiefly about yourself and your private circumstances."[41]

It wasn't enough to declare his own love, he declared that his wife loved Washington too! In reply, the Virginian joked to be careful or else he might steal her affections away from Lafayette. "Tell her . . . that I have a heart susceptible of the tenderest passion . . . that she must be cautious of putting love's torch to it; as you must be in fanning the flame," Washington warned. "But here again methinks I hear you say, I am not apprehensive of danger—my wife is young—you are growing old & the Atlantic is between you. All this is true, but know my good friend that no distance can keep *anxious* lovers long asunder." Even in this playful letter, however, he never called Lafayette his son, or anything more than his friend.[42]

As for visiting France, Washington demurred, pleading his ignorance of the French language as an excuse. For him to have to "converse through the medium of an interpreter . . . especially with the *Ladies* must appr. so extremely awkward—insipid—& uncouth—that I can scarce bear it in idea." It made much more sense, he insisted, for Lafayette's family to visit Mount Vernon. Come "to my rural Cottage, where homely fare, and a cordial reception shall be substituted for delicacies and costly living," he teased. He congratulated the father-to-be and assured him "that I love every body that is dear to you."[43]

In March 1780, Lafayette received orders from King Louis XVI to return to America to confidentially notify Washington that France would, that spring, send six warships and 6,000 troops. That month, Lafayette once again departed France, this time with the blessing of his monarch. "The moment where I will sail for your country, shall be one of the most wished for and the happiest in my life," he wrote. "Oh, My dear general, how happy I would be to embrace you again!"[44]

Upon meeting the French diplomat François, marquis de Barbé-Marbois, Washington immediately asked how Lafayette was doing. Marbois claimed that upon hearing good news about Lafayette, the commander in chief sobbed, "I love him as my own son." Can we take stories like this at face value? It would seem out of character for Washington to shed tears at the mere mention of his friend's name, but other contemporaries recorded similar occurrences. For example, when Lafayette returned to America and reunited with Washington at Morristown, New Jersey, in May 1780, Alexander Hamilton, a reliable source, noted that he hugged and kissed the Virginian, who cried tears of paternal love. One wonders whether these tears were genuine, or whether these occasions were among those staged theatrical moments at which Washington excelled. Upon hearing of Lafayette's safe arrival in Boston, Washington had written that he would soon "embrace you with all the warmth of an affectionate friend."[45]

In mid-May 1780, the two men met at army headquarters to contemplate the logistics of a Franco-American campaign. Hoping to launch a joint movement against New York, the commander in chief wanted Lafayette to persuade General Rochambeau and Admiral Chevalier de Ternay quickly to come south from New England. Their operations could begin once the French fleet took "possession of the . . . Harbour between Staten Island and the City of New York." Meanwhile, to fool the British in New York into lowering their guard, Washington instructed Lafayette to prepare a bogus proclamation announcing a joint U.S.–French invasion of Canada. He confidentially sent the Frenchman's draft proclamation to Benedict Arnold in Philadelphia for printing. As he anticipated, the misinformation was passed to the British—although he did not realize that Arnold, already a traitor, had himself handed it to the enemy.[46]

During the summer, Lafayette represented his superior officer in consultations with the French high command in Newport, Rhode Island. Washington, who remained in New York preparing for the coming campaign, assured Rochambeau that Lafayette spoke for him: "As a General officer I have the highest confidence in him; as a friend he is perfectly acquainted with my sentiments and opinions; he knows all the circumstances of our army and the country at large; all the information he gives and all the positions he makes, I entreat you will consider as coming from me."[47]

The discussions in Rhode Island were interrupted by intelligence that a British fleet would soon attack the French at Newport. Instead of joining an offensive on New York, Rochambeau asked Washington to send Continentals to New England, or to make a diversion against General Clinton in New York. To Lafayette, Washington explained that he could not get his troops to Rhode Island in time to help, and that as much as he would like to hit Clinton, "two things . . . would hinder us . . . the want of men and arms to do it with." Nevertheless, he would do what he could. After the enemy canceled the operation against Newport, Lafayette returned to New York, where he angered the French officers in Rhode Island by imploring them to action. At the Hartford Conference in September, Washington, Rochambeau, and Ternay agreed that more French troops must arrive before a joint offensive could begin. Lafayette acted as secretary and interpreter during the talks, and he drafted the final agreement that all three officers signed. One of Rochambeau's aides was struck by "the marks of affection which the [American] general showed to his pupil, his adopted son."[48]

The following month, Lafayette urged his friend to take offensive action against the British in New York: "The French Court have often Complain'd to me of the inactivity of that American Army who Before the Alliance had distinguish'd themselves By theyr spirit of enterprise. They often have told me, your friends Leave us now to fight theyr Battles and do no more [to] Risk themselves. It is moreover of the greatest political importance to let them know that on our side we were Ready to Cooperate." Both men understood that American inaction might induce the French to accept a mediated peace that might leave large portions of America in British hands. Washington nevertheless responded that it would "be imprudent" to attack without a significant numerical advantage. "To recover our reputation, we should take care that we do not injure it more," he admonished.[49]

In February 1781, Washington appointed Lafayette to march 1,200 Continentals south to fight against the turncoat Benedict Arnold, now commanding British troops in Virginia. Arriving at Head of Elk, Maryland, early in

February, he waited in vain for the arrival of a French fleet to transport his men to Hampton Rhodes. Sending his forces to Annapolis for the time being, the young officer sailed to Williamsburg to confer with Steuben, the American commander in Virginia. Learning that a British squadron had driven off the French fleet, Lafayette called off the campaign and returned to Maryland to march his men back north. Before doing so, he availed himself of the opportunity to visit Washington's mother in Fredericksburg, as well as Mount Vernon. Unfortunately, he did not record his impressions of either.[50]

Already in the South, Lafayette received orders to take his men to Virginia after all, where he would soon face General Cornwallis. Outnumbered six to one, the young Frenchman, like his mentor, resorted to a Fabian strategy. His greatest fear was not Cornwallis, however, but that he would miss a decisive campaign in the North. Washington reassured him that the next big campaign might well be in the South.[51]

In August 1781, with a French fleet headed to Chesapeake Bay, Washington and Rochambeau finally set in motion the Yorktown campaign. Lafayette's orders were to make sure that Cornwallis did not escape from the peninsula between the York and James Rivers as the American and French trap slowly closed in on him. With the French fleet already in place on Chesapeake Bay, Washington arrived at Yorktown to reinforce Lafayette in mid-September. From St. George Tucker, at the time a lieutenant colonel in the Virginia militia, we have an eyewitness account of their reunion: Lafayette "caught the general round his body, hugged him as close as it was possible, and absolutely kissed him from ear to ear . . . with as much ardor as ever an absent lover kissed his mistress on his return." Needless to say, there exist very few accounts of people hugging and kissing Washington—a most unusual circumstance.[52]

During the siege of Yorktown, Lafayette commanded the right wing of the American line. On October 14, his troops attacked and quickly captured a British stronghold called Redoubt No. 10, suffering 9 killed and 25 wounded.[53]

After Cornwallis's surrender, Lafayette headed back to France to lobby for more aid to finish off the war. First, he worked to secure a new six-million livre loan, and then, as a self-appointed, unofficial peace negotiator, he helped convince Spain to recognize the United States. In congratulating Washington on his victory and retirement from the army in 1783, Lafayette begged him to "often Remember Your Adopted Son."[54]

After the war, the retired American general invited the Lafayette family to Mount Vernon, where he promised that they would be received with "friendship & affection." Traveling without his family, the Frenchman arrived at Mount Vernon in August 1784, where he saw his hero in a whole new light. "In retirement General Washington is even greater than he was during the Revolution," wrote Lafayette. "His simplicity is truly sublime and he is as completely involved with all the details of his lands and house as if he had always lived here."[55]

For Lafayette, there was just one problem at Mount Vernon: slavery. During the war, he had joined other young officers in arguing the institution's evils to the commander in chief. Now, he pressed his friend to emancipate. Lafayette even proposed that they jointly establish a model plantation worked by free black tenants. The Frenchman deserves some of the credit for Washington's slow but steady growth on the race issue, and for his decision to free his slaves in his will.[56]

Washington rode with Lafayette as far as Maryland before bidding his friend a tearful farewell. "In the moment of our separation," the Virginian sadly wrote, "& every hour since—I felt all that love, respect & attachment for you, with which length of years, close connexion & your merits, have inspired me." Washington wondered whether he would never see Lafayette again. "And tho' I wished to say no," he mused, "my fears answered yes." As usual, his instincts were correct.[57]

In the years that followed, they exchanged letters and presents. In 1790, during the French Revolution, as Lafayette fought for a constitutional monarchy, he sent the key to the Bastille to Washington as gift from "a Son to My Adoptive father, as an aide de Camp to My General, as a Missionary of liberty to its patriarch." America's first president worried that French radicals would turn on his young friend. Falling victim to both revolutionary extremists and aristocratic reactionaries, Lafayette failed in his attempt to become a French Washington. In 1792, he fled France and was captured by the forces of the Austrian Netherlands and imprisoned for being a violent revolutionary and a traitor to his monarch.[58]

There was little Washington could do to help without violating American neutrality. Attorney General William Bradford noted that the president could not contain his grief when discussing the plight of Lafayette and his family. The only things Washington could do were to send his own personal funds for his friend's relief, to have American diplomats take unofficial steps to aid him, and to write a personal letter to the Austrian emperor asking Lafayette's release as a favor. U.S. envoys Gouverneur Morris and James Monroe saved Adrienne Lafayette from the guillotine and got her out of prison, but they could not free her husband.[59]

In 1795, Lafayette's son, George Washington Lafayette, arrived in America to seek refuge with Washington. But the president could not welcome the young man into his household without insulting the French and British governments, both of whom viewed his father as a criminal. Acting through intermediaries such as Hamilton, Washington made sure the boy was taken care of. In 1796, he finally threw protocol aside by inviting young Lafayette first to the presidential mansion in Philadelphia, and then to Mount Vernon, where he remained until his father's release from prison.[60]

After regaining his freedom, Lafayette wanted to visit America, but Washington urged him to stay away because of the severe tensions between the United States and France in the late 1790s. And so the Frenchman did not make it back to America, and to Mount Vernon, until 1824, by which time a quarter century had passed since Washington's death.[61]

David Clary's claim that Lafayette was the only really close friend Washington ever had is simply wrong. Although Lafayette was in many ways a son to Washington, the friendship must not be romanticized into something it was not. It is significant that Washington's last will and testament, written six months before he died, did not give Lafayette exceptional recognition. Instead, it simply willed to "General de la Fayette . . . a pair of finely wrought steel Pistols, taken from the enemy in the Revolutionary War." Dr. James Craik, in contrast, who perhaps really was the Virginian's closest friend, did receive exceptional recognition in Washington's will, which describes Craik as "my compatriot in arms, and old & intimate friend." Washington's will does not include a tribute like that to Lafayette. About the same time he wrote the will, he privately described his friend as being rather naive, even a bit obtuse. To Timothy Pickering, Washington coldly declared that Lafayette had "a blind side, not difficult to assail."[62]

During the Revolutionary War, Lafayette got as close to Washington as any young man ever did, but he was never Washington's best friend. It was only Lafayette who wrote of himself as "adopted son," while Washington merely referred to him as a "friend." And while the relationship developed relatively quickly, based on compatibility and mutual self-interest, it most certainly was not "love at first sight," especially for Washington, who viewed himself more as Lafayette's protective patron than as his father.

Notes

1. David A. Clary, *Adopted Son: Washington, Lafayette, and the Friendship that Saved the Revolution* (New York, 2007), 431–32; Freeman, picture caption preceding 4:462; James R. Gaines, *For Liberty and Glory: Washington, Lafayette, and Their Revolutions* (New York, 2007), 8–9. For typical representations of the relationship, see Olivier Bernier, *Lafayette: Hero of Two Worlds* (New York, 1983), 46, 49; John E. Ferling, *The Ascent of George Washington: The Hidden Political Genius of an American Icon* (New York, 2009), 162; James Thomas Flexner, *Washington: The Indispensable Man* (New York, 1974), 102; Howard Peckham, "Marquis de Lafayette: Eager Warrior," in *George Washington's Generals*, ed. George Athan Billias (New York, 1964), 217; and Joseph J. Ellis, *His Excellency: George Washington* (New York, 2004), 116. Like Gaines, Edward Lengel eschews the father-son terminology, instead describing a "sincere and lasting friendship" (see Lengel, *George Washington: A Military Life* [New York, 2005], 220).

2. Lafayette to Adrienne de Noailles de Lafayette, 30 May [1777], in *Lafayette in the Age of the American Revolution: Selected Letters and Papers, 1776–1790*, ed. Stanley J. Idzerda, 5 vols. (Ithaca, N.Y., 1977–83), 1:58–59.

3. Benjamin Franklin and Silas Deane to the Committee of Secret Correspondence, 25 May 1777, ibid., 1:51; Silas Deane to Robert Morris, 26 May 1777, ibid., 1:52.

4. Silas Deane to Robert Morris, 26 May 1777, ibid., 1:52; American Commissioners to Washington, [ca. August–September 1777], ibid., 1:108.

5. *Memoir of 1776, Memoir by the Chevalier Dubuysson*, ibid., 1:91, 80.

6. Ibid., 1:100–101n.

7. Resolution of Congress, 31 July 1777, ibid., 1:88 and note.

8. GW to Benjamin Harrison, 20 August 1777, and Benjamin Harrison to GW, 20 August 1777, Fitzpatrick, 9:95, 96n.

9. Clary, *Adopted Son*, 2; GW to George Washington Parke Custis, 28 November 1796, Fitzpatrick, 35:295.

10. Lafayette to Adrienne de Noailles de Lafayette, 1 October 1777, in *Lafayette in the Age of the American Revolution*, 1:116; and Lafayette to the duc d'Ayen, 16 December 1777, ibid., 1:192.

11. GW to Lafayette, 30 September 1779, ibid., 2:314.

12. Peter Henriques, *Realistic Visionary: A Portrait of George Washington* (Charlottesville, Va., 2006), 1–23; Lafayette to GW, 22 July 1783, in *Lafayette in the Age of the American Revolution*, 5:146.

13. Henriques, *Realistic Visionary*, 1–23; Clary, *Adopted Son*, 111–20; Bernier, *Lafayette*, 50–52.

14. Lafayette to Adrienne de Noailles de Lafayette, 1 October 1777, in *Lafayette in the Age of the American Revolution*, 1:116.

15. Lafayette to GW, 14 October 1777, ibid., 1:122–23.

16. GW to the President of Congress, 1 November 1777, Fitzpatrick, 9:480.

17. Lafayette to GW, 26 November 1777, in *Lafayette in the Age of the American Revolution*, 1:157.

18. GW to the President of Congress, 26–27 November 1777, Fitzpatrick, 10:109–10.

19. *Memoir of 1776,* in *Lafayette in the Age of the American Revolution,* 1:91; Lafayette to GW, [ca. 13 January 1778], ibid., 1:233. For Lafayette's written advice to Washington, see ibid., 1:162ff.

20. Stuart Leibiger, *Founding Friendship: George Washington, James Madison, and the Creation of the American Republic* (Charlottesville, Va., 1999), 33, 53; GW to Lafayette, 31 December 1777, in *Lafayette in the Age of the American Revolution,* 1:207–8.

21. GW to Gouverneur Morris, 24 July 1778, in *Lafayette in the Age of the American Revolution,* 2:116–17.

22. Lafayette to GW, 30 December 1777, ibid., 1:204–6.

23. GW to Lafayette, 31 December 1777, ibid., 1:207–8.

24. *Memoir of 1779,* ibid., 1:170–72.

25. Lafayette to the duc d'Ayen, 16 December 1777, ibid., 1:192.

26. Lafayette to Baron von Steuben, 12 March 1778, ibid., 1:353.

27. Lafayette to Henry Laurens, [ca. 5 January 1778], ibid., 1:217; Laurens to Lafayette, 12 January 1778, ibid., 1:231–32.

28. Lafayette to Adrienne de Noailles de Lafayette, 6 January [1778], ibid., 1:223–24.

29. *Memoir of 1776,* ibid., 1:245.

30. Lafayette to Laurens, [26 January 1778], ibid., 1:254.

31. Ibid., 1:248n; Lafayette to the President of Congress, 31 January 1778, *Memoir of 1779,* ibid., 1:267–68, 245.

32. Lafayette to GW, 19 and 23 February 1778, ibid., 1:299–301, 321.

33. GW to Lafayette, 10 March 1778, ibid., 1:343–42; Lafayette to GW, 25 March 1778, ibid., 1:380–81.

34. GW to Lafayette, 18 May 1778, ibid., 2:54.

35. GW to Lafayette, 25 and 26 June 1778, ibid., 2:87; Lafayette to GW, 25 and 26 June 1778, ibid., 2:95–96.

36. Clary, *Adopted Son,* 1–3, 187–201.

37. Lafayette to GW, 6 August 1778, in *Lafayette in the Age of the American Revolution,* 2:132; GW to Lafayette, 10 August 1778, ibid., 2:136–37.

38. Lafayette to GW, 24 October 1778, ibid., 2:195; GW to the President of Congress, 6 October 1778, Fitzpatrick, 13:40–41.

39. *Memoir of 1779,* in *Lafayette in the Age of the American Revolution,* 2:17–18; Lafayette to GW, 5 January 1779, ibid., 2:219.

40. Bernier, *Lafayette,* 78–93; Clary, *Adopted Son,* 225–57.

41. Lafayette to GW, 12 June 1779, in *Lafayette in the Age of the American Revolution,* 2:276–81; GW to Lafayette, 30 September 1779, ibid., 2:313–18.

42. Lafayette to GW, 12 June 1779, in *Lafayette in the Age of the American Revolution,* 2:276–81; GW to Lafayette, 30 September 1779, ibid., 2:313–18.

43. Lafayette to GW, 12 June 1779, in *Lafayette in the Age of the American Revolution,* 2:276–81; GW to Lafayette, 30 September 1779, ibid., 2:313–18.

44. Instructions from Compte de Vergennes, 5 March 1780, ibid., 2:364–66; Lafayette to GW, 7 October 1779, ibid., 2:324–25.

45. Clary, *Adopted Son,* 245, 261; GW to Lafayette, 8 May 1780, in *Lafayette in the Age of the American Revolution,* 3:11.

46. GW to Lafayette, 16 May 1780, in *Lafayette in the Age of the American Revolution,* 3:14–15; GW's Memorandum for Concerting a Plan of Operations, 15 July 1780, ibid., 3:88; Lafayette to Chevalier de La Luzerne, 25 May 1780, ibid., 3:35; Proclamation to the Canadians, [ca. 25 May 1780], ibid., 3:36–39.

47. GW to compte de Rochambeau, 16 July 1780, Fitzpatrick, 19:186.

48. Mediating the Alliance, GW's Memorandum for Concerting a Plan of Operations, 15 July 1780, in *Lafayette in the Age of the American Revolution,* 3:83–88; GW to Lafayette, 22 and 27 July 1780, and 1 August 1780, ibid., 3:106, 112, 122–23; Lafayette to GW, 26 July [1780], ibid., 3:108–11; Light Camp Commander, Summary of the Hartford Conference, 22 September 1780, ibid., 3:175–78; Clary, *Adopted Son,* 285.

49. Lafayette to GW, 30 October 1780, in *Lafayette in the Age of the American Revolution,* 3:211; GW to Lafayette, 30 October 1780, ibid., 3:214.

50. Chronological Outline, ibid., 3:xxxvi–vii; Chesapeake Expedition against Arnold, ibid., 3:327–29.

51. Clary, *Adopted Son,* 291–305.

52. Ibid., 329–30.

53. Ibid., 335–37; Bernier, *Lafayette,* 125–32.

54. Clary, *Adopted Son,* 344–64; Lafayette to GW, 22 July 1783, in *Lafayette in the Age of the American Revolution,* 5:146.

55. GW to Lafayette, 1 February 1784, *PGW: Conf. Ser.,* 1:89; Lafayette to Adrienne de Noailles de Lafayette, 20 August 1784, in *Lafayette in the Age of the American Revolution,* 5:237.

56. Clary, *Adopted Son,* 366; Henriques, *Realistic Visionary,* 161.

57. GW to Lafayette, 8 December 1784, *PGW: Conf. Ser.,* 2:175.

58. Lafayette to GW, 17 March 1790, *PGW: Pres. Ser.,* 5:242; Clary, *Adopted Son,* 403–17.

59. Clary, *Adopted Son,* 410–27.

60. Ibid.

61. GW to Timothy Pickering, 14 July 1799, *PGW: Ret. Ser.,* 4:187.

62. Clary, *Adopted Son,* 432; GW's Last Will and Testament, [9 July 1799], *PGW: Ret. Ser.,* 4:486–87; GW to Pickering, 14 July 1799, ibid., 4:187.

Son of the Army

Captain Robert Kirkwood of the Delaware Regiment

THOMAS RIDER

As the sun rose on the morning of November 4, 1791, warriors of the Shawnee, Miami, and other allied tribes sprang from the woods surrounding the United States Army encampment on the banks of the Wabash River in what is today western Ohio. In little more than three hours of intense fighting, they encircled and virtually destroyed Major General Arthur St. Clair's 1,400-man force. Luckily for St. Clair and those of his panic-stricken men who were able to break out, the Native Americans abandoned their pursuit in order to plunder the camp and finish off the hapless survivors who remained behind. While this decision averted the army's complete destruction, St. Clair's campaign to subdue the Old Northwest nonetheless came to an abrupt end.[1] In writing of this catastrophe to President George Washington, Governor Henry Lee of Virginia estimated the American losses at "between five and six hundred including Officers and followers of the army." Lee went on to name four officers who were among the expedition's casualties. "The Colonels Darke & Gibson will recover" Lee noted, "but the gallant Butler & the entrepid Kirkwood are among the dead, a sad testimony of the doleful casualtys of War."[2]

In the aftermath of this overwhelming defeat, it stands to reason that Lee would report to Washington on the status of the army's important leaders. Lieutenant Colonels William Darke and George Gibson were relatively senior officers who commanded regiments in St. Clair's army, while Major General Richard Butler was the expedition's second in command. But the fourth officer whom Lee mentioned—Robert Kirkwood—was a mere captain, one of dozens of junior officers struck down during the engagement. What made

Lee single out Kirkwood to the exclusion of other lower-ranking officers, and what caused him to emphasize Kirkwood's valor?

Unlike the other subjects of this book, Kirkwood was not a protégé of Washington. Washington was undoubtedly familiar with Kirkwood's name, which appeared infrequently in correspondence to the commander in chief during the American Revolution.[3] As president, Washington nominated Kirkwood as the senior captain in the 2nd United States Regiment for St. Clair's expedition.[4] But despite the unsubstantiated suggestion by an early Kirkwood biographer that he and Washington shared "a strong and abiding friendship," no compelling evidence exists to suggest that the two men ever spoke to one another.[5] While it would be accurate to say that Kirkwood served under Washington during the American Revolution, it was always with numerous intermediary officers and levels of command in between. Kirkwood did, however, work directly for and interact with men who could more properly be called Washington's protégés. John Sullivan, Nathanael Greene, Daniel Morgan, William Washington, and Henry Lee all commanded and had direct interaction with Kirkwood at some point during the Revolution. Greene, in particular, grew to depend on Kirkwood for certain types of missions. Whenever Greene or Lee made reference to Kirkwood, it was always in the most glowing terms. To these disciples of Washington, Captain Robert Kirkwood exemplified the soldierly qualities that Washington prized in junior officers and sought to develop in the Continental Army's subordinate leaders. In this sense, Kirkwood is much more representative of Washington's effect on the Continental Army than are his well-known protégés. There were hundreds of junior officers like Kirkwood that the commander in chief shaped dramatically, albeit indirectly.

As the principal architect and builder of the Continental Army, Washington's influence on the officer corps stretched well beyond those senior leaders who were his immediate subordinates. From the moment he assumed duties as commander in chief, Washington set about establishing a set of values or standards of behavior for his officers. While we might expect these values to include republican virtue and enthusiasm for the cause of liberty, he was far more pragmatic when advising subordinates of his expectations. He did, from time to time, appeal to a notion of selfless service—particularly when trying to convince officers to stay with the army.[6] When exhorting or discussing general officers, he sometimes addressed their sense of virtue or the degree to which they were "zealously attach'd to the Cause."[7] On a day-to-day basis, however, he was far more concerned with the practical matters of building, maintaining, and fighting his army. He had little choice. As he wrote to John Hancock shortly after joining the army outside of Boston in July 1775, "Next to the more immediate & pressing Duties of putting our Lines in as secure a State as possible, attending to the Movements of the Enemy, & gaining Intelligence, my great Concern is to establish Order, Regularity & Discipline."[8]

To establish and then maintain order, regularity, and discipline, Washington required very specific and practical skills from his subordinate leaders, especially from those company-level officers like Robert Kirkwood who dealt directly with enlisted soldiers in camp, on the march, and in combat. His expectations of captains and lieutenants were very clear. In recommending John David Wilpert to the rank of captain in the Continental Army, Washington recalled Wilpert's service in the Virginia Regiment during the French and Indian War. According to Washington, Wilpert had "conducted himself as an active, vigilant, and brave Officer."[9] Washington emphasized these essential qualities of activity, vigilance, and bravery throughout the course of the war. While he prized these traits in all officers, regardless of rank, they were his baseline expectations for the Continental Army's junior officers.

The first of these essential qualities, activity (Washington sometimes used the word enterprise), meant taking initiative. Whether enforcing camp discipline or maintaining the line of battle in combat, Washington needed his officers to act energetically, carry out orders quickly and precisely, and do so even in the absence of senior-officer supervision. As the Continental Army formed in 1775, Washington went so far as to suggest that even though the nascent force lacked "the Order, Regularity & Discipline of Veterans—Whatever Deficiencies there may be, will I doubt not, soon be made up by the Activity & Zeal of the Officers, and the Docility & Obedience of the Men."[10]

Washington believed that an active officer corps would energetically enforce standards of discipline in the army. While discipline is essential to any military organization, it was especially important in the eighteenth century. In camp, ill-discipline exacerbated the spread of disease, and disease was more dangerous to an army than battle. On the march, ill-discipline led to straggling. At all times, lax enforcement of discipline encouraged desertion. When combined, these factors "commonly deprived an [eighteenth-century] army of about one-fifth of its strength in the course of a campaign."[11] Given these challenges, Washington continuously directed subordinate officers to regulate virtually every aspect of their soldiers' lives—from maintaining proper field sanitation and soldier cleanliness to the seemingly mundane prohibition on gambling.[12]

Strict discipline was even more important on the battlefield. In combat, where soldiers needed to maintain close formations and move as one in order to effectively deliver volley fire and the bayonet charge, a lapse in discipline could mean a battle lost. From his experiences in the French and Indian War, especially as a witness to Major General Edward Braddock's defeat on the Monongahela, Washington knew well the importance of maintaining strict discipline in combat, and the consequences for an army when it broke down.[13] He made clear to Kirkwood and the Continental Army's other junior officers their responsibility for maintaining their soldiers in line of battle and for fire discipline. While regimental commanders were "to see that their several Regiments are properly told off," Washington instructed "the supernumerary Officers [to be] so posted as to keep the men to their duty; particular care is to be taken to prevent their firing at too great a distance, as one Fire well aim'd does more execution than a dozen at long-shot."[14]

If also gifted with prudence, active officers could be detached from the main army and counted on to conduct independent operations. When Benedict Arnold led a detachment through the Maine wilderness in an effort to attack Quebec in late 1775, Washington praised his "Enterprizing & persevering spirit," and despite the eventual failure of the operation, remained an advocate for Arnold until his treason was discovered in September 1780.[15]

If Washington prized active officers for their energy and initiative in ensuring army discipline and ability to act independently, he valued vigilant officers for their attention to detail and care of men and material. Vigilant officers helped to establish order and regularity in the Continental Army through the day-to-day accountability of soldiers and equipment as well as the maintenance of arms, tools, and facilities, and the building of systems and standard procedures.

Continuously short of just about everything, Washington depended on his subordinate officers to know what was on hand and to ensure proper care of available assets. Washington continuously emphasized the completion of accurate returns for both men and equipment, and even threatened arrest when officers failed to complete returns in a timely manner.[16] He stressed the role of the junior officer in inspecting soldiers' quarters, kitchens, and latrines, and directed that company commanders personally inspect their soldiers' weapons and ammunition on a daily basis.[17] When battle loomed, the need to ensure the serviceability of weapons and ammunition took on even greater importance. In the summer of 1776, as the Continental Army prepared to defend New York City, Washington noted that "his anxiety for the Honor of the American Arms" and "not a distrust in the officers['] care" prompted him "to recommend a thorough Inspection in the men[']s arms and ammunition."[18]

Likewise, in an army that was still developing a standard way of doing business, it was the responsibility of junior officers to ensure that their men were not only well-versed in daily orders, but also that they carried them out. To facilitate the dissemination of orders, Washington required "not only every regiment, but every Company" to "keep an Orderly-book, to which frequent recourse is to be had." On a daily basis, Washington expected company commanders like Kirkwood to transcribe army, division, brigade, and regimental directives into their company orderly books. He then instructed "that all Orders which are necessary to be communicated to the Men, be regularly read and carefully explained to them."[19] Washington later elaborated on this order, commanding that his officers "be very careful, not only that orders be made known to the men, but that they see [to it] themselves that they are executed."[20] These measures were the only practical way to establish consistent procedures throughout the entire army.

In addition to encouraging his junior officers to be active and vigilant, Washington demanded that they be brave as well. Continental Army officers had to remain calm in battle, make rational decisions under intense stress, and set an example for their soldiers sometimes within reach of British bayonets. Soon after taking command, Washington emphasized the necessity of courage as a quality in junior officers when he cashiered Captain John Callender for misbehavior before the enemy at the Battle of Bunker Hill. He explained that "the Cowardice of a single Officer may prove the Distruction of the whole Army." He went on to encourage "Officers of all Ranks to show an Example of Bravery and Courage to their men."[21] A full year later, as the army prepared to defend New York City, Washington again stressed that officers should posses "great coolness in time of action," and assured his men that those "distinguishing themselves by any acts of bravery, and courage, will assuredly meet with notice and rewards; and on the other hand, those who behave ill, will as certainly be exposed and punished."[22]

Unfortunately, Washington's junior officers did not always live up to his clear expectations. He cashiered officers for cowardice. He reprimanded officers not only for failing to enforce discipline in their men, but for their own egregious lapses. He dismissed officers for being absent without leave, disobeying orders, disrespecting their superiors, and even committing mutiny. Some unscrupulous officers not only failed to properly account for their men and equipment, but they also drew extra supplies and funds for their own personal use. Washington cashiered Lieutenant Thomas Cummings for the vague but apparently serious offense of "behaving in a scandalous and infamous manner, unbecoming the Character of an Officer and Gentleman."[23] It is not surprising, therefore, that when a junior officer consistently and exceptionally demonstrated the soldierly qualities Washington prized, his protégés would take note of that officer's performance. One such junior officer was Captain Robert Kirkwood.

On January 17, 1776, Robert Kirkwood of New Castle County, Delaware, began his life as a soldier when he received a first lieutenant's commission in Colonel John Haslet's Delaware Regiment. Although only twenty years old, Kirkwood was well educated, having trained for the ministry at the Newark Academy.[24] Not much is known of Kirkwood's individual exploits during his first year of war, but the Delaware Regiment is well documented. When Haslet's men joined Washington's army in New York prior to the Battle of Long Island, they quickly developed a reputation for discipline that distinguished them from other units. This distinction stemmed in part from the fact that Haslet's men were better equipped and uniformed than most other Continental regiments. Simply stated, they looked like soldiers.[25]

The influence of Captain Thomas Holland, the regimental adjutant, was another factor that set the Delaware men apart. This former British officer taught the fundamentals of drill, discipline, and basic officer responsibilities to the regiment's inexperienced lieutenants and captains. As one Delaware company commander suggested, Holland was "an excellent disciplinarian and brought on the Regiment fast."[26] Kirkwood not only learned the importance of discipline in camp and on the drill field from Captain Holland, but also quickly gained practical experience in the importance of discipline on the battlefield.

On August 27, during the Battle of Long Island, the Delaware Regiment distinguished itself as part of Brigadier General William Alexander, Lord Stirling's Brigade. Alerted at three o'clock in the morning, Haslet's men and Colonel William Smallwood's Maryland Continentals marched two miles to the extreme right of a defensive line that ran along Long Island's Gowanus Heights. Here, they found Colonel Samuel Atlee's Pennsylvania Regiment already engaged with a 5,000-man column under British Major General James Grant. Further to the east, additional American elements defended other passes through the heights. Although outnumbered, Kirkwood and the Delaware Regiment performed well in their baptism of fire. As Colonel Haslet reported to Delaware congressional delegate Caesar Rodney, the regiment "stood unmoved in firm array [for] four Hours exposed to the fire of the Enemy, nor attempted to retire till they received Orders." Unfortunately for the Continentals, Grant's attack was a demonstration—a trick designed to attract the attention of the inexperienced Americans while other British forces enveloped the defensive line farther east. As British elements converged, Stirling's Brigade discovered enemy troops advancing from their front, left, and rear. Stirling led approximately 250 of the Maryland Regiment in a desperate attack to buy time for the rest of the Continentals to retreat. They did, but Kirkwood and the other Delaware men had to plunge into a mill pond in order to make their escape.[27]

The Delaware Regiment's standing did not suffer as a result of their inglorious flight. To the contrary, in writing about the defeat on Long Island, Washington noted that Stirling's Brigade, to include the Delaware Regiment, "behaved with great bravery and resolution," and withdrew only after "being Surrounded and overpowered by Numbers on all sides."[28] Washington was not alone in his opinion. As Lord Stirling had been captured in the battle, the Delaware Regiment briefly came under Brigadier General Thomas Mifflin's command. Haslet again wrote to Rodney that Mifflin had "complimented" him "on the Behavior of our Troops." Haslet was also pleased to report that the regiment remained "in high Reputation."[29]

Haslet's men continued to distinguish themselves throughout 1776, even as the Continental Army moved from defeat to defeat. The Delaware Regiment acted as part of the covering force when Washington abandoned Long Island, and were among the last troops to evacuate.[30] They suffered with the rest of the army through supply shortfalls and sickness as summer turned to fall, but maintained a reputation as effective fighters.[31] In late October, Lord Stirling, who had been exchanged, hand-picked Haslet to lead the Delaware Regiment and attachments in a nighttime raid against Mamaroneck—the encampment of the legendary Robert Rogers and his Queen's American Rangers.[32] A week later, the regiment again performed well at the Battle of White

Plains, enduring an intense artillery bombardment and twice repulsing enemy cavalry charges. Before leaving the field, Haslet's men covered the withdrawal of Brigadier General Alexander McDougall's Brigade.[33] In November, with the regiment's one-year enlistments set to expire, they retreated across New Jersey with the remnants of Washington's army.[34]

It is at this point that evidence emerges showing Kirkwood as an outstanding officer. Colonel Haslet ordered several junior officers, including Kirkwood, to return to Delaware. They were to help raise a new regiment to serve for the duration of the war—one of eighty-eight such units authorized by Congress in September.[35] On December 1, Kirkwood received his commission as captain of the Second Company in the new Delaware Regiment.[36] Colonel David Hall would command the regiment after Haslet's death at the Battle of Princeton. In February, while the rest of the regiment slowly formed, the Delaware Assembly ordered the companies of Captains Kirkwood and Enoch Anderson to proceed to Philadelphia to receive uniforms before joining the Continental Army in New Jersey.[37]

Kirkwood and Anderson raised their companies more quickly than the regiment's other company commanders. The reenlistment of soldiers who had previously served in the 1776 campaign surely accounts for the speed with which these officers were able to stand up their units. In comparing the April 1776 returns of the entire Delaware Regiment with the January 1777 payroll for Kirkwood's company, it appears as though twenty-one to twenty-six veterans of the regiment agreed to reenlist under Kirkwood. This reenlistment rate, a full one-third of the company's strength, suggests that these soldiers viewed Kirkwood as a capable officer. These men had witnessed Kirkwood's performance in camp and in combat. With this knowledge, they chose to join his company.[38]

Of course, not all of Kirkwood's soldiers were so eager to serve. By the end of January, at least five new recruits had deserted.[39] These AWOL soldiers presented Kirkwood with one of his first leadership challenges as a company commander. Since much of the regiment had yet to form, Kirkwood apparently had considerable autonomy in the oversight of his company, and seems to have been on his own in dealing with this problem. His solution was to publish a newspaper advertisement in which he named and described each man, notifying the public that "whoever takes up said deserters and secures them so that their Captain may have them again, shall receive FIVE DOLLARS for each." In the same advertisement, Kirkwood warned the rest of his company to assemble by March 25 or they too would "be deemed as deserters and treated as such."[40]

The vast majority of the men assembled. By May 19, Kirkwood's and Anderson's companies were in Princeton, New Jersey.[41] At Princeton, the Delaware detachment was part of a growing concentration of Continental soldiers who would eventually comprise Major General John Sullivan's Division for the coming campaign.[42] The rest of Washington's army secured defensible terrain at Middlebrook, approximately twenty miles to the northeast.

After Washington's victories at Trenton and Princeton five months earlier, the British had abandoned much of New Jersey except for a string of outposts on the Raritan River from Brunswick east to Amboy. Washington positioned the Continental Army to threaten any British moves to retake the state. If the British intended an overland advance through New Jersey to Philadelphia, then Sullivan's force at Princeton could block the British path, while from Middlebrook, Washington could fall upon the enemy's right or line of communication.

Sir William Howe, the British commander, preferred to draw Washington out into the open, where the Americans could not benefit from fortified positions and Howe's better-trained and disciplined regulars would have the advantage. In mid-June, Howe struck westward from Brunswick with 11,000 British and Hessian troops. Fearing that Sullivan's small division would be cut off, Washington ordered it north to the safety of the Sourland Hills (west of Washington's position at Middlebrook), where it could readily link up with the rest of the main army. Also, if Howe continued toward Philadelphia, then Sullivan's men could join Washington in any attack on the British line of communication. As Washington would not take Howe's bait and Sullivan could not be cut off, the British withdrew back to Brunswick and eventually abandoned the town as they prepared for a seaborne attack against Philadelphia.[43]

Sullivan's move from Princeton to the Sourland Hills involved a fifty-six-mile march for Kirkwood and his men over the course of three days.[44] On the evening of the third day (June 15, 1777), as the Continentals began to make camp, Kirkwood received orders to establish a picket between the American encampment and the British lines. Kirkwood reported that this "was not very pleasing, as we had been three days constantly marching." Still, he assembled his detachment of one hundred men and began a three-mile march to establish the picket. On the way, the party encountered General Sullivan. Despite being fatigued, Kirkwood requested that Sullivan authorize a nighttime reconnaissance patrol in addition to the picket. Sullivan consented, and Kirkwood left half of his men on guard and proceeded with the rest of his detachment past the enemy picket line. Masquerading as a loyalist officer, Kirkwood tricked a local woman into allowing him to use her young son as a guide. The boy identified a prominent Tory nearby who spied daily on the Continental encampments. With the boy leading the way, Kirkwood went to the Tory's house and tricked the man into incriminating himself. Taking the spy and the man's slave, Kirkwood and his detachment passed safely back to friendly lines.[45] This raid proved Kirkwood to General Sullivan as an active and brave officer. It also demonstrated Kirkwood's knack for independent action, which would serve him well in future campaigns and bring him to the attention of other senior leaders.

Kirkwood not only exhibited his activity and bravery during the 1777 campaign, but also his vigilance. Unlike other company commanders who had failed to heed Washington's directive to maintain orderly books, Kirkwood religiously annotated daily general, division, brigade, and regimental orders so as to ensure his soldiers' compliance. Washington lamented that, as "many regiments have but one orderly book—he in some measure ceases to wonder, that orders are so little known, and so frequently disobeyed." He then ordered that "until each company can be furnished with an orderly book, the officers commanding regiments are to see that their officers and men are clearly informed of every order which concerns them respectively, by reading or causing the same to be distinctly read to them."[46] Kirkwood dutifully transcribed Washington's directive in his company orderly book, just as he did all the others.[47]

The campaign of 1777 was grueling for Washington's main army, Sullivan's Division, and the Delaware Regiment. Between May 17 and October 21, Kirkwood estimated that he and his soldiers marched 796 miles through Pennsylvania, New Jersey, New York, and Delaware.[48] They participated in a division-sized raid on Staten Island and fought in the major battles of Brandywine and Germantown along with the rest of Washington's army. Unfortunately, while some details are known about the Delaware Regiment's involvement in each of these engagements, little was recorded concerning the specific actions of Kirkwood and his company.[49]

As the 1777 campaign came to a close, Washington and the majority of the main army settled in at Valley Forge, where they could threaten British forces in Philadelphia. The Delaware Regiment, Maryland regiments, and the

2nd Canadian Regiment wintered in Wilmington, Delaware, under Brigadier General William Smallwood.[50] While in Wilmington, Kirkwood was again able to come to the attention of his superiors as an active and brave officer, through a successful, independent mission. In late December, several British warships and transports anchored near Newcastle, Delaware, landing several boats onshore. Smallwood informed Washington that he had "detached a good Officer with 100 men & a Guide . . . to scour the Shores, intercept such as might Land, & make discoveries." The "good Officer" Smallwood spoke of was Kirkwood, who returned with seven prisoners who provided intelligence on the activities of the British fleet.[51]

In terms of fighting, the years of 1778 and 1779 proved less eventful for Kirkwood and the Delaware Regiment than the previous two years had been. In June 1778, the Delaware Regiment played a minor role in the Battle of Monmouth. It did not take part in Sullivan's 1779 expedition against the Iroquois, and while a detachment of Delaware light infantry did participate in Brigadier General Anthony Wayne's raid on Stony Point, there is no evidence that Kirkwood accompanied them. This does not mean that Kirkwood and his men were inactive during this time. In addition to camp routines, reconnaissance and security patrols, and efforts to maintain order regularity and discipline, there was a transformation underway in the Continental Army. In early May 1778, while the Delaware Regiment was still encamped at Wilmington, Washington wrote to Smallwood about Baron Friedrich Wilhelm de Steuben's plans "for establishing uniformity of discipline and manoeuvres" in the Continental Army. Washington added that he was sending one of Steuben's deputies to train Smallwood's Continentals. Undoubtedly, Kirkwood spent countless hours with his men learning and perfecting this new system of drill.[52]

Although Kirkwood and the other Delaware officers had little to fear from enemy action in 1778 and 1779, currency depreciation nearly ended their military careers. On May 16, 1779, in a letter to the Delaware Assembly, fifteen officers, including Kirkwood, threatened to resign their commissions, "unless such provision be shortly made that will inable us to continue in the service." Their pay was simply inadequate given the expenses that officers had to cover out of their own pockets. Kirkwood and his comrades made it clear that they wished to continue as officers, and closed their remonstrance by stating that "should we be obliged to withdraw ourselves from the Service of our Country, it will be with the greatest reluctance."[53]

Regardless of the hardships suffered by Kirkwood and his fellow officers, this letter can rightfully be seen as a lapse in public virtue, and perhaps even insubordination to civil authority. The Delaware Assembly did not take offense, however, and acted quickly to address the officers' concerns.[54] While it is unclear if Washington was aware of this specific incident, he was well informed on deficiencies in officer pay. During the encampment at Valley Forge, he had written to a congressional delegation concerning "the numerous defects, in our present military establishment." The first issue he raised was officer pay and benefits. Washington stated that "it is not indeed consistent with reason, or justice, to expect that one set of men should make a sacrifice of property; domestic ease and happiness—encounter the rigors of the field—the perils and vicissitudes of war, to obtain those blessings, which every citizen will enjoy, in common with them, without some adequate compensation."[55] While Washington would have looked askance at junior officers groveling before their state's civil government, he well understood the financial problems that his officers faced.

At about the same time that the Delaware officers were demanding relief from their pay problems, they again found themselves serving alongside their fellow Continentals from Maryland, as part of the 2nd Maryland Brigade under the command of Brigadier General Mordecai Gist. Along with Smallwood's 1st Maryland Brigade, they comprised Major General Johann Baron de Kalb's division. In November 1779, the division set out for winter quarters in Morristown, New Jersey, and to await orders for the campaign of 1780. The Delaware Regiment's assignment under De Kalb, and the eventual campaign in the Carolinas, would have profound implications for Kirkwood's future service in the Continental Army.[56]

In April 1780, with the British besieging Major General Benjamin Lincoln's southern army in Charleston, South Carolina, De Kalb received orders to reinforce the city. While on the march, the Continentals learned that Lincoln had surrendered and that the British were in the process of seizing control of the South Carolina countryside.[57] This information only intensified a sense of foreboding among De Kalb's men. Lieutenant Colonel John Eager Howard of Maryland would later confess that "our march to the Southward seemed to be a forlorn hope and my return very uncertain."[58]

By late July, De Kalb's force had reached the Buffalo Ford on the Deep River, about ninety miles southwest of Hillsborough, North Carolina. Here, Major General Horatio Gates took command of De Kalb's Continentals as well as militia from Virginia and North Carolina. With this army, Gates set out to strike the isolated British garrison at Camden. What followed was a debilitating march. The poorly supplied army advanced up to eighteen miles a day in the summer heat of the Carolinas.[59] Sergeant William Seymour, one of Kirkwood's subordinates, described the expedition's privations: "We were so much distressed for want of provisions, that we were fourteen days and drew but one half pound of flour. Sometimes we drew half a pound of beef per man, and that so miserably poor that scarce any mortal could make use of it." Seymour added that he and his comrades were "living chiefly on green apples and peaches, which rendered our situation truly miserable, being in a weak and sickly condition, and surrounded on all sides by our enemies the Tories."[60]

The leadership of officers like Captain Kirkwood was the chief factor in maintaining order and discipline during this ordeal. At one point during the march, when promised supplies failed to materialize, one Continental officer noted that "being again disappointed, fatigued, and almost famished," the soldiers' "patience began to forsake them, their looks began to be vindictive [and] mutiny was ready to manifest itself." To avert this crisis, the Continental officers moved "among the men and remonstrating with them, appeased [the] murmurs." They showed the men "their own empty canteens and mess cases, [and] satisfied the privates, that all suffered alike." The activity of these officers and the sense of shared sacrifice allowed the army to continue the march in some semblance of order.[61]

Like the approach march, the subsequent Battle of Camden was a fiasco. Lieutenant General Charles, Earl Cornwallis, who had reinforced the supposedly weak garrison at Camden, stood eager for a fight. Gates, meanwhile, not only lacked a clear picture of the enemy he faced, but also had grossly overestimated the size of his own exhausted army. Moreover, in arraying his forces, Gates expected much from the militia and placed them on the left of his line of battle. When the British advanced, the militia fled, many without firing a shot. As they ran from the field, Cornwallis's men moved in to envelop the Continentals' uncovered left flank. Kirkwood reported that as the militia retreated, they "gave the enemy's horse an opportunity to gain our Rear, their Infantry at the same time gaining our Flank, and their Line advancing in our front which Caused the Action to become very Desparate."[62]

With British infantry pressing them from the front and left, and light cavalry threatening their rear, the Continentals fought on. Delaware Lieutenant

Caleb Bennett noted that "the Continental troops . . . were left to sustain the heat of battle, when and where they acquitted themselves like soldiers devoted to their country."[63] But in the chaos some of the Continentals needed the encouragement of their officers. When a portion of Kirkwood's company wavered, he "stepped directly in front of them, and, raising his sword menacingly, said 'By the living God, the first man who falters shall receive this weapon in his craven heart!'"[64] Despite the leadership and courage of Kirkwood and officers such as De Kalb, who was mortally wounded in the engagement, the British eventually overwhelmed and routed the Continentals. Colonel Otho Holland Williams of Maryland reported that "every corps was broken and dispersed." Kirkwood was one of a handful of officers who "formed a junction" in the line of retreat that fleeing soldiers could join as they withdrew northward.[65]

In the aftermath of Camden, the Continentals who escaped made their way to Salisbury, and then to Hillsborough, to rebuild the southern army. As all of the Delaware field-grade officers were among the captured, Kirkwood took charge and informed the Delaware authorities as to the state of the regiment.[66] In October, Gates reorganized the remnants of his army. The Delaware Regiment became two companies. One, under Captain Peter Jaquett, joined the remaining Maryland troops to constitute a single battalion. Gates designated Kirkwood's company as well as a company of Maryland Continentals and a company of Virginia Continentals as light infantry. These three light companies, initially under Lieutenant Colonel John Eager Howard, along with Lieutenant Colonel William Washington's cavalry and a detachment of riflemen, formed an elite partisan corps. These light forces would form the backbone of Brigadier General Daniel Morgan's "Flying Army," and would continue to provide valuable service when Major General Nathanael Greene assumed command of the Southern Department in December 1780.[67]

Kirkwood's soldierly qualities, his sense of enterprise, his vigilance, and his courage continued to serve him well in partisan operations in the Carolinas. Partisans of the eighteenth century were not necessarily guerrilla fighters or irregulars as they are today.[68] American partisan detachments frequently consisted of elite regulars, to include light infantry and light cavalry. Sometimes riflemen and other militia augmented the Continentals. In order to move rapidly over great distances and act independently of the main army, the men in these units had to possess an even higher state of discipline than the average Continental, and the officers had to have the ability to exercise initiative, sometimes independently of supervision by superior officers. The light forces Kirkwood served with excelled at reconnaissance, foraging, raids against enemy detachments, intimidation of loyalists, and covering force operations for the main army. From October 1780 through January 1782, Kirkwood and his men performed these missions, usually as part of a larger partisan force, but sometimes as an independent, company-sized detachment.

Soon after the formation of the light troops and Greene's assumption of command of the Southern Department, Kirkwood's company took part in Morgan's excursion into northwestern South Carolina and the subsequent Battle of Cowpens. On December 16, 1780, Greene ordered Morgan's Flying Army, including the light infantry companies under Howard, William Washington's cavalry, and militia augmentation, to "proceed to the West side of the Catawba River" in order to link up with additional militia forces. Morgan would then "give protection to that part of the country and spirit up the people, to annoy the enemy in that quarter; [and] collect provisions and forage out of the way of the enemy."[69]

When British forces under Lieutenant Colonel Banastre Tarleton moved in to counter the Flying Army's activities, Morgan retreated, but, with the enemy in hot pursuit, could not risk crossing the rain-swollen Broad River. On January 17, 1781, at the Cowpens, he offered battle. He arrayed his army in three defensive lines, with militia to the front to soften up the advancing British, and Howard's Continentals to the rear. At the center of the third defensive line, Kirkwood's company patiently endured artillery fire and witnessed the withdrawal of the militia as the British advanced.[70]

When the British got within musket range of Howard's line, Kirkwood's men suffered heavily. A leading historian of the battle has suggested that "Kirkwood's Delawares saw the most intense fighting of all American units at Cowpens." But despite witnessing as many as one-sixth of the members of the company killed or wounded by this point in the fight, Kirkwood's men maintained order. They contributed to a demoralizing Continental musket volley that broke the British advance. Then, alongside the rest of Howard's infantry, they charged with fixed bayonets and swept the British from the field.[71] In a somewhat self-serving description of this singular American tactical victory, Sergeant Seymour noted that "all the officers and men behaved with uncommon and undaunted bravery, but more especially the brave Captain Kirkwood and his company, who that day did wonders, rushing on the enemy without either dread or fear, and being instrumental in taking a great number of prisoners."[72]

After Morgan's victory at Cowpens, the light forces of the Flying Army continued to act as a partisan corps, but now in direct support of the main body of Greene's army. Upon learning of Tarleton's defeat, Cornwallis began to pursue Morgan. When the Flying Army linked up with Greene near Salisbury, Cornwallis saw it as an opportunity to defeat the Continentals once and for all. What followed came to be known as the Race to the Dan—Greene's epic retreat through North Carolina and into Virginia with the British hot on the Americans' heels. During this retrograde, the light forces, now under the command of Colonel Williams, acted as a covering force protecting the rear of the main body and hindering the British pursuit. Later, when Greene decided to return to North Carolina, the light forces screened his advance.[73]

But when Greene finally decided to offer Cornwallis battle, he reincorporated the light forces into the southern army's main body, where they would play an invaluable role. On March 15, 1781, at the Battle of Guilford Courthouse, Kirkwood exhibited extraordinary autonomy for a company-grade officer. This battle serves to highlight the capabilities of the unit he led, as well as Kirkwood's activity and bravery in controlling his men during the chaos of battle and inspiring them by personal example.

When Greene established his defensive positions at Guilford Courthouse, he arrayed his forces in depth much like Morgan had done at Cowpens. A line of North Carolina militia would be the first to encounter the advancing British. A second line of Virginia militia was some 300 yards behind the first line, and the Continental regulars comprised a third line some 500 yards behind the second. But in adopting this plan, Greene was careful to note Morgan's advice concerning the militia. Morgan advised Greene that "you'l[l] have . . . a great number of militia—if they fight you'l[l] beat Cornwallis, if not, he will beat you and perhaps cut your regulars to pieces." To mitigate the unreliability of the militia, Morgan suggested that Greene "select the riflemen . . . and fight them on the flanks under enterprising officers . . . acquainted with that kind of fighting."[74] Greene followed this advice. One of the "enterprising officers" he chose was Kirkwood, whose light company joined a detachment of Virginia riflemen and William Washington's cavalry on the right flank of Greene's first line. They were to bolster the militia, secure the American right, and provide enfilading fire against the British left flank.[75]

During the course of the battle, despite the difficulties of moving through wooded terrain, the less-than-orderly retreat of the adjacent militia, and continued contact with the British, Kirkwood and his men were able to engage effectively the enemy at each successive American defensive line. Through well-placed musket fire, they inflicted casualties and created disorder among the British until pressed, and then withdrew intact to take up new defensive positions. When Kirkwood's men fell in with their regular comrades in the third defensive line, they not only continued to provide well-directed fire, but also joined in a bayonet charge against the advancing British. When Greene decided to retire from the field, Kirkwood's men were among the last to withdraw.[76]

For such a relatively junior officer, Kirkwood led his men to make a significant contribution in this battle. The disciplined and effective enfilading fire that Kirkwood's light infantry and supporting riflemen delivered at the first and second defensive lines had a devastating effect on the British. Sergeant Seymour noted that "our riflemen and musquetry behaved with great bravery, killing and wounding great numbers of the enemy."[77] Just as significant as the hard-hitting gunfire was Kirkwood's ability to maintain control of his troops as they fell back so that they could continue to resist the enemy at every phase of the battle. Perhaps the best praise for Kirkwood and his men came from Lieutenant Colonel Henry Lee, whose men had a similar mission on the army's left flank. Lee took special note of "the company of Delaware, under Kirkwood (to whom none could be superior)."[78]

While the Battle of Guilford Courthouse was tactically an American defeat, the high British casualties ended Cornwallis's efforts to subdue North Carolina. As the British limped to Wilmington and the safety of the North Carolina coast, Greene set out to retake South Carolina. By early April 1781, Greene had set his sights on the British garrison at Camden and began marching his army, including Kirkwood's light infantry, toward the town. At the same time, Greene dispatched a partisan force under Lee to strike at the British line of communication to the rear of Camden on the Santee River.[79] During the fighting around Camden, Greene clearly demonstrated his high opinion of Kirkwood's activity, vigilance, and bravery through the types of missions he repeatedly assigned the Delaware light infantry.

On April 19, 1781, as the southern army approached Camden, Greene detached Kirkwood's company and sent it in advance of the main body to attack the tiny settlement of Log Town, about a mile north of Camden proper. In a night attack, Kirkwood's men drove off the British defenders. They endured harassing fire through the night and defeated an attempt to retake the settlement as morning broke. Greene soon after arrived with the rest of the army, but Kirkwood's work was not done. Kirkwood and his company set off in support of William Washington's cavalry to destroy a British redoubt west of Camden. This mission accomplished, the party, as Kirkwood recorded, "took 40 horse & 50 Head of cattle & returned to Camp."[80]

Camden proved too formidable to attack. Consequently, Greene moved his army north of Log Town to Hobkirk's Hill. On April 25, the British commander, Colonel Francis Lord Rawdon, seized the initiative and marched the Camden garrison to attack Greene's unsuspecting force. In the ensuing Battle of Hobkirk's Hill, Kirkwood and his light company would once again provide invaluable service.

Greene does not seem to have been fully prepared for the British attack. According to one American officer, "Most of our men were cooking, or at the Spring washing, [when] we were alarmed by a firing from the Piquets, or the light Infantry under Capt. Kirkwood."[81] The Continental picket guard provided security several hundred yards in advance of the army's main body. When they detected the British advance, they opened fire, alerting Kirkwood's men, who quickly moved to support the picket. Sergeant Seymour reported that as the British advanced, the Delaware "light infantry immediately turned out and engaged them very vigorously for some time." As Lord Rawdon brought on additional troops, Kirkwood's men fell back to link up with other American elements and "renewed the fire with so much alacrity and undaunted bravery, that they put the enemy to stand for some time." The alertness of the picket guard and quick action of Kirkwood and his company bought time for the rest of Greene's soldiers to form and meet the British attack in some semblance of order.[82]

The Battle of Hobkirk's Hill was yet another defeat for Greene's southern army, as the British forced the Americans to quit the field. That being said, the American's withdrew in relatively good order and Greene would not long be delayed in continuing offensive operations. The British, although victorious, had suffered heavily in the battle. These losses, combined with American partisan activity along the British line of communication back toward Charleston, forced Rawdon to evacuate Camden by early May. In the meantime, Greene had another mission for Kirkwood. Following the battle, he dispatched the Delaware light infantry along with William Washington's cavalry back to the battlefield to recover any American wounded who remained. Thus, it is no exaggeration to state that Greene relied heavily on Kirkwood and his men at every phase of his operations around Camden. Greene was not stingy in his praise. In his report of the battle to Samuel Huntington, president of the Continental Congress, Greene lauded Kirkwood and noted that "both he and his Corps behaved with great gallantry."[83]

After Hobkirk's Hill, Kirkwood and his men continued to serve the southern army during Greene's reconquest of South Carolina. They performed such partisan missions as attacks against isolated enemy outposts, reconnaissance, covering-force operations, and the suppression of Tories—typically in conjunction with William Washington's cavalry and sometimes with augmentation from other Continental infantry units.[84] They served side by side with Lee's Legion at the Siege of Ninety-Six.[85] Three months later, at the Battle of Eutaw Springs, Greene attributed his "victory . . . to the free use of the Bayonet made by the Virginians and Marylanders, the Infantry of the Legion, and Captain Kirkwood's Light Infantry." It is fitting that in this last major battle of the southern campaign, Kirkwood's men captured an enemy artillery piece and were again among the last Americans to leave the battlefield. Not content with merely seizing the enemy gun, as the Continentals pulled back, Kirkwood personally captured a British officer, dragging him off the porch of the stone house that had been at the center of much of the day's fighting.[86]

Kirkwood received his furlough from the southern army in January 1782.[87] Shortly after his departure, Greene wrote to Governor John Dickinson of Delaware that "the uniform good conduct of the Officers and Soldiers of your Line affords me an opportunity to testify to the World their singular merit and important services." Greene added that "no Man deserves better of his Country than Capt Kirkwood."[88] Even so, a captain Kirkwood remained. Despite his years of service and demonstrated activity, vigilance, and bravery, promotion in the Continental Army was by state, and Delaware had no field-grade vacancies.[89]

Kirkwood married Sarah England after his return to Delaware. They lived in New Castle County and had three children, two of whom survived to adulthood. When Sarah died, in 1787, Kirkwood looked westward to lands that Virginia had granted him for his wartime service. He served as a justice of the peace in the Northwest Territory, but when war with Native Americans threatened his new home, he resumed the role for which he had been so well suited in the Revolution—that of infantry company commander.[90]

When enemy warriors attacked the United States Army under Arthur St.

Clair on the banks of the Wabash, Captain Jacob Slough reported that he saw Kirkwood "cheering his men, and by his example inspiring confidence in all who saw him." Later in the fight, Slough found "Kirkwood lying against the root of a tree, shot through the abdomen and in great pain." As the army fled the field, Slough was forced to leave Kirkwood behind.[91] Although not a witness to this action, Henry Lee described Kirkwood's final moments: "The gallant Kirkwood fell, bravely sustaining his point of the action. It was the thirty-third time he had risked his life for his country; and he died as he had lived, the brave, meritorious, unrewarded, Kirkwood."[92]

It is not hard to imagine Kirkwood calmly attending to his duties in his final moments, for he had internalized the soldierly qualities that George Washington had demanded from his junior officers during the Revolution. Although Robert Kirkwood was no protégé of Washington—no son of the father—he was a true son of the army that Washington had created.

Notes

I would like to thank Professor Samuel Watson of the United States Military Academy at West Point for his assistance in helping me devise the concept which formed the basis of this essay. I would also like to thank Professors Eugenia Kiesling, Steve Waddell, and John Stapleton, as well as Lieutenant Colonels Gail Yoshitani and David Beougher, also of West Point, for reading and listening to various drafts of both the conference and publication versions of this essay. An Omar N. Bradley Foundation fellowship supported the research for this chapter.

1. Wiley Sword, *President Washington's Indian War: The Struggle for the Old Northwest, 1790–1795* (Norman, Okla., 1985), 171–95 passim.

2. Henry Lee to GW, 16 December 1791, *PGW: Pres. Ser.,* 9:290–91.

3. John McKinly to GW, 28 February 1777, *PGW: Rev. Ser.,* 8:465–66; William Smallwood to GW, 25 December 1777, ibid., 12:710–11; Smallwood to GW, 10 January 1778, ibid., 13:200.

4. GW to the United States Senate, 3 March 1791, *PGW: Pres. Ser.,* 7:506.

5. P. Benson De Lany, "Biographical Sketch of Robt. Kirkwood," *Graham's Magazine* 28 (March 1846): 100.

6. General Orders, 18 July 1775, *PGW: Rev. Ser.,* 1:128; General Orders, 26 October 1775, ibid., 2:235–36.

7. GW to John Thomas, 23 July 1775, ibid., 1:159–62; GW to John Augustine Washington, 31 March 1776, ibid., 3:570; GW to John Hancock, 17 June 1776, ibid., 5:21.

8. GW to Hancock, 21 July 1775, ibid., 1:138.

9. GW to Hancock, 8 July 1776, ibid., 5:239–40.

10. GW, Address to the Massachusetts Provincial Congress, 4 July 1775, ibid., 1:60.

11. Christopher Duffy, *The Military Experience in the Age of Reason* (New York, 1987), 167–73 (quotation, 173).

12. Washington's General Orders contain countless directives on regulating soldier behavior. See, e.g., General Orders, 14 July 1775, *PGW: Rev. Ser.*, 1:114; General Orders, 3 October 1775, ibid., 2:81–82; General Orders, 3 January 1776, ibid., 3:13–14; General Orders, 5 January 1776, ibid., 3:27–28; and General Orders, 26 February 1776, ibid., 3:362.

13. Edward G. Lengel, *General George Washington: A Military Life* (New York, 2005), 60–62.

14. While the term "supernumerary officers" sometimes meant excess officers above and beyond a unit's authorization, in this particular context, Washington seemed to be referring to the regimental commander's subordinate leaders—particularly the company-level officers. The historian Matthew H. Spring has demonstrated that officers in British infantry regiments in the American Revolution had four principal responsibilities in combat. They motivated their men through personal example and threat of punishment, engaged the enemy in combat (the least important of their duties), maintained order in the ranks, and controlled the movement and fire of their element. Two of these responsibilities match directly with the responsibilities that Washington mentioned in this quotation. Since Washington sought to follow the British model, it seems reasonable that he would dictate similar officer roles in combat (see General Orders, 3 March 1776, *PGW: Rev. Ser.*, 3:401–2; and Matthew H. Spring, *With Zeal and With Bayonets Only: The British Army on Campaign in North America, 1775–1783* [Norman, Okla., 2008], 169–82).

15. GW to Benedict Arnold, 5 December 1775, *PGW: Rev. Ser.*, 2:493.

16. Among Washington's numerous directives concerning the completion of returns are General Orders, 17 July 1775, *PGW: Rev. Ser.*, 1:123; General Orders, 18 July 1775, ibid., 1:127; General Orders, 20 July 1775, ibid., 1:134; General Orders, 12 December 1775, ibid., 2:539; General Orders, 2 January 1776, ibid., 3:10–11; and General Orders, 8 January 1776, ibid., 3:52–53.

17. General Orders, 14 July 1775, ibid., 1:114; General Orders, 1 December 1775, ibid., 2:466; General Orders, 5 January 1776, ibid., 3:27–28.

18. General Orders, 30 June 1776, ibid., 5:155.

19. General Orders, 1 January 1776, ibid., 3:1–2.

20. General Orders, 16 August 1776, ibid., 6:34.

21. General Orders, 7 July 1775, ibid., 1:71; GW to Hancock, 21 July 1775, ibid., 1:138.

22. General Orders, 2 July 1776, ibid., 5:180.

23. Washington's papers contain numerous examples of officer misconduct, particularly during the Revolution's first campaign. See, e.g., General Orders, 1 August 1775, *PGW: Rev. Ser.*, 1:207; General Orders, 2 August 1775, ibid., 1:212; GW to Hancock, 4–5 August 1775, ibid., 1:229; General Orders, 9 August 1775, ibid., 1:278; General Orders, 10 August 1775, ibid., 1:281; GW to Lund Washington, 20 August 1775, ibid., 1:335–36; General Orders, 22 August 1775, ibid., 1:347; General Orders, 5 September 1775, ibid., 1:414; General Orders, 8 September 1775, ibid., 1:431; General Orders, 13 October 1775, ibid., 2:154; General Orders, 23 October 1775, ibid., 2:220; General Orders, 15 November 1775, ibid., 2:377; General Orders, 17 November 1775, ibid., 2:388–89; and General Orders, 29 November 1775, ibid., 2:455. For the quotation, see General Orders, 23 February 1776, ibid., 3:356.

24. Christopher L. Ward, *The Delaware Continentals: 1776–1783* (Wilmington, Del., 1941), 539; *Delaware Archives,* 3 vols. (Wilmington, Del., 1911–19), 1:34; De Laney, "Biographical Sketch of Robt. Kirkwood," 98. For a brief history of the Newark Academy, see George H. Ryden, "The Newark Academy of Delaware in Colonial Days," *Pennsylvania History* 2 (October 1935): 205–24.

25. Ward, *Delaware Continentals,* 16–17.

26. Enoch Anderson, *Personal Recollections of Captain Enoch Anderson, an Officer of the Delaware Regiments in the Revolutionary War,* Historical Society of Delaware Papers, no. 16 (Wilmington, Del., 1896), 7.

27. Ibid., 21–22; Ward, *Delaware Continentals,* 28–42 passim; Barnet Schecter, *The Battle for New York: The City at the Heart of the American Revolution* (New York, 2002), 141–54 passim. For the quotation, see John Haslet to Caeser Rodney, 31 August 1776, in *Delaware Archives,* 3:1390.

28. GW to the Massachusetts General Court, 19 September 1776, *PGW: Rev. Ser.,* 6:344.

29. John Haslet to Caeser Rodney, 4 September 1776, in *Delaware Archives,* 3:1391.

30. Ward, *Delaware Continentals,* 56.

31. Ibid., 75.

32. Ibid., 78–82.

33. Ibid., 83–89; John Haslet to Caeser Rodney, 12 November 1776, in *Delaware Archives,* 2:1030–31.

34. Ward, *Delaware Continentals,* 96–103.

35. For officers leaving for recruiting duty, see Anderson, *Personal Recollections,* 28–29. For the eighty-eight battalion resolve, see Robert K. Wright Jr., *The Continental Army* (Washington, D.C., 1983), 91–93.

36. *Delaware Archives,* 1:89.

37. Ibid., 1:85; Anderson, *Personal Recollections,* 29; John McKinly to GW, 28 February 1777, *PGW: Rev. Ser.,* 8:465–66.

38. Problems arose when trying to match names between the two sets of records. Common names in the 1776 regiment, including John Smith and John Brown, also appeared in Kirkwood's 1777 company. Additionally, there were some spelling variations between the two sets of records. For example, the 1776 regiment had a soldier listed as Enos Doil. Kirkwood's 1777 company had an Eneas Doyel. Despite these challenges, it is safe to say that Kirkwood's 1777 company had numerous veterans of Haslet's 1776 regiment. For the April 1776 returns, see *Delaware Archives,* 1:39–61. For Kirkwood's January 1777 payroll, see ibid., 1:199–200.

39. *Delaware Archives,* 1:199–200.

40. *Dunlap's Pennsylvania Packet* (Philadelphia), 11 March 1777.

41. Robert Kirkwood, *The Journal and Order Book of Captain Robert Kirkwood of the Delaware Regiment of the Continental Line,* ed. Joseph Brown Turner (Port Washington, N.Y., 1970), 274.

42. By June 1, 1777, Sullivan's Division only had 1,346 Continental troops present and fit for duty at Princeton; 87 were members of the Delaware Regiment (see Return of General Sullivan's Division, 1 June 1777, in *Letters and Papers of Major-General John Sullivan, Continental Army,* ed. Otis G. Hammond, 3 vols. [Concord, N.H., 1930–39], 1:354).

43. Stephen R. Taaffe, *The Philadelphia Campaign, 1777–1778* (Lawrence, Kans., 2003), 36–44 passim. For Washington's instructions to Sullivan, see GW to John Sullivan, 14 June 1777, in *Letters and Papers of Major-General John Sullivan,* 1:389; and GW to John Sullivan, 14 June 1777, *PGW: Rev. Ser.,* 10:41.

44. Kirkwood, *Journal and Order Book,* 274.

45. Captain Kirkwood to his Father, 23 June 1777, in *Delaware Archives,* 3:1397–99.

46. General Orders, 26 September 1777, *PGW: Rev. Ser.,* 11:323–24.

47. Kirkwood, *Journal and Order Book,* 181–82.

48. Ibid., 274–77.

49. For the Delaware Regiment at Staten Island, see Anderson, *Personal Recollections,* 31–33; and Ward, *Delaware Continentals,* 178–85. For Brandywine, see Ward, *Delaware Continentals,* 196–211. For Germantown, see Anderson, *Personal Recollections,* 44–46; and Ward, *Delaware Continentals,* 222–32.

50. Anderson, *Personal Recollections,* 53.

51. William Smallwood to GW, 25 December 1777, *PGW: Rev. Ser.,* 12:710–11.

52. GW to Smallwood, 1 May 1778, ibid., 15:7–8.

53. Remonstrance of Officers, 16 May 1779, in *Delaware Archives,* 3:1271; Ward, *Delaware Continentals,* 285–86.

54. Ward, *Delaware Continentals,* 285–86.

55. GW to a Continental Congress Camp Committee, 29 January 1778, *PGW: Rev. Ser.,* 13:376–78.

56. Ward, *Delaware Continentals,* 288, 312–13.

57. William Seymour, "A Journal of the Southern Expedition, 1780–1783," *Pennsylvania Magazine of History and Biography* 7 (1883): 286; Otho Holland Williams, "A Narrative of the Campaign of 1780," in William Johnson, *Sketches of the Life and Correspondence of Nathanael Greene, Major General of the Armies of the United States, in the War of the Revolution,* 2 vols. (Charleston, S.C., 1822), 1:485.

58. John E. Howard to the Executors of Stephen Shelmerdine, 26 May 1809, Bayard Papers, Maryland Historical Society, Baltimore; Jim Piecuch and John Beakes, *"Cool Deliberate Courage": John Eager Howard in the American Revolution* (Charleston, S.C., 2009), 32.

59. Kirkwood, *Journal and Order Book,* 10–11; Seymour, "Journal of the Southern Expedition," 286–87; Williams, "Narrative of the Campaign of 1780," 485–89.

60. Seymour, "Journal of the Southern Expedition," 287.

61. Williams, "Narrative of the Campaign of 1780," 488; Piecuch and Beakes, *"Cool Deliberate Courage,"* 36.

62. For the best synopses of the Battle of Camden, see John S. Pancake, *This Destructive War: The British Campaign in the Carolinas, 1780–1782* (Tuscaloosa, Ala., 1985), 98–107; and Piecuch and Beakes, *"Cool Deliberate Courage,"* 36–42. For the quotation, see Kirkwood, *Journal and Order Book,* 11.

63. Caleb P. Bennett, "The Delaware Regiment in the Revolution," *Pennsylvania Magazine of History and Biography* 9 (1885): 455.

64. De Lany, "Biographical Sketch of Robt. Kirkwood," 104.

65. Williams, "Narrative of the Campaign of 1780," 497.

66. Kirkwood, *Journal and Order Book,* 11; Seymour, "Journal of the Southern Expedi-

tion," 289; Bennett, "Delaware Regiment," 455–56. While Kirkwood's letter to the authorities in Delaware has not been found, Caeser Rodney made reference to Kirkwood's letter in other correspondence (see Caeser Rodney to Thomas Rodney, 25 September 1780, in *Letters to and from Caesar Rodney 1756–1784*, ed. George H. Ryden [Philadelphia, 1933], 383).

67. Kirkwood, *Journal and Order Book*, 11; Seymour, "Journal of the Southern Expedition," 290; Williams, "Narrative of the Campaign of 1780," 504–5, 508; Ward, *Delaware Continentals*, 355–57.

68. For an overview of eighteenth-century partisan and light forces in Europe, see Duffy, *Military Experience*, 273–79. For a discussion of British light forces in the American Revolution, see Spring, *With Zeal and With Bayonets Only*, 185–90.

69. Nathanael Greene to Daniel Morgan, 16 December 1780, in *The Papers of General Nathanael Greene*, ed. Richard K. Showman et al., 13 vols. to date (Chapel Hill, N.C., 1976–), 6:589–90.

70. For the best monograph on the Battle of Cowpens, see Lawrence E. Babits, *A Devil of a Whipping: The Battle of Cowpens* (Chapel Hill, N.C., 1998).

71. Ibid., 100–123 passim (quotation, 105).

72. Seymour, "Journal of the Southern Expedition," 295.

73. For a synopsis of events between the Battles of Cowpens and Guilford Courthouse, including the Race to the Dan, see Lawrence E. Babits and Joshua B. Howard, *Long, Obstinate, and Bloody: The Battle of Guilford Courthouse* (Chapel Hill, N.C., 2009), 13–51.

74. Morgan to Greene, 20 February 1781, *Papers of General Nathanael Greene*, 7:324.

75. Ward, *Delaware Continentals*, 411; Henry Lee, *Memoirs of the War in the Southern Department of the United States* (1812; repr., New York, 1870), 276.

76. Ward, *Delaware Continentals*, 414–17; Babits and Howard, *Long, Obstinate, and Bloody*, 114–15, 123, 143–47, 165.

77. Seymour, "Journal of the Southern Expedition," 378.

78. Lee, *Memoirs of the War in the Southern Department of the United States*, 284.

79. Greene to Samuel Huntington, 22 April 1781, *Papers of General Nathanael Greene*, 8:131.

80. Ward, *Delaware Continentals*, 427–28; Piecuch and Beakes, *"Cool Deliberate Courage,"* 100–101; Kirkwood, *Journal and Order Book*, 16.

81. John E. Howard to John Gunby, 22 March 1782, Bayard Papers, Maryland Historical Society, Baltimore.

82. Ward, *Delaware Continentals*, 431–32; Piecuch and Beakes, *"Cool Deliberate Courage,"* 102–4; Seymour, "Journal of the Southern Expedition," 381.

83. Ward, *Delaware Continentals*, 435–36; Piecuch and Beakes, *"Cool Deliberate Courage,"* 108–9; Greene to Samuel Huntington, 27 April 1781, *Papers of General Nathanael Greene*, 8:155.

84. Ward, *Delaware Continentals*, 437–40; Kirkwood, *Journal and Order Book*, 17–18; Seymour, "Journal of the Southern Expedition," 382–83.

85. For an overview of the Siege of Ninety-Six, see Ward, *Delaware Continentals*, 445–52.

86. Ibid., 453–65; Kirkwood, *Journal and Order Book*, 22–24; Seymour, "Journal of the Southern Expedition," 385–86; De Lany, "Biographical Sketch of Robt. Kirkwood," 103–4; Greene to Thomas McKean, 11 September 1781, *Papers of General Nathanael Greene*, 9:332–33.

87. *Delaware Archives,* 1:128.

88. Greene to John Dickinson, 1 February 1782, *Papers of General Nathanael Greene,* 10:292.

89. As the war ended, Kirkwood did receive a brevet or honorary promotion to major, but never served in this capacity. When he reentered military service for the St. Clair expedition in 1791, it was again as a captain. For Kirkwood's brevet promotion, see Kirkwood, *Journal and Order Book,* 5. For promotion by state, see Lee, *Memoirs of the War in the Southern Department of the United States,* 185.

90. Ward, *Delaware Continentals,* 540; De Lany, "Biographical Sketch of Robt. Kirkwood," 102.

91. De Lany, "Biographical Sketch of Robt. Kirkwood," 102–3.

92. Lee, *Memoirs of the War in the Southern Department of the United States,* 185.

AFTERWORD

Unanticipated Challenges and Unexpected Talents—Leadership and the Colonial Matrix

JACK P. GREENE

THIS ESSAY DEPARTS SOMEWHAT FROM THE THEME OF THIS VOLume to address the issue of leadership, a subject on which Don Higginbotham did some of his best work about thirty-five years ago. His perceptive essay on the military dimensions of leadership appeared in a volume emanating from a Library of Congress symposium in May 1974 entitled *Leadership in the American Revolution.*[1] To my knowledge, this book was the last to address this subject from a general perspective, but it was hardly the last word on it. Only two of the five pieces it included, Higginbotham's and an essay by Marcus Cunliffe on leadership in the Continental Congress, systematically addressed the problems of definition involved in the study of leadership.[2]

The discussion that follows is a highly speculative effort to untangle and comment on some of the problems that went largely unaddressed in that volume. The general problem I will focus on is how relatively new, dependent, and supposedly underdeveloped societies find leaders—first, for developing resistance movements of the kind that emerged in colonial British America in 1764–65; then, for steering a coalescence of those movements through a successful war for independence; and finally, in the war's wake, for creating a new extended federal polity that drew heavily on colonial experience. To put the question more directly—and more narrowly—where did colonial British America find not only George Washington and his protégés, but also the much larger group of civil stewards who guided colonial polities from resistance to Independence and on to republican statehood and national union?

As the title, "Unanticipated Challenges and Unexpected Talents," is meant to suggest, however, the emergence of previously undetected *talents* for leadership is only one of three elements in the interpretive equation. The second element, and necessary precondition, is the appearance of unanticipated *challenges* sufficient to create the opportunities necessary to bring those talents to the fore. In a 1780 remark, John Adams succinctly laid out the larger parameters of the problem. "When a society gets disturbed," he wrote, "men of great abilities and good talents are *always* found or made."[3] In this expansive pronouncement, which seems to apply to all societies at all times, Adams begs a series of interesting and important questions that together constitute the third element in my interpretive equation: (1) What is the relationship between the "great abilities and good talents" discovered in times of disturbance, and *previous experience*? (2) What is the relationship between that previous experience and the broad social milieus in which it was acquired? and (3) What is the bearing of previous experience and existing social conditions upon the outcomes of efforts to meet contingent disturbances? In brief, what are the social and experiential foundations of leadership in such situations?

Because 90 percent of my intellectual energy over the past few years has been directed toward unraveling the main discourses or languages by which, in the eighteenth century, metropolitan, not colonial, Britons talked or wrote about the wider British Empire, I shall here approach this large topic by focusing on the much narrower question of why so many metropolitan Britons underestimated the colonial capacity for resistance. Certainly, the metropolitan British political and military establishments were deeply surprised by the caliber of the leadership exhibited by the colonists at every stage of the resistance from the Stamp Act crisis onward. Opponents of the government's coercive policy—and they were numerous—liked to poke fun at those people who, largely uninformed about the character of the several parts of the overseas empire, blindly supported administration measures. Thus, in 1778 an anonymous wag calling himself a West India merchant published a series of letters in the *London Evening Post* in which he recounted an alleged conversation among members of Parliament. When one inquired of another whether he ever gave himself "the trouble of examining and considering the subject" of taxing the colonies, his respondent declared: "Oh yes, that I've done in this case long ago.—I'm quite sartin that we are to tax the *West-Indies,* as well as the *West of England.*"

"You mean the *North-Americans,* I suppose, Sir?," asked his interrogator.

"Why, you knows," the respondent answered, "its all the same thing:—*North-America, Bingal, Virginny, Jemaiky,* is all in the *Indies,* only the sea folks that loves to box the compass, calls things North and East and West, as if it wasn't better to say *Piccadilly* and *Whitechapel,* than East and West end of the town; and that makes it so puzzling to understand and to remember the names, and to know where all these *outlandish Colonies* are: but this I'm quite sartin of, they never brought us any good, nothing but charges ever since we had 'em.—I knows *Old England* very well, and if all *the rest* was drownded in the sea, i'm sartin it would be much more better for us."

When the questioner responded to this startling display of geographical mastery that he could "not conceive how my friend here, that does not so much as know what part of the world they are in, should fancy himself their Representative," the respondent said: "*Pho! I knows well enough in the main; but as I never made the tower of Europe,* I can't be so exact as you:—But the *Continental Congress,* to be sure, is in the *continent,* where the *continental wars* are always the plague of us; the *North Colonies* are partly in *Germany,* where *Hanover* is, and partly in *France;* and the *West-Indies* is partly in *Spain.*—We was dam fools for taking 'em from the French and Spaniards . . . and I wish with all my heart they had them, and *Hanover* too, back again; they brought us nothing but mischief and expences, as all *continental kinexions* does."[4]

But ignorance could scarcely have been the principal source of metropolitan British surprise with the leadership resources of the colonials in the 1760s and after. During the previous three-quarters of a century, between roughly 1710 and the outbreak of the American War for Independence, the colonies had experienced a sustained period of growth and development in terms of every possible measure, including territorial expansion, population growth, and overseas trade, stretching not just to Britain, but also to the West Indies, southern Europe, Ireland, and Africa. Although this rapid expansion stimulated the proliferation of economic treatises touting the colonies as "the principal *Cornucopia* of *Great-Britain's* Wealth," metropolitan Britons were initially a bit slow to recognize the colonies' growing economic and strategic importance.[5] Between the mid-1730s and the early 1760s, however, this situation changed dramatically as metropolitan officials and parliamentary leaders developed a deeper appreciation of the centrality of empire to Britain's economic well-being and international standing—an appreciation revealed in increased government spending for imperial defense; the establishment of buffer colonies at the two ends of the continental chain (Georgia in 1734 and Nova Scotia in 1749, the first state-sponsored and state-supported colonies in the British Empire); and a growing recognition of the vulnerability of Britain's overseas settlements to attack from its principal imperial rivals, Spain and France, and of the advisability of using state funds to protect those settlements.[6] The war with France between 1744 and 1748 especially helped to focus attention upon that nation's growing capacity to rival Britain as a colonizing and maritime power at the same time as it underlined, for metropolitan officials, the limits of metropolitan authority within the colonies. Efforts to shore up that authority began immediately in 1748, and the Seven Years' War eventually led to an exponential increase in expenditures to support the naval and military forces required to check French expansion in the overseas colonial world, from North America and the West Indies east to Bengal.

Parallel to this growing official engagement with empire ran a widening and deepening of public interest in all parts of the British overseas world. After 1740, information about all areas of that world poured into print: histories, chorographies, economic treatises, political pamphlets, novels, plays, epic poems, and magazine and newspaper articles fed what was obviously a voracious appetite for knowledge of the empire. Moreover, as Kathleen Wilson shows, this public interest in empire by no means remained confined to London and other major overseas trading centers such as Bristol, Liverpool, and Glasgow; it spread via provincial newspapers over all of Britain.[7] By the 1750s and 1760s, information about the overseas empire was available to Britons wherever they resided, and the wide extent of the empire, as well as the distinctive character of each of its several parts, was well known to large segments of the metropolitan British population, many of which were intimately involved with the colonies through producing items of export to them, exchanging goods with them, supplying them with labor, population, and capital, processing colonial products, or participating in their defense. Probably no part of the empire was better known than the colonies in North America, the West Indies, and the Atlantic islands. Clearly, ignorance was not the explanation for Britain's failure to anticipate the leadership potential in the American colonies.

A far better explanation was an ancient and categorical prejudice against colonials. In metropolitan Britain, the celebration of empire as an enormous stimulant to Britain's wealth and a major element of its international stature, together with the conception of colonization as a noble enterprise to bring civilization to savage and rude new worlds, had always been qualified. If the colonies themselves had been an obvious boon to Britain, the settlers who inhabited them often seemed, to people who remained at home, to be less worthy of praise. The discourses of empire which took shape in the late seventeenth and early eighteenth centuries often involved expressions of a heavy-handed skepticism about the character of the settlers who inhabited the plantations and the character of the societies they had created. From very early on, a significant strand of metropolitan imperial thought used what modern analysts would call the language of alterity or otherness to depict the colonies as receptacles for those who had failed at home: the poor, the unemployed, the unwanted, and the outcasts—the very dregs of English society. Throughout the seventeenth and eighteenth centuries, this widely circulated language ran as a strong undercurrent in metropolitan conceptions of empire. The colonial process thus involved not just enlightening encounters with indigenous and imported others, but also the creation of a new category of others into which colonial participants could be lumped and thereby distinguished from the more successful and refined populations of the metropolis.[8]

While by no means universal, this unfavorable image of colonials and the social spaces they had created was ubiquitous in British publications—in commercial tracts, critiques of colonial slavery, imperial histories, travel memoirs, fake chorographies, novels, poetry, plays, magazine and newspaper essays, political pamphlets, and parliamentary speeches—and it took a variety of forms. Rooted in a conviction that no one would leave England unless compelled to, this image stressed the lowly social origins of migrants and their religious and social deviancy. Furthermore, the malignant and distinctly non-English places where colonials chose to settle, sharing the wilderness with uncivil, savage peoples, and the questionable societies they created in the process, seemed to put these overseas English people in a separate and inferior category. With little learning or religion (or a deviant form thereof), and with few of the other cultural amenities of English life, colonial societies were so crude that cultural degeneration over the generations, not a few metropolitans thought, was inevitable, especially when most colonial populations had started from such a low base. Moreover, their lowly origins, unsavory characters, and narrow pursuit of economic gain, metropolitans charged, produced societies fundamentally dissimilar from what they had left behind—societies characterized by vicious labor regimes, sharp business practices, and legal regimes that catered to the self-interest of the dominant socioeconomic groups, subverted metropolitan efforts to regulate them, and showed little concern for traditional English social mores. This emerging stereotype provided metropolitans with a sturdy foundation on which to construct a language of alterity. Less harsh than the well-developed languages of savagery and barbarity, which were only occasionally applied to the colonies, and less comprehensively exclusive than the language of alienization used to identify foreigners, this language lacked a contemporary name to encompass all of the many elements that combined to form a discourse of social derision and condescension expressing metropolitan misgivings about the genuine Englishness of England's overseas offshoots. At every level, it deeply affected metropolitan-colonial relations.

Neither the widespread colonial protests against this unfavorable image, nor the continuing conception of the American colonies as places of opportunity in which both the outcast and ambitious could find redemption and economic independence, did much to transform the reputation of the colonial world. Throughout the eighteenth century, metropolitan publications continued to depict the colonies as receptacles for the waste population of Britain. Unable to overcome the stains of their social origins, these people had created in America social milieus that in many respects fell short of even their lowly origins. Even Adam Smith subscribed to this image in his *Theory of Moral Sentiments,* published in London in 1759. In a section on the differences in customs between a savage and "a humane and polished people," Smith observed that there was "not a negro from the coast of Africa, who does not," in respect to fortitude, "possess a degree of magnanimity, which the soul of his sordid master is scarce capable of conceiving." "Fortune never exerted more cruelly her empire over mankind," he added, "than when she subjected those nations of heroes to the refuse of the jails of Europe, of wretches who possess the virtues neither of the countries which they come from, nor of those which they go to, and whose levity, brutality, and baseness, so justly expose them to the contempt of the vanquished."[9]

If the legalization of slavery, which was common to all British colonies, was the most glaring deviation from metropolitan British social norms, a variety of other characteristics operated throughout the early centuries of empire to sustain a negative image of the American colonies as not quite British, or even as foreign places populated by people who, even if they originated in Britain, had not recognizably reproduced British society. Living in exotic places among the strange peoples whose land they had taken or who had been imported to labor for them, colonial settlers, as depicted from the metropolitan perspective through the language of alterity, themselves seemed to be a separate breed—a mixture of people unable to make it in Britain, including poor laborers, former servants, transported felons, economic and social adventurers, and religious deviants—demographically and culturally contaminated through their sexual liaisons with native peoples and imported Africans. That societies created by such deviants would be presided over by social upstarts known for shady business practices, harsh labor regimes, immorality and suspect sexual mores, religious deviancy or neglect, social crudity, a lack of civility, extreme provinciality, and long-term cultural degeneration, was, for metropolitans, only to be expected.

Such attitudes were widely evident in metropolitan circles during the debate over how to respond to colonial resistance after 1764, especially among those who advocated a hard line. Thus, in a House of Commons debate in November 1775 over what, in light of its army's misadventures in Massachusetts the previous spring, Britain should do to deal with colonial resistance to parliamentary authority, William Innes, Member of Parliament for Ilchester, spoke at length in favor of strong coercive measures. Emphatically questioning whether the colonists were even "the offspring of Englishmen, and as such entitled to the privileges of Britons," he denounced them rather as a promiscuous "mixture of people" who consisted "not only . . . of English, Scots, and Irish, but also of French, Dutch, Germans innumerable, Indians, Africans, and a multitude of felons from this country." Few members of such a population, he insisted, could possibly have a legitimate claim to the rich inheritance and identity of full Britons. Colonial British Americans, he charged, had created and continued to live in societies that bore little resemblance to that of the home island. He cited, in particular, the massive importation of slaves and the "despotic" exploitation of them. Societies thus drawing their "sustenance from the very bosom of slavery," he declared, "surely [had] nothing in them similar to what prevails in Great Britain."[10]

That societies composed of such false Britons could ever find the leadership or the resolve to mount an effective resistance to a powerful state composed of *true* Britons seemed thoroughly problematic to many people in Britain. To be sure, many metropolitan observers understood that the colonies had become infinitely more wealthy and improved over the eighteenth century. Indeed, their growing wealth made them an attractive source of revenue. But they little associated that wealth with the sort of cultural and political improvement necessary for stable and effective governance. Ignoring the highly positive contributions of money and men to the Seven Years' War from such key colonies as Massachusetts, Virginia, New York, and Connecticut, metropolitan analysts instead used the striking dissimilarities among the colonies, their extreme parochialism, their inability to put the common welfare above provincial interests, and their internal divisions during that war, as evidence to support the contention that colonials were too divided and lacking in common purpose to stand together for long, much less to govern themselves without the direction of the metropolis.

This lack of respect for colonial political capacities made it easy for metropolitans to ascribe colonial resistance to the efforts of a small group of demagogues and agitators, which, without experienced, competent, and prudent political leadership, and with no experienced military men, would quickly wilt under naval or military pressure from Britain. Dismissing the Americans as disorganized rebels, "paltroons, enthusiastics, and cowards," as Manasseh Dawes described them, who, according to a writer calling himself "Janus," "would soon disperse at the appearance of the king's regular troops," members of Parliament, complained an anonymous opposition writer, "descended to the last degree of puerility and meanness, in their invectives against that people." Thus did the "*brave* Colonel [James] Grant" brand them "with the name of cowards" when "he offered to traverse the continent of America with a thousand men," while, as "Janus" maintained, the "first lord of the Admiralty, L[or]d S[andwic]h, spoke freely of driving them with a few hundred soldiers all through their country." Meanwhile, as the anonymous writer recalled, another administration supporter "gave out to the world, that a thousand poles with red coats on them, placed around the *fortress* of Boston, would be sufficient defence," since "the *Yankeys,*" as he "was pleased to stile them, *never felt bold enough* to face a red-coat."[11]

Prejudice was the primary source of this fatal and massive miscalculation, precisely because it blinded so many—though by no means all—in the British political nation to the social and political dimensions of the extraordinary growth experienced by the North American colonies over the previous half century. As a result of that growth, the colonies after 1710 experienced rapid development and impressive accumulation of human, social, cultural, and political capacity that stimulated the production of individual talent.[12] This is not the venue for recounting the impressive list of such accumulations in the economic, social, and cultural spheres.[13] More interesting in grappling with the questions I have raised here are those in the public realm.

In the political and civil spheres, all but a few of the colonies had experienced several generations of practice in governing their households, counties, towns, parishes, and provinces. They had made and enforced law, negotiated disputes among rival contenders, catered to the needs and demands of a free citizenry, and organized their polities to keep civil peace and defend against local enemies. By the middle of the eighteenth century, they had in every province developed a cadre of leaders fully competent to preside over that polity and to thwart unwanted metropolitan interference whenever they thought necessary, while many others had experience in managing public affairs in the localities, and the overwhelming majority of the free population enjoyed access to justice and the right to vote—or not—and was open to the possibility of mobilizing for collective action against whoever might threaten the basic conditions of their existence. At the same time, the increasingly sophisticated newspaper essays, pamphlets, and other treatises that appeared in an expanding volume after 1730 testified to the growing density of the public sphere and the rising level of political expertise, capacity, and engagement.

For the provincial leaders who presided over these late-colonial polities, most of the challenges met between 1764 and 1783 were simply business as usual. To be sure, they found themselves at the head of a generalized resistance movement to resist metropolitan efforts that, in their view, threatened to deprive them of their British and colonial inheritance. In spearheading that resistance, they sometimes found it necessary to overcome the opposition of some of their fellows who were reluctant to carry opposition so far as to constitute what, in British eyes, represented rebellion against the parent state. They also found themselves having to mobilize the larger population and to absorb within their ranks new leaders just coming on to the political stage or cast up by the exigent situation. Through all these challenges, however, they moved ahead cautiously but confidently. When they deemed it no longer possible to achieve their goal of civil equality for colonial Britons within the British Empire, they presided, on thirteen separate stages with thirteen separate sets of leaders, over the transition to republican statehood in provincial contexts with which they were thoroughly familiar. If, outside Connecticut and Rhode Island, few people had the executive experience that would have been ideal for republican governors, the parliamentary state republics they created did not usually leave important matters to unassisted executive authority or demand extraordinary people to fill executive positions. At the state level, early governance, like earlier colonial governance, was very much a legislative or judicial responsibility.

Relatively few of the members of these provincial leadership corps had to meet the new challenge of concerting with others from many different provincial environments to mount a common resistance, run a war, negotiate with potential foreign allies, or create a loose national union. Those few relied on their extensive colonial experience to master the new roles into which they were thrust. As they went through a winnowing process, not all of them were successful. If in the civil realm, to go back to the quote from John Adams used early on in this essay, leaders were easily found from existing provincial leadership reservoirs, in the military realm they had to be made. Few men began with extensive military experience. Through a process of selection on the ground, however, competent military leaders emerged, if not to win, then at least not to lose this war for state independence and a shot at the creation of an American national union.

One part of my message here is that late-colonial societies were emphatically not underdeveloped politically, and not lacking in leadership resources, and that Adams, in his ongoing effort to magnify the challenges and achievements of his generation of founders, may well have underemphasized the capacity of existing pools of leadership at the same time that he exaggerated the degree of the challenges they encountered after 1774.

If colonial polities were thus, in the words of Jon Butler, "far more self-sufficient and self-directing" than British authorities understood when embarking upon their strategies of coercion in 1774, they were also, as both Butler and I have emphasized, altogether more open, mobile, expansive, dynamic, flexible, and participatory than some later historians of the Revolution have posited.[14] Such historians have been so intent upon assimilating the American Revolution to the great European revolutions by emphasizing its revolutionary character and positing a radical discontinuity with the colonial past, that they have by and large neglected to explore the bearing of earlier American social and political experience upon its events and developments.

Politically competent civil societies were not the product of the American Revolution, but its precondition. They were the result, not of independent nationhood or some newfound resources or sensibilities generated by the Revolution, but of an ongoing process of refinement and accumulation that had taken place during the century and a half following the establishment by the first founders of English-American colonies during the seventeenth century. From this perspective, what historians call the American Revolution needs to be understood as an effort to perpetuate the benefits of the civil societies that were already thoroughly in place by the last decades of the colonial era.

The civic autonomy that colonial British Americans sought through independence and the institutional structures that they created during the last quarter of the eighteenth century were at once a part of that effort and expressions of the social, cultural, and political developments that they had already created and were determined to preserve. Continuities, not disjunctures, characterize the transition from the colonial to the early national era in all areas of life. However, until historians of the national era stop relying on the invention of a backward-looking and confining traditional colonial world dominated by venerable provincial hierarchies who presided over societies that were highly deferential and politically exclusionary against which to magnify the changes they wish to chart in the post-revolutionary era, we are unlikely to achieve any very clear understanding of what did change as a result of the Revolution, and how much—or, to return to the point at which I started, to begin to appreciate where the American Revolution obtained its leaders.

Notes

1. Don Higginbotham, "Military Leadership in the American Revolution," in Library of Congress, *Leadership in the American Revolution: Papers Presented at the Third Symposium, May 9 and 10, 1974—Library of Congress Symposia on the American Revolution* (Washington, D.C., 1974), 91–111.

2. Marcus Cunliffe, "Congressional Leadership on the American Revolution," in Library of Congress, *Leadership in the American Revolution,* 41–60.

3. As quoted by L. H. Butterfield, "Opening Remarks," in Library of Congress, *Leadership in the American Revolution,* 3.

4. *The West India Merchant: Being a Series of Papers Originally Printed Under that Signature in the London Evening Post* (London, 1778), 15–17.

5. G.B., Esq., *The Advantages of the Revolution Illustrated, by a View of the Present State of Great Britain* (London, 1753), 30.

6. During Nova Scotia's first four years of parliamentary funding, from 1749 to 1752, Parliament lavished upon it £336,707 (*Proceedings and Debates of the British Parliament Respecting North America,* ed. Leo F. Stock, 5 vols. [Washington, D.C., 1924–41], 5:535).

7. Kathleen Wilson, *The Sense of the People: Politics, Culture, and Imperialism in England, 1715–1785* (Cambridge, U.K., 1995).

8. For a superb study of the English/British encounter with the non-European worlds of others, see P. J. Marshall and Glyndwr Williams, *The Great Map of Mankind: Perceptions of New Worlds in the Age of the Enlightenment* (Cambridge, Mass., 1982). See also *Empire and Others: British Encounters with Indigenous Peoples, 1600–1850,* ed. Martin Daunton and Rick Halpern (Philadelphia, 1999), which offers a collection of illuminating case studies on this subject.

9. Adam Smith, *Theory of Moral Sentiments* (London, 1759), 402–3.

10. William Innes, speech, 8 November 1775, in *Proceedings and Debates of the British Parliaments Respecting North America 1754–1783*, ed. R. C. Simmons and P. D. G. Thomas, 6 vols. (White Plains, N.Y., 1982–86), 6:203.

11. Manasseh Dawes, *A Letter to Lord Chatham concerning the Present War of Great Britain against America* (London, 1777), 7–8; Janus [pseud.], *The Critical Moment, on Which the Salvation or Destruction of the British Empire Depend* (London, 1776), 14; *The Conduct of Administration with Regard to the Colonies* (London, 1775), 20.

12. For a fuller development of this subject, see Jack P. Greene, "Social and Cultural Capital in Colonial British America: A Case Study," *Journal of Interdisciplinary History* 19 (Winter 1999): 491–509.

13. See Jack P. Greene, *Pursuits of Happiness: The Social Development of Early Modern British Colonies and the Formation of American Culture* (Chapel Hill, 1988), 184–87.

14. See Jon Butler, *Becoming America: The Revolution before 1776* (Cambridge, Mass., 2000), 1, 4–6, 51, 90, 229, 235.

Contributors

FRED ANDERSON received his BA from Colorado State University in 1971, and his PhD from Harvard in 1981. He has taught at Harvard and at the University of Colorado, Boulder, where he is currently Professor of History and Director of the Honors Program in the College of Arts and Sciences. He has held fellowships from the National Endowment for the Humanities, the Charles Warren Center of Harvard University, the John Simon Guggenheim Foundation, the Rockefeller Foundation, and the National Humanities Center. His publications include *Crucible of War: The Seven Years War and the Fate of Empire in British North America, 1754–1766,* which won the 2001 Francis Parkman Prize, and *The Dominion of War: Empire and Liberty in North America, 1500–2000,* which he coauthored with Andrew Cayton. His current project, also with Andrew Cayton, is *Imperial America, 1672–1764,* a volume in the Oxford History of the United States.

THEODORE J. CRACKEL has a PhD from Rutgers University and was, from 2004 to 2010, the Editor in Chief of the Papers of George Washington at the University of Virginia. In 2005 the project was awarded the National Humanities Medal by President George W. Bush; in 2007 the project launched a digital edition, and in 2009 it undertook the online publication of Washington's extensive financial papers. From 1994 to 2004, Crackel was the founding Director and Editor of the Papers of the War Department, 1784–1800, at East Stroudsburg University in Pennsylvania. In 2001–2002 he was a visiting professor at West Point during the school's bicentennial year. Among his books are *Mr. Jefferson's Army: Political and Social Reform of the Military Establish-*

ment, 1801–1809, and *West Point: A Bicentennial History.* He is currently at work on a biography of Washington's boyhood years.

WILLIAM M. FERRARO is Associate Professor and Associate Editor of the Papers of George Washington at the University of Virginia. He received his undergraduate degree in American Studies from Georgetown University, and his PhD in American Civilization from Brown University. Since starting with the Papers of George Washington in June 2006, he has coedited Volume 19 of the Revolutionary War Series, which covers the period 15 January–7 April 1779, and edited Volume 21, which covers the period 1 June–31 July 1779. He previously helped edit volumes of the Salmon P. Chase Papers and the Papers of Ulysses S. Grant. Besides topics stemming from his editorial work, he has a long-standing research interest in the family and careers and John and William Tecumseh Sherman.

JACK P. GREENE, who was fortunate enough to be a close friend of Don Higginbotham for almost fifty-five years, taught at Johns Hopkins University between 1966 and 2005 and has published widely on early modern British colonial American and imperial history. His latest books are *Encountering Empire and Confronting Colonialism in Eighteenth-Century Britain,* and *Creating the British Atlantic: Essays in Transplantation, Adaptation, and Continuities.*

JOHN W. HALL is the Ambrose-Hesseltine Assistant Professor of U.S. Military History at the University of Wisconsin–Madison. He holds a BS in History from the United States Military Academy at West Point, and a PhD in History from the University of North Carolina–Chapel Hill. He specializes in early American military history, with particular emphasis on partisan and Native American warfare. He is the author of *Uncommon Defense: Indian Allies in the Black Hawk War,* and numerous essays on early American warfare, including "Washington's Irregulars," in *A Companion to George Washington,* edited by Edward Lengel.

PETER R. HENRIQUES received his PhD in history from the University of Virginia in 1971 and is Professor of History, Emeritus, at George Mason University. He taught American and Virginia history, with a special emphasis on the Virginia Founding Fathers, especially George Washington. His *Realistic Visionary: A Portrait of George Washington,* published by the University of Virginia

Press, came out in paperback in 2008. His other books include *The Death of George Washington: He Died as He Lived,* and a brief biography of Washington written for the National Park Service. A member of both the Editorial Board of the George Washington Papers and the Mount Vernon Committee of George Washington Scholars, he regularly conducts Leadership Institutes at Mount Vernon for various government and private groups and is involved in various teacher seminars conducted by Mount Vernon and other educational institutions, including the Distinguished Lecture Series at Colonial Williamsburg, 2011–12. He is the 2012 recipient of the George Washington Memorial Award given by the George Washington Masonic Memorial Association.

MARY-JO KLINE holds a PhD in American history from Columbia University and a degree in Library and Information Science from Catholic University. Her first book, *Gouverneur Morris and the New Nation,* was published in 1978. She was Associate Editor of the Adams Papers at the Massachusetts Historical Society and headed the Papers of Aaron Burr at the New-York Historical Society. She is the author of the standard text in this field, *A Guide to Documentary Editing.* As a librarian, she was on the staff of the web-based "American Memory" project at the Library of Congress, and served as American History Specialist for the Brown University Library as well as a consultant to the Papers of John Jay at Columbia. She provided the "Archivist" column for the online quarterly journal *History Now.* A resident scholar in the Department of History of the University of Virginia, she is working on a biography of Sarah Livingston Jay, wife of the first chief justice.

STUART LEIBIGER is Associate Professor and Chair of the Department of History at La Salle University. He received his BA from the University of Virginia, and his MA and PhD from the University of North Carolina at Chapel Hill. His book, *Founding Friendship: George Washington, James Madison, and the Creation of the American Republic,* now in its third edition, was published in 1999. He edited *A Companion to James Madison and James Monroe,* published by Wiley-Blackwell, in 2012. He has written numerous articles on the founders for historical magazines and journals, and has been a historical consultant for television documentaries and museums. He has worked on the editorial staffs of the Papers of George Washington and the Papers of Thomas Jefferson. From 2004 to 2009, he served as the Scholar-in-Residence at the National Endowment for the Humanities Landmarks of American History Teacher Workshop at George Washington's Mount Vernon, and he is a former Distinguished Lecturer for the Organization of American Historians.

ROBERT M. S. MCDONALD, Associate Professor of History at the United States Military Academy, is a graduate of the University of Virginia, Oxford University, and the University of North Carolina at Chapel Hill, where he earned his PhD. He is editor of *Thomas Jefferson's Military Academy: Founding West Point,* and *Light and Liberty: Thomas Jefferson and the Power of Knowledge.* He is completing a book to be titled *Confounding Father: Thomas Jefferson's Image in His Own Time,* as well as an edited volume, *Thomas Jefferson's Lives: Biographers and the Battle for History.* He is the first Sons of the American Revolution Distinguished Scholar.

L. SCOTT PHILYAW is Associate Professor of History and Director of the Mountain Heritage Center at Western Carolina University. He earned his MA from the College of William and Mary, and his PhD from the University of North Carolina, where he studied under Don Higginbotham. His publications include *Virginia's Western Visions: Cultural and Political Expansion on an Early American Frontier,* and "A Slave for Every Soldier: The Strange History of Virginia's Forgotten Recruitment Act of 1 January 1781," published in the *Virginia Magazine of History and Biography.* In 2003, he served as Scholar in Residence at the Museum of Early Southern Decorative Arts at Old Salem, North Carolina. He is the recipient of the UNC Board of Governors' Award for Excellence in Teaching, Western Carolina University's Paul A. Reid Distinguished Service Award, and a Mellon Fellowship from the Virginia Historical Society.

THOMAS RIDER is an active-duty lieutenant colonel in the United States Army and a veteran of the wars in Iraq and Afghanistan. He earned his MA from the University of North Carolina at Chapel Hill, where he had the privilege of studying under Don Higginbotham, and has served as Assistant Professor of History at the United States Military Academy. His research interests include the Continental Army and the adaptation of eighteenth-century European military practices to warfare in North America.

BRIAN STEELE is Associate Professor of History at the University of Alabama at Birmingham. He received his PhD at the University of North Carolina at

Chapel Hill, where he studied with Don Higginbotham. His work has appeared in the *Journal of American History* and the *Journal of Southern History.* His book, *Thomas Jefferson and American Nationhood,* was published by Cambridge University Press in 2012.

MARY STOCKWELL is a Research Fellow at the International Lincoln Center for American Studies at LSU Shreveport. Most recently, she was an Earhart Foundation Fellow at the William Clements Library at the University of Michigan. She was previously Professor of History and Chair of the Department of History, Political Science, and Geography at Lourdes University. She is the author of several history books for young students, including *The Ohio Adventure, A Journey through Maine,* and *Massachusetts: Our Home,* which won the Golden Lamp Award for Best Book from the Association of Educational Publishers in 2005. She wrote a major biography of our twenty-eighth president, entitled *Woodrow Wilson: The Last Romantic,* which was published in 2008 as part of a series called First Men: America's Presidents. She recently completed *Many Trails of Tears: The Removal of the Ohio Tribes* and *The American Story: Perspectives and Encounters to 1865.* Stockwell has also won several awards for excellence in teaching and to pursue research, including a fellowship from the Gilder Lehrman Institute of American History.

MARK THOMPSON is Professor of History at the University of North Carolina at Pembroke. He earned his MA and PhD degrees at the University of North Carolina at Chapel Hill. He has presented papers and written essays on a variety of topics related to early American history and American military history, but the focus of his research has been on Henry Knox and his contributions to the early republic.

Index

Recent Books in the
JEFFERSONIAN AMERICA SERIES

Douglas Bradburn *The Citizenship Revolution: Politics and the Creation of the American Union, 1774–1804*

Clarence E. Walker *Mongrel Nation: The America Begotten by Thomas Jefferson and Sally Hemings*

Timothy Mason Roberts *Distant Revolutions: 1848 and the Challenge to American Exceptionalism*

Peter J. Kastor and François Weil, editors *Empires of the Imagination: Transatlantic Histories of the Louisiana Purchase*

Eran Shalev *Rome Reborn on Western Shores: Historical Imagination and the Creation of the American Republic*

Leonard J. Sadosky *Revolutionary Negotiations: Indians, Empires, and Diplomats in the Founding of America*

Philipp Ziesche *Cosmopolitan Patriots: Americans in Paris in the Age of Revolution*

Leonard J. Sadosky, Peter Nicolaisen, Peter S. Onuf, and Andrew J. O'Shaughnessy, editors *Old World, New World: America and Europe in the Age of Jefferson*

Sam W. Haynes *Unfinished Revolution: The American Republic in a British World, 1815–1850*

Michal Jan Rozbicki *Culture and Liberty in the Age of the American Revolution*

Ellen Holmes Pearson *Remaking Custom: Law and Identity in the Early American Republic*

Seth Cotlar *Tom Paine's America: The Rise and Fall of Transatlantic Radicalism*

John Craig Hammond and Matthew Mason, editors *Contesting Slavery: The Politics of Bondage and Freedom in the New American Nation*

Ruma Chopra *Unnatural Rebellion: Loyalists in New York City during the Revolution*

Maurizio Valsania *The Limits of Optimism: Thomas Jefferson's Dualistic Enlightenment*

Peter S. Onuf and Nicholas P. Cole, editors *Thomas Jefferson, the Classical World, and Early America*

Hannah Spahn *Thomas Jefferson, Time, and History*

Lucia Stanton *"Those Who Labor for My Happiness": Slavery at Thomas Jefferson's Monticello*

Robert M. S. McDonald, editor *Light and Liberty: Thomas Jefferson and the Power of Knowledge*

Catherine Allgor, editor *The Queen of America: Mary Cutts's Life of Dolley Madison*

Peter Thompson and Peter S. Onuf, editors *State and Citizen: British America and the Early United States*

Maurizio Valsania *Nature's Man: Thomas Jefferson's Philosophical Anthropology*

John Ragosta *Religious Freedom: Jefferson's Legacy, America's Creed*

Robert M. S. McDonald, editor *Sons of the Father: George Washington and His Protégés*